PROSCRIBED TELUGU LITERATURE AND NATIONAL MOVEMENT IN ANDHRA : 1920-1947

PROSCRIBED TELUGU LITERATURE AND NATIONAL MOVEMENT IN ANDHRA : 1920-1947

PENTA SIVUNNAIDU
M.A., M.Phil.

RELIANCE PUBLISHING HOUSE
NEW DELHI (INDIA)

"The Publication of this book has been financially supported by Indian Council of Historical Research. The responsibility for the facts stated or opinions expressed is entirely of the Author and not of the Council.

First Published 2002

ISBN : 81-7510-150-4

Published by
Dr. S. K. Bhatia *(Life Member ILA, FEPI, HWF, INSA, Common Cause, ISCKON)*
For **Reliance Publishing House**
3026/7H, Ranjit Nagar,
New Delhi-110 008. Ph. : 5737377, 5852605
Fax : 5786769

Composed by
Elegant Printographics
74, Savera Apartments,
Sector-13, Plot-5, Rohini,
Delhi-110085
Ph. : 7567413

Printed by **S. S. S. Printers**
New Delhi.

CONTENTS

ACKNOWLEDGEMENTS

I take this opportunity to express my deep sense of gratitude to the Research Director, Dr.M.S.R.Anjaneyulu, Reader, Department of History and Archaeology, Andhra University, Waltair, for the interest he has taken in the conduct of this study and perennial inspiration and guidance I received.

I cannot but express by heartfelt thanks to all the staff members of the History & Archaeology Department, Andhra University, who encouraged me in my research work.

I express my sincere gratitude to Dr.B.Kesavanarayana, Reader, Department of History & Archaeology, Andhra University, Waltair, for his valuable suggestions and encouragement at various stages of this study.

My special thanks are due to the staff of Andhra Pradesh State Archives, Hyderabad; International Institute of Telugu, Hyderabad; State Central Library, Hyderabad; Andhra Pradesh Government Oriental Manuscript Library, Hyderabad; Osmania University Library, Hyderabad; Tamil Nadu State Archives, Madras; Connemera Public Library, Madras; National Archives, New Delhi; Nehru Memorial Museum and Library, New Delhi; Saraswataniketan, Vetapalem; Tagore Parisodhana Kendram, Vijayawada; Guntur District Regional Library, Guntur; Gautami Regional Research Library, Rajahmundry; District Collectorate Library, Visakhapatnam; Ambedkar Law College Library, Waltair; District Central Library, Visakhapatnam; Regional Office of Andhra Pradesh State Archives, Visakhapatnam for their cooperation throughout the study.

I extend my gratitude to the staff of Dr.V.S.Krishna Memorial Library, Andhra University for their cooperation in my study and thank the U.G.C., for providing me financial assistance in completing my thesis.

I am grateful to Sri M. Suri Babu for his efficiency in typing this work.

Last but not the least to ICHR and my publisher Dr.S.K.Bhatia of Reliance Publishing House, New Delhi.

P. Sivunnaidu

ABBREVIATIONS

A.I.C.C.	:	All India Congress Committee.
A.I.R.	:	All India Reporter.
A.P.C.C.	:	Andhra Provincial Congress Committee
C.I.D.	:	Criminal Investigation Department.
C.P.I.	:	Communist Party of India.
C.S.P.	:	Congress Socialist Party.
Dt.	:	Dated.
G.I.POL.	:	Government of India Home Political Proceedings.
G.O.No.	:	Government Order Number.
I.N.C.	:	Indian National Congress.
I.O.L.	:	Indian Office Library Collection.
I.P. (E.P.) Act, 1931.	:	Indian Press (Emergency Powers) Act, 1931.
J.P.	:	Judicial and Public Department Proceeding IOL.
M.C.	:	Minto Collections.
M.L.C.P.	:	Madras Legislative Council Proceedings.
M.S.	:	Miscellaneous.
N.A.I.	:	National Archives of India.
N.P.R.	:	Native News Paper Reports.

ANDHRA REGION IN MADRAS PRESIDENCE

LIST OF PHOTOGRAPHS

1

INTRODUCTION

The period from 1920 to 1947 was a watershed in the history of Modern India. During this period the people of India and elite-politicians fought for freedom under the unique and inspiring leadership of Gandhiji and made history. To make history the elite-politicians needed the active participation and assured support of the masses. Recognising this significant fact Gandhiji brought the masses to politics. He took politics to the door of the Indian masses. Limited politics and institutional politics gave way to popular politics and mass struggle.

Gandhian phase of national movement offered to the people a number of constructive programmes and political movements. The success of these programmes and movements depended on politicization and mobilization of the masses. In communicating and propagating the political ideas of the nationalist leaders to the masses the nationalist intelligentsia of Andhra played an effecrtive and remarkable role. They were influenced by the Gandhian ideology and political techniques and through their writings influenced the people to a great extent. They made the people to believe, to accept, to support, to involve and to participate in the national movement. They criticised the colonial rule and authorised the national movement. In the process they wrote dramas, songs, books, pamphlets, leaflets and articles in newspapers imbuing the people with patriotic fervour, indomitable courage and heroic-sacrifice to an extraordinary degree. The consequent efflorescence of nationalist literature contributed to the formation of people's national consciousness and their voluntary participation in the national movement to such an extent that the colonial Government began to sense a threat to its own existence and was forced to resort to proscription and suppression of ideas and oppression of the freedom of the press.

The writers in Andhra wrote a number of works to inculcate, keep alive and stimulate patriotic fervour among the people. They mirrorised the then politics in their works. They wrote what they and their leading leaders felt, thought and believed. They used highly powerful literary weapons in the creation of national spirit and enjoyed severe punishments. The writers, some of whom were also freedom fighters, being in close touch with the local people could understand the pulse of the people, their instincts and aspirations. So they acted between the leaders and the lead.

Scope of the Study

The objective of this study is to estimate the contribution of the Proscribed Telugu Literature to the national movement in Andhra between 1920 and 1947. On the basis of the available material an attempt is made in this study to detail the contents of the works, to explain the techniques adopted by the writers and analyse the themes embodied in the literature. The work also studies the reaction of the Government towards the writers and their works. It also highlights the contribution and sacrifice made by four leading nationalist intelligentsia who were writers and at the same time freedom fighters.

The period between 1920 and 1947 has been taken for the research work as that period constitutes a very important unit in the history of Indian National Movement. The year 1920 witnessed the emergence of Gandhiji as the towering leader of the struggle for freedom and starting of the non-cooperation experiment. Further in the history of nationalist literature in Andhra the year 1920 marks a turning point. It was from this year that the nationalist intelligentsia became bold and started attacking the colonial Government without fear or inhibition through their works. They viewed the emergence of Gandhiji as the birth of a new force and hope. This led to the emergence of Gandhian literature, leftist literature, nationalist dramatic literature and literature on economic nationalism and patriotic effusion. Hence the year 1920 is taken as the starting point of this study.

The period between 1920 and 1947 was not only packed with great national movement like the non-cooperation movement, the salt satyagraha, the civil disobedience movement and the Quit India movement but also witnessed besides, the old Repressive laws, the passing of several repressive legislative measures to suppress the freedom of the writers, like the Indian Press, (Emergence Powers) Act, 1931, Ordinance II of 1932, Ordinance X of 1932, the Criminal Law Amendment Act, 1932 and Defence of India Rules, 1939. It was a period of heroic conflict between the nationlist writers and the Imperialist Government in India. This study closes by the "Fifteenth of August", 1947.

The present study is confined to the Telugu speaking area of the composite Madras Presidency i.e., coastal Andhra consisting of the districts of Srikakulam, Visakhapatnam, East Godavari, West Godavari, Krishna, Guntur, Prakasam and Nellore and the Rayalaseema region. The justification for limiting the area of study to Andhra lies primarily in the fact that it is a unit comprising homogeneous population, speaking one language, possessing a common history and culture. It had remained fore long time under the dominant influence of the British which enabled it to receive western cultural trends and develop its own uniform social system and political ideology. However, the Telangana region of erstwhile Hyderabad state was excluded from this study, because the Telangana districts were under the control of a different political authority i.e. The Nizam of Hyderabad.

The study has a limited objective of analysing the nature, contents and the themes of the proscribed literature, pointing out the reaction of the Government towards the literature and its impact on the national movement in Andhra. Hence study is confined only to the proscribed Telugu literature and the nationalist literature that was not proscribed, will not fall under the scope of the present study.

Methodology

In the present study I have followed the historical method which essentially includes the interpretation of evidence from Government Documents, Government Orders, Fortnightly Confidential Reports, Madras Police Abstracts of Intelligence, C.I.D. Reports of Madras Presidency, Proscribed books, pamphlets, booklets, newspapers and periodicals, Gazetteers, Souvenirs, as primary and secondary sources. Almost all the writers of the proscribed literature are not alive today. The only writer and freedom fighter whom I have interviewed was Vaddadi Sitaramanjaneyulu. He too expired on 14th April, 1993. So I was forced to draft this thesis on the basis of the above mentioned primary and secondary sources.

Review of Literature

Nationalist literature in Andhra was a new phenomena and it played an important role in the national movement in Andhra. However, no scholar has done any comprehensive work on this subject.

Some scholars wrote articles, some made passing references to the proscribed works and the colonial Government's repressive policy, but they did not make a special study on the proscribed Telugu literature.

The role of the nationalist organizations like the Indian National Congress and of eminent freedom fighters has to a great extent been assessed by studies at the national and the regional level. A number of books have been published giving an account of the freedom movement in India at the regional and at the national level. Those studies naturally deal with the prominent events and personalities of the movement but they could not make a special study of the contribution of the nationalist literature at the regional level. To understand how nationalist ideas spread, how the programmes announced by the political leaders reached the masses, a study on the role of nationlist literature is essential.

The valuable contribution of Prem Narain's Press and Politics in India, 1885-1905 is to some extent an attempt at estimating the contribution of the press to the national movement of the period at the national level. A. Ganeshan's The Press in Tamil Nadu and the Struggle for Freedom 1917-1937 is concerned with the role of press in the national movement in Tamil Nadu. So fas as Andhra region is concerned K. Subramanyam's The Press and the National Movement in South India Andhra, 1905-1932 is a pioneering work. However for the purpose of this study the author considered "the daily newspapers and periodicals which contained political news" to be the press. Proscribed literature did not form a part of his study. Moreover the period of his study is limited to the period from 1905 to 1932. As far as the banned literature is concerned at the national level N.G. Barrier's Banned Controversial Literature and Political Control in British India 1907-1947 is a pioneering study. This work examines in detail the interaction between the Government and press. It is divided into two parts. Part one deals with "The Politics of Proscription" and part two is "A Guide to Banned Literature". In this work not much significance is given to the analysis of the banned literature and its contribution to the national movement. Though the proscribed literature played a glorious part in the national movement no scholar has made an extensive study of this subject. The fore-going review of the historiography shows that there is a clear gap in the history of modern Andhra. The present study is mainly aimed at filling this gap in the historiography as well as provide new dimensions to the forces that influenced the course and nature of the national movement in Andhra.

Sources

The present study is based on the in-depth and critical study of the primary sources such as the Government Orders, Proceedings of the Government of Madras-Home Department, Public Department – Judicial Department; Fortnightly Reports (Confidential) of Government of Madras, Madras Police Abstracts of Intelligence (secret) Reports; Native Newspaper Reports of the Madras Presidency (Confidential) and History of Freedom Struggle in Andhra (HFS typed material) pertaining to this period. The non-Government sources include the proscribed books newspapers, periodicals, booklets, pamphlets and private papers.

Published and unpublished Doctoral and M.Phil dissertations, books, articles and souvenirs and other secondary source material are also used in this study.

Chapterisation

The collected material has been classified and analysed on the basis of the themes into Gandhian literature, Nationalist literature, Dramatic literature and Leftist literature. In each chapter the contents of the works were detailed comprehensively. This is necessary to understand the theme, nature of the criticism levelled against the colonial Government, the spirit and attempt of the writers to arouse national consciousness of the people and finally to assess the various types of official interference with freedom of press and shifting rationale for interference with printed opinion.

The present study is divided into nine chapters. The First chapter is an introduction to the study, wherein the scope, methodology, sources and the plan of the study are given.

In the Second chapter a comprehensive history of the national movement in Andhra is dealt with. The Third chapter explains the then prevailing conditions pertaining to press and publication and the repressive legislation of the British. It also highlights the Acts passed by the Government to control the Indian press and writings of nationalist writers.

The nationalist intelligentsia of Andhra came under the influence of Gandhian politics and they in their works described Gandhiji as the only leader who could lead the masses and establish Swarajya. The Fourth chapter explains and examines the nature, the content and the attitude of the writers towards the Gandhian phase of national movement during the period under study.

The Fifth chapter explains how the nationalist writers tried through their writings to spread economic nationalism and patriotic fervour among the Andhras.

The writers of Andhra, recognising the influence of Dramas, especially when enacted, on the people, particularly the illiterate, wrote a number of political dramas to generate mass awakening aimed at using it as a method of mass mobilization. The Sixth chapter evaluates the contribution of the proscribed dramatic literature to the growth of nationalism.

The Seventh chapter gives an account of the banned Leftist literature of the period and assesses its role in the national movement, especially its contribution to the growth of socialistic ideas of Andhra region.

The Eighth chapter is an analytical study of the rich contribution and sacrifice made by the four 'Greats' of proscribed literature. They were all writers and freedom fighters. This feature makes their contribution all the more great.

Summary and Conclusion of this study are presented in the last chapter.

2

POLITICAL ENVIRONMENT

The English East India Company – a mere trading body – conquered India and handed it over to the British Crown to exercise imperial sway over it for about a century.

Under the rule of the East India Company the people became impoverished, their general condition deteriorated, their corporate life became disrupted and their religion was subject to fierce attack. Very few positive steps were taken by the Company to promote the material and moral welfare of the people. As a result of the Governmental politics and actions the Indian tradition, social structure and their faith completely broke down. The prospect before them appeared quite dark. In 1857 a mighty popular revolt also called the First War of Indian Independence broke out in Northern and Central India. It began with a mutiny of the sepoys, but soon it spread to other regions and people. Even though the British suppressed the revolt with an ironhand, it played an important role in bringing the Indian people together and paved the way for the rise of the modern national movement.

As a result of the Sepoy Mutiny (1857-58) the administration of the British territories in India was formally transferred from the East India Company into the hands of the British Crown. In 1858 Queen Victoria issued a proclamation. In the proclamation the Queen promised to establish political, economic, social and religious justice but it was a broken pledge. Even there was not much upliftment in all the fields of life of the people.

The foundation of three universities; the importance of the indigenous languages recognised by Indian political leaders, the Press, the National Literature, the religious movements, Associations for political and other purposes paved the way for the establishment of Indian National Congress in 1885. Its first session was held at Bombay in December 1885 – under the presidentship of a Bengal barrister, W.C. Bannerjee.

The freedom struggle in India passed through three stages. The first covered the period 1885 – 1905, the second period 1906-1920, and the third period 1921-1947. In the first phase the struggle was carried on entirely on constitutional lines. Popular demands were presented to the authorities through petitions, meetings, resolutions and speeches.

The partition of Bengal on 20th July 1905 heralded the second stage in the history of freedom struggle in India. The intelligentsia of Bengal condemned the whole scheme as a deliberate plan to strike at the growing solidarity of Bengal nationalism. Agitation of unprecedented magnitude spread throughout Bengal demanding the integration of the province. The more prominent among its leaders were Bal Gangadhar Tilak, Lala Lajapat Rai, Bipin Chandra Pal and Aurobindo Ghosh. To acquire Swaraj with the co-operation of the masses by following Swadeshi programme and boycott of different forms was the basis strategy of these nationalist leaders. Non-payment of taxes was also thought of as a measure of last resort. Vandemataram became the battle cry of the movement. Hence it came to be known as the Vandemataram Movement.

My topic of research is confined only to Andhra. Hence I am giving a comprehensive account relating to Andhra's participation in freedom struggle. The real struggle for freedom in Andhra as in the other parts of the country commenced only in 1905.

Vandematram Movement

In Andhra the politics got a tremendous shape and the Andhra leaders were inspired by national new leaders like Bal Gangadhar Tilak, Lala Lajapat Rai, Bipin Chandra Pal and Aurobindo in the years 1906-11. The Andhra leaders did everything in fruitful manner by following the national leaders' speeches, writings and through their district and Provincial Conferences. Further in 1907 Mutnuri Krishna Rao who was an editor of a significant newspaper namely Krishna Patrika had invited Bipin Chandra Pal. Bipin Chandra Pal accepted the invitation and undertook responsibility for awakening of people in Andhra. From this time onwards everybody spoke about Swaraj and Vandemataram. Because of these new ideas number of young were sent to Japan[1] for getting the training in the modern industries and then people rejected the foreign goods and used the domestic goods. In the same period K. Hanumantha Rao started Andhra Jateeya Kalasala which influenced Andhra people to participate in the national movement.

The other methods adopted by the leaders were opening of reading rooms, composing of songs of exceptionally nationalist and patriotic nature, staging of plays of political nature and utilising the Telugu Press. These methods were adopted by the leaders to sustain the tempo of popular enthusiasm and to make the movement successful.

The Rajahmundry College Incident

Immediate effect of Pal's tour in Andhra was the Rajahmundry College Incident. Mark Hunter, an European, was then the Principal of Government Arts College, Government Training College, Rajahmundry. On the basis of complaints Hunter forbade the students from shouting Vandemataram, from becoming members of the local Bala Bharata Samiti, from participating in the public processions and from displaying Vandemataram medals and badges inside the college. But some of the students violated the said instructions of the principal. The leading students were Ramachandra Rao and Harisarvothama Rao. Ramachandra Rao was debarred from appearing for the B.A. degree examination. The Government debarred Harisarvothama Rao from employment in any office under the Government. It ruined the career of one hundred and forty young men.

The Cocanada Riot

Another important event that occurred in Andhra during this period was the Cocanada Riot (31st May, 1907). On that day Captain Kemp, the District Medical Officer was driving along in his carriage. Seeing him three boys standing at the clock tower on the road started shouting Vandemataram. Feeling grossly insulted he got down from his carriage, took hold of one of the boys and dealt him some blows until the boy became unconscious. Kemp dragged the boy to the police station and left him there without even giving him first aid. This behaviour of Kemp created a sensation in the town. A mob of two or three hundred armed with sticks gathered and attacked the European club where Kemp and his friends were having dinner. Even though the Riot was the outcome of the behaviour of the doctor the Government felt that the law and order at Cocanada had been broken. The Government began to follow a repressive policy with the object of terrorising the people.

A public meeting was held on 5th June 1907. It was presided over by K. Perraju and passed resolution relating to Kemp's deed, but it did not bring about a change in the attitude of the Government and the police. The Government arrested fifty persons in Cocanada suspected of having taken part in the riot. In addition to this they imposed on the town a punitive police the cost of which was to be met by the inhabitants. It was responsible for much resentment among the people. Out of the fifty persons prosecuted for participation in the riot thirteen were finally convicted.

The movement subsided from July 1907 because of the terror created by the Government. Yet such incidents and the reaction of the Government exercised great influence on the younger generation and influenced all the subsequent stages of the freedom struggle.

The passing of 1909 Minto-Morley reforms, the repressive policy of the Government, the annulment of the Partition of Bengal in 1911 and the expulsion of the extremists from the Congress contributed to the lessening of Vandemataram spirit. Until the beginning of Home Rule Movement, the Andhra leaders concentrated their energies on the formation of a separate Andhra Province.

Andhra Movement[2]

The Andhra Movement may be regarded as the Second Phase in the freedom struggle of this period. This was a comprehensive movement which aimed at the all-round development of Andhras – development in the political, economic, social and educational spheres. The leaders of Andhra felt that such development would be easy if all the Telugu areas in the Madras Presidency were constituted into a separate province and it was to the achievement of this aim that they mostly devoted themselves. It was in furthering the cause of a separate province that leaders like Konda Venkatappayya, Bhogaraju Pattabhi Sitaramayya, Vindyamuri Bhavana Chari and Unnava Lakshminarayana came to the forefront. The vernacular newspapers supported the Andhra movement.

For the all round development of the Andhras Deshabhimani, a paper published from Guntur, in its issue of 19th January, 1910 for the first time expressed the need for unity among the Andhras. It urged that the people should take energetic steps to secure their union.[3] In its issue of 4th February, it took up the cause of a united conference of all the districts in Andhra country. The Telugu Press and prominent leaders like N. Narayana Rao, C. Seshagiri Rao highlighted the needs and merits for the establishment of separate Andhra province in 1911. This idea took a definite shape at the Nidadavolu conference in 1912.

A standing committee was formed with Konda Venkatappayya as its secretary and he was asked to make necessary arrangements to convene an all India Conference.[4]

On 26th May, 1913, under the Presidentship of B.N.Sarma of Vizagapatam the first Andhra Conference met at Bapatla. There was heated discussion and stalwarts like Mutluri Adinarayana, Nyapati Subba Rao Pantulu, Mocherla Ramachandra Rao and Gooty Kesava Pillai opposed the idea of formation of separate Andhra Province. The second Andhra conference met at Bezawada on 11th April, 1914 with Nyapati Subba Rao Pantulu as President. Large majority supported the separate province.

The third Andhra conference met at Vizagapatam in May 1915 with the scholar Politician Raja Panuganti Ramarayaningar as President. A resolution was passed requesting the Government to establish separate Andhra province. Another important resolution of the conference was a demand fore making the mother tongue the medium of instruction in secondary schools. The immediate outcome of the Andhra movement was the growth of habit of addressing public meetings and carrying on the proceedings of all conferences in Telugu. The fourth Andhra Conference met at Cocanada in May, 1916 with Mocherla Ramachandra Rao as President. On June 1917 the fifth session of the Andhra Conference was held at Nellore with konda Venkatappayya as President. On the issue of separate Andhra Province some of the prominent leaders of Nellore voted against it.

Unification of the Congress, co-operation between the Congress and the Muslim League and the demand for Home Rule came to the forefront from 1916 onwards. So the Andhra leaders diverted their attention towards them. The national and regional movements came to act and react on each other.

Home Rule Movement

During 1911-18 Andhra leaders took a fairly active part in the deliberations of the Congress. Andhras had also a fair share in the membership of the subject committees and debates. Nyapati Subba Rao Pantulu was the General Secretary of the Congress for some years.

The Home Rule League was formally established on 28th April, 1916. "The object was to educate and mould public opinion in the country under constitutional means towards the attainment of the self-Government within the British empire".

Annie Besant, the President of the Theosophical Society started another Home Rule League in 1916 in Adyar (Madras). Andhra branch of the League was formed with Harisarvothama Rao as its Secretary. Branches of the League were established in all important towns like Vizagapatam, Guntur, Cocanada, Bezawada, etc. Public meetings were held in all important towns.

Besant also undertook a tour of Andhra from time to time during 1916. The watch word of Annie Besant was "Agitation and more Agitation". The Madras Government was naturally alarmed at the growth of the influence of

Besant and her League. Besides the protests the day on which Besant was interned was observed every month as the "Internment day". Everywhere there was an intensification of Home Rule activity. The movement became specially strong in the Krishna and Chittoor districts. In the city of Madras was formed a new body styled "The indignant group of the Home Rule League", the members of which wore the Besant Pendant as a badge and took a pledge to make any sacrifice for freedom.[5]

Government continued its policy of repression. District Collectors were instructed to discourage the public in the matter of holding protest meetings. But the intensity of the Home Rule agitation brought about a change in the attitude of the Home authorities towards India.

In the annual session of the Congress at Calcutta (1917) a resolution was passed recognising Andhra as a separate Congress circle. Telugu speaking districts were separated from the rest of the Madras Presidency and constituted into a new Congress circle. This was a victory for the sponsors of the Andhra movement.

On 22nd January, 1918 Andhra Provincial Congress Committee (A.P.C.C.) was formed with Nyapati Subba Rao Pantulu as president and Konda Venkatappayya as the General Secretary.[6] Andhra conference was held in 1918. For the first time a resolution was passed unanimously requesting the Government to include the formation of an Andhra Province in the new scheme of constitutional reforms.

The publication of the Montagu-Chelmsford Report on Constitutional Reforms did not satisfy the Indians. This Act of 1919 was not upto the expectations of the Congress and it did not bring out the desired changes in the administrative system in India. Most of the people shared the view expressed by Mrs.Besant that "the scheme is unworthy to be offered by England or to be accepted by Indians."

With the enactment of 1919 Act and the repressive policy of the Government Home Rule Phase of freedom struggle came to an end. But the significance of Home Rule movement lay in the fact that it kept alive the patriotic fervour of the people and succeeded in bringing together many top ranking leaders of first rate caliber in a common course of action. Unlike the previous movement the Home Rule campaign placed a concrete scheme of Self-Government before the people. Thus it marked the beginning of a new phase in the struggle for independence.

The Emergence of Gandhiji

In the history of the Freedom struggle the year 1919 was an outstanding year. In this year Gandhiji emerged as the leader and dominated the political scene till the achievement of freedom. The immediate occasion for his emergence was the passing of the Rowlatt Bill in March 1919. The object of this Bill was to give permanence to the repressive legislation of the warriors. It contained numerous clauses of a draconan character denying to the citizen even the most elementary rights. He took the initiative in mobilising public opinion against the repressive Bill. Against the Rowlatt Act, Satyagraha was begun on 6th April, 1919. The whole country responded well to the call of Satyagraha. In Madras Presidency, the Satyagraha was generally peaceful and was more successful in the Telugu districts than in the Tamil ones. Protest meetings were held in many towns in the Telugu area such as Rajahmundry, Guntur, Narsapur, Nellore and Chittoor at which resolutions were passed calling upon the Government of India to repeal the Rowlatt Act.[7] Gandhiji, the apostle of non-violence, was shocked by the violent outbreaks in north India and confessed that he had made a "Himalayan miscalculation".[8]

The most tragic incident in this year was the Jallianwalla Bagh Massacre at Amritsar (13th April, 1919). This was the worst crime that the British committed during the whole history of their rule in the country. It was indeed a turning point in the history of the Indian national movement. In the history of modern India, no other single incident caused so much bitterness against the British as this tragedy. The force of public opinion against the Government became irresistable. The atrocities in the Punjab sent a thrill of horror throughout Andhra although owing to the strict censorship exercised by the authorities information reached the people only slowly and in driblets.[9] What happened in the Punjab was regarded as a national humiliation.

In the meanwhile Muhammad Ali and Shaukat Ali had started the Khilafat movement as a protest against the dismemberment of the Turkish Empire and the treatment meted out to the Khalif. The treaty of sevres announced in May, 1920 however, did nothing to pacify the Muslims. Hence the Muslim masses were very much agitated over what they considered attacks on their religion. The Jallianwalla Bagh tragedy and the Khilafat question fraternised both the Hindus and Muslims in their opposition to the British.

Non-Cooperation and Civil Disobedience

It was in such a tense situation of indignation and resentment, disappointment and disillusionment that Gandhiji's programme of Non-violent Non-Cooperation was launched. The non-cooperation resolution was ratified at the regular annual session of the Congress held at Nagpur in December 1920. The Congress suggested seven boycotts, surrender of titles and honorary offices and resignation from nominated seats in local bodies; refusal to attend Government functions; gradual withdrawal of children from schools and colleges owned, aided or controlled by Government and in place of such schools and colleges the establishment of national schools and colleges in various provinces; gradual boycott of Brirtish courts by lawyers and litigants; refusal on the part of the military classes to offer themselves as recruits for service in Mesopotamia; withdrawal of candidates of their candidature for election to the reformed councils and refusal on the part of the voters to vote for any candidate who may, despite the Congress advice, offer himself for election; and boycott of foreign goods. [10] It is said that it was with the surrender of his decorations and title by Gandhiji on 1st August 1920 that non-cooperation was formally inaugurated.

Andhra was profoundly stirred and bands of volunteers carried the message of non-cooperation to towns and villages. All sorts of propaganda devices were used to popularise the non-cooperation movement. Public meetings were addressed by prominent Andhra leaders. The movement received wide popular support.

When the first elections under the Government of India Act 1919 drew near, in Andhra, leaders like A. Kaleswara Rao, Sabhapati, K.V.R.Swamy, R.Obulreddi and other withdrew their candidatures to the Madras Legislative Council. As the Congress candidates boycotted the election, the non-Brahman Justice party won a clear majority at the polls and assumed the reins of administration in the Madras Presidency. For the next decade and a half the Justice party administration, with the full backing of the British, fought the Gandhian Satyagraha movement. [11]

As regards the relinquishment of titles and honorary offices and resignation of Government jobs, the response was insignificant and negligible. [12]

In such an atmosphere the Congress met in December, 1920 at Nagpur and accepted no-tax campaign as a part of the civil disobedience programme.

Boycott of the Government run state aided educational establishments by students was spectacular. Up to the middle of 1921 altogether forty-four national schools with a total strength of 2,759 pupils were started throughout Andhra. [13] There were also five colleges teaching national education. Average of pupils in each institution was 300. [14] In all, 108 lawyers suspended practice in Andhra. [15] Popular Panchayat courts were founded to decide civil and criminal cases. But they disappeared as quickly as they came to be started.

It may be noted that in Andhra the movement in favour of civil disobedience and the non-payment of taxes started much earlier than 5th November, 1921, the day on which the All India Congress Committee (A.I.C.C.) authorised every province to undertake civil disobedience if the concerned provincial Congress committee was satisfied that the conditions laid down were fulfilled.

Non-cooperation was extended to municipalities with a view to paralyse local administration. Narasaraopet was the first municipality to be thus affected. In 1920, six out of twelve municipal councillors resigned as a protest against the implementation of the Madras Muncipalities Act of 1920. [16] Their resignations did not prove effective. The views of the Government reigned supreme in this case.

Revolt at Chirala – Perala

There was a trial of strength between the Government and non-cooperators in Chirala – Perala, in the district of Guntur. Chirala and Perala are two neighbouring villages in Bapatla taluk of Guntur district. The local inhabitants protests for fear that it would result in increasing the burden of local taxation. In spite of opposition, the Government imposed a municipality upon the people.

The people protested and asked for the cancellation of the Municipality under the leadership of Duggirala Gopalakrishnayya. [17] He believed that mere protest and non-cooperation would not serve the purpose, but that a parallel Government should be set up to discredit the British Government. With this idea, he started a volunteer army, the Rama-Dandu, the army of Sri Rama. This was to be a non-violent army to lead the people to victory. In pursuance of his programme, the people refused to pay the taxes.

Duggirala Gopalakrishnayya with one thousand of his Rama-Dandu volunteers met Gandhiji and other leaders on 30th March, 1921 at Bezwada where Gandhiji and other leaders were present to attend the A.I.C.C. meeting. On the request of Gopalakrishnayya Gandhiji visited Chirala on 6th April, 1921. He placed two alternatives before the people. One was to continue to no-tax campaign in a non-violent manner and face all the consequences and other was exodus from the town which would automatically result in the disappearance of the municipality. [18]

The people choose the second alternative which meant that they had to abandon their ancestral home. Under the leadership of Gopalakrishnayya, Rama-Dandu played an important role in bringing the people and their belongings to Ramanagar in a peaceful manner and they helped in establishment of amenities to the people. A Panchayat was established. There was virtually Gopalakrishnayya Raj. The difficulties the people had to face did not weaken their will.

In the midst of these hardships Gopalakrishnayya was arrested and sentenced to one year imprisonment. No prominent leader came forward to take his place. After spending eleven months in Ramanagar, the people returned to Chirala. They had to reconcile themselves to the continuance of the Municipality and pay the taxes.

Such a mass campaign did not occur in any other region in India during this period. "It anticipated the far greater mass movements later under Gandhiji".[19] The memory of Chirala-Perala continued to inspire the further struggle in Andhra.

While the non-cooperation movement was gradually spreading among the masses the A.I.C.C. held its meeting at Bezwada on 31st March and 1st April, 1921. it passed a resolution emphasising the need for constructive work and asked the people to collect one crore of rupees for the All India Tilak Swaraj Fund, to increase the number of Congress membership to one crore and to introduce ten lakhs of charakhas in India.

This conference created considerable political awakening among the Andhras. After the conference Gandhiji undertook tour of some of the coastal districts and through his meeting addresses he made it a point to make a special appeal to women. As a result, several women took a prominent part in the public life of the country. This marked a new stage in the history of the emancipation of women.

Defiance of Forest Rules

Another aspect of the non-cooperation movement was defiance of forest laws particularly in the Palnad (Guntur District) and Bezwada Taluks. People had to pay prohibitively high fees imposed by the collector himself. Conditions were specially bad in the year 1921 owing to an unfavourable season, great shortage of food and water, and a more rigorous enforcement of forest rules. The people demanded certain concessions such as free permits for cutting wood for agricultural implements and fuel, for cutting and removal of yepi leaves in the hot weather and for removal of earth from forests etc. But the concessions were not secured in time from the Government.

After the conclusion of the A.I.C.C. meeting held at Bezwada the emissaries of non-cooperation visited Guntur and people from distant villages of Palnad taluk attended the public meetings addressed by them. The message of these leaders also helped to conduct successfully the defiance of forest rules. In addition to that social boycott of Forest Department employees was effectively organised.

The A.P.C.C. appointed a committee in July, 1921 consisting of Unnava Lakshminarayana and Madabhushi Vedantam Lakshmi-Narasimhachari to enquire into the grievances of the people of Palnad. These leaders preached to the people the necessity of non-cooperation and exhorted them to observe strict non-violence. Their visit gave more strength to the agitation. At Macherla they were arrested on the ground that their speeches were provocative and imprisoned.[20] This led to a week's hartal in Guntur.

The imprisonment of the leaders infuriated the villagers and they launched a no-tax campaign. They sent their cattle into the reserve forests without paying the usual grazing fees. Government stengthened the number of forest guards and also stationed additional police in the area. There was a danger of the people coming into clash with them and mob violence breaking out. The Congress leaders in the district were not very much in favour of the movement and asked the villagers to pay the grazing fees while continuing the social boycott.

The villagers however, continued their movement. Matters came to a head in February 1922, when the no-tax campaign was at its height in Pedanandipad firka. In many villages the police were overpowered by the rescuing parties. The most serious incident occurred on the outskirts of Minchalapadu. The leader of the campaign in the area was Kannuganti Hanumanthu. On the 26th February there was a clash between the people and the police. The Sub-Inspector ordered his men to fire. In the firing three people were killed and several wounded. Among those that died were the leader Hanumanthu and one of his servants. The death of the leader, the large number of arrests that were made and the continued use of force by the police demoralized the inhabitants. The Bardoli resolutions also weakened the tempo of the civil disobedience movement in the district. Thus came to an end the forest Satyagraha of Palnad.

Boycott of Foreign Cloth

The Congress included boycott of foreign cloth as part of the non-cooperation movement to hit British business in India. Congressmen were advised to discard the use of foreign cloth and instructions were issued to the Congress organizations for the collection of foreign cloth from consumers either for destruction or for use outside India.

The idea of boycott of foreign cloth created great enthusiasm. At some places the boycott was carried out with redoubled zest. On 1st October, 1921, about 70 merchants of Bezwada took a pledge to boycott foreign cloth, not to import it and not to deal even in Indian mill made cloth or yarn till January 1922.[21] At Tenali, a group of 60 students picketed foreign cloth shops from 10th December. Not a single customer purchased foreign cloth on the following two days.[22] The import of foreign cloth began to steadily decline and to that extent the wearing of home woven cloth made from Indian hand spun yarn increased.

The Anti-Drink Campaign

The anti-drink campaign made considerable progress mainly in Anantapur, Kurnool, Guntur, Ballary and Godavari districts. Both the Hindus and the Muslim worked shoulder to shoulder in a remarkable spirit of goodwill to organize the campaign. Their programme included preventing prospective bidders from bidding at sales of arrack and toddy shops and picketing them after they were leased. These activities were attended with much unpleasantness.

The social conscience of the people was aroused, a sort of stigma was attached to indulgence in drink and the ground was silently prepared for the introduction of prohibition at a later stage.

Repression

Non-cooperation movement was more widespread and intense in Andhra than in the rest of the Madras province. This is the reason why the attention of the Government was specially directed to this area. The Seditious Meeting Act was revived and the Criminal Law Amendment Act and the powers under section 144 of the Indian Penal Code were freely used. Meetings, processions and demonstrations were forcibly broken up. House searches were made for getting copies of national ballads, pamphlets and books which were suspected of preaching sedition.

Another form of repression was the prohibition of wearing Gandhi cap. Even Telugu books which were written with a view to infuse patriotic sentiment and consciousness of nationality among the people were gagged.

A simple example to the Government's repressive policy is the punishment given to a village karnam in Godavari district for no other reason than his giving food to a non-cooperator who visited the village in a state of starvation.[23]

The cup of repression was full to its brim, yet it did not succeed in checking the progress of the movement. The arrest and imprisonment of the Ali brothers worsened the situation and on 5th November 1921, the A.I.C.C. adopted a resolution empowering every province to undertake civil disobedience including non-payment of taxes on its own responsibility.

In this atmosphere of frustration and tension the Prince of Wales visited India. On 17th November, 1921, when the Prince landed in India hartal was observed at several places like Cocanada, Peddapur, Rajahmundry, Tuni, Bezwada and Guntur to express people's resentment, it passed off quietly everywhere.

Thereafter the regular session of the Indian National Congress held in December 1921 endorsed the working committee's resolution with regard to the starting of civil disobedience and vested Gandhiji and Vallabhai Patel with full powers to supervise and conduct the course of the campaign. These two leaders planned to start the civil disobedience campaign first at Bardoli.

In spite of Gandhiji's objection a no tax campaign was organized in the three districts of Guntur, Krishna and Godavari.[24] It was not effectively organised in the latter two districts as in Guntur. The idea that inspired the campaign was that when the exchequer was drained, the Government would be forced to come to terms with the nationalist demand. With this spirit, the movement was started in Pedanandipad and other areas in Guntur district. Intensive propaganda had been already started during December 1921 in which Konda Venkatappayya and Gollapudi Sitarama Sastry played the leading role.

The A.P.C.C. at its meeting at Bezwada on 7th January, 1922, unanimously passed a resolution authorizing the commencement of civil disobedience including the non payment of taxes but confining it to the districts of Guntur, Krishna and Godavari. Shortly after the District Congress Committees of the three districts held separate meetings and unanimously resolved to start a campaign for withholding land revenue and other taxes in their respective areas.

In the Pedanandipad firka of Guntur district nearly one hundred villages rallied under the leadership of Parvataneni Veerayya Choudari and Machiraju Ramamurthi and withheld payment of taxes.

The village officers sympathised with the movement because they had some grievances: Low pay, lack of assistance from assistant karnams, and assistant headmen because of the reduction in the village establishment. The civil disobedience movement gave them an opportunity to show their resentment against the Government. The village officers of Pedanandipad submitted their resignations. These resignations created considerable difficulty in the collection of revenue. Another step in the organization of campaign was the raising of a large number of volunteers. These volunteers toured nthe villages to keep up the enthusiasm of the people. As a result only about five percent of the total tax demand could be collected by the Government.[25]

The Government appointed substitutes for the village officers who had resigned or were dismissed. But such measures did not prove effective.

The Congress volunteers prevented people from accepting appointment as village officers. The Government adopted the quartering of punitive police in every village in which the volunteers made themselves conspicuous. On the initiative of L.G. Rutherford, Collector of Guntur, a large number of non-cooperators were whipped.[26]

The repressive measures adopted by the Government at Ramapuram, a small village in Palnad, serves as a significant instance to show how the ordinary villagers could be subdued by such threats. When the villagers refused to pay tax and drove away the tahsildar and the Inspector of Police, the Collector took them unawares by surrounding the village with his mounted men and reserve police before dawn. The Collector accompanied by the District Superintendent of Police and the Divisional Officer woke up the Village Officers, made the villagers assemble and held an identification parade and arrested eighteen men on the spot.[27] This struck so much fear in the villagers that revenue was practically collected by the next morning. The sub-committee of the A.P.C.C. toured the village in Pedanandipad firka and other areas where the campaign was carried on and recommended its suspension. The Government began to take more repressive measures. A number of non-cooperators were whipped. Several were sentenced to imprisonment. Parvataneni Virayya Choudhari was forced to tender an apology as an alternative to being shot dead.

The outbreak of violence at Chouri Choura on 5th February gave a rude shock to Gandhiji's plans and in a mood of introspection he characterized the movement as a "Himalayan blunder". Hence the Congress working committee meeting on the 11th and 12th February 1922 passed a resolution suspending the movement till "the forces of violence were brought under effective control".

The Government of India held the non-cooperation movement responsible for all the disturbances in India during 1921-22.[28] Gandhiji was arrested on 1st March, 1922. At the trial he pleaded guilty accepting full responsibility for occurrences in Madras and elsewhere. He said "I ran the risk, and if I were set free, I would still do the same". He was sentenced to six years imprisonment.[29] A large number of non-cooperators in Madras presidency particularly in the Telugu districts, were arrested. Thus came to an end the non-cooperation movement in the Andhra.

However the non-cooperation and civil disobedience movements were not a total failure. Even though they did not produce any fruitful results, they did contribute to some useful results. They brought about an awakening of the masses. Political consciousness began to spread to villages. People in the villages began to recognise the significance of Swaraj. Increasing recognition of the need to solve the problem of untouchability and emphasis on khaddar were the results of the events of 1921-22.

The non-cooperation movement also contributed to engender the spirit of freedom and fearlessness among the people. As the official Congress historian remarks: Fear had been cast off by the people. "A sense of self-respect developed in the nation. Congressmen realised that service and self-sacrifice were the only means of winning public confidence. The prestige too of Government was materially shaken, and people had received good lessons regarding the ideology of Swaraj."[30]

Controversy Over Council Entry

The suspension of the non-cooperation movement after Chouri Choura incidents created a feeling of frustration among the Congressmen. Some of them like Hakim Ajmal Khan, Motilal Nehru and V. J. Patel advocated a reversal of the old Congress policy of boycott of legislature and favoured council entry with a view to wreck the constitution and expose the hollowness of 1919 Reforms. This was opposed by some of the Congress leaders liked Kasturi Ranga Iyengar, M.A.Ansari and C. Rajagopalachari on the ground that council entry would mean a violation of the principle and spirit of non-cooperation and that it would help the Government to regain its lost prestige.

The clash between the no-changers and pro-changers reached its climax at the Gaya Congress session held in 1922 where the pro-changers were defeated. This led to the organization within the Congress of the Swaraj party by the supporters of the council entry programme.

There was no unanimity among the Andhra leaders also over the issue of council entry. Andhra was a stronghold of no changers. To win support of the new party C.R. Das toured the Andhra districts in 1923 and conferred with prominent Andhra leaders. This led to the establishment of a branch of the Swaraj party with A. Kaleswara Rao as President and D. Gopalkrishnayya and N.V.L. Narasimha Rao as its secretaries. The pro-changers were triumphantly returned in the elections.

But as the Swaraj party in the Madras Legislative Council was in a minority it became impossible for it to adhere to a policy of effective and constant obstruction.

After the 1924 compromise between the no-changers and the Swarajists, the latter were permitted to carry on the work in the legislatures "on behalf of the Congress and as an integral part of the Congress organization". For the first time in its history the Congress assumed direct control of the electioneering campaign in 1926 and achieved amazing success. Though the Congress legislators constituted a majority, the party refused to form ministry and followed a policy of responsive cooperation. But its achievements within the legislature were not striking.

Outside the council, the activities of the Congress were mainly concentrated upon the implementation of constructive programme. One of the important items of the programme was the manufacture of Khaddar by stimulating hand-spinning and hand-weaving. This work was undertaken with a view to improve the economic position of the poorer classes and also to gain support of these classes to the freedom movement. Real efforts aimed at popularising khaddar commenced after the opening of a branch in Andhra of the All India Spinners Association in 1925. District and Taluk Congress committees followed this example and constituted separate khaddar sub-committees.

At the Calcutta Congress session in 1928 the other planks of the constructive programme figured prominently. The Congress adopted a resolution requiring the Congressmen to confine themselves to the party's organizational work and the anti-drink campaign during 1929. The prohibition campaign was carried on through the press and platform by A. Govindacharlu who toured some of the districts in Andhra. The immediate outcome of this campaign was that some of the Taluk boards and District boards in Andhra resolved not to lease out the Palmyra trees for toddy tapping.[31]

Sitarama Raju's (Rampa) Rebellion.[32]

In August 1922 Alluri Sitaramaraju resorted to violence in Rampa sub-division of the Godavari and Vizagapatam agency for achieving independence. He was aided in this task by a small band of devoted and loyal friends. It lasted for nearly two years and caused more headache than the non-cooperation movement. Gandhiji paying a tribute to Raju, characterised his exploits "as an instance of sustained bravery and genius".[33]

After the suppression of the Rampa rebellion there was a lull for about a decade in revolutionary activities. Meanwhile the urge for Swaraj was rapidily increasing. The Andhra Provincial Congress meeting at Masulipatam in December, 1925 and Eluru in the following year passed resolutions recommending to the Indian National Congress to amend its constitution in order to define "Swaraj" as complete independence outside the British Empire. Further, B. Sambamurthi, supporter of the change, formed a small committee to launch intensive agitation for complete independence. But majority of Andhra leaders including K. Nageswara Rao, G. Sitarama Sastri and others were for "Dominion status" and felt that there was no urgency for a change in the Congress objective.

No Government parts with power unless it meets with irresistible pressure and no such pressure could be exercised on the British authorities in India during the years 1924-1927. It was practically a period of lull in the history of freedom movement. The statement of the historian of the nationalist movement in East Krishna that the country was free from all excitement from 1923 to 1930 was specially true of these three years 1924-1927.[34] The controversies that raged in Andhra as in other parts of the country affected only the domestic politics of the various parties engaged in the national struggle. Government was not in any way perturbed by them and the administration went on along its normal course.

The years 1928-29 mark the stage of transition from council-entry to satyagraha as the more effective weapon for achieving Swaraj. Many factors and developments were responsible for bringing about this change in the attitude of the majority. There was increasing realisation during these years that work in the councils was futile and that it was incapable of producing the result which was originally expected of it. More important than this was the re-entry of Gandhiji into active politics and his assumption of the leadership of the freedom movement. After his release from prison in 1924 he devoted almost all his time to constructive work and to work connected with the Sabarmati Ashram. It was only in March, 1928, that he felt himself morally free to take part in politics once again.

The popular indignation of the appointment of the Simon commission consisting of only Englishmen and the ruthless suppression of the black flag demonstrations against the visit of the Commission, the reluctance of the British Government to accept the constitutional reforms recommended by the Motilal Nehru Committee and the unsatisfactory nature of Lord Irwin's declaration of October, 1929, again gave the struggle for freedom, which showed signs of languor after 1922, fresh life and vigour. The Congress, at its session held at Lahore in December 1929, authorised the working committee to start civil disobedience movement whenever the situation had arisen warranting such a step, declared that the country's goal was the achievement of "complete independence" and directed the Congress members of the legislatures and committees constituted by the Government to resign their seats forthwith.

Accordingly V.V.Jogayya and T. Prakasam, Andhra representatives in the Legislative Assembly, V. Ramadas Pantulu and Dr.V.Rama Rao, representatives in the Council of State, Swami Venkatachalam Chetti, R. Kotireddi, B. Venkataratnam, G. Harisarvothama Rao, P. Anjaneyulu and other Andhra representatives in the Madras Provincial Council, tendered their resignations.

Salt Satyagraha and Civil Disobedience

The A.I.C.C. met at Ahmedabad in February 1930, decided on launching a countrywide civil disobedience movement and requested Gandhiji to lead it. Gandhiji chose to start the Satyagraha campaign by breaking the salt laws at Dandi. Accompanied by a large concourse of people, men and women, Gandhiji marched from his ashram at Ahmedabad and reaching Dandi on 5th April, symbolically manufactured illicit Salt. It was a historic event which sparked off a vigorous movement for similar defiance of authority in other parts of the country.

Andhra displayed great enthusiasm in the ferment. Meeting on 23rd March under the presidency of K. Nageswara Rao at Bezwada, the A.P.C.C. unanimously adopted resolution reaffirming the Congress Working Committee's resolution on civil disobedience. The committee urged the Andhra Congressmen to actively participate in the movement and chose K. Venkatappaiah as the Dictator for Andhra region.

Before the Salt Satyagraha campaign was actually initiated mass meetings were held at Bezwada, Eluru, Guntur and other places where inspiring speeches were made appealing for people's support. Training was given to Satyagrahis as to how salt laws were to be defied in a non-violent manner. Special sibirams were opened for this purpose in many places in Andhra.

The first stage in this new phase of civil disobedience in Andhra began with open defiance of the Salt laws at numerous places where people in large numbers deliberately manufactured salt illegally. This continued with vigour till the end of April.

During the first stage the Government did not take the movement seriously. It contented itself only with arrests and convictions of political leaders of the Congress who participated in the movement. Many Andhra leaders were sentenced to various terms of imprisonment. Government's repression fanned the flames and further intensified tension. Fresh leaders took the place of the arrested ones. The tendency to disregard the law began to increase. Therefore the Government adopted stern measures to crush it.

Some of the local bodies like the municipal councils of Guntur, Chirala, Peddapuram, Tenali, Nellore Cocanada and Rajahmundry and some of the local boards like the East Godavari District Board, Anantapur District Board and Ramachandrapuram Taluk Board expressed their sympathy towards the Satyagraha movement in some form or other.[35] Some of them hoisted national flags on their buildings; some issued instructions to their employees to wear Khaddar and conduct propaganda in favour of its use; some prescribed the singing of national songs as a part of the daily programme of work in their schools; some organized processions of students carrying national flags; some passed adjournment motions in connection with the arrests of political leaders; and some others passed resolutions condemning the repressive policy of the Government.

In addition to the policy of repression, Government thought of a plan of counter propaganda against the Satyagraha movement. The publication and circulation of leaflets, the organization of loyalist associations the holding of meetings of cooperators and the financing of newspapers which supported Governmental policies were some of the items which were included in the plan.

The arrests of the leaders and the repressive measures of the police led to the collapse of the spectacular salt Satyagraha in the districts of Krishna, West Godavari and Nellore and in the city of Madras. But the sense of anger went underground. In other places however, the repression gave an impetus to the movement.

Some village officers resigned their offices to express their sympathy with the movement. Village officers suspected of sympathising with the campaign by providing food and shelter to volunteers were dismissed.

With the advent of the monsoon in June the movement declined. The heavy rains in the coastal districts made it impossible to revive the movement for preparation of Salt. In the second week of June when the A.P.C.C. found that picking of Salt was becoming increasingly difficult owing to the monsoon it instructed the volunteers to stop salt satyagraha and to speed up the boycott of foreign cloth and the anti-drink propaganda.

The boycott of foreign cloth proved widespread and effective. It had already made considerable progress at several places as it was one of the weapons in the previous agitation. Foreign cloth shops were picketed to intensify the boycott movement.

The anti-drink campaign of the Congress made remarkable headway in Andhra. It gave rise to considerable difficult in certain parts in carrying on the excise administration.

Hoisting the Congress flag was another means by which the leaders tried to keep alive the patriotic spirit of the people. The Government did not like the spirit of defiance with which the flags were hoisted. Hence it tried to ruthlessly put down all such attempts, though flag hoisting was not an offence.

As the movement was making steady progress the Government increased the repressive measures and tried to curtain the activities of Congress volunteers in various other ways. On the 21st June the Government of Madras, under powers conferred on it by the Criminal Law Amendment Act, declared the A.P.C.C. and the war councils of Guntur, Krishna, East Godavari and West Godavari districts unlawful. Orders prohibiting meetings, processions, demonstrations in public streets, picketing, singing national songs and carrying flags were promulgated at places like Rajahmundry, Cocanada, Guntur, Bezwada, Masulipatam and Nellore. At Guntur, wearing of Gandhi caps was prohibited because "donning such caps appeared as a symbol of one's sympathy for the civil disobedience movement."[36]

People did not meekly submit; many acted openly in defiance of the these prohibitory orders. Sometimes there were clashes between the police and the agitators resulting in the death of a few and injuries to many. There were also large scale arrests of volunteers.

There were sporadic instances of no-tax satyagraha. But no attempts were made to organise such campaign on any large scale.

In the midst of this struggle was signed the Gandhi-Irwin Pact in 1931. The movement was discontinued and political leaders were freed. The agreement however permitted peaceful activities, and during the period of truce volunteers engaged themselves in a vigorous and organised campaign of anti-drink.

On 28th December, 1931 Gandjhiji returned from England (after attending the Second Round Table Conference in London) completely disillusioned and he found that the Government of India was unrelenting and unbending in arriving at a peaceful settlement. As a result the civil disobedience movement was resumed in 1932 under the leadership of Gandhiji. The Government too was ready to face Congress challenge. It took the initiative and promptly arrested Gandhiji on the 3rd January, 1932. This action stimulated the whole of India, and the Andhras, along with others, prepared themselves to conduct the campaign of civil disobedience. Dictators were appointed in all districts to organise and conduct the movement in their areas. The new civil disobedience movement of 1932 differed from that of 1930-31. It was spontaneous in character. It became a mass movement in the real sense of the term. The absence of leaders (clapped in jails) strengthened and not weakened it.

The Government of Madras acted swiftly to supress the movement. No time was lost in promulgating a number of ordinances in Andhra also to effectively counter Congressmen's activities. The Congress committees which were the main organising agencies of the campaign were first dealt with. The A.P.C.C. and the District Congress Committees were banned.[37] The other associations and organizations proscribed in like manner were the Yelamanchili Firka Congress committee, the Hindustan Seva Dal (Ganjam district) and Madras city Congress Boycott committee.[38]

The promulgation of ordinance was followed by the declarations of 'ashramas' which became the backbone of the struggle as unlawful associations. Simultaneously, under the Criminal Procedure Code the activities of influential leaders were circumscribed. As a measure of repression number of books were proscribed and action was taken against the writers and press.

In spite of the fury of Government repression the movement went from strength to strength in the first four months. New leaders stepped into the field directing the operations. Bands of volunteers actively concerned themselves with the civil disobedience activities and continued the struggle with great fierceness. Boycott of foreign cloth, picketing of foreign cloth shops, defiance of salt laws, picketing of foreign cloth shops, defiance of salt laws, picketing of liquor and toddy shops spread to the whole region and continued with great vigour to a great extent on perfectly non-violence lines.

Another important feature of the movement was the distribution of pamphlets issued regularly in spire of police vigilance among the people furnishing information of all that was happening. Unauthorised pamphlets about Congress activity were distributed among the people. By the middle of 1932 Congress volunteers organised political conferences despite the police ban.

In addition to the arrest of prominent Civil resisters the Government quartered extra police as a punitive measure on such villages were found to have taken a leading part in the civil disobedience movement and collected collective fines.

An information conference of Congressmen who were outside jails was held in Poona (on 12th July, 1933) in Gandhiji's presence to take stock of the political situation. It authorised Gandhiji to seek an unconditional interview with the Viceroy and then decide the future course of action. Gandhiji's attempts to seek unconditional interviews with the Viceroy failed because of the cold response from the Government. Gandhiji thereupon decided that in the interests of national honour civil disobedience must be resumed though in the form of individual as distinguished from mass civil disobedience which had already been suspended. He called upon "all those who are able and willing to offer individual civil disobedience on their own responsibilities, without expectation of any assistance from the Congress organisations" to join the new movement. In consequence of this all the Congress Committee and war councils were dissolved by Aney (the president of the Congress at that time) and they ceased to function.

On 31st July, 1933 Gandhiji, Kasturibai, Mahadev Desai and thirty inmates of the Sabarmati Ashram started their campaign of individual civil disobedience. They were arrested on 1st August and Gandhiji was once more taken to Yeravada Prison as a state prisoner. He was released three days later but was served with a notice calling on him to reside within the limits of Poona city. He disobeyed this order of restraint for which he was arrested, tried and sentenced to one year imprisonment. He was now treated as an ordinary prisoner and not as a state prisoner. Andhra Satyagrahis followed Gandhiji's example and were imprisoned by the Government.

By the beginning of 1934 "the progress of events in the line of civil disobedience was none too satisfactory. The prisoners who were released were fagged. The Provincial leaders who had promised at Poona conference to lead their provinces if mass civil disobedience was given up and individual civil disobedience continued, did not carry out their pledges, except in a few cases. Those who were released from jails found themselves unable or unwilling to face another conviction."[39] The movement lost all momentum and it was only a question of time as to when it would be officially end.

During these circumstances Gandhiji gave a statement on 7th April, 1934.[40] In response to it Government lifted the ban on the meeting of A.I.C.C. and some months later the ban on other Congress bodies was also withdrawn. The Working Committee and A.I.C.C. met in Patna on 18-20th May 1934, suspended the civil disobedience movement and accepted the entry into legislatures as a part of the Congress programme. Thus the Satyagraha battle for freedom resumed on 4th January, 1932 was officially ended on 20th May, 1934.

The period of the civil disobedience movement was full of excitement and drama. The symbolic breach of insignificant Salt laws quickly developed into an aggressive civil resistance campaign on large scale. It continued for a long a time, brought forth qualities of fearlessness, devotion and sacrifice in the volunteers. Women vied with men in violating laws enforced by an alien Government. In this movement enthusiasm was irrepressible. The yearning for freedom did not die in spite of Government's repression which grew with the intensify of the movement. The struggle was however suspended before its goal had been achieved. Thus "it started with a bang and ended in a whimper".[41]

Revolutionary Societies

During the days of civil disobedience movement violent activities were also organized by revolutionary societies to hasten the attainment of freedom. The execution of Bhagat Singh revived extremist sentiment more defiantly than ever and the "Ujjivan Bharat Sammelan' a terrorist organization, was set up in the Godavari district in 1931.

Another revolutionary organization called the 'Hindustan Socialist Republican army' (Madras branch) was founded by about twenty persons in Madras on 16th March 1933. They came into contact with the terrorists of northern India like P.C. Ganguli, S.M.Ghosh and others. They pledged to obtain Swaraj through revolutionary means.

The non-violent, civil disobedience movement and the violent revolutionary movement went side by side and each influenced the other. Their methods and programmes were diametrically opposed to each other. Their objective was same – the achievement of complete independence. The two streams however joined together in 1942 to give the last battle for freedom in a new form.

New Parties

The suspension of the civil disobedience movement caused disappointment in certain quarters and led to the formation of new parties within the Congress. On 12th February, 1934, the Andhra Congress Swaraj Party was formed at an informal meeting held at Bezwada. It was, in fact, only a revival of the old Swaraj Party. Prominent among the persons responsible for this were V. Ramadas Pantulu, G.V. Subbarao and others. The party issued a manifesto in March declaring that its creed was the same as that of the Indian National Congress but with greater stress on social and economic uplift of the country alongside political emanicipation.

The emergence of the new ideas of Socialism which convulsed Europe and the progress achieved in the Socialist countries attracted the attention of some Congressmen. About three hundred of them drawn mainly from younger generation met for the first time at Bezwada on 23rd June, 1934 and formed the Andhra Congress Socialist Party. Only members of the Indian National Congress could become its members and every one of them was bound to subscribe to Marxist principles.

The aims and objects of the party were the conversion of the Congress to Socialism, transfer of the administration of the country to the producer and the proletariat class and the abolition of the system of Zamindars, estates – holders and landlords.[42]

The party also decided to form labour and ryot associations in order to organize a powerful peoples movement for the attainment of Swaraj and for a speedy transformation of the society on Socialistic ideals. N.G. Ranga was elected as the president of the new party and M. Annapoornayya as the Secretary.

These two parties came into existence as complementaries to the Indian National Congress to mobilize the people for a major struggle. Besides these wings of the Congress a new party known as the people's party came into existence. It was organized by the Rajah of Pithapuram with the object of working the provincial autonomy under the Act of 1935. But it had very little public support.

Congress in Office

The next stage in the history of freedom movement was marked by the formation and working of a Congress Ministry in Madras as a result of the first general election held for the provincial legislatures under the Government of India Act of 1935.

The election to the two Houses of the Madras Legislature was held between the 15th and 20th February, 1937 and the Congress emerged from it in great triumph. The Justice party which had been the ruling party for years "as also the people's part of zamindars, led by the Maharaja of Pithapuram" was completely routed. In both the houses the Congress secured absolute majorities. [43] In the local bodies, Congress candidates were elected in a majority to the West Godavari district board though the party failed to win a clear majority in the district boards of Chittoor, Anantapur and Kurnool, its nominees were nevertheless elected as their presidents.

In pursuance of the Congress directive, the Congress party refused to form ministry in Madras. The Congress wanted an assurance from the Governors that they would not use their special powers to override ministers in regard to their constitutional activity. After much haggling and bargaining a compromise was arrived at an Lord Linlithgow, the Viceroy of India assured the Congress on 21st June that he would "strive towards the full and final establishment in India of the principles of Parliamentary Government". [44]

Consequently a visible change came over the Congress and Congressmen were permitted to accept office, "where they may be invited thereto".

As a result of this decision a Congress Ministry was formed in Madras on 14th July, 1937 with C. Rajagopalachari as Chief Minister. The Congress ministry remained in office for twenty eight months till 29th October, 1939 when it resigned as a result of political developments caused by the outbreak of the Second World War. This is not the place to describe in detail the work of the Ministry during this period. The important legislation of the Congress ministry were the passing of the Madras Agriculturalist Relief Act which provided for a liberal scaling down of debts and arrears of rent due from agriculturists. [45] The Madras Prohibition Act was passed in 1937. To raise the social and economic status of Harijans the Malabar Temple Entry Act passed in 1938; the removal of Civil abilities Act passed in the same year[46] and the Madras Temple Entry Authorisation and Indemnity Act of 1939 were placed on the statute book. [47] While the Congress Ministry was working successfully, differences arose between the Congress and the British Government after the outbreak of the second world war regarding the war objectives and the Congress Ministers resigned. But the numerous progressive measures of the Congress Ministry taken to ameliorate the condition of the masses and the efficient administration strengthened the confidence of the people in the Congress.

At the time of resignation of Congress Ministers there were a number of leftist organizations active in Andhra. There was a branch of the Forward Bloc with Madduri Annapurnayya as its secretary. There were many workers associated with the Communist party. But as the party itself was banned they worked either underground or infiltrated into the Congress. There were also branches of the All India Students Federation active in many places. Similarly there were branches of the All India Kisan Sabha with N. G. Ranga as their leader.

Though there were certain differences in the objectives of these various leftist organizations they were all agreed that the time was ripe for the resumption of civil disobedience both for securing the freedom of the country from alien rule and for getting rid of vested interests like zamindaras, money-lenders and capitalists. This was the fundamental point of difference between them and the Congress.

All the leftist organistions suffered from one point of weakness. They had no branches in all parts of the country. They had not the same mass following as the Congress had. They had no All-India leader of the stature of Gandhiji. The result was that their appeal proved ineffective.

There was again a constitutional deadlock. The Congress met at Ramgarh in March 1940 and resolved it could not become a party to the war and that nothing short of complete independence was acceptable to the Indian people. Wearied of the unsympathetic attitude of the British Government the Congress working committee authorised Gandhiji to launch civil disobedience movement. Gandhiji was thus chosen again to lead the country. He interviewed the Viceroy but failed to obtain permission for the Congressmen to deliver speeches against the war.

Individual Satyagraha

As a result, the individual civil disobedience campaign was started by Gandhiji on 17rth October, 1940 with Vinobha Bhave as the first Satyagrahi. For the violation of Government order he was arrested and sentenced. Numerous arrests thereafter followed throughout the country. The campaign started in Andhra in the third week of November, 1940 and before the close of the year all the Congressmen in the front rank were arrested. More and more entered the jails during 1941. In Andhra the total number arrested was 882 and the amount collected in the form of fines was Rs.76,533.[48]

About 1,867 Satyagrahis participated in the individual civil disobedience campaign upto the middle of April 1941. In the succeeding days the number of participants as well as arrests considerably declined, although a few continued to offer Satyagraha and court arrests till about the second week of May 1941.

In December the Government of India announced that all civil disobedience prisoners whose offences had been formal or symbolic in character would be set free including Azad and Nehru. Almost all of them were released in the course of the month and although the campaign of individual satyagraha was not formally withdrawn and although Gandhiji was against its withdrawal the movement might be said to have come to an end by the close of 1941.

A change came gradually in the attitude of the Communists after Hitler's invasion of Soviet Russia. They no longer opposed Britain's war effort in India as they thought that it all helped the defence of Soviet Russia which they regarded as their fatherland. This change in their attitude came as a great relief to the Government and it led in course of time to the lifting of the ban on Communists. This was the reason why in 1942 it was left mostly to the Congress to carry on the freedom struggle.

By the middle of March 1942 a Japanese attack on India seemed imminent. It was at this critical juncture that Sir Stafford Cripps, who was deemed a friend of India, was sent with certain proposals on 22nd March, 1942 to win India's support. The Cripps offer envisaged granting of dominion status to India with the right to secede from the British Commonwealth and also the framing of a new constitution by a constitution-making body which would be set up immediately after the cessation of hostilities. Further, the proposals permitted a province or state to take a decision either to join the union or to remain outside enjoying the same full status as the Indian union. The Congress rejected the proposals because its demand that the new Government to be formed be treated as a cabinet was not accepted by the British Government. The Muslim League opposed the proposals for, the latter did not contain a clear promise of Pakistan.

The Quit India Movement

The year 1942 was a momentous one in the history of Indian freedom struggle. It witnessed the rise and growth the Quit India movement which in a sense marked the final stage in the struggle. It looked like a revolution in the ordinary accepted sense of the term. All sections of people participated in it. By July 1942 the Congress was convinced that the British Government was not serious about coming to an honourable settlement about Indian problems and that it could not cooperate with the British in their war efforts. It however persuaded Gandhiji to resume leadership of the Congress and lead the people in the fight for freedom.

The Quit India movement was the inevitable outcome of the failure of the Cripps mission and the frustration it created in Gandhiji and the Congress circles. Gandhiji had already started writing in the 'Harijan' suggesting "orderly and timely British withdrawal from India". This was, in fact the forerunner of the Quit India resolution passed at Bombay by the A.I.C.C. on 8th August, 1942. This famous resolution demanded the immediate withdrawal of the British power from India, entrusting authority to govern the country to a provisional Government, and sanctioned the starting of a mass struggle on non-violent lines on the widest possible scale under the leadership of Gandhiji. The mantra he gave to the people was "Do or Die".

Already the A.P.C.C. had issued an important confidential circular dated 29th July 1942, to all District Congress Committees indicating the lines on which the organization work was to be undertaken and also the programme of the campaign. Briefly stated, the items of the programme were: defying prohibitary orders, lawyers to give up practice, students to leave college, picketing salt and foreign trade and industry, cutting of communications, cutting of spathe of the toddy yielding trees, travelling without tickets, pulling chains, to stop trains, cutting telegraph and telephone wires, non-payment of taxes excepting municipal taxes, picketing of recruitment offices, picketing of troops and hoisting national flags on all Government building as a sign of independence.

The Government had made all necessary arrangements months ahead for firmly dealing with the movement, and immediately after the passing of the Quit India resolution it struck first and suddenly made sweeping arrests of prominent All India Congress leaders in the belief that by this means the movement could be crushed in its infancy. The A.P.C.C. was outlawed and very soon Andhra leaders like T. Prakasam, T. Viswanatham and others were clapped into prison.

When the people found that they were leaderless they grew intensely angry and it led to spontaneous mass upheaval where each one proved a leader to himself. Groups of people in a frenzy of fury and anger resorted to acts of destruction and directed their anger against the symbols of British power with the intention of paralysing the entire administration in the country. In the beginning of the struggle peaceful demonstrations and processions were held but later on they took a very violent turn. These outbreaks of mob violence, started almost simultaneously in towns and villages in Andhra and the damage was quite extensive.

Railway stations were attacked and burnt at several places. Railway communications were the targets of mob attack. For miles together railway tracks were tampered with and the removal of fish plates, rails or sometimes both were secretly organized with intent to derail trains. Police stations also became targets of attack and some of them were burnt. Even post offices were not spared. Telephone and Telegraph communications were put out of order at as many as 1,500 places in Andhra.[49]

Governments reprisals followed, almost simultaneously. To combat this phase of the movement two special ordinances were passed. Strict censorship was exercised over the press so that people might be kept ignorant of the course of development of the movement in the various parts of the country.[50] The Government tried to suppress the movement by prohibiting meetings processions etc. under Section 144 of the Criminal Procedure Code.

At the same time a non-violent, non-cooperation programme was also vigorously conducted. It assumed many forms. One of them was holding public meetings with a view to whip up public enthusiasm and to secure active cooperation of the people.

The students played a very commendable part in the Quit India Movement by trying to bring about an effective boycott of educational institutions as a mark of protest against the Government's repressive policy.

Salt laws were violated at some places. Sporadic attempts were made to picket toddy and arrack shops. Attempts were made to induce public servants to Quit their offices.

By the sixth week of the movement the Government fairly succeeded in suppressing mob violence and other forms of activity. But the most stringent measures which the Government rigorously applied in dealing with the situation helped terrorism to rear its head once again. Bombs and other explosive mechanism were in use. But the terrorist activities were not so successful in Andhra as in Bengal.

During the great national upsurge of 1942 the Communists acted as stooges and spies of the British Government and helped them against their own countrymen for freedom.[51] Communits were becoming more and more isolated from the other political organisations in Andhra.

The outburst of public emotion did not last long. It was at its worst for a few weeks. Then it was suppressed by the Government with ruthless severity.

The Achievement of Freedom

Some time after this Gandhiji was released on grounds of health and thus a beginning was made to improve the political atmosphere. He had discussions with Jinnah, the leader of the Muslim League, to reach an agreement on the basis of Rajagopalachari's formula, which suggested the formation of a provincial Government by the Congress and the Muslim League during the transition period, the appointment of a boundary commission to separate the Muslim majority provinces through a plebiscite if necessary, safeguarding of defence, commerce and communications and a consultation of the view – points of all parties before the plebiscite. The whole scheme was to be binding only in case of transfer of full power by Britain. The talks however failed as Jinnah insisted, among others, that the separation of the Muslim majority provinces should be decided before transfer of power.

On the failure of the talks between Gandhiji and Jinnah the Government made a fresh effort to break the deadlock and help the country to advance politically. On 14th June, 1945, Wavell, the Viceroy, in a broadcast, announced his intention to convene a meeting of all prominent leaders in Simla to assist him in the formation of a new executive council.

The conference proposed by the Viceroy met in July 1945 at Simla, but nothing worthwhile emerged from the babel of talk emphasising irreconcilable differences of opinion.[52]

The defeat of Japan at the hands of the Allied powers and coming to power of the Labour party in England after the general elections created a favourable atmosphere for resolving the crisis in India. The Labour Government ordered general elections throughout the country. Bans on the Congress and other organisations were lifted and all political prisoners were released.

While the general election campaign was at its full swing in India, the trial of the Indian National Army (I.N.A.) personnel that was constituted by Subhash Chandra Bose in Japan, was held by a military tribunal set up by the Government in the Red Fort at Delhi. The trial of these Indian National Army officers roused the emotions of the people. Processions, demonstrations and hartals were held throughout Andhra as in other parts of the country for the release of these patriots. The Government realising the angry mood of the people, remitted the sentences awarded to the Indian National Army personnel.

Meanwhile general elections were held in the country in which the real contest was between the Congress and the Muslim League. In Andhra many of the general constituencies were captured by the Congress which was riding on a wave of patriotic fervour, while the League could win all the Muslim seats. The Congress took office in Madras, with T. Prakasam as chief Minister.

Thereafter the political scene changed rapidly with the visit of Cabinet Mission,[53] observance of 'direct action' days by the Muslim League and communal riots characterised by an orgy of violence too horrid to narrate, the revolt of a number of ratings in Bombay, the decision of the Attlee Government to transfer administration to responsible Indian leaders, the announcement of the Mountbatten Plan, [54] and the decision of the Congress to concede Pakistan.

In spite of opposition in certain quarters the partition became inevitable, and on 15th August, 1947, India became independent.

The freedom struggle in Andhra, as in most other parts of the country, reached its culmination with the election in March, 1947. Throughout the Vandemataram movement and particularly from the 1921 civil disobedience movement the Andhras were in the forefront of the freedom struggle and their consistent enthusiasm for achieving the country's independence was unequalled. This final contribution to the cause of the country's solidarity and independence could be seen in the elections of 1946 when they elected Congress party members by an overwhelming majority.

This was the political environment that influenced the writers in Andhra. They were influenced by the Political environment and the political environment was influenced by them. Under the impact of the everchanging political environment the writers wrote a number of works that attracted prospcription. For banning the works which were thought to be seditious the Government passed series of Acts leading to the confrontation between the native Press and the Colonial Government.

NOTES

1. The victory of Japan, an Asiatric State, over Russia, a big European power, in 1905 shattered the widespread belief among the Asiatrics about the invincibility of the Westerners. This stirring event created a new sense of confidence and strength among Indians and roused new hopes and aspirations of freeing the country from foreign domination. This event awakened into activity the political consciousness of the people in Andhra.
2. For more details regarding Andhra movement see Madala Veerabhadra Rao, Andhrodyama Charitra (Telugu), G.V.Subba Rao (compilor) History

of Andhra Movement, K.V.Narayana Rao, The Emergence of Andhra Pradesh.

3. N.P.R.1910, p.141, para 47.
4. K. Venkatappayya, Autobiography, Vol.I, pp. 203-5.
5. Fortnightly Report, July to September 1917 and M. Venkatarangaiya (Ed.), Freedom Struggle in Andhra Pradesh (Andhra) Vol.II, Document No.128, pp. 446-447.
6. M. Venkatarangaiya (Ed.), Ibid, Document No.144, p.469.
7. M. Venkatarangaiya (Ed.), op.cit., p.136.
8. Gandhi, p.356,; See also R. Kumar (Ed.), Essays on Gandhian Politics: The Rowlatt Satyagraha of 1919.
9. M. Venkatarangaiya (Ed.), op.cit., Vol.II, Document No.170, pp. 505-506.
10. For full text, see, B. Pattabhi Sitharamayya, The History of the Indian National Congress, Vol.I, p.203. Gandhi admits that in the original draft of the above resolution on non-cooperation, there was no reference to Swarajya. It was added later at the instance of the Madras Congress leader, C. Vijayaraghava Charian see, Gandhi. P. 379.
11. For details see Christopher John Baker, The Politics of South India 1920-1937.
12. G.O. No.2082, Law (General) Department, dt.3rd January 1921.
13. The Hindu, 2nd March, 1921.
14. Report of the Civil Disobedience Enquiry Committee, 1922 Appendix IV.
15. Report of the Civil Disobedience Enquiry Committee, 1922 Appendix V.
16. Report on the working of the Reformed Constitution, 1927, p.99.
17. For biographical details, see G.V.Subba Rao, Andhra Ratna Sree Gopalakrishnayya.
18. M. Venkatarangaiya (Ed.), op.cit., Vol.III, p.32.
19. B. Seshagir Rao, History of Freedom Movement in Guntur District, p.94.
20. When the leaders were being led to the court of Macherla in a huge procession accompanied by beat of drums, the District Collector, Guntur, is stated to have said "They (people) say that Swaraj will come some day, but now I see swaraj around me". K. Venkatappaiah, Autobiography, Vol.II, p.41.
21. The Hindu, 3rd October, 1921.
22. Ibid., 2nd December, 1921.
23. The Hindu, 4th June, 1921.
24. S. Gopalakrishnan, Political Movements in South India 1914-1929, p.84
25. S. Gopalakrishnan, op. cit., p.85.
26. The Hindu, 11th February, 1922.
27. **Ibid**.
28. L.F.Rushbrook Williams (Ed.), India in 1921-1922, p.61.
29. B. Pattabhi Sitaramayya, op.cit., p.238.
30. B. Pattabhi Sitharamayya, op.cit., p.223
31. The Indian Annual Register, Vol.II, 1929, p.283.
32. For a detailed account of life and activities of Sitaramaraju. See A.J. Happel's Report on "Rampa Distrurbances". (upto 21-4-1923); M. Krishna Rao, Alluri Sitaramaraju Charitra, (Telugu), J. Mangamma, Alluri Sitaramaraju; P. Radhakrishna, Manyamlo Viplavam (Telugu), Y. Narasimha Rao, History of Alluri Sitaramaraju; Bh. Satyanarayana, Sri Alluri Sitaramaraju Prasamsa. (Telugu).

33. Young India, Dt.18th July, 1929.
34. M. Satyanarayana Sastry, History of the Nationalist Movement in East Krishna (in Telugu), p.38.
35. M. Venkatarangaiya (Ed.), op.cit., Vol.III, Document No.144, pp.476-477.
36. The Hindu, 25th June, 1930.
37. G.O. No.609, Public (General) Department, Dt. 11th June, 1934.
38. Ibid.
39. B. Pattabhai Sitaramayya, op.cit.,p.565.
40. During the informal conference week at Poona in July last, I had stated that while many individual Civil resisters would be welcome, even one was sufficient to keep alive the message of Satyagraha. Now, after much searching of the heart, I have arrived at the conclusion that in the present circumstances only one, and that myself and no other, should, for the time being, bear the responsibility of civil resistance, if it is to succeed as mans of achieving Purna Swaraj.............. I fell that masses have not yet received the full message of Satyagraha due to adulteration in the process of transmission"; D.G. Tendulkar, Mahatma, Vol.III, p.318.
41. B. Kesavanarayana, Political and Social Factors in Andhra (1900-1956), pp.135-136.
42. Andhra Congress Coailist Party, 1937, pp. 5-6.
43. Results are analysed in G.O.No.596, Punblic (Elections), Dt. 29th March, 1937 though there are certain discrepancies in the figures given.
44. The Indian Annual Register, Vol.I, 1937, p.270.
45. Madras Administration Report 1937-38, p.6. This gives details of the provisions in the Act.
46. Ibid., 1938-39, p.6.
47. Ibid., 1939-40, p.6.
48. B. Pattabhi Siaramayya, op.cit., Vol.II, p.264.
49. B. Kesavanarayana, op.cit., p.156.
50. B. Pattabhi Sitaramayya, op.cit., p.359.
51. R.C.Majumdar, History of the Freedom Movement in India, Vol.III, p.689.
52. For details see V.P.Menon, The Transfer of Power in India, pp. 193-205
53. For the text of the statement made by the Cabinet Mission putting forward its proposals see B. Pattabhi Sitaramayya, op.cit., Appendix IV, pp. cl;xiii.clxx.
54. G.V.Subbarao, vide The Partition of India (1947), pp. 67-74

3

NATIVE PRESS AND COLONIAL GOVERNMENT

In the modern democractic world, the press occupies the position of fourth estate beside Legislature, Executive and Judiciary. Nobody today can deny its powers of influencing the legislature and executive policies and therefore its history is as important as that of the other two as well as that of Judiciary. Broadly speaking, the functions of the press are to convey Government policies to public, keep Government informed to public needs and reaction to Government policies and keep the public and Government informed the events and happenings at home and abroad. Each of these functions developed as the need for it was felt.

Beginnings:

The history of the Indian Press begins with the coming of the Europeans. The Portuguese were the first European nation who brought a printing press to India and the first book published in India was by the Jesuits of Goa in 1557. In 1684 the English East India Company set up a printing press in Bombay. For about a century no newspapers were published in the Company's territories because the Company's servants in India wished to withhold the news of their malpractices and abuses of 'private trading' from reaching London.[1]

The first attempt to publish newspapers in India were made by the disgruntled employees of the East India Company who sought to expose the malpractices of private trade. In 1776 William Bolts,[2] being censured by the Court of Directors for private trading, resigned his service under the Company and announced his intention to publish a newspaper and made it known that he had in his possession "in manuscript many things to communicate which most intimately concerned every individual". The official quarters at once reacted and Bolts scheme ended in embryo. It was left to James Augustus Hickey to publish the first newspaper in India entitled **The Bengal Gazette** or **Calcutta General Advertiser** in the year

1780. For his outspoken criticism of Government officials and scrurrilous attacks on the Governor-General and the Chief Justice, Hickey's Press was seized in 1782. Hickey was also imprisoned and deported. The following years saw the appearance of new publications like **The Calcutta Gazette** (1784), **The Bengal Journal** (1785), **The Oriental Magazine of Calcutta** or **Calcutta Amusement** (1785), **The Calcutta Chronicle** (1786), **The Madras Courier** (1788), **The Bombay Herald** (1789) etc. The promoters of these new publications profited from Hickey's bitter experience, exercised caution and restraint in their press comments in order to avoid any confrontation with Government. These newspapers had very limited circulation and the subscribers numbering hardly two hundred were Europeans and Anglo-Indians. Hence these newspapers registered no impact on Indian public opinion. However, the Company's servants were worried that the people in England might read these newspapers and come to know their acts of omission and commission.

Right from press inception, the Press had to face challenges which raised the very question of its survival. The more serious trial for the Press, however, came in the days of Lord Wellesley when, for the first time in its history regular press laws were formulated.

Beginning of Censorship:

The Censorship of the Press Act, 1799:

Lord Wellesley imposed censorship on all newspapers. Apprehending a French invasion of India and engaged in the struggle for supremacy in India, Wellesley could not tolerate the publication of any matter which might have the effect of weakening his influence vis-à-vis his Indian adversaries or the French. The Censorship of Press Act, 1799, imposed almost wartime restrictions on the press. The regulations required:

(a) The newspaper to clearly print in every issue the name of the printer, the editor and the proprietor;

(b) The publisher to submit all material for pre-censorship to the Secretary to the Government.[3]

Breach of these rules was punishable with immediate deportation.[4] In 1807 the Censorship Act was extended to cover journals, pamphlets and even books.

Liberal Approach:

Relaxation of press restrictions came under Lord Hastings. The Governor-General tried to put his liberal ideas in practice and succeeded in establishing in India some of the progressive views which were gaining ground in England. In 1818 the pre-censorship of the Press was dispensed with. Instead a vigilance was maintained over the Press. However, the Government laid down some general rules for the guidance of newspaper editors with a view to prevent the discussion of topics likely to affect the authority of the Government or injurious to public interests.[5] The Governor-General refused much against the wishes of the members of his council and particularly John Adams, to cancel the licence of James Buckingham,[6] the editor of **The Calcutta Journal** or deport him.

In nutshell, the instructions of Lord Hastings sought that the Press should not educate the people of India against the persons in power. This precaution was sought when the Press in India was the exclusive preserve of the Europeans. What the Company administration resented was the criticism of the Government for personal aggrandisement by rival interests was bringing disrepute to the Company in Britain and was endangering its interests in India. Therefore, the Directors of the Company in England were averse to the freedom of the Press in India.

Rise of Vernacular Press

From 1815 onwards Raja Ram Mohan Roy had taken the uphill task of reforming superstitions and decaying Hindu society in India. He was much impressed that "a well edited newspaper was the best instrument to educate people and to propagate new ideas". Therefore, he launched his own weekly, **Sangbad Kaumudi** in Bengali and **Mirat-ul-Akbar** in Persian in 1821 and 1822 respectively. These weeklies aimed at inspiring "the people to fight against socio-religious malpractices, to be acquainted with the lessons of Western culture, and to inform both the ruling class and their subjects the 'real situation'. Obtaining in the country".[7] Sensing a threat from his publications, the other native leaders of the middle class started newspapers in vernacular language in different cities. These vernacular newspapers covered local events and grievances and did not spare the Government of its shortcomings. The conservative group started its own weekly, Samachar Chandrika.

These rival papers developed a healthy debate and brought forth both progressive and reactionary views to their readers. The duel of words also helped in developing democratic consciousness. The vernacular press was also successful in bringing a unity of approach between different groups to resist missionary onslaught on Hinduism. The vernacular press was also educating the people about the constitutional agitation.

The Company Government was getting alarmed on the growth of vernacular press. Besides, the criticism of Government was eroding the sympathy of the powerful people in Britain and endangering the interests of the Company. It appointed Sir Thomas Munro to inquire into and suggest means for improving the relations between the press and the Government. As was the reality, Munro found that it was the indigenous press which could pose the real danger. He said "But though the danger be distant, it is nevertheless there. It could corrupt and disaffect the Indian army and work for the overthrow of the British power. It might spread among the people the principles of liberty and stimulate them to expel the strangers who rule over them and to establish a national Government. A free press and domination of strangers are things which are quite incompatible and cannot long exist together". It was in this context that the infamous ordinance known as Adam's Gag was proclaimed to control this emerging force.

The Licensing Regulations, 1823:

The appointment of John Adams as acting Governor-General in 1813 gave him the opportunity to give a practical shape to his reactionary views. Press Regulations of 1823 proved more stringent than any that had been in force earlier. The new regulations required:

(a) Every printer and publisher to obtain a licence for starting a press or using it;

(b) The penalty for printing and or publishing any literature without the requisite licence was Rs.400/- for each such publication or imprisonment in default thereof. Magistrates were authorised to attack unlicensed presses.

(c) The Governor-General had the right to revoke a licence or call for a fresh application.

From the arguments supporting the ordinance and its subsequent application it is clear that Adams Regulations were directed chiefly against newspapers published in the Indian languages or edited by Indians. Raja Ram Mohan

Roy's **Miral-ul-Akbar** had to stop publication. After Adam's Regulations only three Bengali and one Persian newspapers continued publication in Calcutta. J.S.Buckingham was also deported to England.[8]

The Liberation of the India Press, 1835:

Lord William Bentinck adopted a liberal attitude towards the Press, Although Adams' press regulations were not revoked, considerable latitude of discussion was given to the press, Indian as well as Anglo-Indian. It was however, left to Charles Metcalfe, officiating Governor-General (1835-36) to repeal the abnoxious ordinance of 1823 and earn the epithet of 'liberator of the Indian Press'. Lord Macaulay supported the case for a free press in India. He argued that since the Government possessed unquestionable powers of interference whenever the safety of the state was in danger, it was therefore unnecessary to keep the offensive form and ceremonial of despotism in time of peace. A new Press Act required a printer and publisher to make a declaration of giving a true and precise account of the premises of publication. It was open to a printer and publisher to cease to function as such by a similar declaration to that effect. The result of this liberal press policy which continued unchanged till 1856 was the rapid growth of newspapers all over the country.

The Licensing Act, 1857:

From 1835 to 1857 the Indian Press continued enjoying its liberty. But when the Mutiny of 1857 broke out, the Indian Government had to lay down certain measures to control the press. Act No.XV of 1857 reintroduced licensing restrictions in addition to the existing registration procedure laid down by the Metcalfe Act. The Act prohibited the keeping or using of printing presses without a licence from the Government and the Government reserved the discretionary right to grant licences or revoke them at any time. The Government was also empowered to prohibit the publication or circulation of any newspaper, book or other printed matter. The Act was passed for one year only, yet it continued in force till 1865, being renewed every year.

The Indian Penal Code, 1860:

The Indian Penal Code was passed in 1860. Though the Act was not directed specifically against the press, it laid down offences which any writer, editor or publisher must avoid, e.g., the offences of defamation and obscenity. Later many amendments were introduced in this Act. We shall discuss some amendments in the proceeding paras.

The Press and Registration of Books Act, 1867:

Lord Metcalfe's Act of 1835 was repealed in 1867. The emergency of an Indian publication industry complicated the political life of the British rulers. Books and Journals could be valuable sources of information if channelled into an intelligence network, however, their appearance also raised questions of surveillance and control of mass media.

A century of bureaucratic interest in the content of Indian publications left a legacy of laws and institutions designed to watch and, as necessary, to control the press, Act XXV of 1867, "for the regulation of printing presses and newspapers, for the preservation of copies of books printed in British India, and the registration of such books", became the legal basis for a surveillance system. The legislation facilitated identification of those responsible for a given work. From 1867 onwards, books, and newspapers were required to bear the names of authors, printers, and publishers. Moreover, the Act set up mechanism whereby Indian officials and the India office could be informed about what was being printed. Copies of printed matters had to be delivered promptly to a designated representative of local Government, who then prepared a Quarterly catalogue of books and periodicals. The Act provided that the publishers and printers had to file declarations before Magistrates, regarding the good conduct of their presses and publications.

The effort to construct a standardized registration system proved only partially successful. Reports eventually came to resemble each other because the Central Government instructed local authorities to follow a catalogue model suggested by Madras, but the apparatus for implementing the 1867 Act differed widely. In some provinces, directors of public instruction registered books and prepared the catalogues, in others, special press officers. Regularity, accuracy and comprehensiveness depended on the back-ground of the registrars.[9] This Act was amended in 1890 and again in 1940, 1952 and 1953.

The press now progressed with rapid strides. Many newspapers came into existence. So that by 1870 their number reached as high a figure as 644; 400 of them being the vernacular papers. The art of journalism developed in the country, different types of features began to appear in the papers, and with everyday that passed, the people developed paper consciousness. Legislation affecting the content of publications accompanied the evolving report system. Several amendments to the Indian Penal Code extended bureaucratic authority over the press. In 1870, an apparent threat from Muslim fanatics led to the passage of Section 124 A, a "sedition" clause aimed generally at actions which caused "disaffection". Except for judicial and executive discussion over what "disaffection" actually meant, the law concerned with sedition did not change until 1898, when once again responding to a crisis (disturbances in Bombay), the Government of India enacted a stronger measure. Act IV of 1898 attempted to amplify the nature of Sedition, and in doing so, widened the scope for prosecution. Section 124 A read as follows:

> Whoever by words, either spoken or written, or by signs, or by visible representation, or otherwise, brings or attempts to bring into hatred or contempt, or excites or attempts to excite disaffection towards Her Majesty, or the Government established by law in British India shall be punished with transportation for life or any shorter term, to which fine may be added, or with imprisonment which may extend to three years, to which fine may be added or with fine. Explanation – The expression "disaffection" includes disloyalty and all feelings of enmity.[10]

The Act also introduced Section 153 A, making punishable writings or speeches inciting "class hatred". A final amendment changed Section 505, which covered statements creating public mischief. Previously the Government had to prove that the author or editor printed romours in the knowledge that they were false. The revised Section made this proof unnecessary, and in effect shifted the burden of demonstrating intent from prosecution to defense.[11]

These amendments focused on punishment as deterrent to controversial writings. A simultaneous alteration of the Criminal Procedure Code equipped the British with extended preventive powers Act V of 1898 permitted Magistrates to execute bonds for good behaviour in cases in which individuals disseminated seditious matter (124 A), publications affecting class enmity (153 A), or threats to the judiciary.[12]

Dramatic Performance Act 1876

To prevent performance of Dramas which the Government thought were inciting te feelings of the people, inciting the people against it, the British authorities and the British Government enacted Dramatic Performance Act in 1876 (Act XIX of 1876). It was for the first time introduced in Calcutta to prohibit a social drama Neeladarpan. The old acts were not utilised for this purpose. It was the beginning of prohibition of dramas in entire India. If British Government felt that the dramatic performance was against the interests of Government, the Government might prohibit it by this Act. If anybody did not co-operate to implement this Act the Government might impose fines on them. To implement this Act necessary power were given to Magistrates.

Local officials have rights to disagree to perform the dramas in certain places. The performances may get licences. The performers should inform and present the script of the drama or the summary of the performance to the officers.

According to this Act the British Government prohibited many dramas which advocated anti-British attitude, argued in favour of peoples welfare and encouraged Swadesabhimanam (love towards mother country).

From 1920 onwards this Act became an Iron-leg on Telugu dramas. Many dramas of Damaraju Pundarikakshudu were prohibited as per this Act. A number of prohibitions took place in Krishna, Guntur, West and East Godavari Districts.

This Act was not confined only to dramatic performances which were performed in open places but also to traditional fork story; traditional performances also came under this Act.

The Vernacular Press Act, 1878:

An unfortunate legacy of the Rebellion of 1857 was the growth of the spirit of racial bitterness among the rulers and the ruled. As a result the European press in India after 1858 was always ranged on the side of the Government in all political controversies. The vernacular press, which had developed and grown on an unprecedented scale since 1857 became more vocal and increasingly critical of governmental policies. this in turn created a strong public opinion critical of the Imperialist acts of Lord Lytton. The terrible famine of 1876-78 which took a toll over six million people and the lavish expenditure on the Imperial Darbar at Delhi in January 1877 made the public opinion and the press restive. Lytton on his part considered the newly rising intellectual class in India as 'a deadly legacy from Macaulay and Metcalfe' and tried to stifle their views.

The Vernacular Press Act of 1878 was designed 'to better control' the vernacular press and to empower the Government with more effective means of punishing and repressing seditious writings. The act empowered (1) a District Magistrate with the previous permission of a Local Government to call upon the printer and publisher of any vernacular newspaper to enter into a bond undertaking not to publish anything likely to excite feelings of disaffection against the government or antipathy between persons of different races, castes and religions among Her Majesty's subjects. The Magistrate could further require a publisher to deposit security and to forfeit it if the newspaper contravened the regulation. If the offence reoccurred, the press equipment could be seized.

1. The Magistrate's action was final and no appeal could be made to a court of law.
2. A Vernacular newspaper could get exemption from the operation of the act by submitting proofs of the paper to a Government censor.

The act came to be nicknamed Gagging Act. The worst feature of the act was that it discriminated between the English Press and the Vernacular Press and no right of appeal to a court of law was given. Under the Act, proceedings were instituted against the **Som Prakash, The Bharat Mihir, The Dacca Prakash, The Sahachar** and a few other newspapers. The act succeeded in its objective and the tone of the vernacular press became submissive and the vernacular newspapers of the period showed very little originality in thinking and more often largely borrowed from the English press.

Lord Cranbrook, the new secretary of State, objected to the pre-censorship clause of the act on the ground that the censors would have to be Indians and that would have to, in point of fact, re-write the newspapers. Consequently in September 1878, the pre-censorship clause was deleted. At the suggestion of the Secretary of State, a Press commission was appointed charged with the duty of supplying authentic and accurate news to the press.

The Vernacular Press Act was repealed in 1882 by the Government of Lord Ripon. Ripon, the nominee of the Liberal Government of Gladstone, held the view that the circumstances which justified the Act of 1878 no longer existed.

The Indian Government was invested with additional sanctions that were useful in checking circulation of printed matter. Modelled on English law the 1889 Official Secrets Act prohibited unauthorized entry into Government offices, divulgence of confidential information and publication of such material Section 26 of the Indian Post Office Act empowered the Governor-General in Council to order interception of postal articles, and Section 19 of the 1878 Sea Customs Act extended similar authority to intercept items imported into India.1

The Newspapers Act, 1908:

The disaffection created by the unpopular acts of Lord Curzon resulted in the growth of an Extremist party in the Indian National congress and led to acts of violence. The newspapers of the time often commented adversely on the Government policies. The Government followed a repressive policy and enacted the newspapers (incitement to Offences) Act, 1908. According to this Act.

(a). The Magistrates were empowered to confiscate printing presses, property connected thereto of newspapers which published objectionable material which served as incitement to murder or acts of violence;
(b) The Local Government was empowered to annul any declaration made by the printer and publisher of an offending newspaper made under the Press Registration of Books Act of 1867;
(c) The newspaper editors and printers were given the option to appeal to the High Court within fifteen days of the order of forfeiture of the press.

Under the Newspapers Act of 1908, the Government launched prosecutions against nine newspapers and confiscated seven presses. As a result of this measure papers like **Yugantar, Sandhya** and **Bandematram,** which had become the mouthpiece of emerging nationalist movement ceased their publications.

The Indian Press Act, 1910:

On 18th November 1909, a bomb bounced harmlessly off the carriage in which Lord and Lady Minto were touring Ahmedabad. Magistrate A.M.T. Jackson of Nasik was not so fortunate. Members of the Abhinav Bharat, a terrorist organization, riddled him with bullets on 21st December, 1909. A week later, the police discovered bombs in front of the District Commissioner's home in Ambala, Punjab. Indian revolutionaries obviously had moved into an accelerated phase of violent protest.

The recrudescence of terrorism opened another chapter of British repression in India. Minto tended to make light of the attempt on his own life, but he viewed differently the well-planned shooting of Jackson and the Ambala bombs. Conspiracy and plots, he wrote Morley, seemed to be everywhere. [14] Consequently, force met force, as the government attempted to destroy revolutionary groups and reassert its authority. Trials, expansion of police activities, and greater protection for informers followed. Panicked and unclear as to the enormity of revolutionary threats, Minto suggested to Morley's horror, that martial law might be required. [15]

The prevailing atmosphere of fear and insecurity among the Governor-General and his Council produced new legislation on the press. The Home Department revived the earlier files and gathered opinion on the press situation. They key assumption during the resulting debate was that tracts and newspapers created a political ethos conducive to revolution. H.H.Risely, Secretary to the Government of India was of the opinion that certain measures against the extremists should be taken, otherwise they would gain power and terrorise the entire population.[16] So in order to curb the extremists challenge the Government passed a new legislation regarding control and regulation of the press. This was embodied in the press Act of 1910. The Indian Press Act of 1910 revived the worst features of Lyttons Press Act of 1878. All press proprietors who made a declaration under the 1867 press Act for the first time would be required to deposit security unless it was dispensed with by a local Magistrate. Owners of existing presses would make the deposit only if they printed objectionable matter. [17] The Indian Press Act of 1910 empowered the Local Government to demand at the time of Registration security of not less than Rs.500 and not more than Rs.2,000/- from the keeper of a printing press or publisher of a newspaper and to forfeit the security and annul the declaration of Registration of an offending newspaper. The Government could allow fresh Registration and may demand a security of not less than Rs.1,000 and not more than Rs.10,000 and forfeit the fresh security and annul the fresh declaration of Registration as well as confiscate the press and all copies of such newspapers, books, etc., if the newspapers persisted in publishing objectionable material. The aggrieved party could appeal to a Special Tribunal of the High court against orders of forfeiture within two months. Further, the printer of every newspaper was required to supply to the Government free of charge two copies of each issue of the newspaper published. The Act gave powers to the Chief Customs Officer to detain all imported packages which contained objectionable material. The Press Act therefore provided for new deterrents (securities) and executive action to remove publications from circulation.

Under the Act action was taken against 991 printing presses and newspapers. Out of these 286 were warned, in 705 cases heavy securities were demanded. During the first five years of Act the Government confiscated securities amounting to about five lakh rupees.

Criminal Law Amendment Act, 1913

The rigours of the Act of 1910 were further enhanced by the Criminal Law amendment Act of 1913. It was used to stifle criticsm and silence agitation.

Defence of India Rules:

During the First world war, 1914-18, the Defence of India Rules were promulgated. These Rules were not only used for war purposes but for all political purposes so as to carry out the policy of the Indian Government in regard to repression of political agitation or free public criticism of the normal acts and the methods of administration in India. The Act was indeed welcomes as a useful addition to the normal armoury of arbitrary executive power in India. The officials used them whenever they deemed fit, irrespective of any real war emergency or necessity. By resorting to the simple formula of acting in the interests of "public safety", they were able to deal with anything which in their eyes was prejudicial there to by directions to the press and penal orders of every conceivable character. The time of war was also found convenient for the abuse and misuse of other rarely used powers under existing Acts, such as the Post Office Act, the State Prisoners Acts etc. The total number of orders under the Defence of India Act to which presses and papers were subjected for purposes unconnected with the war were very large, varied, arbitrary, contradictory, and often ludicrous to a degree.

The Montagu-Chelmsford Reforms were introduced in the disturbed atmosphere of Gandhi's non-co-operation. In 1921 a press committee was appointed under the chairmanship of Tej Bahadur Sapru, then Law Member of the Viceroy's Executive Council, to consider the question of repealing the Press Act of 1910 or amending it. As a result of the recommendations, the Newspapers (Incitement to offences) Act of 1908 and the Indian Press Act of 1910 were repealed.

The Cinematograph Act, 1918 (Act II of 1918) was passed on 6th March 1918. It was an Act to make provision for regulating exhibitions by means of cinematographs.

Official Secrets Act, 1923

The next important law on the subject is the Official Secrets Act, 1923. It is a general Act but has an impact on the press. It is aimed at maintaining the security of the State against leakage of secret information, sabotage, and the like.

The Ordinances of 1930

Communal literature persisted as a source of disharmony. Alterations of the Press law had temporarily dampened religious attacks, but by 1930, the hostility of the writings had resumed and now probably exceeded the levels in the earlier publications. Tracts and newspapers mirrored growing communal antagonism fed by riots and the inability to make political compromises. In 1930 the Civil Disobedience movement was launched.

In the face of a situation that appeared to be a plunge into anarchy Irwin quickly consulted with London and provincial chiefs and then activates contingency plans.[18] The British anticipated that mass arrests and a harsh policy towards demonstrations would cripple the Congress. They arrested Gandhi on 5th May, and also the members of the higher echelons of the Congress. On 30th June, the Government proclaimed the Congress Working Committee an unlawful association.

Irwin simultaneously promulgated emergency ordinances calculated to strengthen British power drastically. Seven ordinances came into effect between 19th April and 7th July. They extended executive prerogative and in effect suspended normal criminal procedure in cases relating to terrorism or disruption of vital services (loosely defined as administration police, the military, and communications).[19] Two ordinances directly affected the press ordinance II (27th April) re-established a system of security demands and enhanced officials' ability to seize publications. The new restrictions were to cover an assortment of printed matter, not just "blatant sedition". Securities could be seized and books banned if writers incited "hatred", attempted to influence troops, put persons "in fear", caused annoyance, or tampered with the law and payment of revenue. Statements introducing the ordinance claimed that its primary use would be limited to returning India to peace, and called on "sober citizens" to unite with Government to achieve that goal. [20] In fact, the Government of India intended to muzzle all segments of the Press defying its dictates. Noting that success of the Congress "depends largely on publicity, and that it is mainly through the Press that publicity is secured", Delhi privately instructed officers to guash any publication that consistently lauded civil disobedience. [21]

A related ordinance for control of unauthorized news sheets and newspapers dealt with material that was slipping through loopholes in the law. By halting the output of daily bulletins mimeographed by Congress units, the British hoped to put the nationalist communication network into disarry. [22]

The embattled bureaurcracy immediately activated the ordinances. By the end of June, the British had issued formal warnings to 150 publishers and banned approximately 400 books and tracts, 40 posters, and 50 numbers of newspapers. [23] During the same two months period, atleast 125 newspapers and 153 presses came under security provisions.

The Indian Press (Emergency Powers) Act, 1931:

The national movement was gaining momentum under Mahatma Gandhi and other leaders and, therefore, the Government wanted to arm itself with extraordinary powers to deal with the situation created by resurgent nationalism. The Indian nationalists were using the weapons of satyagraha and civil disobedience against the Government. Hence the India press (Emergency Powers) Act was passed in 1931 to deal with matters which were likely to incite violence or unrest in the country. The wide and sweeping powers conferred by this Act were fully exercised by the Government in order to weaken the national movement. Even the leading newspapers which espoused the cause of the nationlists were heavily penalised and made to furnish unusually heavy security deposits.

On the 5th March, 1931 the Delhi Settlement was entered into between Lord Irwin and Gandhiji. The chief provisions of the settlement were that civil disobedience was to be discontinued, as well as the boycott of British commodities as a political weapon, Government on their part engaging to withdrawn ordinances connected with the civil disobedience movement and notifications declaring associations unlawful. In terms of the settlement the ordinances in force were repealed on the 6th March, 1931 by the Government of India.

The Indian press ordinance, which had been re-enacted by the Governor-General a day or two before the opening of the year, was, as has been explained above, repealed on the 6th March in terms of the Delhi Settlement, but the hope that the press would respond by the exercise of restraint and moderation was soon disappointed. The Government of Bengal was compelled to sanction a large number of prosecutions for seditious articles and the promotion of class hatred. A marked feature in many papers in Bengal was the glorification of political assassins and the encouragement of the cult of terrorism. The danger of such propaganda both in Bengal and elsewhere was too great to be ignored and the Government of India were again compelled to legislate for the control of the press. So the Indian Press Emergency Powers Act, 1931 (XXIII of 1931) was passed by the Legislature and became law on the 9th October, 1931. The Act gave sweeping powers to the Provincial Governments in suppressing the propaganda for the civil disobedience movement. Section 4(1) of the Act sought to punish "words, sings or visible representations which (a) incite to or to encourage the commission of any offence of murder or any cognizable offence involving violence or (b)directly or indirectly express approval or admiration of any such offence, or of any person, real or fictitious who has committed or is alleged or represented to have committeed any such offence." The Gandhi-Irwin pact introduced an interlude of peace, but after the arrest of Gandhiji on his return from the

Second Round Table Conference, the earlier Press Act of 1931 was amplified into the Criminal Law Amendment Act of 1932. Section 4 was made very comprehensive and expanded to include all possible activities calculated to undermine the Government's authority.

Defence of India Act and Defence of India Rules 1939:

The Press (Emergency Powers) Act of 1931 remained in force throughout the pre-war years, and when the war broke out in 1939, the Government of India armed themselves with further powers under the Defence of India Act, which provided for precensorship of material published in the press relating to certain matters. The Official Secrets Act was amended to provide a maximum penalty of death, or transportation, for the publication of information likely to be of use to the enemy. The Press (Emergency Powers) Act, was amended to provide against the confidential information to the enemy or the publication of any prejudicial report, which amounted to incitement to the commission of a prejudicial act as defined in the Defence of India Rules. When Gandhiji launched his Individual Satyagraha movement a notification was issued by the Government of India:

In exercise of the powers conferred by clause (b) of sub-rule 11, of rule 41 of the Defence of India rules, the Central Government is pleased to prohibit the printing by any printer, publisher or editor in British India of any matter relating to the holding of meetings or the making of speeches for the purpose, directly or indirectly of fomenting such opposition as aforesad.

Provided that nothing in this order shall be deemed to apply to any matter communicated by the Central Government or a provincial Government to the press for publication.

The notification was withdrawn as the result of an understanding between the Government of India and a conference of newspaper editors, which later was constitute into the All-India Newspaper Editors Conference. The special powers assumed by the Government during the Second World War (1939-45) ended in 1945. Thus, after the end of the World War II, the press in India heaved a sigh of relief.

However, it is exaggeration to say that during the pre-independence period, Indian vernacular press groaned under the weight of censorship and other stringent restrictions. But the freedom loving writers, editors and publishers educated the public opinion during the course of Indian national movement even at the risk of confiscation of their security deposits. Their services to national independence were invaluable. The names of such newspapers which mobilised Indian public opinion in the teeth of government's opposition would ever be remembered with gratitude in annals of the India press.

While the Draft constitution was under consideration in the Constituent Assembly, the Government appointed a Press Laws Enquiry Committee to review the Press Laws of India with a view to examine if they are in accordance with the fundamental rights formulated by the Constituent Assembly of India". Among the recommendations of the Committee were the repeal of the Indian Emergency Power Act of 1931, amendments in the Press and Registration of Books Act, modifications of Section 124-A and 153-A of the Indian Penal Code, repeal of the Indian States (protection against Disaffection) Act, 1932 and the Indian States (protection) Act, 1934.

The Growth of Telugu Press:

To a large extent the origin of Telugu journalism bears a close resemblance to the beginnings of journalism in Bengal. The first Telugu journal to be published is believed to be the monthly Satyadoota, a missionary journal started around the year 1836 for the propagation of Christianity by the Christian Association of Bellary. It was printed in Madras. In its wake followed the **Vrittantini** (1840), the **Sujana Ranjini** (1845) of Chinnaya Suri, the **Dina Vartamani** (1860), the **Hitavadi** and the **Ravi**. All these journals were published in a high-flown Sanskritised literary language.

To counteract the Missionary propaganda, a few newspapers were started, the most notable among them being the **Tattvabodhini** in 1864 by the Ved Samaj from Madras.

Kandukuri Veeresalingam Pantulu (1840-1919), the father of the renaissance movement in Andhra and the founder of modern Telugu, started in 1874, [24] in Rajahmundry, a weekly called the **Vivekavardhini** intended for introducing reforms in the social and literary fields in Andhra. About the same time he started a separate journal for women called the **Satihitabodhini**, then the **Hasyavardhini** and the **Satyavadini**, wherein he advocated the removal of social evils like child marriage, caste system and prostitution. In literary aspect he began to propagate popularisation of simple Telugu. In order to countract his teaching journals like the Andhra Bhasha Sanjivini of Mahamahopadyaya Kokkonda Venkataratnam Pantulu, and the Purushartha Pradayani (1874) from Masulipatam were started.

The first political news weekly in the Telugu language was **Andhra Prakasika**, started in the year 1885, the year which saw the birth of Indian National Congress. This was edited by A.P. Parthsarathi Naidu from

Madras. Naidu was an ardent nationalist who carried on the publication of this weekly with vigour for more than 25 years.

The earlier newspapers confined themselves mostly to social, economic or educational matters; the tone of the newspapers changed considerably from the beginning of the 20th century, when they started showing a keen and critical spirit on political issues.

Another journal, the **Sasilekha**, originally stated as a weekly in 1894 by G. Seshacharyulu and later converted into a daily, played a notable part in the early Andhra Movement. The journals like the **Godavari** and the **Andhra Kesari** served the cause of the Andhra Movement creditably.

The Vandemataram Movement, which began after the partition of Bengal in 1905, heralded a new era not only in Indian politics but also in the history of the India Press. From 1905 the press in India became outspoken in propagating the nationalist cult and in attacking the foreign Government in India.

The wave of national resurgence became strong in Andhra, as in the rest of India, after 1905. Writing about the importance of the year 1905. Writing about the importance of the year 1905. Harisarvothama Rao mentions, "even though the **Andhra Patrika** and **Sasilekha** were to some extent writing about political matters before 1902, a new National resurgence started in Andhra, with the establishment of the **Krishna Patrika** in 1902".[25]

The **Krishna Patrika** a weekly, was founded originally in 1902 by Konda Venkatappayya and edited by Mutnuri Krishna Rao. His writings were poignant and inspired the Andhra public a great deal. This paper was started as a fortnightly in 1902 and became a weekly in 1908.

The **Andhra Patrika** was originally started from Bombay as a weekly in 1908, by the great patriot Desoddharaka Nageswara Rao Pantulu (1867-1938). Later it was transferred to Madras in 1914, and published by the daily. It played leading part not only in the struggle for independence but also in the struggle for the creation of a separate Andhra province.

The press in this period was centered round politics. Hence it was a period of "concentrated political Journalism".[26] The Press became a powerful political institution and it was increasingly used for mobilising public opinion.

With the growth of nationalistic journalism the importance and influence of the Anglo-Indian Press or Pro-British Press declined. The strength of the

Pro-Indian Press was derived from the faith and support which it had from the people.

In 1905 there were 30 Telugu journals.[27] This number steadily went upto 63 in 1931.[28] But in 1932 the number of newspapers in Telugu declined to 46.[29] This was not due to the decline in the importance of vernacular Journalism. It was due to the closure of a number of newspapers, because of the rigours imposed on them by the Government. The decrease in the intensity of the civil disobedience Movement in 1932, might have also contributed to a slump in the number of Telugu Journals in 1932.

Each political movement provided stimulus for the rise of Vernacular Journals. The Vandemataram Movement, the Home Rule Movement, the Non-Cooperation Movement, the Salt Satyagraha Movement, and the Quit India Movement, provided good opportunities for the growth of Journalism in Telugu.

The circulation of the Telugu papers also increased remarkably. The total circulation for all the Telugu papers in 1901 was 16,025.[30] By 1930, the circulation of the Telugu papers reached the figure of 69,338.[31] The speedy increase in the circulation of the Telugu papers was a natural consequence of the increase in the number of journals and the increase in the popular interest in the vernacular journals, as most of them strongly supported the national movement. The linguistic affinity between the people and the Vernacular Press was the most important cause for the growth of vernacular journalism.

The English papers even if they were conducted on nationalistic lines by Indians, were not able to satisfy the craving of the rural people for news and views in their own language.

The rise of local press was also an important feature of the press in Andhra. The local press developed as a part of the Vernacular press. The number of such local newspapers were very large for example **Nellore Patrika, Guntur Patrika, Andhravani** of Berhampur etc. During the period of this study, there were many bi-lingual papers in the Andhra region. These bi-lingual papers were mostly Anglo-Telugu papers, containing news, both in English and Telugu. Besides Anglo-Telugu Journals, there were also some Telugu-Kannada. English-Telugu-Oriya and English-Telugu-Tamil Journals during this period.

During the civil disobedience movement in the 1930s Andhra also had its paise newspapers like the **Gandivamu**, the **Janmabhoomi** etc. These papers were very popular not only because they were cheap, but also because they propagated the nationlist message in an interesting and humorous manner. In this period newspapers catering to the needs of the particular castes and communities like the **Reddy Prabha**, **The Setty**, **Balija**, **The Adi Velama** etc. also came into existence. It was one unfortunate feature of the press during this period.

There was underground newspaper circulation during the Salt Satyagraha and Civil Disobedience movements; the cessation of the out-spoken nationalist newspapers and the prohibition of the publication of the news of the national movement, in the published papers, gave rise to such papers, which were circulated secretly.

The other newspapers like the **Congress** of Modduri Annapoornaiah and **Janmabhoom** inspired the people by their writings. The **Andhra Prabha**, founded in Madras in 1938 by the Express Group of papers, also served the nation under the able guidance of Khasa Subba Rao and the virile Andhra Journalist Narla Venkateswara Rao.

Realising the necessity of focussing the attention of the general public on economic and labour problems, persons with a socialistic bent of mind started journals like the Navasakti in 1936 (by Madduri Annapoornaiah) but it was proscribed by the Government in 1939. Then a Communist weekly, the **Prajasakti**, was started in 1941 which was converted into a daily in 1945, by Madduri Chandrasekhar Rao. It was also proscribed in 1948. The same paper once again was started in 1951 as a bi-weekly and now since 1952 under the title of **Visalandra** it is being published from Bezwada.

The undivided Godavari District was the chief center of Journalism in Andhra. Rajahmundry in those days was the chief center for literary, social and cultural activities in Andhra. It was the headquarters for a number of Journals published from the Godavari District. Madras was another center for the journalistic activities of the Andhras. The other important centers for Journalism were Masulipatam, Guntur, Nellore, Vizagapatam, Ganjam and Anantapur.

During the period of this study the Journalism in Andhra was dominated by towering political personalities, as in the rest of the country.[32] Chief among them were Gadicherla Harisarvothama Rao, Pattabhi Sitaramayya Tanguturi Prakasam, Kasinathuni Nageswara Rao of **Andhra Patrika**, Mutnuri Krishna Rao of **Krishna Patrika.** Madduri Annappornaiah and Krovvidi Linga Raju of **Congress** and Atmakuri Govinda Charyulu of Satyagrahi. They happened to be eminent politician-cum-Journalists of this period.

One important feature of the press of this period was that it existed for a purpose. The patriotic press existed for serving the country and the Pro-

British press stood for shielding the Government. Journalism in those days was not a profession but a mission for liberating the country.

Conclusion:

In the beginning the press and literature concentrated on social reform and political concessions, but the starting of mass movements for achieving political ends provided ample scope for the growth of national press and literature in India as well as in Andhra. Literature played a glorious part in rousing national consciousness among the Andhras. It was also responsible to a great extent for the participation of a large number of people in the Indian Freedom Movement. Due to the effective role played by Telugu Press the people became patriotic. With indomitable courage and heroic self-sacrifice they vigorously supported the various phases of the national movement converting the fight against the British into a heroic struggle of the people for a national cause. So in order to curb the role of Press and Literature the British Government passed a series of repressive laws as mentioned above. In this work an attempt is made to estimate the contribution of Telugu (proscribed) Literature for India's struggle for Independence with special reference to Andhra.

NOTES

1. Cowper commented on the 'get-quick-rich' pursuits of the Company's servants.
2. Author of the book **Consideration on Indian Affairs** (1772).
3. The Secretary in turn had been instructed not to permit publication of any information regarding military movement of troops, ships, stores or specie, all speculation in regard to relations between the Company or any Indian power or information likely to cause alarm or dissatisfaction among residents in the Company's territories.
4. See Margarita Barns The Indian Press, London, 1940, p.86.
5. Editors were required not to publish news concerning
   (b) the doings of the Court of Directors or other public authorities in England connected with the Government of India; to avoid remarks on the conduct of the Members of the Governor-General-in-Council or Judges of the Supreme Court or political transactions of local administration.
   (c) Discussions likely to create alarm or suspicion among the native population;
   (d) Republication from English or other newspapers of passages coming under any of the above heads and
   (e) Private scandals or personal remarks on individuals tending to excite dissensions in society.
6. See Mukul Gupta, "A Fearless Friend of India", **Amrita Bazar Patrika**, 3rd February, 1963.

7. Nataranaj, **The Press in India, p.361.**
8. Barns, op.cit., p.121.
9. Notes and correspondence in GI Public, 24th September, 1870, 23-30 A. Also noting in **GIPOL** January 1912, 41-49A.
10. Roy, Law (1922), p.104 A discussion of the circumstances surrounding the various laws is in Secretariat noting, **GIPOL** July 1907, 178-180 A.
11. **Ibid.,** pp. 106-108.
12. Roy, **Law** (1922), p.129.
13. In 1878 there were 62 vernacular papers in the Bombay Presidency, 60 in the North-West Provinces, Oudh and Central Provinces, 28 in Bengal and 19 in Madras. It was calculated that there were probably more than a lakh readers of such papers.
14. Minto to Morley, 19th November, 23rd December, 1909, M.C.
15. Minto to Morley, 13th January, 1910, M.C. Background on the various trials of and attacks is in Guha, Spark, pp. 125-78.
16. Home Political A July, 1910 File No.5-32 Simla Records NAI, p.5.
17. For details see Appendix , Section 4 (1) Indian Press Act, 1910.
18. On tightening of controls, documents in the following, J and P, 1929, 2926, **GIPOL** 1930, 50-3 I-III, Civil Disobedience, pp. 1-12, Gopal, Irwin, pp. 70-87; India in 1930-31, pp. 73-75.
19. On ordinances, documents in GIPOL 1930, 503 I-III, J and P 1929, 2926.
20. Copies of ordinance and correspondence on implementation in J and P 1930, 1962, GIPOL 503 I.
21. Telegram to Local Government, 1235 S (April 25, 1930) GIPOL 1930, 503, I.
22. Documents on the Ordinance, GIPOL 1930, 503, III.
23. Based on quarterly reports on proscriptions, 1930, **GIPOL** surveys of banning notifications in Provincial Gazettes suggested that official cumulative lists were incomplete. Also, see listing and discussion in **GIPOL** 1930, 28.
24. M.Venkatarangaiya (Ed.), **The History of Freedom Struggle in Andhra Pradesh (Andhra),** Vol.I, Document No.61, p.219.
25. G. Harisarvothama Rao, "Telugunaati Jatiyodyamamu Toli Rekalu" from Vavilala Gopala Krishnaiah's Collections, **S.A.H.**
26. 1. S. Natarajan, A History of the Press in India, (Bombay, 1962), p.188.
27. Government of Madras, Letter No.425, Public (Confidential) Dt. 7th June 1906.
28. Government of Madras, G.O.No.1021-22, Public (Confidential) Dt. 26th July, 1932.
29. Government of Madras, G.O.No.577-78, Public (Confidential) Dt. 12th July, 1933.
30. Census of India 1911, Madras, Vol.XII, Part-I, Report – Table on number and circulation of newspapers, p.134.
31. Census of India, 1931, Madras, Vol.XIV, part I-Xtable on Newspapers circulation.
32. Margarita Barns writes, "In India from Raja Ram Mohan Roy to Keshab Chandra Sen, Gokhale, Tilak, Feroz Shah Mehta, Dadabhai Naoroji, Surendranath Banerjee, C.Y.Chintamani, M.K.Gandhi and Jawaharlal Nehru there is a distinguished line of public men who have used.....the press as a medium for the dissemination of their ideas and moral values"; Margarita Barns, **Indian Press**, p.XV.

4

THE NEW FORCE AND HOPE - GANDHIJI

The new force in India's struggle for freedom was Mohandas Karamchand Gandhi. [1] His personal involvement in political developments in India began rather late, only in 1918. Till then he had been engaged in an important mission in South Africa. He championed the cause of his countrymen there. They were being exposed to hardship at the hands of the British Government. It was in South Africa that he experimented with Satyagraha (Passive Resistance) against the policy of racial discrimination practiced by the Government against the non-whites. [2]

Gandhiji returned to India in 1915. Instead of directly plunging into active politics, he considered it prudent to make a thorough study of the Indian political situation. The awakening of the Indian people through the activities of the Home Rule League prepared the way for his rise to the leadership of the Indian national movement in 1919. While Gandhiji was imparting lessons in self-reliance, self-sacrifice, self-help and self-purification to his people, he was suddenly thrown into the vortex of Indian politics and into assuming the leadership of the nation as already stated by the Rowlatt legislation (February-March 1919) followed by the Jallianwallah Bagh Tragedy (13th April 1919).

These events hurt the nation's self-respect deeply and transformed a constitutional agitation for modest political rights into a great national struggle based increasingly on popular sanctions. Gandhiji embodied in his person the wounded feelings of the nation and its will to assert self-respect, and thus commenced the Gandhian era in Indian history. Gandhiji appeared on the scene with his background of struggle against colour and race prejudices in South Africa and with his strange appearance of a common man dressed in his famous loin cloth and shawl covering his body. India was known for its many ascetics and religious leaders but here was a politician who beat them all in his ascetic way of living, and his rustic appearance made a tremendous appeal to the people of India, while he proved to be a puzzle and a nuisance to the British rulers.

At the time of Gandhiji's arrival in India the prevailing mode for politics was limited politics. Gopala Krishna Gokhale was the center of the political stage and politics was confined to the intellectuals. The masses were in the excluded area. The Servants of Indian Society was the forum of the intellectuals and Gandhiji's entry into the society was opposed by a number of members. Further Gandhiji did not like Institutional politics (limited politics). Apparently he wanted to be free from the trammels imposed by it.

The first thing he did was to bring the masses to politics. He took politics to the doors of the Indian masses. This he did mainly by identifying himself with local causes. At Champaran, then at Kaira and lastly at Ahmedabad he entered the arena with the people behind him to remedy their local grievances. When he was assured of the support of the masses, he launched forth into the wider sphere of all-India politics. He brought majority of the people into the streamline of freedom struggle, through his principles, programmes and movements. The writers and poets were influeced by Gandhiji's principles and programmes and began to write many books on Gandhiji's principles and programmes to popularise and intensify the freedom movement. As a repressive measure Government proscribed number of books. Some of the books were investigated. The entrance of Gandhiji into the freedom struggle was the new force and his entrance opened a new chapter in the history of Indian freedom struggle. The people finally succeeded in fulfilling their hope. Therefore I entitled this chapter as The new Force and Hope – Gandhiji. The following description of the various kinds of books and pamphlets on Gandhiji proves the value and relevance of this chapter.

The first Telugu book on Gandhiji, entitled **Navayugam** or **Gandhi Mahodayam** (New Era or the Rise of Gandhi) was a drama, written by Damaraju Pundarikakshudu, Guntur was prohibited by the Government of Madras (the performance of which) within Madras Presidency in 1921.[3] In this drama the author highlighted the principles of Gandhiji and stated that Bal Gangadhar Tilak was the eleventh and Gandhiji the twelfth incarnations.[4] The main intention of the author was to spread the ideology of Gandhiji among the people because his new theory had enormous strength in the principles themselves. So the author realised the new force of Gandhiji and began to propagate it. The details of the drama are furnished in the "Pillars of the Proscribed Literature" chapter.

The second book on Gandhiji is **Swarajya Kolatam,**[5] written by Balakavi Dantu Veeraraghavayya, Siddipalli, Guntur district. Kolatamu was one kind of popular folk dance. In this work the writer praised Gandhiji and his principles. He stated that the British Government skirted the issue of independence to Indians by saying that the Indians were not civilised and intelligent enough for self Government. He stated that Gandhiji, like Sri

Krishna, who protected the Pandavas, assured that he would bring independence to Indians and Gandjhiji also exhorted the people not to indulge in Asatya and Adharama, refrain from drinking, wear khaddar cloth and participate in the non-cooperation movement. The kolatam song went on to highlight the valour and leadership qualities of Konda Venkatappaiah, a domicile of Guntur and a mirror image of Gandhiji.

In this work the author propagated Gandhiji's new theory and encouraged people to participate in the movement through a new technique, kolatam. He also propagated Gandhiji's political economy and encouraged local leaders like Konda Venkatappaiah to lead the people effectively. The Government of Madras, satisfied with investigation of this work, did not proscribe it.[6]

The third book on Gandhiji, entitled **Gandhi Mahatmuni Jivitam**[7] (Life of Gandhi) was published by Kala Venkta Rao, Amalapuram, Godavari district and printed at the Maruti Printing House, Amalapuram.

In this work the author described the grievances, harassment of the Indians in South Africa by the Britishers and praised Gandhiji's spontaneous impulse to do justice through the instrument of satyagraha in South Africa. Later he applied the same technique to inhuman acts like Rowlatt Act which showed scant respect for human rights. 76th April 1919 was an evil day for the whole of the nation. So Gandhiji made people to undergo fast on the above mentioned date and asked them to prepare themselves for hardships.

The writer also stated that the Jallianwallah Bagh tragedy and the British attitude towards Muslims after the First World War encouraged a majority of nationalists to approve the principle of self determination. The Indian National Congress (INC) also gave unstinted support to the non-violent, non-cooperation movement and expressed their confidence in the leadership of Gandhiji.

The intention of the author in this work is to show the hardships of Indians in South Africa, the importance of Satyagraha, the inhuman legislative nature of the British, the propagation of unstinted support of I.N.C. to Gandhian new theory. It was a well investigated work.[8]

The fourth book on Gandhiji, entitled **Navayugam-Gandhi Vijayamu** is a political drama, written by Damaraju Pundarikakshudu, Guntur. It was printed at Andhra Grandhalaya Press, Bezwada. The Telugu translator to Government of Madras translated some passages from the book.[9]

The details of this drama are discussed in the "Pillars of the Proscribed Literature". The intention of the author in this work was to propagate the actual deeds which happened in India from the beginning of Gandhiji's entrance into Indian freedom struggle till the completion of Nagpur Session.[10] The object was to encourage the people to participate in the struggle for independence. The actual deeds were brought to the notice of the people for their active participation.

He compared Gandhiji with God and stated that he was one of the incarnations. He asked the people to follow Gandhiji and use his weapon of non-cooperation in the freedom struggle. He was responsible for the unification of moderates and extremists. He paved the way for the elimination of Brahmin and non-Brahmin feelings and eradicate caste and religious distinctions.

Gandhiji criticised the British for using force in ruling the nation. He prepared to fight against the British with his new theory and asked people to follow it. In Calcutta and Nagpur sessions the leaders opined that Gandhiji's new theory was the way to prevent similar Punjab atrocities to solve Khilafat issue and to get Swaraj to India. Gandhiji urged the people to implement the non-violent theory in certain aspects with British administration. It would protect national education and industry.

In this work the author did not advocate violent methods. Even then the Government of Madras felt that it would create hatred and contempt among the people of the country against the British Government. Hence it was proscribed and the dramatic performance of the drama was prohibited.

The fifth book on Gandhiji, entitled Gandhi Mahatma Prabodhamulu[11] was printed at the Rama Press, Ellore in 1921. The author and place of publication are not known.

In this work the author compared Gandhiji with Hari[12] and he said that Gandhiji gave to the people eight rules of conduct which, if observed, would lead to Swaraj. The eight principles were the using of Swadeshi goods and the boycott of foreign articles; to establish Panchayat and stop gambling in the courts of justice; to give up Government service and follow Indian mode of life; to give up English education and study National education; the boycott of toddy and arrack; the boycott of the Legislative Councils; adherence to truth; and the bringing about of unity.

If people followed what Gandhiji had told them, they would secure their well being. The rulers stooped to oppress the ruled. The British Government derived a revenue of one hundred and ninety three crores every year and spent only twenty three crores for the welfare of the people. This twenty three crores for the thirty three crores of people came to less than ¾ of a rupee per head. The Government took the remaining one hundred and seventy crores. The people had no right to ask for an account. They carried on the administration with bureaucratic power which was like Indrajala (magic).

Their occupation was trade. India was the place for them to derive their income from. It was for this reason that they became rulers. Before this trade in cloth was started, the British people had no food to fill their bellies with. They destroyed the trade of the country, professing to act under the mandate of their sovereign. They subjected the weavers to restraints and had their thumbs cut off, destroyed the livelihood of the Indian,s reduced them to a state of destitution and plunged them in mid-ocean to secure prosperity of the ruling race and plundered crores of rupees. If Indians used their own cloth they can lay by much money and the Britishers would be bereft of food. Further the author said "If that is done, their pride will come down and they will prevail upon their sovereign to welcome the Indians and do good to them. Having amassed immense wealth they have forgotten their pinch of stomach, your food has gone to them, and have no conjee to drink". So Indians should establish Raatnams and purchase Swadesi goods.

If the Munsiffs and Karnams resign, the foundation slips away. If they resign the wall of the British would come down without any violence, Indians would have swaraj. Further the author denounced the British courts of justice, entry into the Legislative councils and their elections.

In this work the author concentrated on the propagation of Gandhiji's non-cooperation, and British exploitation of revenue. The author particularly stressed on trade. In his opinion the trade was an important cause for the British rule and their exploitation. Therefore he encouraged swadeshi trade for the establishment of swaraj.

The Government of Madras felt that it would create hatred and contempt among the people in the country against the British. But the Advocate General reported that the passages, like 'the English had the thumbs of the weavers cut off and were plundering crores of rupees' were written with a view to encourage the use of swadesi goods. He denied the allegation that during the time of the East India Company the British cut off the thumbs of certain weavers. But in spite of this allegation the stanzas taken as a whole would not come under the criminal law. Hence it remained as a well investigated work.[13]

The sixth book on Gandhiji entitled Gandhi Mahatmuni Nirbhandamu (The imprisonment of Mahatma Gandhi) [14] was a translation into Telugu of a book written in Hindi by Giridhar Sukla by Gorrepati Venkata Subbaiah. It was printed and published at the Krishna Swadesi Press, Masulipatam.

In this work a detailed account of the social and political activities of Gandhiji both in South Africa and in India were given. It also traced the reverses and the sufferings experienced by Gandhiji, the success of Satyagraha in places like Champaran and Kaira, the progress of the non-cooperation movement and so on. At the Calcutta Congress and at the Nagpur Congress, Gandhiji asked the Indians not to work in Mesopotomia and also not the support the British Government. The Indians strictly followed Gandhiji's advice. In the preface the author remarked that the Government had committed a mistake by arresting Gandhiji to suppress the non-cooperation movement and asserted that it would 'never die'.

In 1920 Gandhiji made Satyagraha a positive force. The authorities of Natal shot down many people. The British Government could not collect taxes from Kaira Ryots because of non-cooperation. Due to the Jallianwallah Bagh incident Indians lost their confidence in British law and justice. The author provoked the Indians to destroy the British Government which could not protect the honour of Indians and asked them not to honour the Prince of Wales on his arrival. The author expressed his view that if all the Indians including Muslims united together they could fight any force in the world; he suggested that the civil and military forces (Indians) should resign.

The author advised Indians to boycott the foreign goods and cloth. The British Government harassed the weavers and destroyed their industry intentionally for their selfish ends. The Government was thus looting the common man of India. Their law and justice was only favourable to the Britishers. The author pointed out the injustice in the Punjab courts. The author advised Viceory, Lord Reading, to leave India. He said that the Indians should totally discard British Government in India. He warned that the non-cooperators would wage a war with weapons if necessary and strongly warned Lord Montague and Lord Birkinhead that this movement was nothing but final war of Swaraj.

The intenion of the author was to inspire and keep alive the non-cooperation spirit among the people by describing the socio-political activities of Gandhiji in South Africa and India. The author openly propagated Gandhiji's new theory and asserted that it would 'never die' even if Gandhiji was arrested. He condemned the British law and justice for their partiality. He criticised the British rulers for their immoral administration and cruel deeds. Like other writers he too propagated political economy.

The Government of Madras felt that it induced intense hatred and contempt among the people of the country against the Government. The Government decided that it contained seditious matter, the publication of which was punishable under Section 124A of the Indian Penal Code and proscribed it as per the powers conferred by Section 99-A of the Code of Criminal Procedure 1898.[15]

The seventh book on Gandhiji, entitled **Gandhi Mahatma Anu Kaliyuga Prahlada**[16] was composed by Damaraju Pundarikakshudu and printed at the Chandrika Press, Guntur and was published at the same place. This is the fifth book in the series of publications entitled the Swarajya Sopana Pangthi (the flight of steps to Swaraj). It waas in Harikatha form[17] and described Gandhiji's activities and was a compilation of some portions from the **Navayugarambham** or **Gandhi Mahodayam, Gandhi Vijayam**, a drama and **Panchala Parabhavam,** a drama.

The author calls Gandhiji Prahlada.[18] Prahlada had most bitterly been tormented by his father for his intense devotion to God Vishnu till he was rescued from such a miserable state by the latter who killed his father. Kaliyuga Prahlada means the Prahlada of present age. The book is a history in easy verse of the Satyagraha movement from the time of the Punjab murders, and the appearance of the Khilafat question. The details of this work is furnished in the "Pillars of the Proscribed Literature" chapter.

The zeal of the author is evident in the compilation of this work in the form of Harikatha. Harikatha performance was one of the most attractive arts in those days. So it was used as an instrument to inclulcate a sense of political awareness among the people. He also used another technique i.e., he compared Gandhiji with Prahlada. Prahlada conquered his father with his deep devotion while Gandhiji would conquer the demon rulers with his great weapon, Satyagraha. That was the belief of the author. So he began to propagate it. In addition to that the Hindus were the deep believers of mythological stories and paid keen interest on them. So the author used this as an instrument to create political awakening among the people.

The author praised Gandhiji's activities and principles with an idea to make Gandhiji's movement a mass movement. He highlighted Satyagraha vow because it did not touch weapons. He condemned and began to spread the news of General Dyer's cruel deeds at Jallianwallah Bagh in order to prevent such an offence in future. The unification of Hindus and Muslims was a major problem in those days so the author emphasised its significance in this book. He condemned the repressive policy of the British, because they had introduced the Martial law, shot and killed people. He condemned Montague reforms and Council entry. He too preached political economy and preached Swedeshi programme of Gandhiji to get Swaraj within a short period.

The Government of Madras felt that it would bring the Government into utter hatred and contempt among the people of the country. Hence the book was forfeited.[19]

The eighth book on Gandhiji entitled "Gandhi Vijayadwaja Natakam[20] (a drama of the banner of the victory of Gandhi) was a drama in nine acts, written by Kaviraja Sripada Krishnamurthi Sastri of Rajahmundry and printed at the Vidyanilaya printing works, Rajahmundry. The writer was a modern poet of some reputation. He began this drama with a preface containing a short life sketch of the 'Mahatma' in which he represented him as an avatar,[21] like Sankara, Ramanuja or Buddha, possessing manifold virtues.

The principal characters were Gandhiji, Shaukat Ali, Satyasandha, Sindhula, Guna, Narada (Rishi) Parvata (a fellow of Rishi) Tilak, Kelkar, Patel, Devendra (the lord of Gods) Brihaspati (the preceptor of Gods) Chelmsford, Michael, Rowlatt, Annie Besant, Jawaharlal Nehru, Madan Mohan Malavya, Jinnah, Lajpat rai, Kitchlew, Satyapal, Mother India, Chittaranjan Das, Syam Sundara Chakravarti, Jitendra Lal and so on.

The author stated that in 1893 Gandhiji witnessed with his own eyes the hardships to which the Indians in South Africa were subjected to by the British Government. Gandhiji said that victory was certainly assured by means of passive resistance. To support this principle he explained to them the principle of passive resistance, exhorting them to hold fast to non-violence and truth in the midst of all their suffering and cited the example of Prahlada. Gandhiji accordingly decided upon resorting to it saying. 'The adamant may have its edge blunted, the sun may lose his splendour and the fire its heat but passive resistance can never lose its power'. Gandhiji shared the sufferings of the Indians in South Africa and went into Jail and did menial work connected with the clearing of night soil and urine, without feeling any sense of disgust.

Gandhiji condemned the British Government for its brutality in Jallianwallah Bagh, discovered the principle of non-violence and non-cooperation, and secured universal acceptance of it. Through the National Congress, he became universally known to all countries as an **avatar** and devoted himself to the elevation of the country with great self-sacrifice. There is great truth in what Gopala Krishna Gokhale remarked about Gandhiji: that like Salivahana he had the power of creating great persons from dust.

The author further described that Gandhiji was an incarnation of Parasurama (an incarnation of Vishnu who destroyed the Kshatriyas 21 times) and that while Parasurama incarnation of Vishnu was all violence, the Gandhi incarnation was all non-violence. Gandhiji relieved the distress of the ryots of Champaran and Kaira and mill hands of Ahmedabad by making them follow passive resistance and himself fasting in the last stages. When he settled down at the Satyagrahasrama with his family, Montague the Secretary of State craftily declared that responsible Government would be given to India. Gandhiji had memorials sent by thousands of people rejecting the reforms. All the same, the reforms were issued. While it brought a little benefit to the people, they led to increased taxation. Gandhiji and others extended their help to the Government with men and money during the war and expected Swaraj in return, but they issued useless 1919 reforms, instead of Swaraj. On account of this, the taxes, which had already grown beyond limit and consumed the people like fire,were augmented by the addition of some more.

Rowlatt Act was passed by the Government. Malavya, Jinnah and Narasimha Sarma resigned their offices. To achieve victory passive resistance was the only way. Its success exclusively depended on the power of truth, love and soul. For the success of Satyagraha, Indians should face any kind of hardship.

At Amritsar, Kitchlew and Satyapal were arrested for preaching Satyagraha in an assembly of thirty thousand. That demon of O' Dwyer had evil laws enacted and the ancient rights of the Indians were denied and brought calamity to the country. They arrested innocent people.

Dyer came there and saw in that assembly children, women and oldmen, rubbing shoulders with one another. Dyer had machine guns brought up and gave in order to fire at them. They fell all over the ground. The shower of bullets, felled children, young men, old men and women in large numbers and blood flowed freely. Everywhere were to be seen trunks, hands, legs, entrails, calves and fragments strewn and forlorn. Dyer, not content with this had martial law proclaimed and had honour of the people defiled, had millions imprisoned and lawyers arrested, and belaboured and abused. He made them to crawl, salute and tortured them crushing and stabbing them with bayonets. The Rowlatt Acts thus proved to be demonial and unleashed a reign of terror on the people.

The Hunter committee was constituted to enquire into the Punjab disorders. In pursuance of their report the Home Government upheld the action of O' Dwyer and the Viceroy and only held that Dyer's action was hastly and Dyer was granted a pension by the Government and a reward for his meritorious work.

The author criticised the taxation system through the character of a citizen. There was a tax for profession, a tax for lending money for interest, a heavy tax for any gain, a tax for building a house, a tax for drawing toddy, a tax for ippa trees, a tax for salt, a tax for inams, a tax for crops, a tax for a marriage pandal, a tax for the back-yard, a tax for opium, a tax for water, a tax for grass, atax for road, a tax for walking, a tax for sitting. The foreign rulers devised and inflicted so many taxes on the oppressed Indians. The author also explained the need of unity among the Hindus and Muslims.

Gandhiji introduced non-cooperation resolution in the special session of the Calcutta Congress, which discussed the oppression of the Government. While introducing the non-cooperation resolution Gandhiji delivered his speech about the boycott of councils, courts, schools, foreign goods etc. In the course of his speech he said Indians were horribly massacred and insulted in the Punjab. The National Congress could not maintain the prestige of Indians. At Calcutta session the above mentioned resolution was adopted by a majority of 1852 against 889. At the Nagpur Congress non-cooperation resolution received the assent of all.

In this work the author represented Gandhiji to be an avatar and he tried to propagate his belief. He glorified the principle of passive resistance of Gandhiji and its power in the Society.

The author vividly described General Dyer's cruel deeds at Jallianwallah Bagh and the atrocities of British by Rowlatt Act to create hatred among the people against the British Government. He criticised the ruthless system of taxation of the British with a view to bring to the notice of the people the economic exploitation of the British and exhort them to act against them. The author briefly reviewed the political economy and the Calcutta and Nagpur Congress sessions on non-cooperation resolution.

On 1st October 1923, the public prosecutor, Rajahmundry sent a report to the Madras Government. In it he stated that he agreed with the Government Translator that it contained many objectionable passages. It was no doubt a political drama the object of which was the praise of non-cooperation movement. Most of the statements and arguments put forth in the book were no doubt copied from the political speeches of either the leaders of the extremist or moderate parties in the country. Taken individually they might not be sufficient to induce a court of law to pronounce them as seditious. The book contained the usual denunciation of the imposition of tax, Municipal or provincial or Imperial, the Rowlatt Act and the Punjab wrongs. The effect produced on the reader, who might read the whole book would be that, in the opinion of the author, the then Government of the country was the most wicked and unjust, so unjust that a new incarnation of the Deity (Vishnu) was needed to implant justice in the land. The Government of the country which it represented was carried on by trickery. It also alleged that the injustice, was done under His Majesty's commands.

The public prosecutor opined that action should be taken under Section 99-A of the Criminal Procedure Code and not under the Indian Penal Code as the latter course would only unduly advertise the author and his book. "I do not think that any action can be taken under the Dramatic Performances Act unless it can be shown that it would be enacted".

Therefore the Madras Government as per the powers conferred by section 99-A of the Code of Criminal Procedure, declared that the said Drama and all other documents, containing copies or translations or extracts, contained seditious matter, the publication of which was punishable under section 124-A of the Indian Penal Code. [22] Hence it was proscribed and forfeited by the Government. [23]

The nineth book on Gandhiji, entitled **"Mahatma Gandhi Bhajana Gitamulu"** [24] was written by Sitapati Sarma and Gandham Chalamayya and printed at the Desabhimani Press, Guntur. This booklet consisted of two parts. The first part consisted of five verses and contains songs in worship of Mahatma Gandhi. The authors paid their homage to Mahatma Gandhi by depicting him as one of the many incarnations of Kesava (Vishnu).

Gandhiji had lieutenants like Ali Brothers, Aurobindo, Chittaranjan Das and Lala Lajpat Rai. They were compared to the Puranic personages of Jaya and Vijaya, Sankara, Kubera (the lord of riches), and Indra, respectively. The authors questioned Gandhiji, why, with such eminent men at his beck and call, he had not yet rooted out injustice in the country and established justice.

Lord Vishnu was born as Mahatma Gandhi to establish righteousness and to relieve Bharata Mata from her servitude, just as he took up Avatara of Narasimha, Dwarf (Vamana), Rama and Sri Krishna to save his devotees who were in distress.

Even great men were not free from difficulties, though, in their case they were short lived. The authors gave four illustrations. God hid himself in the pillar in the shape of semi-man and semi-lion. He, in the person of a dwarf Brahmin, begtged Bali; Sri Krishna was born in prison. Therefore people need not fear that Gandhiji 'is now in prison'; because "he is only a man in shape but an angel in reality".

In the second part, the authors described how the British first came here as traders and took the kingdom by illegal means by Indian's own help and how they began ungratefully to impose new taxes and cruel bills upon Indians.

The authors stated that the leaders protested against Rowlatt Bill, but it was of no use. So Gandhiji made people resort to Satyagraha. Then, while on the 6th April, 1923 he observed fast, people convened mass meetings in every large village, made festivities to God and were peacefully preaching the greatness of Gandhiji. The Government had no sense of righteousness and Dyer mercilessly had all the meetings in Amritsar disrupted by throwing bombs. The British rulers committed many other atrocities on this occasion. Innocent leaders were imprisoned, chaste and virtuous women were dishonoured in many unspeakable ways.

The authors further described the greatness of Gandhiji in many aspects. For example, he relieved Indians in South Africa of their hardships. Once when the people of the Kaira district were suffering from famine, he had their taxes cancelled by making them observe "Satwic Nirotham" (peaceful obstruction). He had also invented the non-cooperation movement which gave Indians happiness in this world as well as in the other. The authors appealed to the people to use charaka, boycott foreign cloth and English courts, where there was no justice and to establish village Panchayats.

In this work the authors took the two famous epics, Ramayana and Mahabharata and the mythological story, Bhagavata and compared the famous leaders with famous personalities in those stories. These two writers too used the epic personalities, to imprint them in the hearts of the people and to create devotional feeling and inspiration among the people towards the struggle for independence. The authors believed Gandhiji to be an incarnation and propagated the idea. It indicated how the intellectuals (elite), influenced by Gandhiji and his principles, recognised the force of the 'invented' theory.

The Government of Madras felt that it would create hatred and contempt among the people against the British Government. Therefore it was forfeited by the Government of Madras as per Section 99-A of the Code of Criminal Procedure 1898. [25]

The tenth book (Pamphlet) on Gandhiji, entitled **"Santi Sangramamu"**[26] (The peaceful war) written by Vedantam Venkata Subramanya Sarma and printed at the Bhavani printing press, Masulipatam was forfeited by the Government of Madras.[27] It contained seditious matter the publication of which was punishable under Section 124-A of the Indian Penal Code.

The author encouraged Indians not to have fear of war of independence but to face it bravely. He assured that eminent and able persons like Mahatma Gandhi, Jawaharlal Nehru, Konda Venkatappaiah of Guntur, Bulusu Sambamurthi of Cocanada were behind this war and they will surely win it.

The author criticised the Britishers for many reasons such as not giving independence to Indians, not giving food, compulsion on wearing foreign (British) made cloth. When we refused to wear their cloth they threatened to beat us with canes etc. The author invoked God Rama, incarnated as Mahatma Gandhi, to drive out the Satanic Government (British Government).

The author expressed sorrow as India passed into the hands of foreigners. He wrote that Mahatma Gandhi, being son of Mother India, remained in Jail with a lofty mind, turning the spinning wheel in the hope of putting an end to the wicked British Government.

The author prayed to Mahatma Gandhi to bless the Indian people and lead them towards independence. He compared the white people with a flock of monkeys who were spoiling India in every aspect. The British were able to divide the Indian rulers by instigating quarrels among them. Thus they exploited every occasion to gain commercial benefits. With the same mind they destroyed all Indian crafts and ruined Indian ryots.

Bal Gangadhar Tilak hoisted the flag of independence, saying that Swaraj was our birth right and carried on the boycott of (foreign) goods on a large scale in order to destroy the British people's trade and secure self government for Indians. At one stage during freedom movement almost all the National leaders were put in jails including their wives and children. Among those the prominent were Lokamanya Bal Gangadhar Tilak, Lala Lajpat Rai and C.R. Das. All these leaders struck terror in the hearts of the Britishers.

The author said that the Indians were determined not to pay the salt tax because one of the reasons was that salt gave strength to all creatures and was favoured by all poor people. In order to break the Salt-Act Gandhiji went to Dandi and knocked down to the earth the cruel action of the British Government by means of the Salt-Satyagraha.

Gandhiji successfully managed to make the Indian people wear khaddar and boycott all the British-made foreign cloth. This made the British industrialists close down their spinning mills incurring huge losses.

In the Punjab women and children, including pregnant women, were to tortured in many ways by the British Government. Pregnant women were made to crawl on their bellies so that their wombs got displaced. Tender children were made to walk on rough grounds in the hot sun so that they would be terrorised.

Gandhiji was arrested and imprisoned by the British Government, thinking that Gandhiji would become helpless in managing the Indian people towards national movement. But to their (British) surprise the movement reached every nook and corner of India and he (Gandhiji) managed to see the Indian flags hoisted in every village.

Bhagat Singh, though young, showed extraordinary courage and tactics in terrorising the British Government, but finally he had to sacrifice his life as a true patriot and obedient son of India. The author was tactfully provoking the Indian masses by his skilful poetic words and advised them to follow the example of Bhagat Singh, Rajguru and Sukhadev who sacrificed their lives to release India from the British bondage.

The author praised Alluri Sitaramaraju, an Andhrait leader of the Agency Fituri of 1922-23, who by using simple weapons, but implementing brilliant war tacties, became a nightmare to the British Government.

In this pamphlet the author tried to encourage people to participate in the freedom struggle by showing and saying that they had the backing of the prominent leaders and assured the people, that they would achieve Swaraj. He criticised the economic exploitation and divide and rule policy of the British.

The eleventh book on Gandhiji., entitled "**Gandhi Mahatmuni Dasavatara Lilalu**" [28] was written by Nalamu Krishna Rao of Rajahmundry, printed at the Eswara Press, Rajahmundry. [29] The author compared Gandhiji with Sri Krishna and the Government with demon Kamsa who was the uncle of Sri Krishna in Mahabharata. Kamsa who wanted to kill Sri Krishna and in return was killed by Sri Krishna.

Previously God took Ten Avatars to punish the wicked and protect the good. "Now he has come in the form of Gandhiji to redeem the world from the wicked Government". Gandhiji restored the lost Vedic principles of the art, education and virtuous deeds and established peace. By using the weapons of non-violence and satyagraha Gandhiji united thirty three crores of Indians against the British. Gandhiji established non-violence as the real weapon. Like Vamana, Gandhiji crushed the British Government under his feet. He achieved this by using the weapons of violation of Salt Act, boycotting of liquor and boycotting of foreign cloth. Like Parasurama, Gandhiji was a simple but disciplined man. He opposed the mighty world dominated by the British Government.

Irwin was compared with Ravana (the villain in the great Epic Ramayanam), MacDonald was compared with Ravana's son Meghananda, Gandhiji to Sri Rama and wealth of India with Sita (the wife of Rama).

Lanka was compared with Lancashire and volunteer army with monkey army. Irwin took away India's money and deposited it in England. Gandhiji with his satyagraha army would crush the pride of the foreign Lords, Irwin and MacDonald etc. and establish independent, just and peaceful rule in India. The author stated that the "Political diplomacies" of the West were based purely on "deceit, fraud and cheating".

In this work the author widely used the great theme of incarnation of Lord Vishnu to create clear understanding and political awakening among the masses. These are the most popular dependable and commendable works on the life of the Hindus. He stated that Gandhiji was another incarnation to protect the people from wicked British Government.

The Government of Madras decided that it would create hatred and contempt among the people in the country against the British. Hence it was forfeited as per powers conferred by section 19 of the Indian Press (Emergency Powers) Act 1931[30] (Act No.XXIII of 1931).

The twelfth book on Gandhiji, entitled **"Gandhi Mahatmuni Nitimanjari"**[31] which was the first publication of the series known as **"Palleturi Grandhamandali"**, was a collection of some teachings of Mohandas Karamchand Gandhi, rendered into Telugu buy Mudiganti Jagganna Sasri and printed at the Cocanada Printing Press, Cocanada. It was a collection of passages from Young India and other papers. It was not an original work. The first edition printed in April 1927 sold 1000 copies. There was no objection to these books, from any quarter at any time. The second edition printed in 1929 also was not objected to. The third edition was printed in about the middle of 1933. The printer was not aware of any objection to his reprinting this book, till the notice under review was actually served on him.

The author (Gandhiji) suggested that if all the boys could boycott schools, then the national spirit would develop. If all the people of the country collectively resisted a Government such a Government could not exist for long. The people were divided and ruled and looted by the British Government. Freedom was not a thing which could be given to a country by some other Government. Freedom could be attained by shedding blood.

The people need not obey the Government, which depended on the wrongs and atrocities done by its authorities. It was better not to allow the Government to function which pretended as if it was imparting knowledge to the people. It was the duty of the educated Indians to provoke dissatisfaction in the people with the British Government. In schools the Indian children were humiliated by the British officers. Satyagraha was giving strength to Indians. Violence and lawlessness were running away before Satyagraha.

The author thought that even though it was a crime to resist the Government, he would resist it for the sake of freedom. The author was confident that Indian people could establish a self Government. He said that the laws were made to suit the commercial purposes of the British Government. The author pointed out that the Independence would also be won within the jail walls and sometimes only on the scaffold. It could never be secured in schools or Legislative Councils. Civil disobedience redeemed both the king and the people. Freedom was the birthright of Indians and the British Government swallowed it. Englishmen were ruling India to satisfy their own interests. The author pointed out that boycott of foreign cloth would cause very serious losses, not only to the Englishmen, but to all foreign nations as well.

The author wrote implying that the British Government was of a satanical type. The author was expected that the people living under the British Government would suffer jail life.

The British Government was disarming the Indians but at the same time spending huge funds for its military and civil services. For this it exploited all the resources of India and its man power. The Government was ruling India with a business mind. The author warned the British Government that if it failed to do justice to India it would be destroyed. The author advised the Indians to disobey the British laws and said that it was the main weapon to obtain freedom.

In this work the author (Gandhiji) asked the students to boycott English education for the development of national feeling. The united fight would get Swaraj; so he stressed on unity in the diversity of India. He stressed that for achieving freedom shedding of blood might also become necessary.

He urged the intellectuals to make the masses recognise the useless and lifeless rule of the British and bring them to the forefront of the struggle for freedom. Satyagraha would give enormous power to the Indians. He appealed to the Indians to protest against unjust rule and stated that the protest against a Government was a crime but it was justified for the sake of liberation. The British enacted law with a commercial point of view. So the people should give a death-blow to their trade. For continuation of their rule and protection, they were spending huge amounts of money, on military. The author threatened the Government that if it failed to do justice, it would be destroyed and he encouraged people to disobey the British rule.

The Government of Madras felt that it contained matter which came under the purview of Section 4(1) of the Indian Press (Emergency Powers) Act, 1931 as amended by Section 16 of the Criminal Law Amendment Act, 1932 (XXIII of 1932). Hence it was forfeited.[32]

Another book written on Gandhiji was **Round Table Rayabharam** or **Round Table Negotiations**[33]. It was written by Ravipati Kameswara Rao[34] of Guntur district. It was in the form of Harikatha. The author was born in 1897 at Ravipadu, Narasaraupeta Taluk, Guntur District. He was influenced by Satyagraha Movement and began to participate in freedom movement. He was a devotee of Gandhiji and worked in Harijan movement. So the traditionalists expelled him from their society. Even then he was not discouraged. Through his Harikatha he tried to awaken the people towards freedom movement. While he was performing this Harikatha at Vinaya Ashram, Kavur on 23rd December, 1934, he was arrested. On 30th December 1934 the District Superintendent of Police, Guntur, forwarded the manuscript of this book for proscription.

The book was on the lines of religious discourse, containing songs, verses and prose. It was written in four parts as follows:

1. Part 1. Pages 1 to 27. Gandhiji's departure for England to attend the Round Table Conference.
2. Part 2. Page 28 to 61. Failure of the Round Table Conference.
3. Part 3. Pages 62 to 94. Gandhiji's return to India. Resumption of the Civil Disobedience Movement.
4. Part 4. Pages 95 to 123. Picketing – High-handedness of the Police – The White Paper.

"Round Table Rayabharamu" as the title indicated deals with Gandhiji's ambassadorial mission to the Round Table Conference. The author gave a very detailed account in chronological sequence of the Irwin-Gandhi Pact, Gandhiji's participation in the Round Table Conference on behalf of the National Congress, the proceedings of the Conference, the effect of the General Election in England and the advent of the National Government on the Indian question, Gandhiji's return to India with belied hopes, the revival of the civil disobedience and its progress and finally Gandhiji's arrest and imprisonment followed by the rounding up all the Congress leaders. The Communal Award and the white paper came within its purview.

The author glorified the Satyagraha movement and declared that it was the only weapon to succeed over the autocratic British Government. He gave Satyagraha an epic status and raised it to the height of the Hindu mythological Mahabharata War and the patterned his characters after the heroes of Great Epic. Gandhiji was elevated to Godhood and termed 'Lord

Krishna'. His followers, as representatives of the Indian people, were equate with Pandavas and the British with Kauravas (their enemies). Vallabhai Patel was made Dharmaraja, the first of Pandava brothers and Messrs Gafoor Khan, Jawaharlal Nehru, Ansari and Tyabji were called Bhima, Arjuna, Nakula and Sahadeva respectively the other four brothers. Of the British 'Kauravas', MacDonald was termed King Duryodhana, Lord Sankey was called Dhritharashtra, Sir Samuel Hoare was named Karna and Churchill Dussasana. The qualities and character of these Kauravas, were compared and contrasted with those of their epic prototypes. He described how they were inferior to the epic heroes. Just as Lord Krishna had failed to achieve his (ambassadorial) mission to the Kauravas and returned to the Pandavas to appraise them of the inevitability of war, Gandhiji was represented to have failed to achieve his mission at the Round table Conference, returned to India and started Civil disobedience. This was the background of the picture. The author pointed out that the details were meant only to add to the effectiveness of the background. "Repression" (ordinances, lathi charges etc.) was described at length.

The boycott of liquor and foreign goods was advocated in strong terms and Communal Award and the White paper were condemned. The author glorified Satyagraha, pictured the Indian cause as righteous and the British as unfair and dishonest and held that truth (righteousness) would ultimately win.

In this work the author took many personalities from Mahabharata and compared famous Indian political leaders with Lord Krishna and Pandavas. Lord Krishna and the Britishers with Kauravas. After failure of Lord Krishna's negotiations with Kauravas, Pandavas along with Lord Krishna declared war on Kauravas. This negotiation was the heart of the Mahabharata. This context in Mahabharata was most interesting and ever ringing in the hears of the entire Hindu Community. So the author took it as a weapon and described the failure of Round Table Conference, and declaration of civil disobedience war by Gandhiji. The author attached epic status to Satyagraha of Gandhiji. The author also preached boycott of liquor and foreign goods as part of political economy. He condemned communal award because it divided the people on communal grounds.

The book contained matter which tended to bring into hatred or contempt His Majesty, or the Government established by law in British India and to encourage or invite any person to interfere with the administration of the law, or with the maintenance of law and order. It contained matter of the nature described in Section 4 (1) of the India Press (Emergency Powers) Act 1931 as amended by Section 16 of the Criminal Law Amendment Act, 1932 (Act No.XXIII of 1932). So the book and all other documents containing copies, translations of or extracts were forfeited by the Madras Government and prohibited the performance of Harikatha.[35]

The fourteenth book on Gandhiji, entitled **"Dakshinafrika Satyagraham"**[36] was a substantially accurate rendering by Gollapudi Sitarama Sastri of Part I of Valji Govindji Desai's English translation of M.K. Gandhiji's Gujarati work, "Satyagraha in South Africa". The Telugu book was printed at the Saraswati Power Press, Rajahmundry, East Godavari district, and published as No.12 of the series of books known as **"Suryanarayana Grandhamala"**, by the Andhra Geervana Vidya Peethamu of Kovvur, West Godavari district.

The book is a 'mainly historical work'. The President of the Academic council of the Vidya Peethamu, which was in charge of Grandhamala, observes in his prefatory note that the founder of the Grandhamala cherished a high regard for and a keen interest in the ideas and tenets of Mahatma Gandhi, and that one of his objects was the publication of books calculated to enlighten the people of the Andhradesa on 'the principles of Mahatma Gandhi's Satyagraha and their underlying Philosophy'.

The said book dealt with the origin and development of the Satyagraha campaign in South Africa under Gandhiji's leadership, upto the conclusion of the first pact with General Smuts by the end of January 1908, through the mediation of Albert Cartwright, the editor of 'The Transvaal Leader'. The author described the various handicaps the Indian emigrants had been labouring under till the inauguration of the Satyagraha campaign which lasted eight years.

The author pointed out that during the Boer war (1899-1902), Boer women captives received harsh treatment by the Lord Kitchener. Boer women understood that their religion required them to suffer in order to preserve their independence and therefore patiently and cheerfully endured all hardships. Lord Kitchener left no stone unturned in order to break their spirit. He confined them in separate concentration camps, where they underwent indescribable sufferings. They starved, and suffered biting cold and scorching heat. Sometimes soldiers, intoxicated with liquor, became mad with passion, and molested these unprotected women. Still the brave Boer women did not draw back. During these circumstances King Edward wrote a letter to General Kitchener. In it he said, "I could not tolerate and I would prefer any sort of peace than the treatment which you were giving to Boers", and asked him to bring the war to a speedy end.

The Boer cry of severe mental pain reached England. The English people were deeply pained. They were full of admiration for the bravery of Boers. The fact that such a small nationality should for a long period fight with their world-wide empire was rankling in their minds. The Boers' cry reached England, not through Boers or their representatives, but through a few high – souled Englishmen and women who were then in South Africa. The English people began to react. The late Sir Henry Campbell – Bannerman read the mind of the English nation and raised his voice against the war. The late Mr.Stead publicly prayed and invited others to pray, that God might decree the English a defeat in the war. This was a wonderful sight. Real suffering, bravely borne, melts even a heart of stone. Such is the potency of suffering or tapas and there lies the key to Satyagraha.

In the opinion of the author, regarding the supply by the Government of India of the indentured labourers from India to the British settlers in Natal, the Government of India were not well advised in taking the action they did. The British officials in India consciously or unconsciously were partial to their brothern in Natal. It was true that as many times as possible, professing to safeguard the labourers interests, were entered in the indentures. Fairly good arrangements were made for their board. But adequate consideration was not given to the question as to how these illiterate labourers who had gone to a distant land could fulfil their religious needs or to preserve their morality. The British officials in India did not consider that, although slavery had been abolished by law, employers were not free from a desire to make slaves of their employees. They did not realise, as they ought to have realised that the labourers who had gone to Natal would become salves for them.

Further the author described the difference between the Indian traders and the European traders in their dealings with the African customer. The Indian traders were a source of great convenience to the Negroes, who very much feared the European traders. The European trader wanted to trade with the Negro, but it was too much for Negro customers to expect courtesy at his hands. They would think it a great good fortune if he gave them full consideration for their money. Some of them had bitter experiences. When they purchased an article worth four shillings, and placed a sovereign on the counter, and they received four shillings as balance instead of sixteen, and sometimes received nothing whatever. If the poor Negro asked for the balance or showed how the amount paid him was less than his due, the reply would be gross abuse. Sometimes the abuse would be reinforced by a blow or a kick. All the English traders did not behave like this, but the number of such cases was fairly large. On the other hand Indian traders had a good word for the Negroes and even laughed with them. The Indian might not miss an opportunity, if it was offered, of cheating his Negro customer, but his courtesy made him popular with the Negroes. Moreover, the Negro never feared Indian traders.

The British rule in the Transvaal, after the Boer war was contrasted with the Boer regime which succeeded the British. The British constitution was old and stereotyped, and officers under it had to work like machines. Their liberty of action was restricted by a system, of progressive checks. When British power was established in the Transvaal, all laws adversely affecting the Indians began to be more and more strictly enforced day by day. Soon after the establishment of the British rule in the Transvaal and the Free state, Lord Milner appointed a committee whose terms of reference were to prepare a list of such of the old laws of both the republics as placed restrictions on the liberty of the subject or were opposed to the spirit of the British constitution. The anti-Indian laws could clearly have been included in this description. But Lord Milner's object in appointing the committee was not to redress the grievances of Indians but those of Britishers. The committee repealed many acts which adversely affected the Britishers. The same committee prepared a list of anti-Indian acts and were published in the form of a book which served as a handy manual that could be used easily. In the opinion of the author the peace preservation ordinance was passed and remained in force for a long time (without any necessity) in order to harass the Indians in South Africa.

The author dealt at some length with the Western civilisation and the Westerners' trade jealousy and colour prejudice and urged a liberal outlook as an essential qualification for a true Satyagrahi. Such large-mindedness and such patience were essential to the understanding of Satyagraha and above all to the practice of that principle. Satyagraha was impossible in the absence of these qualities. The author stated that "my object in writing the recent volume is that the nation might know how the Satyagraha, for which I live, for which I desire to live and for which I believe I am equally prepared to die, organised and how it was practised on a large scale and knowing this, it might understand and carry it out to the extent that it is willing and able to do so". In passive resistance there was always present an idea of harassing the other party and there was a simultaneous readiness to undergo any hardships entailed upon Indians by such activity; while in Satyagraha there was not the remotest idea of injuring the opponent. Satyagraha postulated the conquest of the adversary by suffering of one's own person.

The Madras Government felt that the book came under seditious law, but after its scrutiny the Government decided that it was neither to be proscribed nor was it actionable[37] and that no action was taken by the Bombay Government against Gandhiji's Gujarati work. So it remained as an investigative work.[38]

Conclusion

Till the emergence of Gandhiji in Indian politics, the struggle for Independence was confined to elite class. But after his emergence he recognised the strength of Indian masses and imbibed among the masses the spirit of struggle for independence. For example the ryots felt Gandhiji was their liberator, and they credited him with extraordinary powers. He moved about in villages asking them to lay their grievances before him, and he was daily transfiguring the imaginations of masses of ignorant men with visions of an early millennium. So he acted as a new force in the freedom struggle. The writers were influenced by him and intensified Gandhiji's various movements through their writings. Thousands of people were influenced and participated in the struggle. So the writers acted as indirect leaders of the people. Gandhiji, throughout the freedom movement, acted as a new force and hoped, by introducing new movements, for the liberation of the mother India.

Almost all the writers thought that Gandhiji was one of the incarnations of Lord Vishnu. The same thing they tried to propagate among the people. They took epics and mythological characters and through them they preached the then political and economic explitation of British Raj. This was really a great technique, which was introduced by the writers. Through their writings they imparted enormous impetus to the struggle for Independence.

In the above books the writers propagated the principles and movements of Gandhiji. They portrayed Gandhiji as the leading personality of the nationlist movement and gave a call to the masses to involve themselves in the freedom struggle under his leadership and face the challenges without fear and with a spirit of dedication.

Almost all the writers propagated the boycott of foreign cloth, education and courts, and encouraged Swadeshi and upliftment of Harijans as one of the constructive programmes of Gandhiji. If the British trade declined they might leave the country. That was the intention of Gandhiji. So it was vigorously propagated by every writer. The failure of British trade would contribute for the liberation of the country. With this hope people actively participated in various movements which were inaugurated by Gandhiji with the call of Gandhiji, lakhs of people participated in the struggle even though they were subjected to many hardships. Thousands of people lost their lives with the hope that Gandhiji would get Swaraj to India. Thus the writers treated Gandhiji as the new force and hope of the Indian masses

NOTES

1. Gandhiji was born at Porbandar, Gujarat State on 2nd October, 1869; son of Karamchand Gandhi; educated at Kathiawar High School, London University and the Inner Temple; married to Kasturibhai 1881, having been betrothed at the age of 8; Advocate, Bombay High Court, 1891, visits South Africa, 1893; enrolled as Advocate, Supreme Court in spite of White Opposition; founded Natal Indian Congress, 1894; agitation in India on behalf of South African Indians, 1895; mobbed almost to death under the lead of Attorney – General Escombe on landing in South Africa on return and saved by the heroism of the wife of the Police Superintendent; led the Indian Ambulance Corps in the Boer War, 1899, whose services were well appreciated in South Africa as well as in England; returns to India to recoup health, 1901; attends the Calcutta Congress under the Presidentship of Mr.Wacha; called to Natal to place the Indian case before Mr.Chamberlain appointed to consider the question; helps Transvaal Indians in the same manner, though right to lead the deputation was refused by the White authorities; enrolled as Attorney of the Supreme Court of Transvaal; founds the Transvaal British Indian Association and becomes its Hony. Secretary and Legal Adviser; founds also the Indian Opinion; also the Phoenix Settlement, 1904, under the influence of Ruskin and the experience of the conflict between Capital and Labour in South Africa; anti-plague work in Johannesburg in 1904; led the Stretcher Bearer Corps in the Native Revolt in 1906; anti-Asiatic Law Agitation, 1906; Passive Resistance struggle; arrest and imprisonment; Gandhiji – Smuts compromise; nearly killed by his own followers who thought the compromise was a betrayal of Indian interests; General Smut;s repudiation of the compromise; the recommencement of the struggle; arrest and imprisonment; Indian Home Rule written, 1908; visit to England, 1909; 1911 settlement; Gokhale's visit to South Africa; repudiation of promise to repeal the £ 3 poll tax, 1913; recommencement of the great passive Resistance struggle; its success; visit to England, 1914; raises Ambulance Corps in London, 1914; return to India, 1915.
2. An appropriate term for M.K.Gandhi's struggle in South Africa was coined by one Maganlal Gandhi. It was Sadagraha which was accepted by M.K.Gandhi who modified it into Satyagraha (Sat-truth Agraho-firmness). For details see, M.K.Gandhi, An Autobiography or the Story of My Experiments with Truth, p. 239.
3. Government of Madras, Public Department, G.O.No.520, Dt. 17th August, 1921.
4. God Vishnu had ten incarnations according to Puranas.
5. Government of Madras, Public (General) Department, G.O. No.738, Dt. 27th October, 1921.
6. Government of Madras, Public (General) Department, G.O. No.738, Dt. 27th October, 1921.
7. Government of Madras, Public Department, G.O.No.763, Dt. 2nd November, 1921.
8. Government of Madras, Public Department, G.O.No.763, Dt. 2nd November, 1921.
9. The contents of the drama are in Pages 1-12 of G.O. No.93 Public Department Dt. 1st February, 1922.

10. The Nagpur Session was held on 36th December 1920. The object of the Congress was for the first time declared to be "The attainment of Swaraj by Peaceful and legitimate means".
11. Government of Madras, Public (General) Department, MS. Series, Confidential, G.O.No.311 Dt. 6th April, 1922.
12. Hindu Mythological God Vishnu.
13. Government of Madras, Public Department, G.O. No.324, Dt. 21st April, 1923.
14. Government of Madras, Public (General) Department, Ordinary Series, G.O. No.413, Dt. 18th May, 1923.
15. Government of Madras, Public Department, G.O, No.324, Dt. 21st April, 1923.
16. Government of Madras, Public (General) Department, Ordinary Series, G.O. No.413, Dt. 18th May, 1923.
17. Harikathas are, as the name indicates, stories of Vishnu. Actually this art was in existence in Maharashtra for spreading devotion to God from the times of Santu tukaram. From time time of Santu Tukaram it gradually developed into Harikatha. **Kalakshepam** was a term at first used along with Harikatha, to mean "whiling away of time (usefully) with the story of Hari". But in course of time, the name was used for a particular branch of literature. When the literal meaning is lost, there may be Harikathas of any deity or personality. We have now Harikathas of Raja Ramamohan Roy, of Gandhi and of Potti Sriramulu.

    The founder of this art in Andhra was Azzada Adibhatla Narayana Das of Vizianagaram (1864-1945). He was an outstanding personality in this art; a great Sanskrit, Telugu, English and Persian Scholar; an accomplished musician and melodious singer; and wrote a Harikatha works such are Ambareeshu Charitra, Gajendra Moksham, Prahlada Charitra, Bhisma Charitra, Savitree Charitra. He got name and fame for the performance and contribution to this art.

    The Harikatha performer delivers his Harikatha in prose, verse and song to the accompaniment of the harmonium, a stringed instrument like the violin and a drum and he holds a pair of castanets in his hand. The composition may be his or another's. This is one of the most powerful weapon to inculcate deep devotion to a deity or principles of a personality.
18. Prahlada was the son of Hiranyakasepa, in a mythological story of Bhagavata. He was a passive devotee of God Vishnu.
19. Government of Madras, Public (General) Department Ordinary Series, Confidential G.O. No.413 dt. 18th May, 1923.
20. Government of Madras, Public (General) Department, MS. Series G.O.No.839 dt. 30th November, 1923.
21. Incarnation of God Vishnu. He was a mythological God, who had a number of incarnations.
22. Government of madras, Public (General) Department, MS Series G.O. No.839, Dt. 30th November, 1923.
23. **Ibid.**
24. Government of Madras, Public Department, Ordinary Series, G.O.No.283, Dt. 16th April, 1924.
25. Government of Madras, Public Department, Ordinary Series, G.O.No.283, Dt. 16th April, 1924.

26. Government of Madras, Public (General) Department, G.O.No.895, Dt. 2nd September, 1931.
27. **Ibid.**
28. Dasavatara Lilalu means the Ten incarnations of God Vishnu and his deeds. Ten incarnations of God Vishnu were : Sri Krishna Matsyavataram, Kurmavataram, Varahavataram, Narasimhavataram, Vamanavataram, Parasuramavataram, Sri Rama Avataram, Buddha Avataram and Kalki Avataram.
29. Government of Madras, Public (General) Department, G.O.No.1006, Dt. 21st July, 1932.
30. Government of Madras, Public (General) Department, G.O. No.1006, Dt. 21st July, 1932.
31. Government of Madras, Public (General) Department, MS Series, G.O.No.318, Dt. 27th March, 1934.
32. Government of Madras, Public (General) Department, MS Series, G.O. No.318, Dt. 27th March 1934.
33. Government of Madras, Public (General) Department, G.O. No.437, Dt. 12th March, 1935.
34. It was edited by Jaidhir Tirumala Rao in 1991, published by Telugu University, Hyderabad, August 1991.
35. Government of Madras, Public (General) Department, G.O.No.437, Dt. 12th March 1935.
36. Government of Madras, Public (General) Department, MS. Series, G.O. No.814, Dt. 24th April, 1941.
37. Government of Madras, Public (General) Department, MS. Series, G.O. No.814, Dt. 24th April, 1941.
38. **Ibid.**

5

BANNED WRITINGS ON ECONOMIC NATIONALISM AND PATRIOTIC EFFUSION

The writers in Andhra, during the period of this study, gave considerable importance in their writings to economic nationalism and patriotic nationalism from the Swadesi movement in 1905 to the Salt Satyagraha and Civil Disobedience Movement in 1932. Economic matters like the use of indigenous goods, promotion of Indian trade and industry, opposition to the oppressive taxes of the Government, and various aspects connected with the exploitationist policies of the Colonial Government were inextricably linked with the fight for the freedom of the country. Hence the Telugu writers devoted considerable space in their writings for matters of economic importance. The general theme of the writers in Andhra on economic matters was the promotion of economic nationalism. They looked at all economic matters from national point of view, exposed and condemned the economic imperialism of the Colonial Government, and rendered great service in preparing the minds of the people against the economic policies of the British Government and in favour of the economic ideology of the Indian national leaders.

The chief contribution of the Telugu literature towards economic nationalism lay in its appeal to the people to develop the Swadesi spirit. Throughout the period of this study, appeals were made for the boycott of foreign goods, and for the use of Swadesi goods. The charka of the spinning wheel and Khaddar became the symbols of the Swadesi spirit, after Gandhiji's emergence as the leader of the national movement, and virtues of spinning and wearing khaddar were extolled.

The Literature in Andhra between 1920 and 1947, played a glorious part in rousing national consciousness among the people. It preached patriotism to the people in several ways and appealed to them to take an active part in the national movement. In trying to inculcate the national spirit among the people, the literature glorified India. Love for one's own country, it was pointed out, was the primary duty of all the citizens in the country. The nationalist Literature in Andhra, like its counterparts in the rest of the country, ably performed the mission of preaching the gospel of nationalism. The writers wrote that patriotism was a unifying force and that it would foster national progress.

The writers urged Andhras to be patriotic in order to repay the debt that they owed to the Mother land. They praised virtues of patriotism. Religious fervour was introduced into nationalism, and love for one's own country was preached as a sacred duty to be performed by all the citizens. They preached patriotism as a solution for all the problems of India. They wrote that every individual should completely surrender himself to the nation.

The writers advocated every aspect of the constructive programme of Gandhiji and Congress. The writers drew from the ancient traditions, Puranas and other religious works to convince the people that the movement was a just one and that it was in accordance with the culture and traditions of the country.

The writers of Andhra explained to the people the virtues and inspiring qualities of great men and appealed to the people to imbibe their spirit of service to the Mother land. They preached nationalism, published the life stories and teachings of great nationalists and the independence movements in other countries to inspire the people. The writers believed that suppression by the Government would not 'throttle' the movement but would educate the people and further strengthen their resolve to overthrow imperialism. The British could not tolerate the political awareness spreading among the common people. That was nothing but sedition. The British authorities pushed further the policy of Ban to counter the growing-nationalist movement. The Britishers realised that the growing unity of the Indian people posed a major threat to their rule. So they followed a policy of ruthless repression to put down the growth of nationalism.

Bharatha Gitamulu

A pamphlet in Telugu entitled **Bharatha Gitamulu**[1] written by Subramanya Bhagavathulu, a teacher in National College, Guntur and printed at the Chandrika Press, Guntur, was proscribed and forfeited by the British India Government as per the powers conferred by sub-section (1) of Section 12 of the Indian Press Act, 1910.[2] The Government felt that the pamphlet would encourage hatred or contempt towards Government established by law in British India and was therefore of the nature described in Section 4 (1) (c) of the India Press Act 1910.[3] The pamphlet was priced at two Anas and sold openly prior to its proscription.

"India is pioneer in civilization while other countries are just learning the rudiments. Our great leaders like Tilak are in jail. We are not allowed to think and write for ourselves. The right of freedom is denied. The rulers are exhibiting contempt towards the religion. The people wanted to expose their grievances and problems to the Government. They were not given patient hearing and but were killed as hunted animals. There was no fixed number of statistics for the huge masses massacred by the Government. When these people went to appeal to the Government".

The write in **Bharatha Gitamulu** deplored the fact that even though India as a country had all the natural resources and also the skills necessary to make use of those resources, the people were held in bondage. They were unable to express their ideas and put them into practice.

Hindudesamu Purvaprastutastitulu (Leaflet)

Immediately after the approval of non-cooperation movement of Gandhiji at Calcutta Congress conference (session) the entire India was subjected to great awakening and it gave new force to Swadesi movement. Moderates in Congress Party thought that the movement should be limited to discussions and submission of petitions to Government. But the youth thought that the movement should reach the ordinary people. So they began to publish many leaflets to educate ordinary people and also change the attitude of the educated rich and selfish people. These three categories were then against non-cooperation. Under these circumstances a leaflet in Telugu entitled **Hindudesamu Purvaprastutastitulu**[4] was written by Madduri Annapoornaiah and printed at the V.R.Press, Rajahmundry. It was prices at 9 paisa. The Government felt that the leaflet would encourage hatred or contempt towards the Government established by law in British India and was therefore of the nature described in Section 4 (1) of the Indian Press Act, 1910.[5]

The author in Hindudesamu Purvaprastutastitulu compared the earlier rule of Hindus and Muslims to the rule of Britishers. The Muslim rulers settled in India. So the wealth of the country was not transferred to another place and appointed Hindu people in jobs. Whereas Britishers transferred Indian wealth to Britain and used discriminatory methods in appointing people to the jobs. Arts, science, and industries were completely neglected and even food had became scarce. The writer advocated that people should take up the vow of non-violence and non-cooperation as propounded by Gandhiji.

People enjoyed peace, tranquility and life of stability under Hindu and Muslim kings whereas they were lacking under Britishers.

Under the caption **The British Rule** the author narrated how the Britishers captured political power in India by a series of frauds and forgeries. The writer described the deeds of Robert Clive, Warren Hastings and Dalhousie. The army was unable to bear such illtreatment and revolted in 1857 which could be dubbed as grand war of Independence. The Britishers on the other hand called it as the Sepoy Mutiny. But the war failed because the army had no preconceived notions of how to conduct it. The native population was exploited mercilessly. One hundred and fifty crores worth of goods were being exported to England every year. The farmers who produced the wealth of the land were ruthlessly exploited and the education given to youth was meant to make them clerks. Many laws like Press Act, Defence of India Act and Rowlatt Act were passed to repress the people. Many leaders were unable to tolerate the cruelty of the Britishers and rebelled against the satanic Government. The great leaders like Lokmanya Tilak, Lala Lajpat Rai and Gandhiji were imprisoned.

Further the writer stated that Indians did not have right to freedom of speech to communicate their grievances to the authorities. They were preventing the meetings, freedom of writing and took assurances from number of presses not to publish news against the Government. These matters made the Government proscribe this leaflet as per sub-section (1) of Section 12 of the India Press Act 1910.[6]

Swarajyamantramu

The booklet in Telugu entitled **Swarajyamantramu**[7] written and published by Yenamandra Krishna Rao, Secretary, Village Congress Committee, Sekur and printed at the Sitavilasa Press, Tenali, Guntur District was proscribed and forefeited by the British Government as per the powers conferred by sub-section (1) of Section 12 of the India Press Act, 1910,[8] because it contained matter of the nature described in Section 4 (1) of the Indian Press Act 1910.[9]

In the above mentioned work the writer described the methods which were followed by Whitemen to occupy political power in India and how the whitemen stupified the Indians with opium and arrack. The British plundered the Indians wealth and placed begging bowl in the hands of Indians and even the burial ground was not exempted in their taxation. In the First World War they used Indian wealth and army and after the war, cheated the Indians. There seemed to be no relief to the sufferings of the Indians. Hence the writer suggested that the Indians should follow satyagraha, the only force to bring victory. The writer encouraged Indian youth ro rise with the sword of peace in hand and rush to the Satyagraha battle. The author gave an account of Punjab massacre.

Sri Bharatiya Vilapam (Pamphlet)

A Telugu pamphlet entitled **Sri Bharatiya Vilapam,** [10] was in the form of a colloquial song, composed by Somayajula Suri Dasakavi of Vizianagaram and was printed in the Navvulamuta press, Vizianagaram.

In this pamphlet the writer explained India's wealth in various forms and how the Indians were suffering from their economic exploitation. The writer said that the British came to India for their livelihood but in course of time they captured political power and they began to export India's raw materials to Britain and sent it back in the shape of various goods. In this process they were carrying away many crores of rupees. They were carrying away many crores of rupees by selling liquor. "Imposing on us professional taxes they carried away huge amount of money in the shape of taxes. As a result of this we were left with nothing but dust".

Further he said that there was no unity among the Indians, so the Britishers were benefiting a lot. If they committed an offence they left them alone and if the Indian committed, they caught us by the neck. Their salaries were by the thousands and that of Indians by the ten. The king gave an assurance that day in the Assembly that he would rule the people with impartiality. That assurance was made a dead letter and they began to oppress us like enemies. Indians could not represent or dispute. People could not express it in writing, it would be set down as sedition and visited with punishment. This must be considered as the Dharma of Kaliyuga.[11] (Justice of the present day).

They considered the lives of the Indians as of little value, and would kill them without any hesitation. They had been punishing the Indians without any offence being committed by them. The Indians stood bravely and fought and won victory in the First World War. That good service turned at to be an evil. Indians got the Rowlat Bill in return for it. They first accustomed Indians to woollen garments and chinaware, and then the prices of these were raised with a view to amass wealth.

Understanding Indians power, they enacted laws prohibiting the establishment of large factories here. Asking Indians to act in conformity with their wishes they had been keeping Indians under restraint and annoying them.

The author further described "The Punjab Massacres" and gave a pathetic description of the sufferings of the wounded Indians in the Punjab and the torture of students, children and old men. The sufferings of the women of the Punjab were greater than those to which Panchali[11a] (the wife of the Pandavas) was subjected.

Then follows a brief description of the patriotic life of Talk, who was said to have bequeathed his mantle to Mahatma Gandhi.

The author said that Mahatma Gandhi had, out of mercy, taken in the incarnation from Lord Krishna[12] for saving Indians. So, Indians should open their eyes now. Indians could reach their goal, if they listened to the teachings of Gandhiji. Under the leadership of Gandhiji Indians should release their Mother from her restraint.

Further the author said that the Indians must adopt non-violence, truth and associate with the good and virtuous. If Indians did this their troubles would be removed. Asuras like Narakasura[13] and Ravana[14] and other Rakshasas met with ruin on account of their wickedness. Kauravas met with destruction on account of the outrage they committed on Panchali. So Indians should act with faith in the teachings of Gandhiji and people would meet with victory. They should put an end to the satanic Dharma (Justice) of persons like Dyer.

The Government felt that this ballad was composed with the intention of creating disaffection towards the Government established by law in British India. Therefore the above pamphlet and all other documents containing copies of translations of or extracts were forfeited, [15] under Section 4 (1) of the India Press Act 1910.

Sahayanirakaranamu

A Telugu pamphlet **Sahayanirakaranamu**[16] (non-cooperation) was written by Vennelakhanti Ragavaiah[17] the secretary of the District Congress Committee, Nellore. It was printed in the Kistna Swadeshi Press, at Masulipatam and was published by the Congress Committee of Koruturu.

It was proscribed on the basis of Section 99-A of the Criminal Procedure Code 1898. The pamphlet contained 14 pages.

The author gave an account of the Muhammadans conquest of India and described the progress in trade, arts, industries and in other directions. He stated that the British entered India and by using the difference between Hindus and Muslims they established their Empire in India. The British established the railways, the post and the telegraph to benefit the Government, rather than the people.

The author criticised the Whites because, through prodigious salaries paid to the British, and by means of commerce and other means fifty six crores of rupees were reaching England every year. All offices in India with high salaries were for the Britishers. There was road tax, the railway tax, the land tax and the income tax. The taxation was increasing from generation to generation. It seemed that they might impose tax on education also. If the Indians criticised the irregularities of the British Government either in speech or writing in the papers there was punishment. In March 1919 the Government passed the Rowlatt Act. According to this act, if any person criticises the actions of the Government the police could put him in jail without an enquiry.

The author described the Punjab 'Slaughters' of 1919. He regarded the Punjab occurances "as a tale of tears, a tale of national humilation, a wholesale destruction of justice; and an eternal stain on the same and fame of the British Empire". The Britishers applauded the heroism exhibited by Dyer and gave him three lakhs of rupees as a reward and the British Government gave Dyer a pension, at the rate of Rs.13,5000 a year. Incited by the Punjab massacre the Indians killed six Whites. The Government gave five lakhs to the six families, but for the thousands of Indians that were killed by the Britishers they gave only twenty thousand as compensation.

In Khilafat issue the British Prime Minister did not keep his word and cheated the seven crores of Indian Muslims. Hence the author appealed to the readers to boycott schools, courts, Government services, foreign articles etc., so as to establish self-Government for themselves within a short period.

In the British Dominions such as South Afirca, Australia and Fiji the Britishers were treating the Indians worse than dogs, flogging them and subjecting them to several hardships in jail.

For the establishment of Swaraj for Indians the author suggested two ways. The first was the forbidding of killing Government officials whether openly or secretly, and the second was non-cooperation. If the Government did not concede Swaraj, as a result of the constructive part of the non-cooperation programme, all the Indians should resign to the civil and military services and also withhold the payment of taxes of the Government.

Swapnaprayanam

A Telugu book entitled **Swapna Prayanam**[18] was written by Nelluri Venkatrama Naidu. It was printed at Madras and the Government reported that it was published by the author. The book was in the form of songs. It contained 38 pages.

It was the first book of the author. He was a poet, writer, freedom fighter, critic, and a social worker. He was a good singer.

The book was a political work. In this work the author described the activities of the freedom struggle in 1920 in India. He highlighted the activities of Bal Gangadhar Tilak's ideology and its practicability in Andhra region. The author compared the Indian freedom struggle with Kuru-Pandava war[19] Indian leaders woith Lord Krishna, Arjuna and other leaders, and the Britishers with Kauravas. The author had compared the Britishers with monkeys. The author did not mention the names of Tilak and Gandhiji, but he described their ideas vividly.

The Madras Government felt that it would create hatred and contempt in British India and it was against the law established by British in India. Therefore it was proscribed by the Government within a few days of its publication.

Swarajyaprapti Sadhanamu

Swarajyaprapti Sadhanamu[20] (The means for the attainment of Swaraj) was a Telugu booklet. Its stanzas to the end of page 7 were composed by Pisipati Narayana Sastri of Vidupalapadu, while rest of them were written by Gouravajjhala Sitarama Sarma of Anantavaram Agraharam. The booklet was printed at the Rama Press in Ellore. It was proscribed and forfeited by the Government as per the powers conferred by the Section 99-A of the Code of Criminal Procedure 1898.[21] It incited a feeling of intense hatred and contempt towards British Government and British institutions in India. Hence it was punishable under Section 124-A of the Indian Penal Code.[22]

In this work authors stated that the Indians were leading a life of 'servile profession'. The authors compared Gandhiji to 'thunderbolt', 'treasure house of intellect' and 'destroyer' for his courage and activity. They used the words 'Westerners' 'Huns' "Demons' and 'Vile wretches' to describe the evil nature of the Britihsers. They exhorted the Indians to fight for independence overcoming religious differences. Muhammad Ali and

Shaukat Ali were waiting for an opportunity to destroy the Britishers. The authors encouraged the Indians to give up the western education. Indians should try to abandon the servile profession. On the cover of the booklet there was an extract from a speech of Gandhiji in which he exhorted the graduates to spin yarn on the charka. This work strongly advocated the non-cooperation movement.

Abhinava Bharata Charitra

A Telugu book entitled **Abhinava Bharata Charitra**[23] (Modern Indian History) written by Tumuluri Sivaramayya was printed at the Rajata Press, Tenali, Guntur district. The book was a Telugu rendering of the Hindi original **Bharata Vidrohi**. It was proscribed under section 99A of the Code of Criminal Procedure 1898. The book is not available. The available contents are, it gives a brief history of the Indian revolution from the end of the 19th century to the beginning of the Non-cooperation movement. The author traced the origin and development of the revolutionary movement, taking each affected province separately. Extracts from the writings, speeches and journals of the revolutionaries were also incorporated in the book.

Swarajya Jhanda-Swarajya Sanku

Booklets in Telugu entitled **Swarajya Jhanda** (Flag of Swaraj) and **Swarajya Sanku**[24] (Conch of Swaraj) were also proscribed by the Government as they contained matter the publication of which was punishable under section 124-A Indian Penal Code.[25] **Swarajya Jhanda** was written by Srungavarapu Sitaramacharya of Rajahmundry. It was printed at the Sitaramanjaneya press, Rajahmundry and the publisher was Kondapalli Veera Venkaiah.

Swarajya Jhanda contained 26 ballads, each ballad contained 5 stanzas, some 6 stanzas and some 7 stanzas. In this booklet the author exposed the policy of the Britishers which was "divide and rule", by creating differences among the sections of Indians. In order to counteract this Gandhiji resorted to Satyagraha. Gandhiji without delay organised Salt Satyagraha and advised Indians not to pay taxes due to salt production, completely boycott foreign cloth and thereby not to allow the drain of Indian money to British.

Having introduced Section 144 the Britishers punished Indian people indiscriminately with lathies. Their intenion was to show their might and whatever they said was the law. The Britishers imprisoned all the Indians who wore Gandhi cap and who chanted the slogan "Vandemataram". By becoming very rude and unmannerly the Britishers removed all the Swaraj flags in the town and tried to scare the people.

The British Government declared that the Congress committees were unlawful and imprisoned all the innocent and non-violent Indian people and subjected them to all sorts of suffering. The British police created a lot of havoc in the marriage function of Sri Vadapalli Venkateswarlu by using lathies and introducing panchamas into marriage function.

The British police roamed about posing as if they were maintaining law and order and shot down a number of innocent Indians. They soon found the fallacy of resorting to repressive laws. They recognised the strength of the Congress, and withdrew their extraordinary laws.

In order to break the Congress, Lord Irwin ordered cruel massacres and was determined to hang Bhagat Singh though the whole country asked him to let off Bhagat Singh. He was hanged with Sukhdev and others.

This was the brief summary of the twenty six ballads. The Government thought that this booklet provoked the people to question the authority of the Government and proscribed it.

The second booklet "Swarajya Sanku" (Conch of Swaraj) was written by Kalaga Satyanarayana. It was printed at Sree Prabhasi printing press, Rajahmundry. In this booklet, the author printed Mother India photo and Vandemataram slogan on the front page. The booklet was in the form of songs. The author compared India with milch cow and Indians as its tender calves. The Britishers were compared to shrewd shepherds who were completely swallowing the milk without leaving even a little to the calves (Indians).

The author expressed his opinion that whatever the Britishers did, was only for selfish benefits. In the name of Indians the Britishers were ruling India and were grabbing everything from India. It was better to discard drinking. The education provided by the Britishers would impart in Indians the salvery and no benefits whatsoever. The Britishers made huge debts in the name of India and ruined this country. They grabbed our land and instead returned a bowl. He advised Indians to have strong beliefs in the attainment of Swaraj. He said "Brothers accept no compromise except victory to obtain Swaraj". He exhorted Indians to wake up soon and jump into the non-violent fight with the Britishers. He suggested to the Andhras to declare fight against the Britishers.

The author requested Indians to donate for the Swaraj movement. He assured Indians that Mahatma Gandhi was about to go to London to put an end to the While rule. He advised Indians not to tolerate any more the rule of the Whites.

Generally the Government of Maderas sent Telugu books to Telugu Translator to the Madras Government to translate the objectionable passages into English and then they scrutinized the contents. But whereas in this case the full powers were given to the East Godavari District Magistrate. Hence the said Magistrate on 20th August, 1931 suggested that to the said booklets should be proscribed. Therefore the Government of Madras proscribed the two booklets under one G.O.

Jatiya Swarajya Pathamu

A Telugu booklet entitled **Jatiya Swarajya Patamu**[26] was written by Kalaga Satyanarayana of Rajahmundry. It was printed at Lakshmi Press, Rajahmundry and published by Kalaga Satyanarayana.

Jatiya Swarajya Pathamu consisted of national songs in Telugu. The author treated the birth of Gandhiji as one of the incarnations of Vishnu. He criticised the Bruitishers for taxing the Indian people heavily. By transporting silver and gold the Britishers destroyed the economic base of the country. The author explained the miserable conditions of the masses. Describing the Punjab atrocities he criticised the British Government for promulgating the Martial law and killing innocent people.

Satyanarayana also abhorred the conditions prevailing in jails, especially the Koraput jail, and the treatment meted out to the internees by the jail authorities.

In view of these facts the author proclaimed that instead of living under the foreign rule and leading a miserable life, it was better to face death valiantly and courageously. He exhorted the people, with all their valour, manliness and endurance, to become satyagrahis and fight for the independence of the motherland.

It was forfeited under Criminal Procedure Code Section 99-A of 1898. It was calculated to incide hatred against the European community and contempt and rebellion against the Government established by law.[27]

Bardoli Satyagraha Vijayam

A Telugu book entitled **Bardoli Satyagraha Vijayam**[28] (Success of the Bardoli Satyagraha Movement) printed at the Andhra Gandhalaya Press,

Bezwada, by Kondandaramayya, Keeper of the press. It was seized by the British Government on 6th January, 1932. This book contained some extracts of Bardoli taluk no tax campaign.

The 'No tax movement' that was launched in Bardoli taluk of Surat district in Gujarat in 1928 was also in many ways a child of the non-cooperation days. Bardoli Taluk had been selected in 1922 as the place from where Gandhiji would launch the civil disobedience campaign, but events in Chauri-Chaura had changed all that and the campaign never took off. However, a marked change had taken place in the area because of the various preparations for the civil disobedience movement and the end result was that Bardoli had undergone a process of intense politicization and awareness of the political scene.

In 1901 the land tax was at Rs.2 per head in the Bombay presidency. It was highest in the Surat District at Rs.5-9-0. It was decided to enhance the taxes further. At the request of the Legislative Council in 1924 one Special Committee was appointed. Nevertheless the taxes were enhanced.

The Government had not accepted the advice given that water tax should not be collected on account of the underground source of water supply. The told tax of Rs.5,14,762 was enhanced to Rs.6,72,273 and 30% of additional tax was imposed. It was proved by the people that the enhancement was illegal and unfounded but the Government would not listen to their words. At last to get rid of their troubles the people decided to start Satyagraha and sought the help of Vallabhai Patel, the right hand of Mahatma Gandhi.

On 6th February, 1928 Vallabhai Patel wrote to the Governor that the settlement was unjust and that it would be good to have it decided by some disinterested mediators and that if their request was not acceded to he would have to advise people not to pay taxes and take the consequences peacefully. A degrading reply was sent to it. Patel had no further reply from the Governor. The ryots assembled on 12th February. Patel consulted them and made them take oaths that they would not pay taxes.

Patel told the people again that they had no means of meeting animal power of the Government and that they should be prepared to undergo suffering. He also said that until the Government agreed to ryots' conditions they should not pay taxes to the Government. This was a peaceful war concerning people's self respect. The Government might punish the leaders among the people. Thus commenced the peaceful war. Patel was the commander. He got all the people ready for war. The person responsible for this movement was Gandhi Mahatma.

The Government commenced attachments. The Government announced that if the taxes were not completely paid before 18th February a penalty of 25% would be imposed. Not satisfied with this they began to beat and abuse people. On account of these attempts only a few yielded but the rest stood firm.

Even the village officer who came to attach the land felt ashamed when he saw the Satyagraha. Though it was April, Satyagraha had not given way. The whole country supported the movement. The Collector encouraged the village officers to collect taxes. The ryots shut their doors against the Collector. The movement was strengthened. Patel said "We should stop words and take to sacrifice". The Government commenced to take illegal measures. Land worth of three lakhs of rupees was sold for eleven thousand. To purchase buffaloes the Government brought butchers from elsewhere. They began to confiscate utensils and instruments for ploughing the fields. They broke open the doors. They seized the paddy bags but left them as there were none to carry them.

May ended. Seeing all these some Council members resigned their posts. 63 village Munsiffs and 11 Karnams resigned their posts. Vetties also gave up their service.

To put down the movement the Collector began to punish the volunteers who stood in front of his bungalow. Their places were occupied by many others. To disgrace the people the accused were made to walk in chains. To kill the movement under any circumstances the Satyagrahis were accused of all sorts of offences and given rigorous imprisonment.

The Government said that they would order an enquiry if the movement was stopped. Gandhiji went to Bardoli on 2nd August to discuss about the compromise. The Government agreed to certain conditions and appointed a committee to enquire into the matter. After enquiry for some months one lakh and forty thousand rupees of the new taxes was reduced and the village Munsiffs and Karnams were reinstated and the Government returned their confiscated lands. It was proved that the contention of the people was just. The success of the movement created a faith in the people that Satyagraha was sure to result in success to the party which had Dharma as its criterior.

The Publisher also said that to get Swaraj, people should know the necessity of mass movement, offer peaceful resistence by taking the vow of Satyagraha, join as members of the Congress and form Congress associations in each village, give donation for Satyagraha fund and maintain the families of the Satyagrahis and follow with success the Congress programme.

By the use of Mahatma's wonderful weapon several people won victory. The Akali Sikhs in Punjab to decide their question about their "Gurudwaram", the untouchability movement in Travancore, the illegal taxes in Borsad (Gujarat), the national flag in the Central provinces etc. in all these cases people used this weapon successfully.

The said publication was proscribed by the Madras Government as per Section 4 (1) of the Indian Press (Emergency Powers) Act, 1931 as amended by Section 63 of the Emergency Powers Ordinance II of 1932. [29]

Akhila Congress Karya Sangham Teermanamu (Pamphlet)

A Telugu pamphlet **Akhila Congress Karya Sangham Teermamamu**[30] (Resolution of the All India Congress Committee) was printed at the Krishna Swadeshi Press, Masulipatam, by Kota Subbarao, Keeper of the press and published on 7th January, 1932.

The Working Committee heard Mahatma Gandhi's account of his visit to the West and considered the situation created by the extraordinary ordinances promulgated in Bengal, the United Provinces and the Frontier Province and the actions of authorities, including the numerous arrests made, among others, of Khan Abdul Ghaffar Khan, T. A. K. Sherwani and Pandit Jawaharlal Nehru and also the shooting in the Frontier province of innocent men, resulting in many deaths and many more being injured.

These acts and other actions betrayed no intention on the part of bureaucracy to hand over power to the people and they were calculated to demoralize the nation. They also betrayed want of faith in the Congress from which co-operation was expected by the Government.

The Working Committee yielded to no one in its abhorrence of terrorism on any account whether resorted to by individuals such as witnessed in Bengal, or the terrorism practiced by Government, as evident by its acts and ordinances.

The Working Committee expressed deep national humiliation over the assassination of two girls in Comilla and was firmly convinced that such a crime did a great harm to the nation, especially when, through its greatest political mouth-piece, the Congress, it pledged itself to non-violence for achieving Swaraj.

The Committee stressed that non-violence must be observed in thought, word and deed in the face of the gravest provocation, it being understood that the campaign was not one of seeking revenge or inflicting injuries on the oppressor, but was one of converting him through self-suffering and self-purification.

Social boycott with the intention of inflicting injury on Government Officers, police or anti-nationalists, should not be undertaken and was wholly inconsistent with the spirit of non-violence. It should be borne in mind that non-violent campaigns were independent of pecuniary assistance. Therefore, there should be no hired volunteers but the bare maintenance of dependent of poor men and women, who might have been imprisoned or killed was permissible wherever it was possible.

Further the committee resolved that boycott of all foreign cloth, whether British or of other countries, was obligatory under all circumstances. All Congress men and women were expected to use hand-spun and hard woven khaddar to the exclusion of even cloth manufactured in indigenous mills. Picketing of liquor shops and foreign cloth shops should be vigorously conducted chiefly by women, but always ensuring perfect non-violence. Unlicensed manufacture and collection of salt should be resumed. If processions and demonstrations were organized, only those should join them who would stand lathi charges or bullets without moving from their respective places. Civil breach of non-moral laws and of laws and orders injurious to people wherever it considered possible and advisable might be practiced. All important orders issued under the ordinance might be destroyed.

In exercise of the powers conferred by Section 19 of the Indian Press (Emergency Powers) Act, 1931, (Acrt XXIII) of 1931) the Government of Madras declared to be forfeited[31] the publication and all other documents containing copies or translations or extracts as it contained matter of the nature described in Section 4 (1) of the India Press (E.P.) Act 1931 as amended by Section 63 of the Emergency Powers Ordinance, II of 1932.

Daridranarayanam

A pamphlet in Telugu entitled **Daridranarayanam**[32] was printed at the Andhra Grandhalaya press, Bezwada, and issued under the auspices of the West Krishna District Congress Committee. The pamphlet contained matter of nature described in Section 4 (1) of the India Press (E.P.) Act 1931 as amended by Section 63 of the Emergency Powers Ordinance 1932. Therefore as per powers conferred by Section 19 of the Indian Press (Emergency Powers) Act, 1931 the Government forfeited it.[33]

The Committee opined that the British Government was forced on Indians who were robbed of all the privileges and so it was better to destroy it.

Independence could not be obtained by begging but only by use of force. The author criticised those Indians who were afraid of 'whites' and helped them., and criticised those Indians who were adopting the British culture and losing their self-respect and privileges. The author declared that the British establishment was a forced Government on Indians. So they would not do any good to the Indians. Those who were following western culture were loosing health and wealth. The British Government taught the Indians slavery devoid of independent development.

The Indians were rendered economically poor by the Britishers by various means such as ruining of Indian industries, giving false assurances to Indians, not giving facilities for education and agriculture. They misused Indian wealth for the military and civil services and also enhanced taxes without reason.

The British Government had curtailed the freedom of speech and turned Indians from kings and ministers into slaves and clerks. In addition to the other illegal acts of the Government were alcohol drinking, salt tax, enhanced rate of land tax, increased salaries of civilians.

Indians lost their confidence in obtaining justice from the British Government and so started freedom struggle under the leadership of Mahatma Gandhi by self help. To obtain Swaraj Gandhiji adopted civil disobedience and Satyagraha movements. The author advised Indians not to pay taxes and not to obey the British laws.

British Vastu Bahishkaramu

A Telugu booklet entitled **British Vastu Bahishkaramu**[34] (Boycott of British goods) was printed at Sowbhagya Press, Bezwada and published by the West Krishna District Congress Committee.

The publishers stated that though India was producing different crops, it was subjected to famine. Though it was a birth place of gold, diamonds and treasure, starvation was the result, though there was sea on the three sides, scarcity of salt was being felt. Although India was a seat of silk and cotton industry, people had to depend upon others for clothes.

Ever since the British came to India as traders they began to destroy Indian industries and improve theirs. They destroyed Indian weaving, shipping and other industries. They took the raw material from India. They began to send to Indian clothes, soaps etc., at high rates and to suit their interests they kept control over currency in their hands. They promulgated various laws, imposed taxes, and settled the steamer and railway fares only to suit their convenience. They refused to give Swaraj to Indians lest they should modify all these illegal matters. Though they said outwardly that they were ruling the country for the good of the Indians, in reality they used the country to sell their goods, especially Lancashire cloth, and did not leave their hold.

The publishers questioned how to escape from the firm hold of the British who carried away Indian wealth and suggested that it was in the hands of the Indians themselves. Boycott of British goods was the only weapon by which Indians could open their eyes and make them accede to the request of the Indians. All the people should treat the foreign goods as equal to poison, boycott them and use only national goods. If Indians boycotted the cloth and other articles manufactured in their mills besides the goods imported from England it would cripple their industry. Indians should stop the flow of the wealth into England, improve native industries, give food and cloth to the people and try to release Mahatma Gandhi and other leaders from jails.

In exercise of the powers conferred by the Section 19 of the Indians Press (Emergency Powers) Act, 1931, the Madras Government forfeited the book and all other documents containing copies or translations of or extracts on the ground that the said book contained matter of the nature described in Section 4 (1) of the India Press (Emergency Powers) Act, XXIII of 1931 as amended by Section 63 of the Emergency Powers Ordinance, 1932 (Ordinance No.II of 1932).

A Telugu book entitled **Prabhutwa Dhanamu Mana Bidathanamu** (Public Finance and our poverty) was written by Professor J.C.Kumarappa, printed at the Cocanada Press, Cocanada,and published by Sanivarapu Subba Rao and Balanthrapu Satyanarayana Rao of Jatheeya Grandhamala, Pithapur.

A Telugu book entgitlted **Purnaswathanathram** was written by Kona Venkataraya Sarma of Peda Cherukoor, Parachin Post, Guntur district, printed at the Rajatha press, Tenali, and published by the author.

A Telugu book entitlted **Bharatha Desa Swathanthramu** (a translation of C.F. Andrew's book) was published by Upendra Publishing House, 17, Narayana Mudali Street, George Town, Madras. Pages 1 to 28 were printed at the Tata printing works, Madras, and pages 29 to 44 at the India Printing Works, Madras.

A Telugu book entitled Swarajyame Saranyamu (translation of C.F.Andrew's speech) was published by the India Agency Bureau, Post Box

No.420, Triplicane, Madras and printed at the Central Co-operative Printing Works Limited, Madras.

The above mentioned books were forfeited by the Government as per the powers conferred by Section 19 of the Indian Press (Emergency Powers) Act 1931[36] (Act No.XXIII of 1931), as they contained matter of the nature described in Section 4 (1) of the said Act as amended by Section 77 of the Special Powers Ordinance, 1932[37] (Ordinance No.X of 1932).

Prabhutwa Dhanamu Mana Bidathanamu (Public Finance and our Poverty): In this work the author criticised the irresponsible British Government. Further he said that it was the meanest and basest of all Governments that exploited and lived upon other nations. Under these circumstances any other country would have severed its connections with such a devil long time back.

Purna Swathanthram: In this book the author explained the vexation in making their representations and prayers to the Britishers. From the existing circumstances, British rule had become quite useless. The Britishers were robbing the wealth of the Nations which they were ruling and also degrading them. The author expressed his anguish and wished the destruction of British Government. The author believed that as long as the Indians were under the rule of the British Government, they would lose their rights and privileges.

Bharatha Des Swathanbthramu: In this work the author felt unhappy regarding the slavery of India under the British rule; he advised the Indians not to join the British army he, suggested to the Indians to do everything seriously in order to get freedom. He felt pity on Indians who were treated by British as brutes and slaves.

Swarajyame-Saranyamu: In this book the author expressed his feelings at the deplorable state the Indians had been reduced to; and also felt that it was an everlasting disgrace to thirty three crores of living Indians if their country remained a prostrated slave to a small island called England situated in a corner of the world. When that plague of British Government was eating away our very vitals, how could Indians rest in peace. It was enough if Indians abstain from serving the British Government. In a month the English Kingdom would come to an end.

Bharata Swarajya Yudhamu

Bharata Swarajya Yudhamu (War of Indian Swaraj) [38] was an account in Telugu of the attempts made by the people of India for attainment of Swaraj from Alexander's invasion down to present times. It was written by Gadepalle Suryanarayana Sarma, edited by Mudignti Jagganna Sastry, printed at Jagapati Printing Press and published in 1928 as, 9-10 production of **Palleturi Gramdhamandali**. In the preface, a vivid contrast was drawn between the 'ancient glory' and present alround degeneracy of India.

The first chapter contained in detail the system of administration in Vedic times. The author wrote that India had been maintained independence continuously for 10,000 years prior to Alexander's invasion of India. In those days Aryan civilization was identical with Hindu civilization. Hindu kings ruled India according to the Divine law and there was perfect democracy based on village Panchayats. The author maintained that Indians had a community of interests and the essential requisite of nationhood. So he advised the Indians not to have any doubts in this respect in which the western rulers had intentionally created misunderstanding with the object of imposing perpectual tyranny in India.

The second chapter dealt with the gradual down fall of Hindu independence. The first symptom of disunion started in India with the birth of Buddhism, Jainism and such other anti-Vedic religions and gradually increased with the multiplication of sub-castes in the Hindu society and the spread of false philosophy and ritualism. The author expressed that every small ruler tried to become independent and began to make wars against his neighbouring rulers with the intention of attaining for himself an emperor's status. During these circumstances Alexander invaded India. According to the author the first foreign rule was established in India with the defeat of Purushottama in the battle with Alexander. After this Chandragupta Maurya and his brilliant Prime Minister Chanukya and the Sangam Dynasties brought the whole of India. Under one rule and thus India enjoyed good days again. Then the author described in detail the early Muhammadan invasions and the rule of the Muslims culminating in the establishment of Mughal Empire. In this context the author expressed his high regard for the personality, universal tolerance and harmonising influence of Akbar attributing the downfall of Muhammadan empire to the fanatical and unilateral policies followed by Aurangzeb.

The author further wrote that insipite of occasional outburst of Muhammad religious madness the Hindus never felt that they had been under a foreign rule and such a great country like India would have gone to ruins in a period of two hundred years, if the Muhammadans had followed the very same policy as the British had done.

The author wrote that the Marathas established an Empire in India which upheld the Hindu Swaraj in the major part of India. The author further described the advent of Westerners into India and the constant quarrels between the British and the French for the establishment of their power. He also traced how the British succeeded in the establishment of political power in India and how the policy purused by the British East India Company completed the downfall of Hindu Swaraj rendering the whole country a huge bural ground devoid of any brightness of life and prosperity.

In the third chapter the author discussed the causes for the defeat of the Great Indian Mutiny of 1857. He considered this Mutiny to be the first attempt to Indians to get independence on a nationwide base. The author said the formation of Indian National Congress was the second national attempt of Indians to get independence. The independence movement crossed various stages and finally went to the leadership of Gandhiji in 1920 with all its implications. In Chouri-Choura some violence had occurred at the instance of some Congressmen. Keeping this in view Gandhiji called off the Civil Disobedience at Bardoli and this was considered to be a temporary failure of the freedom movement.

The concluding chapter traces the course of the Congress upto its Madras Session of 1927 'a remarkable session of account of its resolution defining the goal of the Congress as complete independence'. The book ends with the prayer by God's grace that the freedom movement may continue on non-violent lines in future also, resulting in the establishment of Indian Swaraj.

The Government of Madras felt that in spite of this prayer, the wholesale condemnation of Britishers and the British Government in which the author has indulged can have only one effect, namely, incitement of hatred and contempt for the British people and the Government constituted by law in India. The book accordingly falls under the purview of Section 4 (1) of the India Press (Emergency Powers) Act of 1931 as amended by Section 16 of the Criminal Law (Amendment) Act of 1932. Hence it was forfeited by the Madras Government. [39]

Rajaniti Saramu

Rajaniti Saramu (Essence of Political Science) [40] which forms the second of the series of publications know as **Palleturi Grandhamandali** is said to be a Telugu translation of an English work. The name of the English original is not given. The book under report, which is a copy of its third edition, was written by Mudiganti Jagganna Sastri, who was the editor of the series. It was printed in 1933 by D.V.Syamala Rao at Syamala Art Press, Tanuku, West Godavari.

After thoroughly analyzing the political and cultural aspects existing in India at that time, the author felt that it is good and necessary for the Indians to accept and follow with great faith the leadership and the principles of Mahatma Gandhi.

The author considered Gandhiji a born leader of high qualities whose actions, principles and deeds were such that they can drive away the innocence and ignorance of the Indian people and ultimately lead them to a better desired future. The author characterises journalists, logicians, statesmen and lawyers as the worst enemies of a subject country. The author considered Britishers as the capitalists who established their rule in many countries only to secure their capitalistic benefits.

The author described the characteristics of a foreign Government and the people ruled by it. The foreign Government after conquering a country should disarm the people of that country in order to strengthen their own Government. The author expressed that a nation, fallen to the foreign Government would lose its manliness. The people should adopt the foreign language and follow their methods which can build up love of ease.

The author said that it is incorrect to think that retaliation means torture and slaughter of the enemy. The methods of retaliation will depend upon the strength, talents and other conditions of the two parties involved. For a nation, especially for a subject nation, it is better to die soon than to live with too many leaders in the country. The people who disobey the command of an honest and efficient leader will face defeat. It is but proper to pardon the enemy as the occasion demands. But it is foolish and dangerous to tolerate traitors and cowards who are time servers. The desire to acquire power is natural with every man. Since England has to fulfil its desire, she would conquer and exploit nations. But the fault of that the British nation lies in the fraud played by it.

Describing the evils of the present system of education, the author wrote that the modern system of education not only fails to rouse the latent abilities of students but is even ruining their natural intellectual power. It is the grave of that power. This is why we do not find at all any great artists, vedantins or warriors now-a-days (in India). The present 'constitution' (of India) is "a miserable hell, a crooked doorway".

Commending some features of Communism, the author writes : A Government under which one dies out of starvation for want of work, a Government under which a man cannot educate his children for want of means, a Government under which men of genius have to 'stoop' to 'service' or business for the sake of their bellies, unable to find any means for their livelihood, such a Government is wholly unworthy of that name. A

Government under whose regime there remains fallow even one acre of cultivable land (in the country) for any or no reason, stands self-condemned. A Government under whose regime there is an opportunity for 'beggars' to exist is a pauper Government which is unable to fully utilise the natural resources of the country.

It would be enough if she (India) can completely do away with foreign cloth and foreign education, she would be able to enjoy her political independence in the very next movement.

Writing about Gandhiji's leadership in the freedom movement the author says – The weapon used by Gandhiji i.e. "Non-cooperation" is the greatest and the best in the world. This weapon sets the whole world in the right path. The author advised everyone to use this weapon even though it is very difficult to use it in the initial stages. In order to conquer untruth, first cultivate truth. May action conquer truth (untruth)afterwards.

Highly academic and pedantic in style and most unsystematic in delineation of the subject matter, the book is least calculated to leave any permanent impression on the readers mind or fire up the latter's heart with an all sacrificing devotion to Gandhiji as desired by the author. And yet a scrutiny of the book would show that it contains matter which comes under the purview of Section 4 (1) of the Indian Press (Emergency Powers) Act, 1931 as amended by Section 16 of the Criminal Law amendment Act 1932. Hence it was forfeited by the Madras Government.[41]

On 20th November, 1933 West Godavari District Magistrate searched the author's house and Syamala press, took into their possession 750 copies of the book from the press. Then he wrote a report to the Madras Government. In it he stated that as per Section 4 (1) of the Indian Press (Emergency Powers) Act, 1931 as amended by Section 16 of the Criminal Law Amendment Act 1932, the book contained anti-Government matter. So it was confiscated and he also demanded Rs.1000/- as a security deposit and he recommended to the Government to bring the press into Black list.

Symala Rao was the printer of the third edition of the book. He was surprised to receive on 30th March, 1934, a notice to pay security deposit. The first edition was printed in 1926 in Cocanada press, Cocanada. There were number of copies in circulation. He never showed anti-British deeds and did not have political relations and was not a member of any organisation. He did not understand why the Government imposed prohibitary orders on his press. He started a press, for his livelihood. So, he approached a lawyer and wrote a petition to the Government and in it he expressed his apology if the printing of the said book was a crime. In adition to that he gave an assurance that if necessary, he was prepared to write a bond not to print such books in future. He requested the Government to withdraw their order for security deposit.

The District Magistrate sent another report. In it he reported that the owner of the Press had a property of Rs.5000/- and he could pay the security deposit. He did not participate openly in the activities of the Congress party. But, he was a sympathiser of the activities of the Congress in 1932. Without knowing facts, on the basis of the local officials recommendations, the Government imposed prohibitary orders on the Press.

The Government issues a notice to the owner of the press. It demanded Rs.1000/- to be paid before 10th April, 1934. So, once again Syamala Rao wrote a representation to the Government. In it, he expressed his inability to pay the amount and that from 11th April, 1934 onwards, the press was to be closed and he also stated that he was losing his only livelihood. Even then the Government did not respond positively and he was forced to close the press.

As a result of it, a number of press owners became afraid of it and lost their courage to print such books. Some of the writers became silent. Some of the writers said good-bye to writing of political works. Some of the writers changed their attitude and began to write to gain the good will of the authorities. Yet some of the writers did not care the prohibitory orders of the Government and continued their writing to create awakening among the people.

Moplah Tirugubatu

A Telugu book entitled **Moplah Tirugubatu**[42] (Moplah Revolt) by Tummala Venkataramaiah was a substantially accurate, though literal translation of S.N.Tagore's booklet in English entitled **peasants Revolt in Malabar in 1921**[43].

During British rule, Malabar became a single administrative unit under European Collectors. Feudalism on which land tenures and landlord-tenant relationship in Malabar were based was destroyed. The worst sufferers by this change were the Mappilla peasantry. The majority of them were cultivators beholden to big landholding families who looked after them as feudal overlords. When these landlords began to enforce their rights without fulfilling their corresponding obligations., relations became strained. The landlords were caste Hindus, while the peasants were mostly the Mappillas. In August, 1921, peasant discontent erupted in the Malabar district of Kerala. Simultaneously, the Khilafat movement was also extending its sweep. In fact there was hardly any way one could distinguish between Khilafat and tenants' meetings. The leaders and the audience were the same, and the two movements were inextricably merged into one.

The Khilafat-cum-tenant agitation had received considerable impetus from the visits of Gandhiji, Shaukat Ali and Maulana Azad. On 5th February, 1921 the Government issued prohibitory orders on all Khilafat meetings. So on 18th February, 1921, all the prominent Khilafat and Congress leaders were arrested. Thus the leadership passed into the hands of the local Mappilla leaders. Hence the Mappillas began to exhibit increasing sings of turbulence and defiance of authority. But the final break came only when the District Magistrate of Eranad Taluk, E.F.Thomas, on 20th August, 1921, with police force tried to arrest Ali Musaliar, a Khilafat leader and a highly respected priest. They found only three fairly insignificant Khilafat volunteers and arrested them. Soon Mappillas from Kottakkal, Tanur and Parappanangadi converged at Tiruranagadi and their leaders met the British officers to secure the release of the arrested volunteers. The people were quiet and peaceful, but the police opened fire on the unarmed crowd and many were killed. A clash ensued, and Government offices were destroyed, records burnt and the treasury looted. The rebellion soon spread into the Eranad, Walluvanad and Ponnai taluks, all Mappilla strongholds.

The targets of attack were the unpopular Jenmils (landlords), mostly Hindu, the symbols of Government authority such as kutcheris (courts), police stations, treasuries and offices, and British planters. Lenient landlords and poor Hindus were rarely touched. Rebels would travel many miles through territory populated by Hindus and attack only the landlords and burn their records. Leaders like Kunhammed Hoji did not discriminate in favour of Muslims: he ordered the execution and punishment of a number of pro-Government Moppillas as well.

The British declared martial law and repression began in earnest. The character of the rebellion underwent a definite change. The communalization of the rebellion completed the isolation of the Mappillas. British repression did the rest and by December 1921 all resistance had come to a stop. 2,337 Mappillas had lost their lives. Large number of rebels were captured or had surrendered. Since then the Mappilas neither joined the national movement nor the peasant movement that was to grow in Kerala in later years under the Left leadership.[44]

The English book referred to above had been proscribed by the Government of Bengal, vide Home Department G.O.No.6308 Public, 4th August, 1937. In June 1937 author Tummala Venkataramayya declared in Vahini news paper that he was going to translate S.N.Tagore's booklet, but when he came to know about its proscription, he stated in the preface of the book that he obtained the material from Government reports, articles in **Young India** and S.N.Tagore's book. The author did not admit anywhere in the Telugu version that it was a translation, and made his own interpolations combined paragraphs, arranged them under headings and occasionally transposed sentences. It was printed by Vasa Suryanarayana Sastri at the Srinivasa Press No.70, 8th Ward, Rajahmundry, its title page alone was printed at the Bharat press, Rajahmundry.

The Telugu translator felt the contents of the following passages as objectionable:- The author on page 6 expressed the opinion that the hatred of Moplah peasants was based on class-antagonism and not on communal hatred. He also felt that the soldiers were ignorant of the fact that they too were poor men like the peasants and were also being exploited. Their thinking that they were eating the money of the landlords was incorrect. In fact while working for the Government of landlords and capitalists they were killing their own brethern. In this connection he observed "The army intended for the protection of the landlords and oppression of the poor people shot dead the peasants". As a result the revolts were increasing but as the peasants had no unions and were unable to forege a front they were short lived.

In other passages the author criticised the nature of the rule of the British and the collusion of the Zamindars with the Imperialist rulers. The Imperialists, while declaring that there was no unity between Hindus and Muslims and they as rulers were trying to maintain peace and safe-guard the property of the people, in practice, used their military strength on the poor peasants and put down ruthlessly the peasants upraising. He also criticised the firm relationship that existed between the Zamindars, who betrayed the country and masses and the British Imperialists. "Though the uncivilized Zamindari system has died out in other countries, the British have been preserving it here from dying out. Like the Zamindars, Imperialists also have a share in the exactions made from the exploited masses. The British Empire protects the Zamindar class and the Zamindary system that gets ready to counter revolution if it shoul break out in India. Zamindars and Imperialists are helping each other in this manner".

The author also justified the raid on the Mosque saying that the leaderas who attacked the Mosque were fighting for their rights against Zamindars. The peasants wanted to have an armed uprising against their enemies, the Zamindars and "Imperialism" aiding these Zamindars. Their aim was only to fight for their rights and to protect themselves against their exploitation.

Referring to the death of 56 'Moplah prisoners in the train on their way to Ballari, the author observed that "It is the lasting blot on British administration". He considered these prisoners who died as a result of the

Governments highhandedness as heroes "who sacrificed their lives in the struggle for freedom."

Even though the Moplah rebellion failed, the author stressed that "the revolutionary struggle is not dead. The self sacrificing zeal of the Moplah heroes has not gone in vain. The revolutionary fight is going on. It will be going on till independence is achieved. Therefore, let us say may revolution thrive, though the Moplah Revlolution has failed".

The police department felt that the Telugu account was more lucid effective and would win the sympathy of the reading public not only for the revolt but also for Socialist principles and ideology by decrying the British Government and "its creation" the Zamindars and landholders class.

The Madras Government wrote a letter to the Secretary to the Government of Bengal, Home Department. In it the Government wrote that the book in English entitled "Peasants Revolt in Malabar in 1921" was written by S.N.Tagore and proscribed by the Government of Bengal and it was desirable that all translations should be on the same footing. The Government of Madras would like to know if Bengal Government would take steps to amend the proscribing order to cover all other documents containing copies, reprints or translations of or extracts from, the English book referred to above. It seemed to the Madras Government that the basic proscription by any provincial Government ought to cover all translations in any language, in order to a void republication of orders. According to the law as it stood, such orders issued by the Government of any province had effecting all Provinces. Therefore the Madras Government requested that if there was no objection the Government of Bengal might be pleased to amend their original order of the proscription as suggested above.

On 21st November, 1938, the Secretary to the Government of India Home Department, Delhi, issued suggestions to the chief Secretaries to Provincial Governments (except Madras), and all Chief Commissioners that a case had been brought to the notice of the Government of India in which a Provincial Government issued a notification under Section 19 of the Indians Press (Emergency Powers) Act, 1931, proscribing a publication, but omitting to proscribe also other documents containing copies, reprints, or translations of or extracts from, that publication. As the Provincial Government was aware, orders issued by the Government of any Province under that section had effect in all Provinces. A suggestion had been made that, in order to avoid a multiplicity of notifications, the original notification should always be so worded as to proscribe as well "all other documents containing copies, reprints or translations of, or extracts from" the proscribed publication. He was directed to commend this suggestion to the Provincial Government, in case it was not already adopted.

Bengal Government issued orders on 20th December, 1938 proscribing the said Telugu book in exercise of the power conferred by Section 19 of the Indian Press (Emergency Powers) Act 1931 (XXIII of 1931) on the ground that it appeared to the Governor that the book contained words of the nature described in clauses (b) (d) and (f) of sub-section (1) Section 4 of the said Act, that is to say, words which directly or indirectly expressed approval of any offence of murder and which tender directly or indirectly to bring into hatred and contempt the Government established by law in British India and to excite disaffection towards the Government, and to incite persons to interfere with the maintenance of law and order and to commit an offence. Notification copies were sent to the concerned departments in Bengal Province and to the All India Library Association. Forfeiture notification of the Bengal Government was republished in Public (General) Department, G.O.No.141, dated 24th January, 1939.

As already stated that the book was printed at the Srinivasa Press Rajahmundry and must have been printed in June 1938. Its owner was Vasa Suryanarayana Sastri. The foreward was dated 5th June 1938. This Press had already been warned on 5th May, 1938 for publishing a proscribed book. In memorandum No.18669-2 dated 18th August, 1938 on p.8 of G.O.No.1430 Public General dated 18th August, 1938 the District Magistrate of East Godavari had been asked to warn the Press again that translations of proscribed books which recommended the use of force to destroy Parliamentary institutions could not be permitted and that the Government trusted that such activity on the part of the press would not be repeated.

1857 Bharata Swatantra Pradhama Yudhamu

A book in Telugu entitled **1857 Bharata Swatantra Pradhama Yuddhamu** (The First Indian war of Independence of 1857) [45] was written by P.S. Acharya and A. Kesavaraya Sastri. It was published by Satprohita society, Brahmacharya Asramam, Katur, Krishna District. It was printed in 1939 at the Swarajya Mudraksharasala, Bezwada, Krishna district. Foreword to this book was written by N.G.Ranga.

The authors described the condition of India during the regime of East India Company in the following strain:- Since the days of Plassey (1757) there was growing discontent in the hearts of the Indian youth against the British and their Government. From the days of Clive to the days of Dalhousie the representatives of East India Company broke their pacts, scrapped their treaties, dethroned several Indian rulers, annexed one by one their territories, destroyed Indian arts and crafts, threw mud in the mouths of lakhs of Indians, broke into the zenanas of helpless Begums and Queens and dishonoured them, looted their wealth, destroyed the territories of the zamindars, and destroyed the scions of the ancient nobility. Thousands of poor ryots at Gorakhpur and Benares were bereft of their family lands, and such atrocities were committed on account of these violent acts the hearts of the Indian princes and the populace were aflame with anger and indignation against the British.

The authors discussed the capabilities of Mangal Panday, on March 26th when the battalion was called to parade ground. Mangal Panday at once snatched and loaded his gun. He roared like alion calling upon his fellow sepoys to wage a righteous war against the British. When sergent Major Hughson saw this, he ordered Panday's arrest. But none came forward to arrest him. Panday fired his gun and sent Hughason to eternal sleep immediately. Just at this time Lieut Baugh came upon the scne. Before the horse could come forward Panday sent both the horse and the rider to the ground with another bullet. Panday drew his sword and dispatched Baugh to hell. Colonel Wheeler ordered Panday's arrest but the sepoys did not obey him. The Colonel ran to the General's bungalow in a fright.

The sepoys tore away their uniforms with pleasure and had a bath in the river as if to wash away the sins of slavery. Thgousands of caps began to fly in the air. But due to the force of gravitation, they fell again on Indians soil. The sepoys trampled upon the polluted caps. This disgrace of the caps was unbearble. The British officers saw all this, petrified with astonishment and rage.

In April, 1857 there were incendiary fires in British houses in Lucknow, Meerut, Ambala and other places. Every effort was made by the British officers to trace the offenders. But no clue was obtained because the police too had joined the revolutionaries. The police and the people of Muradabad joined the rebels.

At Allahabad, the town folk helped the revolutionaries. The houses of the Englishmen were burnt. Prisons were broken and prisoners released. The banks were looted. The railways was wrecked and telegraph wires cut. The rebels got about thirty crores of rupees from the banks. The flag of independence was hoisted in the city and in the military camp with great pomp and also one was hoisted at the city police station.

The police, the servants, the cooks and even the water carriers in the British stations participated to a large extent in the 1857 Sepoy Revolutionary Movement and increased its splendeour.

Khan Bahadur Ali Khan (Rebel) issued a proclamation to inspire the people. It was posted throughout Rohikandis residents of Hindustan. The gist of the proclamation was that if the Hindu-Muslim bretheren allowed the Britishmen to remain in India, they would butcher all and destroy Indian dharma. The English never kept their promises. They were unrivalled in the art of deception. They had cut Indian throats with our own swords. So Indians must avenge this sin of treachery to our country. They had even tried to root out Indian religions and to spread Christianity. They had pushed aside the rights of adopted children. They had swallowed native kingdom. They had created internal troubles between Hindus and Muslims and kept both sides under their heel. Hindus and Muslims should forget the minor differences and unite and jump into the arena of the freedom struggle and wash away the name of English from India.

In another proclamation issued by him, Bahadur Shah stressed the need of Hindu-Muslim unity to struggle for independence under one leader and conduct themselves in such a way, increasing mutual good will and love and keeping the poorer classes contented. Further he suggested that the copy of the proclamation should be affixed in prominent places.

The leaders of the Indian War of Independence were dead. The war was unsuccessful. Slavery had once again taken deep root in the country. The author reported that the British historians had treated very meanly in their writing of Nana Saheb, the leader of the First Indian War of Independence who made the British soldiers tremble. Indian readers should understand that the British historians had committed a greater sin by withholding correct particulars than the sin of massacre committed by British Generals, Neil, Nicholson and others.

The summary of the report of an officer of the Special Branch, C.I.D. was as follows:- The said book was a true version of the incidents connected with the Sepoy Mutiny of 1857. It was dedicated to the heroes of the freedom struggle, who sacrificed their wealth, status and life for liberating the country from slavery. That it was not intended for mere academical study was patent from the very outset and much of the material in this book was based on the English version of "The Indian War of Independence of 1857" by V.D.Savarkar (proscribed). N.G.Ranga, who had written a foreword entitled 'Hero Worship', congratulated the authors for bringing out such a thought-provoking publication which stimulated the readers to follow as an ideal at this moment, the love for freedom, capacity for military organization and secret work, chivalry to women, and patriotism shown by Indians of those days. Referring to the punishment meted out to the revolutionaries by the Britishers, Ranga stated that "The British rulers have done worse unjuswt acts in this country during the days of revolution than the atrocities perpetrated in China by Japan today, than that the Germans did in the last war, and the inhumanities done by Mussolini recently in Abyssinia". He paused to question "will the present day army also join us today or tomorrow? We must always endeavour to gain the sympathy and help of our sepoys". He believed that the authors were staunch in their resolve "to have as their ideal the lives of these heroes of independence, to overthrow the present day exploiters, to over throw British autocracy and the poswer of their allies, the Indian traitors, and win not merely independence but a Swaraj of peasants and workers."

The officer of the Special Branch C.I.D. further in his observations said that the authors of this book to prove that the so-called Mutiny was really an organised revolt, carefully planned and carried on with admirable secrecy under the very nose of the Company servants by powerful chiefs, with a view to drive the British out of India and re-establish the Empire of Mughals. If the rul;er of Hyderabad in the South, Sikhs and the Gurkhas of the North abstained from active support to the British, the Mutiny might have been successful. The British military officers, Neil in particular, were condemned for their ruthlessness in torturing the civil population whereas the rebels were extolled for their moderation, their high sense of duty, their regard for women and children and their excellent behavior throughout the campaign.

The C.I.D. reported that the trend of the book was highly objectionable and it contained passages which fell under Section 4 (1) of the Indian Press Act (E.P.) 1931. Hence he recommended it to be proscribed. Therefore the book was proscribed and forfeited by the Madras Government.[46]

The Government also gave a warning to the keeper of the press that action would be taken against him under Section 3 (3) of the Indian Press (Emeregency Powers) Act, 1931, if he printed or published matter of nature described in Section 4 (1) of the said Act.

Swatantra Garjana

A Telugu book entitled Swatantra Garjana[47] (The Roar of Independence) was written by V.V.Subramanya Sastri, Bezwada. It was printed at the Andhra Vani press, Bezwada and published by the author. The first topic went by the name of the title of the book, and the second and the third topics were "Telugu Ravvalu" and "Sankranti" (Pongal) respectively. There was a Gandhiji's photo on the cover page.

In the first topic, "Swatantra Garjana" the author described the then degradation of India and said that the lions of heroes, who tried for the freedom of the country were being shot down by machine guns and had to face many cruelties. He wrote, that the hunters (this expression is probably meant to refer to the British) thrust in sharp knives into the bodies of young married couples, knocked down pregnant ladies and dragged them until the ambroyo came out, left the weeping children in the midst of deserts and strangled those who refused to take water etc.

Communal discord arose from differences of opinion in general and Hindi-Muslim clashes in particular. Even in spite of such a grave danger, and when India was on the deathbed, the Hindus and the Muslims were fighting with each other without caring to secure the freedom of India. Moreover the Panchamas were trodden down by the caste Hindus. To save the country, the author said that Mahatma Gandhi with Charka appeared on the scene and admonished the people to become united and follow his leadership.

The second topic is "Tenugu Ravvalu" (Andhra Diamonds). In it the author praised Subhas Chandra Bose and described him as a strong bull, which was capable of digging up the earth (here England according to popular usage) to be very roots. He was also described as "the lion of Bengal", the spear capable of being pierced into the heart of England and as "the hero who would destroy all shackles of slavery".

The third topic is "Sankranti"[48] (pongal) which has got an allegorical meaning addressed to time. The cock fight, which is a common feature in the Andhra country during the pongal anmd described here, may be compared to the fight for independence by India and the cocks killed during the fight may be compared to the heroes who had laid down their lives in the fight for independence of their country. The author further exhorted the people to drive away the British who made India poor and he also appealed to time to see off the dolls that have reduced Indians, well-known for their riches and practical benevolence, to the position of beggars. This has a reference to the custom prevailing in Andhra desa by which young girls display and worship their toys for four days in connection with the pongal festival. Thus by implication the expression "dolls" may mean Britishers who were worshipped by some people of India.

Madras Government directed that wherever found the book and all other documents, copies, tracts, reprints, translations be forfeited.[49] The Government gave powers to Krishna District Magistrate to take action against the management of the Andhravani Press, Bezwada and the Government tried to prosecute the author.

Vinayaka Savarkar Jeevitamu

Vinayaka Savarkar Jeevitamul is an account in Telugu of the life of Vinayaka Savarkar written by Mudiganti Jagganna Sastri of Rajahmundry and printed at the Cocanada printing works, Cocanada (the book under report being of the second edition brought out in 1932). The author states that he has gathered this information from the Report of the Rowlatt Committee, 'The Story of My Exile' by Byrendra Kumar Ghosh (brother of Aurobindo Ghosh), "Life of Barrister Savarkar".

The author attaches high value to Vinayaka Savarkar's influence from his boyhood for martial valour. Savarkar was influenced by his father Damodar Pant Savarkar in virtues and war-like spirit. At the age of thirteen in 1895 he led a small army of Hindu Urchins against a party of Moslem lads and gained victory by means of such terrible weapons as pen, knives, thorns and pins.

Messrs Rand and Irst who oppressed the people of Poona and resorted to maladministration were murdered in Poona by Chapekar Brothers on 22nd June, 1897 the very day of Jubilee celebration of Queen Victoria's reign. Subsequently Chapekar brothers were executed.

Referring to the execution of the Chapekar Brothers, the author wrote as follows:- Some of the Indians began to condemn Chapekar Brothers as murderers while others were secretly praising them as patriots who sacrificed their lives for the freedom of their motherland. Vinayaka Savarkar also praised Chapekar. Indians were surprised to know that Ranade was also executed along with Chapekar in Yerrawada Jail. Vinayaka Savarkar could not control his grief and felt ashamed he was not able to do anything appreciable for his Motherland. He later founded 'New India Association'.

Savakar organised a secret association called 'Mitra Mela'. The objectives of Mitra Mela were to gather and unite Indian people, to teach them patriotism, to impart fighting spirit and to lay their lives if necessary for their motherland.

Vinayaka Sarvarkar advised the people to boycott foreign cloth and in place of it to use Indian made Khadi. Bal Gangadhar Tilak thought that the people might be hostile to such a movement. But to his surprise the people strictly followed the boycott of foreign cloth. Seeing all this Tilak had his doubts dispelled and assumed the leadership of the movement.

Vinayaka Savarkar took his B.A. degree in 1905 and left for London on a scholarship offered to him by the late Shyamji Krishna Varma of the

Indian Home Rule League. Bombs were used for the first time in Bengal by Khudiram Bose which resulted in the death of Kennedis. The author wrote as follows:- This news roused both India and the Government from deep stupor and shook them. The advent of bombs marked the beginning of a new era in Indian politics. When India was resounding with echoes of bombs, the Savarkar camp in England was brimming with enthusiasm.

Referring to The Indian War of Independence (the Great Indian Sepoy Mutiny of 1857), written by Vinayaka Savarkar, the author wrote as follows:- That book tremendously attracted every body in the world. The Government banned that book before it was completed. Savarkar criticised all the false statements made by English historians, making out the Indian War of Independence of 1857 to be a mutiny of sepoys and a conspiracy. But it was a national war with the attainment of independence for India as its sole object, in which the whole of India comprising Maharajahs, Emperors, sepoys, men and women fought in defence of Dharma (Righteousness).

The author discussed Vinayaka Savarkar's secret revolutionary propaganda among Indian students in England his trip to Paris and return to London, his adventurous voyage to India under police custody after preliminary inquiry in London, in order to stand his trial at the High Court in Bombay, his sentence to transportation for life, his stay as a convict in the Andamans and his conditional release about ten years ago and finally the magnificient welcome accorded to him on his arrival at Nasik.

It was forfeited by the Madras Government because it contained matter of the nature described in Section 4 (1) of the Indian Press (Emergency Powers) Act 1931 as amended by Section 16 of the Criminal Law Amendment Act 1932 (Act XXIII of 1932).[51] A similar book entitled Vinayaka Savarkar, published in Tamil was proscribed by the Madras Government.

The forfeiture order was cancelled by Government of Madras, Public (General) Department, MS. Series, Confidential in Government order No.1236, dated 9th October, 1946.

Atma Tyagi

Atma Tyagi (Sacrificer of Self)[1] is an account of the life of a Bengali youth named Jatindranath Das, an under trial prisoner in the Lahore conspiracy case of 1929, who had been on hunger strike for more than 60 days, as a protest against the treatment accorded by the Government to the martyr and an ideal patriot. Indian young men are exhorted to cultivate his spirit of self sacrifice and win liberty for their motherland. A book in

Hindi about the life of Jatindranath Das by Auditya Prasanna Roy, entitled Mrityu Vijaya Jatindra Das was proscribed in G.O. MS. No.789 Dated 2nd July, 1930. This book in Telugu is admitted by the author, Kuchibotla Prabhakara Sastri of Kolluru, in his preface, to be a translation of the above-mentioned book in Hindi. The Telugu book was printed at the Ramakrishna printing works, Tenali and published by Kommuri Kasi Viswanadham, Tenali, Guntur district.

The Government behaved very badly towards the prisoners arrested in connection with the Lahore conspiracy case. There upon, Jatindranath Das along with thirteen other prisoners started hunger strike. He asked for an explanation from the hard hearted Government having grown indignant over the instances of ill-treatment to which he was subjected. But the Government was unable to comply with his request. Though the Government gave an indication to release him on bail, it did not agree to release him unconditionaly. On Friday (the 13th day) in September 1929 at 1.5 P.M., the heroic Jatindranath Das, of adorned Valhalla (peace be to his sacred soul). He was a true son of Bengal.

The author described the funeral procession at Lahore immediately after the demise of Jatindranath Das. The procession was one and half miles long. They reached the Bengali Tola with the reverberating "Down with Imperialism Jatindranath Ki Jai". At Moti Chowk, many people scattered one rupee, one quarter rupee, one quarter anna and other coins over the corpse of Jatindra. Many respectable persons began to pick them up and when questioned as to why they were picking up those coins, they said at the top of their voices. "We take them home and cause them to be worn by our children as pendants round their necks. We believe that by doing so they (our children) too, would become daring, fearless and well known patriots like Jatindra".

Writing about the funeral procession at Calcutta, the author says, "There were nearly one lakh of people in the procession which carried placards bearing the words 'Long live revolution Down with Imperialism".

Vikram Bihari Das the father of Jatindranath Das sent a message just before setting fire to the funeral pyre of Jatindranath. In his message he wrote "I pray that as a result of his (Jatin's) self sacrifice India may be awakened".

In India today a social and political revolution was necessary and inevitable. "Body is perishable; work should be achieved" was the principle, the mantra, for which Jatin gave up his life. "Bear this in mind and practise it in thought, word and deed".

India cannot attain independence and broad-cast her ideas in foreign countries so long as we do not resolutely stand on the side of justice as opposed to injustice without wavering in the face of any number of hardships and do not make sacrifices, bearing all those hardships. Be not afraid of dying for the country's cause. This land India would get rid of the fetters of slavery and attain independence, when it is wetted with the blood of the people.

The exhortation is ambiguous. The author has carefully avoided the use of the word 'violence' and as it stands, it can be construed either as an idealistic appeal to his countrymen treading the path of non-violence or as a fervent appeal to the people to take to violence. The latter view may be taken in as much as the writer praises the life of Jatindranath Das, a revolutionary. Therefore the Madras Government forfeited the above said book and all other documents containing copies, reprints or translations of, or extracts containing matter of the nature described in Section 4 (1) of the Indian Press (Emergency Powers) Act, 1931, as amended by Section 16 of the Criminal Law Amendment Act 1932 (XXIII of 1932).[53]

Sardar Bhagat Singh Jeevita Charita

A book in Telugu entitled Sardar Bhagat Singh Jeevita Charitra[54] was edited by C. Krishnaswami Sarma and printed at Gopalakrishna Press in 1931. Only the wrapper containing a photograph of Bhagat Singh was printed at the Kesari printing works, George town, Madras. The name of the authbor of the book has not been given. The style of the book is simple.

Sardar Bhagat Singh Jeevita Charitra is a short sketch in Telugu of the life of Bhagat Singh, a violent revolutionary of Lahore who threw bombs in the Legislative Assembly on the 11th April 1929 in the dead of night, injuring Sir George Schuster and another. He was subsequently tried for the offence of waging war against His Majesty George V, the King of England and Emperor of India, and awarded capital punishment. He was executed in the Lahore Jail along with Raj Guru and Sukh Dev in the same case at 7 P.M. on the 23rd March, 1931.

Bhagat Singh was born in 1907. He is reported to have been nursed from his very childhood on the milk of firmness and courage which are characteristic of the leonine Sikh community of the Punjab. It is stated that he received his lesson in patriotism from his father, Kishin Singh, who' was one of the Lieutenants of the late Lala Lajpat Rai and who was also deported by the Government shortly after Lajpat Rai's deportation to Mandalay in 1907. Bhagat Singh's patriotic career commenced from the

13th year when he left school in obedience to Gandhiji's call to his countrymen in 1920 to boycott Government Services, Law Courts and educational institutions. An idea of his humanitarian service is conveyed to the reader from the manner in which he and another worker named Dutt helped the distressed people of Delhi when it suffered from torrential rains.

Bhagat Singh had been studying conditions in his country from his very boyhood. He was observing the ways of administration of the foreign Government. He was overpowered by a passionate longing for independence. Recollecting the Jallianwallah Bagh atrocities he used to experience hereoic excitement. His heart was grieved over the system of administration. He was of the opinion that it would take very long for Indians tlo attain Swaraj by the peaceful and moral means. He was determined to obtain independence quickly by any means. He made up his mind to follow the western method, the method of force, for that purpose.

The book contained passages which extolled revolutionary movement, self-sacrifice and appointed out that the main object of the people was to put an end to the present autocratic system of the Government.

The Nava Jawan Bharata Sabha was reported to have passed a resolution at its conference held in Karachi in the last week of March 1931 along with the Congress session. This Conference, while commending the wonderful self-sacrifice of Bhagat Singh, Raj Guru and Sukh Dev who offered their lives for the sake of the independence of India condemned unanimously the brutal and uncivilized policy adopted by the Government of India in hanging three persons.

Bhagat singh when he was in jail expressed and wrote his views in the newspaper The People. He opined that the revolting nation would be able to concentrate all its energies and destroy the Government of autocrates straight away. All these events occurred in the annals of Russia.

Therefore the Madras Government forfeited the above book and all other documents containing copies, reprints or translations of or extracts containing matter of the nature described in Section 4 (1) of the Indian Press (Emergency Powers) Act, 1931 as amended by Section 16 of the Criminal Law Amendment Act 1932 (XXIII of 1932).[55]

The 1922 Ryot Revolt in Manyam (Agency)

A Telugu book entitled The 1922 Ryot Revolt in Manyam (Agency) (Alluri Sitarama Raju)[56] is an elaborate account of what is known as the Agency Fituri of 1922 and of the life of Alluri Sitarama Raju, its leader. It was written by Ponnaluri Radhakrishnamurti, 'after a long and laborious tour in the Agency at great personal inconvenience', and was printed at the Krishna Printing Press, Sattenapalli Guntur district and published by Annapragada Kameswara Rao of Guntur under 'The Extremist Publication series'.

In the introduction the author said that he had gathered "all the story which has been freely let loose the public and placed it on the other side. I have kept the (Communist) Manifesto of (Karl) Marx in the seat of justice. The whole of this book is only the judgement delivered by that Manifesto".

In this Agency many Rampa Fituris had taken place. In those times, when the campaign which was originally started against the Government, failed to receive popular support in an adequate measure, it used to be turned in the last resort against the people themselves owing to lack of endurance. It then created the impression that it was a dacoity and proved to be an internecine quarrel among the people. In such circumstances, the Government had a good opportunity to crush it with the help of the people themselves. But the revolution of Rama Raju easily and dexterously transcended these internecine quarrels. Just like Abyssinia's fight with Italy, the revolution continued long and only sustained defeat in circumstances that rendered a defeat inevitable.

The following message of S.S.Hardikar, Secretary of the Hindustan volunteer corps is reproduced: "India today in need of heroes like Srirama Raju to obtain independence from the hands of the foreign rulers. I exhort the youth of India to emancipate from her bondage and shine like heroes in the world".

The author discussed the motives of Sitarama Raju in leading the Fituri in the following way:- As one who had read and understood history thoroughly, Rama Raju did not want the monarchical system for the country. In the monarchical age, the countries wealth was buried underground within the high walls of forts. The imperialists spirited away that Goddess of wealth out of Forts, leaving the latter desolate. The world ought to feel glad for this change. Under the monarchical system, one individual's ambition for territorial expansion led to fomented wars resulting in the wasteful flow of the people's blood. The imperialistic ambition of the many was the sole cause in the modern times of fomented wars resulting not only in the wasteful and territorial flow of the people's blood but also in their improvement. The Imperialists had given life to that Goddess of wealth but placed fetters on (her) hands and legs. One man was drinking nectar, while some people were vomitting blood. In such an Empire Rama Raju was a poor member of a race (Kshatriya) which was devoid of any progress. Rama Raju was trained in the art of war to libterate the poor from the oppressive Government. It was due to his love of the class (of poor, workers and peasants) and not to his caste-instinct. Rama Raju was a revolutionary. He would invoke the deluge itself for the wiping out of injustice.

The causes of revolutionary spirit among the Agency people were stated at length in the following style:- It was with the object of leading the forest areas also along with the rest of India to be 'best civilization', that the British imperialists had established their Government departments there and thereby restrained the independence of Agency people. To facilitate their commerce, they had reserved these forests and created obstacles to the livelihood of the people. In other words the uncivilized Agency tribes could not freely move about in the forest as before. According to the forest laws, the tribes should not utilize as much timber as they want. The Government appointed civil officers with stringent laws to administer this Agency. The British created here the Muthadari system to crush the great revolutions that might arise in this forest (area) from a desire for independence, just as they created the Zamindari system in the country for the protection of their Empire, immediately after the defeat of the people in the War of Independence (the Sepoy Mutiny) in 1857. Though the names were different a Muthadar's rank did not fall short of a Zamindar's. The authorities and the officials in the Agency become selfish and tried to get rich by taking bribes from Muthadars and ryots through intimidation. In the same way Muthadaras tried to increase their riches by doing injustice to their ryots. In addition to other inconveniences, the greed of officials and Muthadars was the fundamental cause of a great revolution.

In this agency, there were big mines and dense forests full of giant trees which yielded good timber. There were also huge waterfalls. Since these were a source of considerable profit, the British had established their commercial rule here. As cultivable and mining lands constitute two 'arts', 'labour' also was divided into two classes, namely workers (coolies) and ryots. These two labour classes were exploited by the British Government and Muthadars. Bastian was an awaful miser and an ambitious person. His object was to get labour from the coolies without paying wages to them. The coolies were therefore, carrying on strike after strike against Bastian. Muthadars alone must supply coolies to the Government whenever necessary.

The author said that the exploitation and humiliating policy of the Bastian and the harassment of the police forces led to the Fituridars' looting of the Krishnadevipeta police station on 23rd August, 1922.

In addition to the facts which are described in foregoing paras the author further explained how the Muthadars and British Government were responsible for the creation of Fituri. Muthadars were like trustees for the revenue on cultivable lands. They should collect some money from the ryots as rent and improve the agricultural facilities with its aid. But besides their salaries, they swallowed the rent amount without spending even a pie on agricultural improvements. The advent of British gave way to indifference and internal quarrels among the people. Courts of law did not uphold justice.

The forest tribes had no personal right to the forest wealth. All this wealth was concentrated in the hands of the Government. As soon as the people got impoverished on account of this reactionary system, they would wage war in order to break the doors of that center and fill their stomachs. This is known as economic revolution. Instead of establishment of peace the Government used its satanic powers to fill the Agency area with heaps of corpses. It was only for this the Government had brought civil police to the Agency from every nook and corner in order to check Rama Raju and the Revolution.

These helpless Agency people were prepared to resist the Government with the same degree of cruelty with which the Government wanted to rule them. The Government thought that some people were armed. The author said that it was not correct. These revolutionaries were innumerable. All the people belonged to such a category.

Referring to the raids by the Fituri rebels on police stations the author said that Rama Raju conducted surprise raids only in respect of Chintapalli, Krishnadevipeta and Rajavommangi stations in the beginning but afterwards he used to give pre vious notice before raiding any police station. The Government with all its gigantic military strength could not resist the revolutionaries.

Further the author says on the morning of the 19th October, 1922 at Rampachodavaram the revolutionaries fired their rifles on approaching the Taluk Office. In the face of strategy of Rama Raju the British forces under Mr.John retreated. On this occasion the people of the village honoured and garlanded Rama Raju and his party. The Government never published these incidents in their reports. Such publication would be a disgrace to them. To crush the revolutionaries the Government brought additional military forces in December, 1922.

Describing the decisive night engagement between the Government forces and the rebels at Lingapuram on 16th December, 1922 the author wrote that the revolutionaries fought valiantly though wounded and dying. But they did not retreat. When a man died and dropped another would step into his place and get ready to fall down. Meanwhile the Government soldiers stopped firing. The revolutionaries also stopped it. The revolutionaries began to flee in one direction carrying such of their associates as had fallen unconscious. Seeing this and fearing that the fituridars might lie in ambush on the way to the village, Mr.Swiney also began to run in another direction.

The author says after inspecting the places where Rama Raju had set his foot, the Collector listened to the accounts of love and respect which the people had for Raju. He then notified that he had imposed a punitive tax of four thousand rupees on Annavaram village. The people gladly agreed to abide by Raju's law. The British Government began to harass the people in many places in order to compel them to submit to its authority.

The British Government seized the food-stuff going to the Agency for sale and detained the retain merchants with an idea that the people would soon surrender, if food supplies were cut off and if they were subjected to starvation. The Government itself issued orders that the people alone should bear the cost of maintenance of the forces which were formed for the preservation of its won authority. But Rama Raju rendered entire villages deserted. The people would not in the least transgress Raju's commands. Then the Government took steps to divide the people.

Rama Raju's heart was like a wonderful mirror that reflected the forms of such world saviours as Karla Marx and Lenin. When the Agency people were rolling in such a sad plight, Rama raju was unable to bear it and got ready for self sacrifice.

In the concluding chapter the author says the people were suffering extreme hardships and were helpless. Deprived of the collective (people's) strength, the followers of Rama Raju who were at large in forests were undergoing starvation for want of food. The whole Agency was greatly perturbed by military anarchy. Old men, women and children had no protection. In the beginning of May 1924, Rama Raju rallied all his followers and enjoined heroic death on them. Persons like Aggi Raju, Gantama Dora and Padulu all agreed to die like heroes, but they did not agree to Rama Raju courting death. They wished that Rama Raju might live long.

The same day on which Aggiraju was captured, Rama Raju, it was said, reached the village Mampa at 10 O'clock in the night. People were forced to believe this report. The very next morning a man in the garb of Yogi was seen by a Koya boy near a stream. The Yogi gave a letter to the boy with instructions to hand it to the (Government) forces which was moving about close by under the command of an Indian police officer. On reading the letter given by the boy, the officer started for the place where the Yogi was. The officer questioned him who he was. The Yogi answered "I am Sita Rama Raju". This officer had never seen Rama Raju.

The Yogi was very quickly escorted to Gudal, a white officer. Camping with his force in close proximity to that place. Even Gudal had never known Rama Raju. He forthwith had the Yogi fastened to a tree with chains and shot him dead. Cremation of the corpse was ordered and a public secret was concealed. There the story ended.

The author had criticised the attitude of the Congress and its leaders towards the Fituri, because it did not shown sympathy to the people. T. Prakasam Pantulu the then President of the Andhra Provincial Congress Committee, advised the Peddapur Taluk Congress bodies to remain strictly neutral in respect of the Fituri. Prakasam Pantulu condemned as 'dacoits' persons who looted police stations and carried away rifles and cartridges without doing any harm to the people.

The gist of the Telugu translator to Madras Government's report on the book was that the author was an unreserved admirer of Sita Rama Raju and had spared no pains to portray him as a Communist hero and the Fituri led by Rama Raju as 'a popular revolution of the workers and peasants', directed against 'British Imperialism . The author compared Rama Raju to 'victorious' shivaji in his depredatory marches from one police station to another in the East Godavari Agency and to Rana Pratap Singh in his reverses. The Fakir of Ipi is referred to and acclaimed as 'the present living embodiment of all the virtues and powers of Raju'. In the author's opinion, movement of these two 'heroes' as well as the Rampa fituri of 1879-80,[57] and the Lagarai Fituri of 1914-16[58] in the Agency were only 'the inevitable consequences of the open exploitation by British Imperialists particularly in the uncivilized areas of India'. The violence with which these revolts were associated was attributed to the 'the favourable nature' of the jungle and the hill areas involved and was sought to be explained away as an educative measure for the ultimate introduction of non-violence in wild regions. The reader was earned not to be deluded by the Government's description of Sita Rama Raju as 'an ambitious Kshatriya full of racial hatred against the British, who had fomented the Fituri with the sole object of becoming an independent Raju of one of the Agency Taluks'. He characterised Sita Rama Raju as 'a heroic Sanyasin' 'who recognised the principle of non-violence' and considered the story of his revolution worth recounting 'as he conducted it on scientific lines'.

The opinion of the Madras Government was that the author portrayed Sita Rama Raju as a Communist hero and depicted the out break as a spontaneous revolt in the class-war between the labouring classes and capitalists. Such interpretations might be harmless when a stage of history was reached, but this movement was not suitable for such propaganda. The violent methods adopted by participants in the Fituri were applauded and it was represented as a glorious attempt at revolution to be emulated by other labourers. The Government considered that the book contained passages tending to incite and encourage ignorant people to the commission of offences involving violence and that the circulation of such literature in the Agency areas was dangerous to peace. Therefore the book and all other documents containing copies, reprints or translations of or extracts were forfeited by the Madras Government.[59]

Conclusion

Thus the nationalist writers during this period stressed on the various aspects of economic nationalism and patriotic nationalism in their economic critique of imperialism, they took note of all the three forms of contemporary economic exploitation, namely, through trade, industry and finance. They clearly grasped that the essence of British economic imperialism lay in the subordination of the Indian economy to the British economy. They vehemently opposed the British attempt to develop in India the basic characteristics of a colonial economy.

With a view to create patriotic effusion among the people they described the patriotic spirit of historical personalities and urged the Andhras to imbibe the virtues of nationalism. They especially advocated every aspect of the constructive programme of Gandhiji and Congress.

NOTES

1. Government of Madras, Public Department G.O.No.212, Dt. 12th April, 1921.
2. **Ibid.**
3. **Ibid.**
4. Government of Madras, Public (General) Department G.O.No.594, Dt. 14th September, 1921.
5. **Ibid.**
6. Government of Madras, Public (General) Deapartment, G. O. No. 594, Dt. 14th September, 1921.

7. Government of Madras, Public Department G. O. No. 812, Dt. 18th November, 1921.
8. **Ibid.**
9. **Ibid.**
10. Government of Madras, Public (General) Department, G.O. No.367, Dt. 29th April, 1922.
11. Panchali was the wife of Pandavas in the epic of Mahabharatham.

11.a According to Indian Mythology the time was divided into four yugas. They are Krutayuga, Thretayuga, Dwaparayuga and Kaliyuga.

12. Lord Krishna was the mediator to Kauravas and Pandavas in epic of Mahabharatham. He finally fought on behalf of Pandavas and succeeded.
13. Narakasura, was a Villain in a mythological story.
14. Ravana was the Villain in the epic Ramayana.
15. Government of Madras, Public (General) Department, G.O.No.367, Dt. 26th April, 1922.
16. Government of Madras, Public Department, G.O.No.844, Dt. 21st October, 1922.
17. He was born on 4th June 1897 in Singapeta village, Kovuru Taluk, Nellore district. He belonged to middle class family. His father was Papayya and mother Subbama. After many ups and downs he completed B.A., B.L. in 1928. In the first year of B.L. education, he heard the speech og Gandhiji at Madras beanch and was attracted by boycott of foreign goods and non-cooperation movement. He came to Nellore in 1920 and worked as a Secretary to Nellore District Congress from 1920 to 1929. In 1929 he resigned the office of the secretary. For details. See, Adusumalli Poorna Chendra Rao, Vennela Velugulu, Padmabhushan, Sri Vebbala Kanti Raghavaiah Jeevita Charitra.
18. Government of Madras, Public (General) Department, MS. Series, G.O.No.904, Dt. 3rd November, 1922.
19. Kauravas and Pandavas were brothers in Mahabharatam, an Epic of Indians. Pandavas fought with Kauravas for righteousness.
20. Government of Madras, Public Department, G.O. No.80, Dt. 6th February, 1923.
21. **Ibid.**
22. **Ibid.**
23. Government of Madras, Public (General) Department, Confidential, G.O. No.1044, Dt. 21st August, 1930.
24. Government of Madras, G. O. NO. 906 Public (General) Departmnt Confidential, Dt. 4th September, 1931.
25. **Ibid.**
26. Government of Madras, Public (General) Department, G.O. No.1215, Dt. 3rd December, 1931.
27. Government of Madras, Public (General) Department, Confidential, G.O. No.1215, Dt. 3rd December, 1931.
28. Government of Madras, Public (General) Department, MS. Series, G.O. No.121, Dt. 20th January, 1932.
29. Government of Madras, Public (General) Department, MS. Series, G.O.No.121, Dt. 20th January, 1932.
30. Government of Madras, Public (General) Department, MS. Series, G.O.No.121, Dt. 20th January, 1932.

31. Government of Madras, Public (General) Department, MS. Series, G.O.No.121, Dt. 20th January, 1932.
32. Government of Madras, Public (General) Department, MS. Series, G.O.No.134, Dt. 22nd January, 1932.
33. Government of Madras, Public (General) Department, MS. Series, G.O.No.134, Dt. 22nd January, 1932.
34. Government of Madras, Public (General) Department, MS. Series, G.O.No.171, Dt. 30th January, 1932.
35. Government of Madras, Public (General) Department, MS. Series, G.O.No.171, Dt. 30th January, 1932.
36. Govt. of Madras, Public (General) Department, G. O. No. 1006 dt. 21st July, 1932.
37. **Ibid.**
38. Government of Madras, Public (General) Department, Confidential, G.O.No.209, Dt. 5th March, 1934.
39. Government of Madras, Public (General) Department, Confidential, G.O. No.209, Dt. 5th March, 1934.
40. Government of Madras, Public (General) Department, G.O. No.317, Dt. 27th March, 1934.
41. Government of Madras, Public (General) Department G.O. No.317, Dt. 27th March, 1934.
42. Government of Madras, Public (general) Department, MS, Series Confidential, G.O. No.141, Dt. 24th January, 1939.
43. Among the various theories advanced regarding the origin of the term, Mappilla (Also spelt as Moplah), the most appropriate one is that the word is derived from **Mahapilla** i.e. **Great Child** or **Bridegroom** considered as a title of honour applied to the colonialists on the western coast of India. The Christians were differentiated from the Muslims, the former being called Nasrani (Nazarene) Mappila and the latter Jonaka Mappilla., The Moppillas are the descendants of the Arab traders who settled down in Malabar, most probably in the first decade of the seventh century A.D. This was stated by M. Wilk, in his **Historuical Sketches of the South of India** in an attempt to trace the history of Mysore, Vol.11, p.129.
44. For more details see K. Madhavan Nair, **Malabar Kalapam** (The Malabar Rebellion in Malayalam); K.N.Panikkar, "Peasant revolts in Malabar in the Nineteenth and Twentieth Centuries", in A.R.Desai, Editor, **Peasant Struggles in India**, New Delhi, 1979; Conrad Wood, Peasant Revolt: "An Interpretation of Moplah Violence in the 19th and 20th Centuries"; in Dewey and Hopkins, Editors, **The Imperial Studies in the Economic History of India and Africa**, London, 1978' S. Gopalakrishnan, **Political Movements in South India 1914-1929**, Madras, 1981.
45. Government of Madras, Public (General) Department, G.O. No.1948, Dt. 7th November, 1939.
46. Government of Madras, Public (General) Department, G.O.No.1948, Dt. 7th November, 1939.
47. Government of Madras, Public (General) Department, G.O.No.1834, Dt. 25th August, 1941.
48. An important festival in India particularly in Andhra Pradesh.

49. Government of Madras, Public (General) Department., G.O.No.1834m, Dt. 25th August, 1941.
50. Government of Madras, Public (General) Department, MS. Series, Confidential, G.O.No.73, Dt. 25th January, 1934.
51. Government of Madras, Public (General) Department, MS. Series, Confidential, G.O. No.73, Dt. 25th January, 1934.
52. Government of Madras, Public (General) Department, G.O. No.1277, Dt. 2nd August, 1935.
53. Government of Madras, Public (General) Department, G.O.No.1277, Dt. 2nd august, 1935.
54. Government of Madras Public (General) Department, G.O.No.1882, Dt. 11th November, 1935.
55. Government of Madras, Public (General) Department, G.O.No.1882, Dt. 11th November, 1935.
56. Government of Madras, Public (General) Department, G.O.No.1451, Dt. 24th August, 1938.
57. The tribes of Rampa area revolted against the exactions of the mansubdar of Rampa, the police, the money lenders and the newly imposed excise policy. The revolt lasted for about 22 months and the area affected by it was 5000 sq. miles. The important leaders were Bodulur Ambul Reddy, Karem Tamman Dora, Kundala Bhim Reddy, Dwarabandala Chandraiah etc. For details of the revolt see G.O. No.109 Judicial, Dt. 6th Januaruy, 1880. Report of the Administration of Madras Presidency for the year 1879-1880 and 1880-1881.
58. The Kammaras and Koyas of Lagarai Kondapalli and adjacent areas in the Godavari Agency rose against the authorities and resorted to looting the wealthy. The area affected by it was around 2000 sq.miles. The important leaders of the revolt were Garamalla Mangadu, Manga Pentadu and others. The important incidents of the revolt were the murder of Dharakonda Muttadar and the Sardar of Kondapalli. For the details of the revolt See G.O.No.231, Home (Judicial) dt. 3rd February, 1917.
59. Government of Madras, Public (General) Department, G.O.No.1451, Dt. 24th August, 1938.

6

POLITICAL ACTION THROUGH DRAMAS

As stated in the chapter "Political Environment" the establishment of Universities in India contributed to the spread of English education among the Indians. It enabled them to imbibe the political ideas and the humanitarian social ideals of Western thinkers and thereby created an urge to build a new India, synthesising all the best in western and Eastern culture. It also stirred the dormant Andhra mind to action, revolutionise the outlook of educated Andhras and truly laid the foundation of real great progress.

Number of people were influenced by English education. Among them Korada Ramachandra Sastri, Kokkonda Venkataratnam Pantulu, Parvastu Venkattaranga Charyulu were the first writers in Telugu drama literature. They began to translate dramas into Telugu from Sanskrit. Among the three, Korada Ramachandra Sastri was the first person to write dramas in Telugu.

Manjarimadhukariyam was the first Telugu play by Sastri as well as in Andhra. As per available sources it was written in 1860. In 1871 Pantulu translated Narakasura Vijayavyagamu into Telugu. It was printed in 1872 and it was the first translated work into Telugu from Sanskrit. Venkataranga Charyulu translated Abhijnana Sakuntalam into Telugu in 1872 and it was the first translated work into Telugu from Sanskrit. Venkataranga Charyulu translated Abhijnana Sakuntalam into Telugu in 1872.

In 1875 Vavilala Vasudeva Sastri translated Shakespear's Julius Caesar into Telugu entitled Caesar Charitram. He was the first person to translate English plays into Telugu. He was also the first person to write independent social play entitled Nandakarajyam. It was printed in 1880.

But the above mentioned author's plays were not performed on the stage.

Kandukuri Veeresalingam Pantulu established students Dramatic Association in 1880 and through it he began to give performances of his own plays. With this many dramatic associations began to be established in important towns. Among them the important earliest associations were Guntur Hindunataka Samajam, Bandar Hindu National Theatrical society, Rajahmundry Natakojjivaka Samajam, and Vizagapatam Jaganmitra Nataka Samajam. In the early years of 20th century dramatic assoiciations were also established in Narasaraopeta, Tenali, Gudivada, Masulipatam, Ellore, Nellore and few other places.

Plays in Telugu were staged with a view to keep alive the ideas of Swadesi and boycott of foreign goods. A play called Lala Lajapat Rai was staged at Masulipatam in December 1907. The drama commenced with the exhortation of V. Parabrahmam, who played the role of Lajapat Rai, to boycott foreign goods and encourage home industries. He was arrested and this led to a riot. Another drama called Vandemataram, composed by Veluru Vasudeva Sastri, was enacted at Kottapalli (Cocanada Taluk) in April 1908.

As per the opinion of the critics the dramas may be divided into three kinds.[1] They are mythological, historical and political. The details are furnished in the "Pillars of the Proscribed Literature" chapter. During the period of my study political dramas were published in large number, under the influence of Gandhiji.

The period from 1920 to 1947 was the heart of the struggle for independence. So during this period number of works were written on Gandhiji and others to inspire and popularise the national feeling among the people and to propagate and create mass movement with non-violent and non-cooperation theory among the people. Works were also written for propagating Socialist and Communist principles among the people. From the year 1920 onwards the writing of political dramas began in Andhra. These political dramas mirrored the then political conditions.

The writers and dramatic associations realised and recognised the importance of the performance of the dramas on the stage. Some of the writers also established dramatic organizations. They chose this art to awaken people in political matters and for their active participation in the struggle for freedom. The dramas acted were the most powerful weapons to bring people into the streamline of the freedom movement because the decorations of the characters, the application of the then politics to the old mythological characters, the arrangement of scenery as per context, the dialogue delivery of the actors, and the musical instruments conveyed a message to the audience. So the people began to participate actively on the freedom struggle. As a result the Government of Madras began to proscribe a number of dramas as per their repressive laws. A separate act i.e. Dramatic Performance Act was passed to impose control on dramas. Even then the writers did not lose their courage and wrote number of dramas to appeal and encourage the people to participate in the freedom struggle.

Telugu dramas Navayugarambham or Gandhi Mahodayam[2] (New Era or the Rise of Gandhi) and Panchala Parabhavam[3] were written by Damaraju Pundarikakshudu. The details of the drama are discussed in the 'Pillars of the Proscribed Literature' chapter. These two dramas were proscribed and the performance of these dramas was prohibited.

Swarjya Radhamu

Swarjya Radhamu[4] (The Swarajya Car) a drama was written by Samaraju Ramanuja Rao and printed at Chandrika Press, Guntur. Tilak Nataka Samajam, Guntur cooperated for the publication of this book. The author attracted by non-cooperation movement in 1921-22, actively participated in the movement.

The author introduced the characters like Mother India, God Indra, tilak, Queen Victoria, Shaukat Ali, Gandhiji, a Citizen of Amritsar, Ratna Devi, Panchali (A Punjab Lady), Kali, Indians, Annie Besant, Srinivasa Sastry, Aurobindo Ghosh.

Swarajya Radhamu was a drama in five acts in which the author stated that the sages like Vyasa and Valmiki, great like Nala and Harischhandra, incarnations like Rama and Krishna and truly noble poets like Kalidasa flourished in India, but at present it was in slavery. Indians should leave off connections with the rulers, live without violence, largely follow Indian customs in the matter of dress, language and business, establish universities throughout. India for national education and keep up the functioning of village Panchayats. All these things enrich the non-cooperation movement to get Swaraj to Indians.

Further the author described the role played by Hindus and Muslims in the First World War. The British Government could not keep up their promise. The Indians had lost their wealth, honour and life. The Government had passed the time with false promises. The whole Government became a demonical rule. The Indian religion at present became eroded. The author questioned what Hiranyakasipa and Kamsa, Napolean and Kaiser gained through their cruelty. Peaceful methods alone are useful to gain victory. The author gave an account of the Punjab massacre.

The author compared Lala Lajapat Rai, Shaukat ali, Chittaranjan Das, Muhammad ali, and Satyapal with Pandavas of Mahabharatam. Once more the Mahabharata war (the great war of India) would take place with peaceful means. In the war Dussasana – Dyer would be punished.

While a sum of sixty crores of rupees was reaching England under the pretext of cloth, while one hundred and ninety two crores of rupees were being collected in the shape of taxes, fifty lakhs of starving people perish every year crying to God Rama for food. Besides the Britishers were treating the Indians as "brutes". The author suggested non-violent non-cooperation as the only means by which the above mentioned evils could be removed.

In this drama the author took the religious as well as political figures as characters. It was one of the techniques to mobilise the people towards freedom struggle. To create enthusiasm and to intensify the participation of the people in the liberation of the mother country he highlighted the past glory of India. With this background he explained the then slavery of Indians to inculcate the sense of Swaraj in the hearts of the people. To achieve it he encouraged the people to do war against the British but it must be non-violent. He also criticised the economic exploitation of the British through this drama.

The Government of Madras thought that it would create intense hatred and contempt among the people of the country against the British. Therefore the Government prohibited the performance of this drama and proscribed the book.[5]

Navayugam – Gandhovijayam,[6] a drama was written by Damaraju Pundarikakshudu. It was proscribed and forfeited by the Government. His another drama entitled Snagha Samasya Anu Samskarini[7] was an investigative work. These two dramas are discussed in the "Pillars of the Proscribed Literature" chapter to avoid repetition.

Another Telugu drama entitled Gandhi Vijayadwaja Natakam[8] was written by Kaviraja Sripada Krishnamurthy Sastry. It was proscribed by the Government. It was discussed in "The New Force and Hope – Gandhiji", chapter.

Jebunnisa a Telugu drama was written by Pingali Nagendra Rao in 1923. To prohibit this drama Muslims[9] conducted a movement against its performance. Therefore the performance of this drama was prohibited by the Government of Madras in 1923, on the ground that it would disturb the religious harmony among the Hindus and Muslims. At the same time another drama entitled Ramaraju which was written by Kolachalam was also banned by the Government of Madras. The details of these dramas are not available.

Another Telugu drama entitled "Avatara Parivartanam" was written jointly by Viswanadha Satyanarayana and Kodali Anjaneyulu (between 1920-25) on freedom movement, but the manuscript of this drama was burnt by the Government.[10]

Some of the newspapers published dramas also in their columns to promote political consciousness and active participation of the people in the nationalist movement.

Among them "Congress"[11] was a Telugu weekly started by Madduri Annappornaiah. It was one of the most powerful and popular newspapers published in Telugu during the Indian struggle for freedom. It played a prominent role in rousing the national sentiment among the Andhras. From inception in 1922 till its extinction in 1932 it carried on a fearless fight against the British Government in India..[12]

Several objectionable articles[13] were published in the "Congress" during the years 1922, 1923, 1924 but the Government did not take any action as the Advocate General was of opinion that the articles did not offend against the seditious sections of the Indian Penal Code.[14]

The policy of the paper was to uphold the ideas and methods of the Indian National Congress and the ideology of Mahatma Gandhi. It advocated the cause of complete independence even from 1925. The Madras Government thought that the tone of the Congress was scurrilous.

Chichulapidugu or A Thunderbolt of Fire:

In 1929 the "Congress"s published one Act drama entitled Chichulapidugu or A Thunderbolt of Fire.[15] It contained three scenes and was written by Rama chandra Venkatappa (co-editor of the Newspaper Congress). To write this drama the author referred to Indian War of Independence written by V.D.Savarkar. History of Mutiny written by Charles Bal and Roberts Forty years of my life in India written by Lord Roberts. This drama was published by Madduri Annapoornaiah in Congress newspaper from 8th May 1929 to 10th May 1929. It offended the Sections 124A, 153A of Indian Penal Code. The Government filed a case against the editor of the Congress, Madduri Annappornaiah. In the court he declared that he was the author of the said drama. He wrote a letter to Ramachandruni Venkatappa in which he stated "I saw your drama and published it in the newspaper so I was responsible for it". The Government sentenced him to punishment. It was discussed in the last para of this drama.

On 7th April 1930 at Chollangi, the Congress party sent Ramachandruni Venkatappa and five others to violate the Salt Act. The police beat them. In this context Venkatappa declared that he was the author of the Chichulapidugu drama but Annapoornaiah was subjected to two and half years rigorous imprisonment at Vellore Jail.

The summary of the said drama is as follows: In the drama the hero is one Mangal Panday a Sepoy. The first scene consists mostly of monologues by Pandya. In monologues he expressed his hatred towards the British and compared them with robbers because of their injustice, violence and robbery methods. Britishers, men of another religion, took away Indian Swaraj and suppressed Indian Swadharma. Panday addressing his sword gave the details of how Mother India was teased by them and occupied provinces such as Burma, Satara, Nagpur, Brahmavarta, Jhansi, etc. by evil methods. He proceeded to detail inequities committed by the British, culminating with the charge that they are destroying the religion of Hindu and Muslim by making them use cartridges smeared with the fat of the Cow and the Pig. If the three lakhs of Indian soldiers in the British service in India made up their minds to rebel against the rulers they would lose everything in India. He exhorted the Indian sloldiers to fight the Britishers.

In the second scene Panday's exhortation to his co-soldiers to kill the British, achieve Swaraj and come to discharge their indebtedness to the mother country is given. Panday's object was to start a war of Independence to attain Swaraj and drive out the British from India.

In the third scene Panday expressed his last wish to Herse, the executioner as 'May your nation, if it has got any desire to live, leave our country and go away soon'. This scene ended with the execution of Pandya. The writer is to hold up Pandya as a hero and patriot for others to follow.

Stage performances of Chichulapidugu was conducted by Amancharla Gopala Rao on behalf of Youth League in Guntur prior to its proscription.

The primary object of the author in writing this drama was the encouragement of heroic sacrifices to free the nation from foreign yoke. The author compared Britishers with 'Robbers' and criticised the deceitful methods of British for the occupation of India with a view to create aversion towards the British rule and prepare the people to fight against the British Raj. He tried to mould the Indian soldiers towards struggle for Swaraj.

Hence the British Government felt that the writer attempted to bring into hatred and excite disaffection towards the Government established by law in India. Therefore it was proscribed by the Government.[16] The writer also attempted to excite enmity between the British Indian subjects and Hindus and Muslims, respectively. So, as per Sections 124A, Indian Penal Code and 153A Indian Penal Code Madduri Annapoornaiah was sentenced to two years rigorous imprisonment and Rs.500/- fine, and in default, six months rigorous imprisonment for the charge under Section 124A Indian Penal Code and to one year's rigorous imprisonment for the charge under Section 153A, Indian Penal Code the sentences of imprisonment to run concurrently.[17]

Maharani Jhansi Lakshmi Bai Natakam

Maharani Jhansi Lakshmi Bai Natakam[18] was a Telugu drama depicting the story of the Rani of Jhansi of the great Indian Mutiny of 1857. It was written by Chukkabhatla Satyanarayana and printed and published by Duvvuri Sambamurti at the Iswara press of Messrs Duvvuri Brothers, Rajahmundry in 1930. It was forfeited by the Madras Government.[19] The drama which consisted of five acts is couched from start to finish in a simple and spirited style. It contained matter, the publication of which was punishable under Section 124A and 153A of the Indian Penal Code.[20]

The author introduced the characters like Manu Bai (the name of Maharani Lakshmi Bai, Rani of Jhansi, before she was married) Nana Saheb (adopted son of the last Peshwa Baji Rao II), Tantiya Tope (one of the most loyal servants of Nana Saheb, who won immortal fame by his patriotism, determined fighting and skillful guerilla operations during 1857 revolt) Baji Rao (the 1st Peshwa Moropant (the father of Manu Bai), Raghuramchandra Panth (Prime Minister of Gangadhara Rao, Raja of Jhansi), Ellis (the political resident at Jhansi), Ministers, Dharma Singh and Pratap Singh (two soldiers in the army of the Raja of Jhansi), Ahmud Hussain (a Muhammadan Soldier) Servant, Soldiers, Lakshmi Bai, Baker (a general of the British army) and Ramachandra Rao Deshmukh (one of the Sardars of Lakshmi Bai).

The author, in the preface to this drama declared that he was dedicating this book to patriots who were fighting the British Government either by violent or by non-violent methods.

The play opens with Nana Saheb, Tantiya Tope and Manu Bai meeting in a forest near Benares and holding a conference on the 'fallen' conditions of India. Afterwards all of them proceeded to meet Moropant at Peshwa Baji Rao's residence Benares. Here the whole group expressed their regret for the dependence on the British Government. After Baji Rao left the scene a message was received from the Governor-General stating that money due to Baji Rao could not be sent till the Governor-General returned from the camp. It made Moropant furious and he delivered a heated speech against the British Government.

Ellis misbehaved with Raghuramachandra Pant who met him. Later it was shown in the drama that Ellis offered his apology to Raghuramachandra Pant. Moropant advised Nana Saheb and Tantiya Tope not to hesitate to kill the British people who were traitors and responsible for India's slavery. Moropant appeared as a Hindu Monk and created hatred among Indian soldiers against the British Government.

Nana Saheb and Tantiya Tope hatched a plot to encourage the Indian sepoys to overthrow the British Government. The British Government issued an order declaring the adoption of a boy by her deceased husband invalid. Basing on this Jhansi Lakshmi Bai decided to wage a war against the British Government with the help of Nana Saheb and Tantiya Tope.

Nana Saheb and Tantiya Tope received the news that Mangal Pandya killed three British soldiers at Berhampur and was himself executed and the whole country was in a blaze and so they expressed grave concern. Basing on this Nana Saheb and Tantiya Tope decided to send their spies to all military stations to convey to all sepoys to start revolution at once. At Jhansi, Moropant received this message and advised Ahmud Hussain a local leader of the revolution to capture the British treasury and arsenal and prepare the soldiers for the revolution.

The sepoys revolted and were trying to capture the treasury of Jhansi and Ellis was trying to make arrangements for the survival of his family. Lakshmi Bai held her last Darbar and assigned specific military duties to her Sardars and Ministers and ordered the soldiers to fight till the end and liberate India from British rule.

Lakshmi Bai encountered general Baker on her way to Kalpi and killed him. In the Gwalior battle she attacked British soldiers and killed all of them, but finally she fell down after receiving a fatal blow from a sword.

In this drama the writer exhorted the people to resist foreign rule and lay down their lives for the country's independence. He appealed to the people to read the story of Jhansi and pay homage to her in the appropriate manner.

The Government thought that it would "incite hatred against the British people and the Government established by law and tamper with the loyalty of the Indian forces......". It contained seditious matter, the publication of which is punishable under Section 124A and 153A of the Indian Penal Code. Hence it was proscribed and forfeited by the Government.[21]

Zamin Ryot

A manuscript copy of the drama in Telugu entitled Zamin Ryot[22] in three Acts was written by Vedantam Venkata Subramanya Sastry of Maddulaparva, P.O.Vissanna, Krishna district.[23] It was forwarded to the Senior Translator to the Government. The Senior Translator was requested to obtain from the Telugu translator a copy of the book and the report forwarded to Government.

Anti-Zamindari movement was the foundation for the writing of Zamin Ryot drama. Ryots were subjected to many hardships. So they established Ryot Sangam[24] (Ryot Association) in 1928. The procession of 1938 from Ichchapuram to Madras created awakening and great change among the ryots.

The summary of the drama is as follows : Some coolies who were on their way to lands of the Zamindar of their village for transplantation work exprssed their discontent that they were not properly paid for their work by the Zamindar. Particulalry the coolies Venkanna and Ramanna criticised the exploitation by Zamindars. They appreciated the ryots who paid better wages to their labour. Choudarayya, one of the influential ryots of the place, met them on the way and dissuaded them from going to the Zamindar's lands and took them with him to his own lands promising them a higher wage. The Zamindar after coming to know this sent one of his srevants to bring the coolies back by force. But coolies refused to come with him. Choudarayya gave an assurance to secure the coolies.

The author vividly described the slavish conditions of tenants of Zamindars. The Zamindars used the tenants for the cultivation of their own lands without paying anything. The servants of Zamindars exercised meaningless supremacy over the tenants and other people. The Zamindars used to threaten the tenants to vote in favour of their own candidates in District Board elections.

A kavi (poet) approached the Zamindar for help in his attempts to dedicate some of the patriotic works to Gandhiji. The Zamindar treated the kavi very rudely and set his manager, Pantulu, who was also a poet, against him. Pantuluand kavi abused each other in verse.

Meanwhile the Zamindar sent Anjai and Gopalam, who were the servants of Zamindar, to bring back the coolies to his field. After prolonged arguments between Choudarayya, coolies and Anjai and Gopalam, choudarayya agreed to let the coolies go and the coolies also agreed to go to the field of Zamindar.

Kavi met Choudarayya who promised him help and explained how he was insulted by the Zamindar. Choudarayya, said only Zamindars were responsible for the poverty and evils of the country. Their exploitation was increasing day-by-day. Fearing trouble from Choudarayya the Zamindar caused his house to be looted and all his cattle to be killed and got Choudarayya and his wife Hyma beaten. While Choudharayya, his wife and son (Kumara Rao) were talking together over the incident, Kavi met them and advised Choudarayya to go to another village and work with him for enlistment of workers and peasants to Gandhi Seva Sangh. Accordingly a meeting was held under the Presidentship of Choudarayya in another village.

Kavi in his speech explained how the Zamindars were exploiting coolies and ryots keeping in their hands the Legislative Assemblies, Governors, District Boards, collectors and Police Inspectors. Those who opposed the deeds of Zamindars were severely punished and oppressed. The real wealth producers, coolies and ryots were suppressed. The coolies did not have cloth, food and shelter and did not have equal status in society. Kavi also spoke of how Choudarayya was deceived by the Zamindar. He stressed that only when coolies and ryots took over the reins of administration the country would flourish, unemployment might be solved and dictatorial Zamindari administration would come to an end. To achieve this goal he advised the entire coolie and ryot community to enlist their names in the Gandhi Seva Sangh and wait for his orders. India would destroy slavery and establish independent India, he declared.

Choudarayya next addressed the meeting. In his speech he pointed out that the wealthy and Zamindars were leading their lives exploiting the labour of coolies and ryots. After occupation of India by the Britishers the collection of tax became a problem to them. So, they appointed Tabedars from various parts of India. Their duty was to collect taxes from the ryots and send 2/3 of the tax to the Government and retain 1/3. To collect taxes from the people they should have some powers. So the Government granted them some powers. With these powers the Tabedars occupied forests, poramboku and funeral grounds. With this kind of wealth these Tabedars became Zamindars and they began to collect rupees ten or twelve per acre instead of real tax of rupees two. They would send rupees two to the Government and remaining was retained in their own treasury. Against them and their exploitation the collies and ryots were helpless. Some of them were deceived by their words and helped them in suppressing the others. Before he concluded his speech, hew as arrested by the police on a false charge, preferred against him by the Zamindar that he had burnt down his hay-stack and killed four of his cattle.

Zamindar created false witness. So, Choudarayya was tried and sentenced by a Magistrate to two years rigorous imprisonment. Even in prison Choudarayya thought of the problems of the coolies and ryots. The Warder trired to stop it but he continued it. Hyma the wife of Chopudarayya led a sad life under Kavi's protection. While making cloth through spinning wheel she sang a song of Raatnam. While in jail Choudarayya was given oil-mill work and whipped by the jail Warder for not performing his work properly in the presence of Kavi, Hyma, Kumara Rao and a number of ryots who came to the jail to see him. Kavi began to address the ryots present on the "Sad plight" of zamin ryots. The ryots who came to see Choudarayya decided not to see the face of Zamindar and hated him. While the ryots asked Choudarayya to leave the jail, Choudarayya told them not to try for his release and advised them to work for the removal of sufferings of the coolies and ryots. The whole party was turned out of the jail by the jail-warder. The Telugu Translator commented on the drama that it looked like a piece of anti Zamindari propaganda.

In this work the zeal of the author was to create unity among the working class. He gave a detailed account of the origin and growth of the Zamindars and explained the nature of exploitation. He cruiticised the exploitation of Zamindars and tried to prepare the working class to fight against the Zamindars. He also described how the Zamindars used the ryots in getting votes in their favour in the elections. In this aspect the intention of the author was to prevent the ryots to be used as tools for the selfish ends of the Zamindars. The author stated that Zamindars were resoponsible for the impoverished conditions of the people. He also showed how the believers of Gandhiji were insulted by the Zamindar, within a view to show the Zamindar's favourable attitude towards British Raj. He encouraged the working class to establish their rule. He appealed to the working class to extend their full support and active cooperation to the Gandhian movement.

The District Collector, Guntur sent a report to the Secretary to the Government of Madras. In it he stated that the drama "Zamin Ryot" from the beginning to the end depicted the ill-treatment mmeted out by the Zamindars to their tenants and the resulting hardships of the latter. The enactment of the drama might therefore create unnecessary hitch and disaffection between Zamindars and their servants. It was not a fit drama to be enacted as it was apt to create class and communal hatred. Therefore he requested the Government to consider the advisability of prohibiting the performance of this drama in Guntur or any other district in the Presidency under Section 3 of the Dramatic Performance Act.

The drama was an outright condemnation of the Zamindars. It was an indirect attack on the police and the jail administration.

The Government of Madras decided that the drama "was of Scandalous and defamatory nature". The prohibition order was prepared by Legal Department on 12th October, 1938. Hence, in exercise of the powers conferred by clause (a) of Section 3 of the Dramatic Performance Act 1876 (XIX of 1876) the Government prohibited its performance in any public place in the Province of Madras.[25]

Tirugubatu (Revolt)

Tirugubatu (Revolt)[26] was a Telugu play written by Muni Manikyam. It was printed at Usha press, Telaprolu and published as No.18 of the Adarsa Grandha Mandali Series, Elamarru, Krishna district by Gadde Lingayya, the editor of the said series. In the course of his preface, the editor said that he had published the play, to popularise socialist ideas through appealing forms of literature such as plays, stories and ballads. The plot of the play was short and simple.

The summary of the play is as follows:- Poornayya Sastri a rigid orthodox Brahmin, and his unemployed graduatge son, Sundaram entered into a discussion about the propriety of caste Hindus dining with Harijans. Sundaram questioned his father what harm there was if they dined with Malas and Madigas and in which way they were inferior to Brahmins. Sastri replied "you are casting to the winds the Vedic Dharma of the Vyakarnam family and we belong to the highest (Brahmin) caste", Besides the Harijan led a low life, drank toddy and ate meat. Sundaram again questioned his father by saying Doras (Europeans) also ate pork and beef and drank intoxicating liquors, which were worse than toddy and even they did not clean their teeth. "We not only associate with such people but dine with them we consider it a great honour". Sastri questioned, "Are Malas and Madigas equal to Doras". Sundaram in response to his father, said that they were equal, except the difference in colour. Then Sastri said that the Doras were rulers and association with them was a duty enjoined by necessity. In response to his father, Sundaram had questioned his father, "How can you sanction the friendship of 'Wretches' who eat the flesh of the sacred cow and condemn our deities and customs? They have become worthy of our respect, while a member of the lowest caste who worships our Rama and chants his name was an untouchable. There is no fairness in it."

Conversation took place in respect of temples between Sundaram and Subba Rao (one of the characters in the play) Sundaram began to describe to Subba Rao, saying that all those things that were done in the so-called famous temples were only henious sins. As stated in the newspapers that the Mahant of the Tirupati temple had been living with five or six prostitutes and wasted money in an indescribable manner. When men and women who visited temples at places like Mangalagiri, Kotappakonda, Govada and Ponnur on the occasions of festivals of the deities there, committed all sorts of foul deeds inside the precincts of those temples, at the back of their shrine-rooms and behind trees and when the thieves stole the jewels adorning the deities, would God keep quiet, if there was God. These idols had no power whatever. A mad belief was propagated for the sake of livelihood of priests etc.

Another conversation took place between Sundaram and some Harijans. In it Kannamadas informed that Subba Rao gave his word to bring the Harijans to enter Shiva's temple. It seemesd that he would bring Gandhiji also. Sundaram had discouraged them and questioned if any one had seen God and said it was nothing but succumbing to sort of delusion.

When Poornayya Sastri's wife and some orther Brahmin ladies were drawing water from the village-well, some women folk of the Harijan ward came there and drew water from the well in spite of the Brahmin ladies protests, returning abuse for abuse. Kotayya, the village Headman, Veeraya, his brother-in-law, Guravayya, the merchant, and Nancharayya, the Priest of Siva temple and Poornayya Sastri gathered round the village banyas tree and discussed the incident and the meeting closed with the vow of Kotayya to burn the Harijan ward and thus teach a lesson to the Harijans, 'who are getting more and more arrogant day by day'. One day Venkatesi, a Harijan labourer under Kotayya asked the latter to return the dowry money of his daughter, Lachchi, which he had kept in Kotayya's custody three years ago, together with the interest thereon, Rs.50/- in all. Kotayya then offered to give the money provided Venkatesi sent his daughter alone to him that evening and said that in the event of her husband abandoned her, he himself would maintain her decently. Venkatesi who understood and resented this insult, sternly demanded his daughters dowry money as well as his wages upto that day. But he got in return foul abuse, a flat refusal of his money and threats of violence and he left Kotayya's hoiuse in utter disgust curşing him.

Kotayya and Veerayya hid themselves behind a tamarind tree in a garden through which Lachchi and another Harijan woman, Ratti, would go home with baskets of grass on their heads. They came out of their ambush on seeing the women. Kotayya attacked Lachchi, while Veerayya tried to assault Ratti. Lachchi was thrown on her back on the ground and Kotayyan began to roughly handle her. Veerayya received a blow with the sickle and asked Kotayya to come to his help leaving Lachchi and both of them took to their heels. Lachchi and Ratti went home and informed all the Harijans of the assault made on them by Kotayya and Veerayya. After returning to the village, Kotayya and Veerayya represented to Poornayya Sastri and others that Ratti and Lachchi assaulted them when they questioned their behaviour at the village well. Kotayya instigated Veerayya to burn the houses of Ratti and Lachchi. One night Veerayya executed his mission successfully, undiscovered by any body, with the result that the whole Harijan ward was reduced to ashes and poor old Venkatesi was burnt alive. Lachchi exhorted the Harijan men to take up arms and wreak vengeance on Kotayya and Veerayya. Improvising a red flag out of a piece torn from her saree and holding it in her hand, she led them to the accompaniment of war cries in a campaign against those that had oppressed Harijans and robbed Harijan women of their honour.

In this work the author crititicised the caste restrictions on Malas and Madigas. He compared Malas and Madigas with Britishers in their habits, with a view to establish equal social status in the Hindu society. He denounced the temple activities and priesthood. One of the objects of the author was to propagate the Gandhian Harijan upliftment. The author also described the atrocities of higher castes on Harijans, with a view to create a sense of confidence to face and oppose them with courage. The financial exploitation by the higher communities was also shown with a view to make them unpopular. He tried to create awareness among the Harijans to fight against the exploiting class even with arms.

The Telugu translator to Madras Government, opined that the play seemed to be designed as a piece of propaganda partly for Mahatma Gandhi's Harijan Movement and partly for Communist principles.

The summary of the opinion of the Madras Governmenrt was that the said book tended to incide and encourage people to the commission of offences involving violence, and to promote feelings of enmity or hatred between different classes of people. Therefore the Madras Government directed that copies of the book, wherever found, and all other documents containing copies, reprints or translations of or extracts from it be forfeited.[27]

The Government of Madras prohibited the performance of the Telugu dramas Rajakota and British Gayopakhyanam.[28] Rajakota was written by Vedantam Venkata Subramanya Sastri. On 16th October, 1939 the author wrote an application to the Krishna District Magistrate to allow the performance of the drama and along with the application a manuscript copy was also sent to the Government of Madras for scrutiny. Manuscript copy was not returned but he received orders of prohibition of performance, order No.6097 dated 24 November, 1939. So the manuscript was not found in Andhra Pradesh State Archives, Tarnaka, Hyderabad. The available information was that the drama was written on the basis of political incidents which happened in Rajakota court.

Roshanara

A Telugu drama entitled Roshanara was written by Kopparapu Subba Rao. It was very popular for some years in Andhra. His other dramas were Tarasasankam, Ranapratap, Nurjahan, Neti Natudu etc. Except Rana Pratap the remaining dramas were published.

Roshanara was the sister of Aurangazeb one of the Mughal rulers of India. But this story was fiction. She used to go to war fields alongwith her brother. Once she intentionally allowed herself to be caught by Sivaji's spies (Sivaji was the ruler of Maharatha Kingdom). They brought her before Sivaji. For his heroic deeds she fell in love with him. But he refused to marry her. So she declared war against Sivaji and she was killed on the battle field. This is the plot of the drama. The author included songs on patriotism relevant to the then political conditions to inspire the people towards freedom struggle with a view to get Swaraj to Indians.

The performance of this drama attracted the attention of the people and thousands of people became inspired. But the Muslims were displeased with it. The Muslims thought that it was an insult to their religion. So the Muslims in Andhra collectively sent memorandums to the Collectors of Guntur and Krishna districts pleading a ban on the performance of this drama. So the collectors issued prohibitary orders on the performance of drama in the Krishna and Guntur. The dramatic association also sent memorandums to the Collectors. In them they stated there was nothing in it against Muslims or to their religion. The anti attitude towards this drama also spread to the West Godavari district. The West Godavari district Collector called the two parties before him. Negotiations were held. But the Muslims did not agree to the performance of this drama. At last they agreed to the performance of the drama if the dramatic association changed its title to a Hindu woman. They also imposed a condition that the name of Aurangazeb must be removed. Therefore the association accepted their conditions and changed its title as Jahwari Bai. It was also successfully performed in Andhra.[29]

Girijavilapam

Girijavilapam is an article in the shape of a drama contributed by Allamaraju Narayana Rao of Bobbili and published by P.T.Jagannadha Rao, in his Telugu Journal Kanti[29a] issued from Tirupati, Chittoor district on 16th June, 1940.

The article represented the men of the Arya-Vysya community as of deteriorated character and the women as unchaste and immoral and suggested that Vasavi Kanyaka (who is worshipped as a caste-deity on account of her self-sacrifice to maintain her virginity) should have eloped with King Vishnuvardhana. It made the Goddess Durga pronounce terrible cruses on the men and women of the community, insult the men by calling them black-dogs, bull-calves, robbers, rakes Rakshasas, impotent creatures and beings with heads shaven as a mark of disgrace and the women as the worst of prostitutes, exulting in the depravity of their husbands and sets the Brahmin community especially of the Saivite persuation, against the Arya-Vysya community.

Arya-Vysya Mahasabha, central committee, 85 Govindappa Naick Street, George town, Madras submitted a memorandum giving instances of vilification of the Arya-Vysya community and excitement of class-hatred by writings in journals and books and by characters introduced into dramas and cinemas.

The said central committee applied to Government on the 21st August, 1940 for sanction to prosecute the author and publisher of the article in question. The reply contained in Government order No. MS. 3689 dated the 9th September, 1940 is as follows:- "The Government regrets that they are not prepared to agree to the prosecution proposed". The editor of the Journal was warned by the Madras Government.[30]

Nedu is a Telugu Drama written by V.S.R. Somayajulu and proposed to be enacted at Repalle in October, 1940. It required the intervention of the District Magistrate of Guntur on account of excitement created in the minds of the members of the Arya-Vysya community, owing to its vilification.

Class-mates or Premavallika is a drama written by Giddhalur Guruswami and published at Rajahmundry. Navina Vikramaditya a cinema was exhibited by the Gemeni Pictures Corporation, Broadway, George Town Madras. Chintamani is another drama. Sakkubai is a devotional drama enacted in the Victoria Public hall and an article also appeared in this regard in the Telugu daily. Janarani in 1939 Garam Soda is a short story contributed by Kanchanapalli Ranga Rao of Berhampur to the Telugu monthly Garjana published from George Town, Madras, in its issue dated November, 1939. Kovvali Lakshmi Narasimha Rao's novels published from Rajahmundry and Vysya Vadokta Kriya Vichara Vyavasta is a book published under the auspicies of the Sringeri Mutt.

All these works depicted the Arya-Vysya community as a ridiculous, shameless one and intended to bring down the prestige of the Arya-Vysya community. Therefore the committee made their protest to the Madras Government. But the Government did not react on them because these dramas were not against the interests of the Government or the Britishers. They were only against the Arya-Vysya Community. It indicates the escaping nature of the British in the social affairs of Hindus with a view to strengthening their divide-and-rule policy indirectly.

However the publication and propagation of caste degrading literature was a most tragic feature of then society. It indirectly worked as a helping factor for the continuation of the repressive rule of the British. When there was a tremendous opposition for a work based lon religion in the case of Indians, then only the British Government declared proscription and forfeiture.

Guru Babu

A manuscruipt drama in Telugu entitled Guru Babu[31] was declared forfeit by the Madras Government on 18th September, 1941. The author of the drama is not known. The essence of the drama is as follows:-

Guru Babu was the president of the provincial labour union and also the leader of the workers movement. Kranti, a young woman worker, was a member of the labour union. She took keen interest in the welfare of the women workers and was in love with Guru Babu. A labour colony was attached to the union, as a sort of shelter from pursuit, for unemployed workers. Bhattu was also a member of the labour union. He was noterd for his ardent pleading in support of the movement, but was considered not firm and reliable. He assumed that Kranti loved him. Jiyyar was another member of the labour union. He was a singer who went from village to village, and did propaganda for the movement through his songs.

Guru Babu and other leaders of the workers' movement found instances of highhandedness on the part of landholders increasing day by day. While Bhattu and some other workers including Kranti advocated violent measures in return, Guru Babu advised caution and stressed steady constructive work as the required condition for any successful workers' revolution. At last they decided to declare a general strike of workers all over the province in reply to the notice of reduction by fifty percent of the wages of farm-labourers given by Sankarayya, the most influential landholder of the place. At this juncture Kranti said that at every step the workers' should demonstrate their strength to landholders. Workers' should make them understand that without workers the world itself could not exist and if the workers were so minded, they would swallow even the world.

And she also resolved that the coolies should not work for the reduced wages, though they might die of starvation. She went on to say that the workers should not keep quiet any more and there should be a revolution and workers Karmikapuram alone should be its center. The workers movement should be crowned with success in this province. In this context Bhattu said that the coolies should not work, even though they might die. If even the original wages were to be offered, workers should not move. Unless the wages are doubled, they should not step into the farm. Further he said, that the fields had with bumper crops. At nights, they should raid the fields, cut and bring as much (produce) as workers could get hold of. All the harvest represented the sweat of workers labour. All the money in the rich people's boxes belonged to workers. If the society and the Government should stand in workers way of taking what was theirs, they should defy them and fight with them.

The demand for a cent percent increase in the workers wages was summarily rejected by Sankarayya. The workers went on a strike and labour union sent out its members to propagate among workers through out the province. To neutralise the strike Sankarayya deputed his well-to-do tenant ryots, Bapayya and Kotayya to carry on a counter-propaganda in every village among the ryots and landholders. Clashes took place between the groups of the two parties. The first encounter was between Sankarayya's party including a policeman on the one hand and a procession of women workers under the leadership of Mani, a close friend of Kranti on the other. The policeman attempted to attack hostile Mani and was roughly handled by Kranti. At that stage Guru Babu and other men workers entered in large numbers. Realizing that they were outnumbered, Sankarayya and his men silently departed from the place.

Jiyyar, in the course of his propaganda through songs came into clash with a Mokhasadar. The Mokhasadar gave him a sharp blow with the palm of his hand in the face and he fell down. He was found again in the same place in company with Mani, preventing a group of women workers from going to their fields under the influence of Jiyyar's songs. The landholders gave a fatal blow on his head with a stick. Under these circumstances Sankarayya consulted Kotayya and Bapayya and finally they decided to make short work of Guru Babu as they did in the case of Jiyyar. For this purpose, Swarnasri, the educated daughter of Kotayya and her brother Raghavan offered their services. Swarnasri took ten thousand rupees from Sankarayya, gave one half of it to her brother and retained the other half with her. She instructed her brother to influence the police to file a case against Kranti for Jiyyar's murder and prepared a plot to separate Kranti and Guru Babu. Swarnasri joined the labour union in the guise of worker and supported the condolence resolution on the death of Jiyyar, saying that she was a disciple of his.

On the death of Jiyyar a meeting was convened to mourn. In it Guru Babu, the president of the labour union, said that the workers should harass and destroy Capitalism which was operating as a thorn in the side of humanity. Till then Jiyyar's soul would not-have peace. If uni versal equality was to be attained, imperialism should be ended. If the fire of hunger was to be quenched the stomachs of Capitalists should be torn to pieces.

Gradually Swarnasri made Bhattu a tool in her hands by means of her good looks and money and persuaded him to hate Guru Babu, saying that Guru Babu forcibly won over Kranti in spite of all her earnest love for him. She instigated him to assume the presidentship of the labour union by murdering Guru Babu. Raghavam succeeded in his attempts to introduce surreptitiously a case on Kranti for Jiyyar's murder and had her interned in the village. At a meeting of workers in Karmikapuram, Mani announced that Kranti had been implicated by the police in Jiyyar's murder case and kept in remand and conveyed the meassage of both Kranti and Guru Babu to the audience to carry on the strike bodly and non-violently. All entry into the village of the interned labour leaders from outside was banned. Guru Babu carried a propaganda in surrounding villages about the workers movement and that Kranti was not the culprit.

Swarnasri got Bhattu to give a telegram to Guru Babu to start immediately and attend a very important meeting of workers to be held near a particular coffee hotel the next evening. Under her instructions Raghavam manipulated the bus driver to delay the trip purposely. So that Guru Babu might be alone. She gave Bhattu a flase hope of marrying her and becoming the president of the labour union himself. Guru Babu fell into the trap and arrived at Karmikapuram in the bus. He thought thart due to his late arrival the meeting had dispersed. Bhattu entered dressed in black, and approaching Guru Babu stabbed him while pretending to embrace him. Guru Babu drew his sword and injured Bhattu on the shoulder, but Bhattu again stabbed him. Guru Babu fell down and tried to get up. Then Bhattu tried for help. Immediately Raghavam rushed with a sword and fatally stabbed both Guru Babu and Bhattu. When about to die Guru Babu told Raghavam that the worker's movement would surely swallow up the whole world like a great flood and that such murders of individuals could not check its course and appealed to him and his capitalist friends to come to terms with workers in their own interests and establish Communism everywhere.

In this work the author encouraged the establishment of unions to get due share of their labour, and tried to make them realise the real value of their labour and their role in the economic survival of the society. To achieve their goal he encouraged strikes against the exploiting class. He described the cherting policy of the landlords. He also explained the deceitful role of the Government and police on behalf of the landlords. The author also encouraged the singers to propagate the righteous cause among the people in the country. He stressed that Capitalism was the responsible factor for the starvation and loss of life of the workers. So he encouraged workers to destroy it. The other important point stressed by the author was his appeal to women workers to participate in the workers movement. The author gave advice to the capitalists to come into terms with workers for the establishment of communistic form of Government.

The opinion of the Madras Government was that the author through speeches and songs from the different characters depicted Capitalism and capitalists as atrocious and attributed everything that was meanest to them and thus tended to incite class hatred between the working class and the capitalist class. He further had shown that Capitalism was identical with imperialism and that the latter safeguarded the interests of the former. It was clearly shown that it was the intention of the author to bring about a mass revolution by resorting to violence. Therefore the manuscript of the Telugu book contained the matter of the nature described in clauses (a) and (d) of sub-section (1) of Section 4 of the Indian Press (Emergency Powers) Act, 1931. So the Madras Government directed that the said manuscript book and all other documents containing copies or translations, be forfeited.[32]

Paschattapamu

A Telugu drama entitled Paschattapamu[33] (Repentance) was written by Dr.G.Raja Rao of Pornki of Bezwada Taluk, organiser for the Andhra country of the people's cultural propaganda committee, a branch of the All India People's Threatre's Association, in furtherance of the manifold objects of the Association of educating the masses on principles of democracy and for creating unity among the masses through dramas, songs, dances etc. It was printed at the Prajasakthi Press and was published by the Prajasakthi office, Governorpet, Bezwada, as its 46th publication in December, 1943.

The summary of the drama was that Suguna was a college girl studying in Madras, whom Mohan loved. But Suguna did not return the love and wished to throw her lot with Rao who was also a college student and interested in educating the masses on politics and for the attainment of freedom for the country. Suguna and Rao set out to the native place of the latter in response to a letter received by him from his father. Rao upset the plans of his father to marry him to a girl whom he had chosen by refusing to marry her and went out into the country educating the working classes as to how they could secure their rights in getting proper wages for their work. Rao married Suguna under the Civil Marriages Act. His mother got ill and died. This event made his father love him once again. Mohan turned out a villain and he took a vow to bring Rao into trouble, assumed the role of a Congress worker, dressed himself up as such and talked freely of having secured bombs, money etc. for acts of sabotage.

In one meeting, Rao addressing the audience, said that the world had divided itself into two parties and was fighting. Soviet Russia, china and United States of America stand on one side while Japan and Germany stood on the other. The Communists, as well as Congress leaders, wished, that the first party should become victorious. Both the Congress and the Communists had realised the need for the establishment of a national Government for the achievement of that end. But the Congress passed a resolution to the effect that it would resort to Satyagraha if the British Government failed to grant Indians a national Government. Taking this opportunity, the British Government arrested Congress leaders. Destructive measures which followed the arrests were not the Congress programme. But, the Communists had been doing propaganda to the effect that it was an error on the part of the Congress to have passed such a resolution, that Communists should obtain national Government by helping war effort and by increasing popular strength and that this was the only method which would give an impetus to the fight for freedom. The Congress Socialist Party should counteract the programme and activities which the fifth columists like the Forward Block was carrying on against the war and in favour of Japan.

Mohan, accompanied by his co-workers Sangayya and Das, attended a meeting organised by Rao. Sangayya dealt a blow at the instance of Mohan on Rao's head while he was addressing a meeting. Rao fell down. Das, the former follower of Mohan, was convinced that the path that Mohan and himself had been following was mistakes and declared that he would follow hence forward Rao as the preachings of the latter were bound to free the country saying that he and the Congress had no connection with the disturbances created by Mohan. The police arrested Mohan and Sangayya for having bombs with them. Sugana and Rao lived happily and worked for the country.

The District Superintendent of Police, Krishna district and the Krishna district Magistrate recommended the drama for proscription to the Madras Government on the ground that the drama was meant for scoring a hit against the National students organisation as opposed to the Communist controlled students organisation. It was written in free colloquial language to effectively appeal to young and innocent blood to organise for an anti-Government drive. The author covertly devoted a considerable portion of the drama to advocate sabotage and pro-facist activities. The play bristles with the then politics in a considerable form and as such did not deserve to reach the hands of the students. Therefore the Government might be pleased to take necessary action under Section 99A of the Criminal Procedure Code. But the Government did not proscribe it and it remained as a well investigated work.[34]

Kashta Jeevi (Toiler)

Kashta Jeevi[35] (Toiler) was a short story (street drama) written in Telugu song interspersed with prose by Sunkara Satyanarayana and swas printed at Prajasakthi Press, Bezwada. It was a copy of the third edition of the 101st publication of the series. The story appears to be an attempt at describing the ways of life of the Zamindars and their highhandednbess towards their ryots and the means available to the latter for getting themselves released from their clutches.

In the beginning of the story the author wrote a prayer. In it he described the Zamindars robbing the ryots continuously with the result the ryots starved and fell to the ground. If ryots and coolies united and attacked the mean fellows (Zamindars), the Zamindars could not face the ryots and coolies even a minute. Therefore ryots and coolies had to march forward.

The summary of the story is as follows:- Rama Rao a Zamindar of a village known as Rampuram in the North. The inhabitants were very poor. Despite their untiring efforts, the yield of their fields was very meager for, the tanks were dry and were not repaired, the kist rate was high and no remission was granted, the Estate officials were corrupt and the ryot generally was neglected. The Zanmindar was depicted as a licentious man and a tyrant, always indulging in drink and cock-fighting and the villagers were virtually afraid of him. Hanumayya, one of the leading ryots of that village, won the respect of his fellow ryots by his patience and righteousness. He had three sons and one daughter. Nagayya the eldest son, completed his vernacular education by the time he attained his sixteenth year and began to help his father in tilling the soil. He wanted to give English education to his brother, but due to poverty, Bheemaiah, the brother next to him had to discontinue his studies while studying in III form. But the next brother, Narayana Rao was continuing his higher education. Nagayya, became the president of the village Ryots Association. He engaged himself in organising the ryots and educating them to free themselves from the bondate of landlordism.

Enraged at the activities of the Nagayya, the Zamindar confiscated Hanumayya's cattle for non-payment of Pulavari amount. Hanumayya approached the Zamindar who threatened him and asked him to take care of his son. He paid the Pulavari amount immediately and released the cattle. The ryot youths in the village were humiliated and were seeking revenge. Nagayya warned them against future troubles. He suggested that in case of violence by them, the Government would be there under the pretext of maintaining law and order and suppress them and therefore advocated patience and unity. A meeting was then held and a resolution condemning the action of the Zamindar was passed. The Zamindar then began his atrocities on Hanumayya's family. He sued Nagayya on false chargesd, created parties against them in the village. But Nagayya went on organising and strengthening the Ryots' Association without caring for the Zamindar.

Meanwhile Narayanarao a student of Intermediate class, studied politics and economics from the works of Marx and Engels. He returned home for the summer vacation, educated the illiterates, taught politics to the coolies and ryots and told them of the war news and the atrocities of the Axis powers. He propagated unity through which they could bring the irresponsible Government to mend its ways. Gradually the village disputes subsided and unity was established.

It enraged the Zamindar still more and he was determined to have Nagayya murdered. There was a rowdy in the village by name Narigadu whom the Zamindar persuaded to murder Nagayya by promising him lands and money. One night while sleeping in the fields Nagayya was murdered by Narigadu. The Zamindar escaped from the clutches of law by spending large sums of money. The whole village was shocked at the outrageous act and joined with the bereaved family. Narayanarao heard this news and came to the village and at the corpse of his brother took a vow to fulfil what his brother had started. He then told his sister to join him to work for the unity of the people.

Narayanarao stopped his studies and stayed in the village. A meeting was held by the ryots and with boiling blood in them they resolved to wipe out the Zamindar. Narayanrao pacified them and asked them to unite first and be patient. He then toured in villagers and preached unity.

Retribution began to dog the foot-steps of Narigadu. When once his object was achieved, the Zamindar began to treat him with contempt and did not pay him even a pie. After some days, the wife of Narigadu was in great danger being unable to give birth to a child. Having no other person to whom he could turn for help, he went to the Zamindar and begged him for some monetary aid, but the Zamindar beat him with a heavy arrack bottle and necked him out of his compound. He was heavily wounded and lying groaning on the roadside, when Narayanarao who was coming that way, saw him, rendered him first aid and took him home. Narigadu confessed his guilt moved by Narayanarao's tenderness both towards his wife and himself, and begged him to forgive him. Sometime afterwards the wife of Narigadu died on account of extreme weakness, though she was able to give birth to a child. The baby died for want of milk and then Narigadu sought the shelter of Narayanarao. Narayanarao told a 'Burra Katha' (Street drama) to him and he went out to do propaganda to unite coolies. He narrated that Zamindars were deceiving and creating splits between ryots and coolies and requested them to unite. He assured them that the Communists who would create a paradise for toilers like him wanted them all to unite for unity alone would get 'Swaraj' and dispel famine. Thus Narayanarao worked for the unity of ryots and Narigadu for that of coolies.

One day, the Zamindar happened to see Sumati, the daughter of Hanumayya. He was bewitched by her extraordinary beauty and wanted to possess her. He waylaid her with the help of some accomplices and was preparing to take her away by force, when Bheemaiah, the second brother of Sumati, came there. Narigadu who was attracted by the cry for help from Sumati, also came there. They both succeeded in rescuing Sumati from the hands of the rowdies, the Zamindar received good blows in the scuffle that followed.

The next day, the Zamindar bribed the police and got Bheemaiah and Narigadu arrested on the plea that they both assaulted him. On hearing these news the villagers all took up cudgels and planned to demolish the palace. Narayanarao arrived then and persuaded them to be patient and appealed to the people to petition to the Government and to observe hunger-strikes for the release of the comrades. Sumati also joined her brother in propaganda. A great agitation soon spread and the Government not being able to resist peoples' pressure, released Bheemaiah and Narigadu and arrested the Zamindar and the four rowdies. But through money and recommendations the Zamindar escaped.

From that day onwards ryots began to defy him and stopped giving mamools to the servants of the Zamindar. Further they stopped ploughing freely for him, put an end to the practice of gathering their cattle in one of his gardens for dung; abstained from sending their children into the tobacco garden for free labour; avoided giving the first harvest of fruits and vegetables. The Zamindar found himself at his wit's end at the sudden change of affairs. He closed all the public paths around the village with a view to harass the villagers and kept rowdies to guard these paths. Narayanarao negotiated with Zamindar but failed to reopen them, then the ryots and coolies took up crow bars and began to open the closed paths. When the rowdies obstructed them they beat them and routed them till they ran for their lives. During these circumstances the Zamindar shifted his residence to a town unable to bear the dishonour into which he descended.

On hearing this news, the ryots and coolies assembled to celebrate over their success. Narayanarao addressed them and said this was only an initial success but not final victory. The capitalistic Government always protected such 'scoundrels'. The grievances of the ryots and the coolies would never be redressed, unless they got rid of this kind of rule. At this juncture they must overcome their difficulties and secure national Government.

The love of freedom rose high and people took up the hammer and the sickle. When all Europe jopined and fell on them, they suppressed the enemy and established people's government. The red army flowed on to break the Facist hearts and to build their tombs everywhere. Further the author stated through the character of Narayanarao if Hindus, Muslims, Ryots and Coolies, all united together, they could stop the game of Churchill and Amery and secure freedom in a minute. Imperialism, would never give freedom to Indians. That was why Indians must unite and achieve it. Union itself was a fight and he said "comrade work for it, get the elders out of jail and tell it is the way for Swaraj".

In this work the author described the hardships of the working class and criticised heavy taxation system and corrupt estate officials with a view to bring to the knowledge of the entire working class. He explained the luxurious life of the Zamindars at the cost of working class. He stressed the need for unification of working class and educate them to overcome their troubles. He narrated the mischievous activities of Zamindars to destroy the labour. He appealed to the educated people to educate the working class on Communist principles. He tried to unite and prepare them to fight against the injustice. Thus the main object of the author was to encourage the working class to devote their energies for the establishment of people's rule in India.

On 25th April, 1945, the Superintendent of Police, special Branch C.I.D. forwarded a copy of the booklet 'Kashta Jeevi' and suggested that it might be proscribed, on the grounds that it contained an imaginary story aiming at uniting the ryots and labourers in order to get rid of the Zamindars. It was in fact anti-Zamindari propaganda. He said that there were several objectionable portions in the book which brought Government into contempt and also tend to incite, class hatred. Further he pointed out that it would promote feelings of enmity between zamindars and ryots.

The District Magistrate, Nellore, was of the view that it was a matter for Government to decide whether anti-Zamindari propaganda of this nature should be stopped or not. He started that there were indications to show that Government themselves were considering whether the smaller Zamindaries should be acquired and settled on the ryotwari system. That being so, he was of the view that one should not seriously object to this form of propaganda simply because they were carried on by Communists.

Therefore the Madras Government did not proscribe it. It remained as a well investigated work.[36]

Sitaramaraju

A Telugu booklet Sitaramaraju[37] (Burrakatha or Street drama) was written by Sunkara Satyanarayana and published at the Prajasakthi Press, Bezwada as publication No.152, wherein the revolt of the people of the Agency tracts in the circars under Sitaramaraju's leadership was described in verse in the form of a ballad.

The author stated in the preface, after the flames of the civil disobedience cooled down, that Alluri Sitaramaraju organised people's revolt in the Agency tracts. He gained experience from the Terrorist Movement as well as from the civil disobedience movement. He understood that it was useless to sacrifice lives like the terrorists to kill autocratic Government servants. He also understood that limitations should not be imposed for the people's movement, as Gandhiji did in the name of non-violence.

In this agency area, Koyas, Chenchus and other forest tribes were living. These people ate fruits, roots and bamboo rice in the forest and lead a free life. The foreign Government which robbed the whole country and whose civilisation was only to exploit and rob, went to the forests promising enlightenment. As soon as the Government stepped in, it did not respect those people. As it wanted to suppress the freedom there, it at first converted the forest into reserves and declared that they were the owners. The Government made the people not to touch even the roots and greengrass. The British Government began to exploit the Agency tracts. For this area, Bastian was the Tahasildar. He was a hard task-master. He was extortionate, cruel and extremely selfish. He compulsorly enlisted the labour and denied wages to the workers. He was extremely corrupt and a sinner. He subjected the hill-tribes to severe hardships and harassment. There the British Government created Muttadars just as they created Zamindars who sucked Indian blood. As companions to Muttadars corrupt fellows were given appointment to ruin the people in the Agency. The agency in which there were no class differences, was split up and three groups called Muttadars, coolies, and ryots were created.

Sitaramaraju wanted to stop this plunder. He met some people of non-violent creed. He attended their meetings. He felt very happy when he met people who attended those meetings and at the manner in which they met together. But these people wanted to keep the revolution within certain limits. He did not relish it. Thereafter, he met some who believed in the use of bombs. He was overwhelmed with joy at their bravery, valour and sacrifices. But these people had no contact at all with the people. So he decided to carry out a revolution by taking the good from the both creeds; it would be a success.

The people and their leaders got enraged. Their rage took the form of a revolt under the leadership of Sitaramaraju. Gantam Dora, Malludora, Padalu and Aggiraju were his trusted lieutenants. They were great fighters. The rebels looted police stations and took hold of guns and released the persons imprisoned there and enlisted them in their revolutionary army and now and then holding meetings in villages and impressing on them about the revolution. The heroic fighter Raju had thus strengthened his army. One class was armed while the other was unarmed. Those who fought with arms belonged to the first battalion. The coolies who helped the revolution by strikes, the ryots who refused to pay even a pie of the tax formed the second battalion of the revolution and were its heart. The third section consisted of the secret agents who destroyed the enemy's plans.

The Government took steps to put down the revolt. They first tried through the District police, but they failed. Next, they tried through the Malabar police. Even then they failed. Lastly, they dispatched military forces. They too fared no better. Realising the impossibility of routing the rebels in open battle the Government came to the conclusion that they could not suppress the revolution in this manner, in open fight. It thought of attacking the people hereafter. To harass the people, the Government promulgated Martial law.

The employment of torture by the military authorities for eliciting information from the people about the whereabouts of Raju and other leaders was described as follows:- One day the Government troops attacked a village at midnight and set fire to it. It began to burn, the fire having spread to all the four corners. When the people woke up in panic and left their houses in bare clothes, the forces rounded them up into a herd at one place. The forces said, to them "If you show that universal hero Raju, we will reward you ten thousand. If you bring Gamu brothers tied up we will grant you lands and support you. Show us soon the ten leaders of the revolution". In response to it, no agency man would talk. The soldiers finding them silent flew up into a rage like revengeful snakes and they tied men to trees and whipped them till they bled. Their commander was not satisfied with that. He saw that it was no good be labouring the men; he wished to frighten the women-folk who witnessed the unbearable sight of this torture and were weeping, and see whether that would have any effect. One of the women was consoling her four-yeasr's old boy who was crying.

The commander rushed at her, pulled the child from her arms, swing him round and threw him up and caught him and handled him as if he were a ball. He thrust his dagger into the boy's breast and flung the boy aside. The British soldiers killed children before their mother's eyes at one place. At another they killed mothers before the eyes of their children. They would first cut legs and arms into pieces and then kill.

Seeing all this the Gantam Brothers decided to give fight. One was killed and the other was taken prisoner. Padalu was also killed and Aggiraju was taken prisoner. The author said Sitaramaraju was the only enemy free. The inhuman activities of the military authorities made him leave his retreat and rush to the rescue of his suffering countrymen in the burning villages. The military opened fire and he was killed.

The author further stated that for the salavation of the motherland, Raju infused into the Agency people bravery and mobilised them. With the cooperation of the people, he organized the revolution. For over two years, he made the British Government shiver. But to spread the revolution throughout the country neither the Andhra leaders nor the All India leaders rendered any help. The author questioned how long could the people of an Agency and their leader Raju, oppose the mighty forces. On account of this weakness alone, the Agency heroes had to perish. Truly in the history of the independence movement of the Andhras, the history of the Sitaramaraju deserves a chapter in golden letters.

The remarks of the Telugu translator to Madras government on the book are: it idolises a rebel leader and his lieutenants and holds them out as objects of emulation for the Telugus in their struggle for independence and the establishment of a popular Government in Andhradesa.

Europeans like Bastian, Cowart, and Haiter were painted in black colours and presented as specimens of heartless and degraded humanity. This sort of presentation might rouse popular feelings against Europeans.

The book was written in verse and the ballad form was adopted. Ballads were meant to be sung and when sung their appeal was powerful.

The book was published at the Prajasakthi Press, Bezwada, obviously under Communist auspices. This was also a noteworthy fact.

In these days of labour strikes, communal clashes, political unrest and Communist propaganda, the book was not a desirable addition to Telugu Literature.

But the Madras Government did not proscribe it and it remained as a well investigated work.[38]

Cinema

J.M.Sengupta was a famous Congress leader during the freedom movement in India. He led civil disobedience movement. He was imprisoned in jail for a long time as a detenue. He faced many hardships in the jail and died. The Government declared it was due to ill-health. His funeral procession was led by students.

Entire India had declared 6th August, 1933 as memorial day of Sengupta. So, on this context a short film on Sengupta was released on 6th August, 1933 at Panduranga theatre in Ellore, west Godavari district. But the District Magistrate made a condition i.e. after its observation the film could be allowed to be exhibited. Hence its exhibition on 6th August, 1933 was prohibited.

District Magistrate, Local Sub-Divisional Magistrate, District Superintendent of Police, privately saw the film on 6th August, 1933 and they sent a report to the Government. They suggested cancellation of the exhibition certificate to Sengupta film. At that time there was much more awakening among the students of East and West Godavari. The three officials felt the film might create more anti-British feelings among the students.

In fact there was no anti-British attitude in the film. But on the basis of the political conditions prevailing then, it might create some anti-British impact on the public.

The film picturised large number of people and youth participating in the civil disobedience movement. If the film was allowed to be exhibited the people might respect the civil disobedience movement, people might show sympathy towards the political ideas of Sengupta and people might lead processions against the Government. The District Magistrate suggested cancellation of the censor certificate to this film. In Madras also the performance of this film was prohibited. This news came to the notice of the West Godavari District Magistrate. He also brought this news to the notice of the Madras Government. He had prohibited the exhibition of the Cinema in the West Godavari District as per sub-section (5) of Section 7 of Cinematography Act 1918 (II of 1918). He sent a prohibitary order copy to the Madras Government.

On 18th August, 1933 the Madras Government asked the opinion of the Madras police department. The Police Commissioner reported that this film had Bombay Censor Certificate No.12476 dated 31st July, 1933 and Bengal Censor certificate No.18456 dated 31st July, 1933. So, it might be allowed to be performed in the region of Madras Government.

After all these observations the Madras Government on 11th September, 1933 agreed to allow the performance of the film in Madras Presidency. However the film was to be shown in entire India on the memorial day of Sengupta, but it was prohibited in some places on that day. In this way the object of the film was affected.

The Zamindars of Bobbili and Venkatagiri influenced the District Magistrate to prohibit the exhibition of a Telugu Film entitled Ryot Bidda in their Estates in 1939-40. So the Magistrate prohibited it. The theme of film was the unification of Ryot community. It appealed to the ryots to crush the exploitation system of Zamindars. Later on the exhibition of this Film was prohibited by the Government of Madras in Madras Presidency.

Photos

During the freedom movement photos exercised tremendous influence over the people. The fact that photos would influence the people to work for the independence of their mother country was proved during the period between 1931 to 1940.

The British Government hanged Sardar Bhagat singh, Raja Guru and Sukhadev on 23rd March, 1931. After their hanging every Indian began to feel that they had great heroes of whom they could be proud of. To get inspiration and to work in their foot-steps, the photos of the three hanged leaders were distributed throughout India. People began to keep the printed photos of these three hanged carefully. The distribution and preservation of Bhagat singh photos became a problem to British Government from 1931 to 1940.

On 20th April, 1932 photos of Bhagat singh appeared in East Godavari district. The Government gave powers to Handerson to take them into his possession. The Deputy Director, Intelligence Bureau, New Delhi in his letter No.32/R.A./32-II dated 12th January, 1932 stated that any police officer could treat the photos as unauthoirsed newssheets. So, as per Section 16 (1) of the Indian Press (Emergency Powers) Act, 1931, he might take into his possession the photos. But in the letter of the C.B. C.I.D. on 13th December, 1939, the District Magistrate of North Arcot ordered to handover the photos to concerned persons from whom they were collected. Once again the Government was subjected to confusion.

However, at last the Government came to a conclusion that they might take the photos or pictures into their possession and destroy them. The photo or picture was "a document" containing a visible representation which indirectly expresses approval of the offences of murder".

Gramaphone Records

Not only books, newspapers but also cinema songs and private songs did not escape from prohibition. Hindi gramophone record Shahidon Ki Toli number 5095, was prepared by the Star India Company, Benares. It was forfeited as per book and publications clause (c) of sub-rule (1) of rule 40 of the Defence of India Rules by United Province (U.P.) Government.

On 26th January, 1940 the United Province Government sent this information to Madras Presidency. The Madras Government also under G.O. No.354 dated 13th February 1940 implemented the same G.O. in Madras Presidency. It was published in Fort St. George Gazette.

The Andhra writers also tried to spread the freedom movement through the Gramophone records. For this purpose Sun Record company asked the Gramophone Company of India Limited, His Masters Voice, Madras to make a Gramophone record (No.N.V.233).

But, prior to this the Government proscribed the Gramophone records in Hindi, Tamil languages and also the Government issued orders not to make such records against the law established by the British Government. So, the Company wrote a letter to Government and asked the details of proscription orders.

Government of Madras wrote a letter to the Company. In response to the letter, the Company on 29th February, 1940 wrote a letter to the Government and asked for permission to make Gramophone record But the Government did not give reply to the letter. So, the Company again on 5th March 1940 wrote a letter to the Government. In response to that the Government arranged an interview with the Manager of Gramophone Record Company.

The Government examined the written scripts of songs. Andhra Raastram (Andhra State), Gandhi, Lendi Karmikulara (wake up labourers). These three songs were written by P. Suri Babu.

The content of the songs, the praise of past glory of Andhra repeatedly was not useful to the establishment of Andhra state. The entire Andhra community should be united and fight (by peaceful means) for Andhra State. In the second song the author highlighted and praised the sacrifice, and the non-violence principle of Gandhiji. In the third song the author questioned the ryots and labourers why they were living without independence and without due share of their labour and he stated that it was useless to live as subordinates.

The songs were written in moderate style of language. But the writer wrote the songs on the then problems of the people like establishment of Andhra State, Independence and to wake up of ryots and labourers. That he tried to propagate them through Granmophone records was a great thing. All these details were available in Government order No.556 dated 12th March, 1940. Whether these songs were Gramophonised or not, was not known. The details were not available.

The Government of Madras asked the script while preparing a Gramophone record by the Saraswati Stores.[39] They sent it to the Government. The first song was on propagation of Raatnam (spinning wheel). The second song was on praise of Gandhiji and Independence. The Government did not impose any restrictions on the first song, but in case of second song government of Madras imposed restrictions and communicated to the stores., "If you Gramophonised the song Government will take action under Rule 34 (7) of the Defence of India Rules". So the complete second song was not available. The Saraswati stores stopped completely the preparation of Gramophone records.

Madras Government tried to take action on Telugu song Rare Podamu, but they did not take any action. The reason was not known. Whatever it was the Gramophone reclords also created fear in the hearts of the Brirtish rulers.

During this period the writers wrote dramas with the object of educating the masses on principles of democracy and for creating unity among the masses. Some writers tried to popularise Socialist ideas through this appealing form. In addition to the political dramas the writers used Burrakatha (Street drama) to popularise national feeling among the people.

NOTES

1. P.S.R. Appa Rao, Andhra Nataka Vikasam (Telugu), p.346.
2. Government of Madras, Public (General) Department, MS. Series, Confidential, G.O. Nbo.520, Dt. 17th August, 1921.

3. Government of Madras, Public (General) Department, MS. Series, Confidential, G.O. No.792, Dt. 12th November, 1921.
4. Government of Madras, Public (General) Department, G.O.No.83, Dt. 28th January, 1922.
5. Government of Madras, Public (General) Department, MS, Series, Confidential, G.O. No.93, Dt. 1st February, 1922.
6. Government of Madras, Public (General) Department, MS, Series, Confidential, G.O.No.942, Dt.15th November, 1922.
7. Government of Madras, Public (General) Department, MS, Series, Confidential, G.O. No.839, Dt. 30th November, 1923.
8. Umrali Shah led a movement against this drama in 1923.
9. Manikonda Satyanarayana Sastry, "Krishna Zilla Jateeyodyama Parivartanam" (Telugu).
10. It originated from the Sitanagaram Asram and was published by the Andhra Yuvajana Swarajya Sabha of Rajahmundry. On the front page the slogan 'Swaraj is my birth right' was printed. At the end of the Journal the slogan 'Vandemataram' was printed. It had a circulation of about 300 copies in the early period of its existence. Later it increased to 600. The entire paper contained news and comments of the freedom movement in India.
11. It was a bi-lingual paper, published both in English and Telugu. The annual Report of the Madras Government on the Press, for the year 1928 (G.O. No.933-34 Public (confidential) dated 16th September, 1929) mentioned it as an Anglo-Telugu paper.
12. Government of Madras, Public (Confidential), G.O.No.404 Dt. 5th June, 1924.
13. In November, 1928 the Congress published certain articles entitled Lakshmi Bai of Jhansi and the war Dance (an ode in praise of Jhansi and Jhansi Lakshmi Bai (on the valour and heroism of Jhansi). It also published the life stories of many other revolutionaries to instill patriotism and courage among the youth. Articles on Bhagat Singh, Chandrasekhar Azad, V.D.Savarkar, Jatin Das and others were published. The issue of the 11th June, 1929 contained a serial feature on the lives of the advocates of bombs. While writing about the revolutionaries the paper formally condemned their violet methods but praised their valour and supreme sacrifice.
14. Government of Madras, Public Department, G.O. No.404, Dt. 5th June, 1924.
15. Government of Madras, Public (General) Department) MS. Series, G.O. No.713-14, Dt. 13th July, 1929.
16. Government of Madras, Public (General) Department, G.O.No.906, Dt. 6th September, 1929.
17. Government of Madras, Public (General) Department, G.O.No.713-14, MS. Series, Dt. 3rd July, 1929.
18. Government of Madras, Public (General) Department, G.O.No.643-A (S-12), Dt. 8th June, 1931.
19. Ibid.
20. Ibid.
21. Government of Madras, Public (General) Department, Confidential, G.O.No.643-A (S-12), Dt. 8th June, 1931.
22. Government of Madras, Public (General) Department, G.O.No.576 Dt. 19th October, 1938.
23. Edited by Jaidhir Tirumala Rao, Telugu University, Hyderabad, Published by the said University in October, 1991.

24. Andhra Provincial Ryot's Association was founded by M.B.Needu and Prof.Ranga in 1928 at Guntur, when the first Andhra Provincial Ryot's Conference was held under the Presidentshuip of B.V.Ratnam, M.L.A. It was led by the people of all political parties till 1934 when the Justicities in whose control the organisation remained in 1931-33, had found it impossible to stem the upsurge of radical elements among the peasants. Since 1934 it came to play a very prominent role in the organized life of the Andhra peasants with Prof.Ranga and his devoted band of peasant workers at its head. It was registered on the 4th June 1936 under the Act XXI of 1860 and its official Headquarters was at Nidubrole.
25. Anti-Zamindari movement gained momentum in Andhra under the leadership of N.G.Ranga. On 13th July, 1938 ryot procession started from Ichchapuram to Madras, it gained historicity. The object of the process was to explain the ryots' troubles and to protect ryot's from Zamindar's dictatorial activities. The other important participants in this procession were Jammalagadda Ramalingayya, chundi Jagannadham, Chelasani Vasudeva Rao, Pullela Syama Sundara Rao, K.S.N.Murthy, C.H.V.Rao, Gautu Lachchanna. In this procession from five hundred villages, 1100 petitions were collected. On 27th August 1938 the ryot's procession reached Madras and submitted memorandum to the then Prime Minister Rajagopala Chari. Throughout their procession for 45 days they were welcomed and encouraged by road-side villagers.
26. Government of Madras, Public (General) Department, G.O.No.576, Dt. 19th October, 1938.
27. Government of Madras, Public (general) Department), G.O.No.1464, Dt. 8th September, 1939.
28. Government of Madras, Public (General) Department, G.O.No.1464, Dt. 8th September, 1939.
29. On 16th November, 1990, Jayadhir Tirumala Rao, Telugu University, Hyderabad, interviewed Parvati Devi, the wife of Vedantam Venkata Subramanya Sastri at Kovvuru. In the interview she gave the above information. In concern with Gayopakhyanam, Gayudu was one of the kings in a mythological story in Maha Bharatam.

29a. Sthanam Narasimha Rao, Natasthanam (Telugu) p.193, The Character of Roshanara was performed by Sthanam Narasimha Rao a great stage actor of Andhra.

30. Government of Madras, Public (General) Department, MS. Series, G.O.No.1920, Dt.26th September, 1940.
31. Government of Madras, Public (General) Department, G.O. No.2049, Dt. 18th September, 1941.
32. Government of Madras, Public (General) Department, G.O. No.2049, Dt. 18th September, 1941.
33. Government of Madras, Public (General) Department, MS. Series, Confidential, G.O. No.3577, Dt. 13th December, 1944.
34. Government of Madras, Public (General) Departmenbt, MS. Series, Confidential, G.O.No.3577, Dt. 13th December,, 1944.
35. Government of Madras, Public (General) Department, MS. Series, Confidential, G.O.No.1413-A, Dt. 12th June, 1945.
36. Government of Madras, Public (General) Department, MS. Series, Confidential, G.O.No.1413-A, Dt.12th June, 1945.

37. Government of Madras, Public (General) Department, MS. Series, G.O. No.1391, Dt. 10th May, 1947.
38. Government of Madras, Public (General) Department, MS.Series, G.O.No.1391, Dt. 10th May, 1947.
39. Government of Madras, Public (General) Department, G.O. No.2153, Dt. 1st November, 1940.

7

PROSCRIBED LEFTIST LITERATURE

The Communist Party of India (CPI) was unofficially established outside India. Several Indians who were staying in Russia at the time of the Revolution along with those who had left India on Hijarat came together in Moscow and formed the CPI in 1921. Many of them came back to India. Some of them while crossing over to India were arrested at the border and kept in Peshawar jail. In 1923, they were sentenced to various terms of imprisonment.

An Indian Communist group was also formed by Indian emigrants in Germany. M.N.Roy was a leading participant in the formation of the party groups at Moscow as well as in Germany. Marxism also began to penetrate into the Indian political life in the wake of the Russian Revolution. Communist groups began to be formed in Indian industrial centers and towns. By 1923, there were Communist pockets in Bombay, Calcutta, Madras, Kanpur and Lahore. Their formation at different places signified that the ideas of marx and Lenin were spreading throughout the country. The CPI was formed in 1925. However, the CPI remained weak until 1926. But in between 1926 and 1929 the party gained considerable strength. The imprisonment of their most important leaders in the Meerut conspiracy case weakened the organization and strikes organised by them failed. In July 1934, the Communist Party was declared unlawful by the Government of India.[1] During the time of ban on Communist party, the Communists worked with Congress Socialist Party to achieve their goal.

For the formation of Congress Socialist Party many external and internal factors were responsible. The external factors were the First World War,the Bolshevik Revolution, Labour movement, Western literature and education. Internal factors were the character of the Indian National Congress, British policy, post-war economic crises, Gandhian leadership, rise of the Left Wing in the Congress, Indian Trade Union Movement, the CPI, Youth Leagues and Revolutionary Movement, Role of M.N.Roy and Jawaharlal Nehru, and Civil Disobedience Movement.

In the early 1930s the move towards the formation of a Socialist Party was made in jails during 1930-31 and 1932-34 by those who were dissatisfied with Gandhian strategy, tactics and leadership. Many of the founders of the Congress Socialist Party (CSP) were active in the youth movements of the 1920s. Almost all of them had joined the civil disobedience movement during 1930-31 and 1932-93. They were disillusioned by the Gandhi-Irwin Pact in 1931. Many of them opposed the Pact at the Karachi session of the Congress and felt frustrated by the ruthless suppression by the Government of the second phase of the movement. In jails they had the time to study and discuss Marxian and other Socialist ideas. They looked for an alternative to Gandhism and liberal nationalism. Revolutionary terrorism had already declined. Many individuals and groups were groping towards an alternative. Ultimately they came together and formed the Congress Socialist Party at Bombay on 22nd October 1934. Important founding members of this party were Jayaprakash Narayan, M.R.Masani, Ashok Mehta, Achyut Patwardhan, N.G.Gore, S.M.Joshi, M.V.Dantwala, Purushottama Tricumdas, Yusuf Meherally, and others.

Emerging as a political force in early 1930s, the CSP came to play a significant role in the Indian national movement. In particular, it contributed to the movements socio-economic radicalism and political militancy. Alongwith other left-wing individuals, groups and parties, it succeeded in making socialism the accepted creed of the youth of India during the 1930s and 1940s. Within the National Congress the left was able to command influence on important issues.

The genesis of the Communist Party in Andhra may be traced to as far back as 1934. Dissatisfied with the progress of the freedom struggle under the leadership of Mahatma Gandhi, a section of Congressmen, mostly youths, founded the Congress Socialist Party in that year to steer the Congress on the line of Socialism. These youths received inspiration from Marxist philosophy. [2] Communist literature flowed abundantly into the country from Russia and the definite switch-over by a few Congressmen also could be attributed to the impact of this literature. For instance, D.Chechayya, a leading Communist, says that Dr.Sherwood Eddy's 'The Challenge of Russia and Russia Today' caught his imagination and converted him into the Communist creed.[3] He further mentioned that C. Rajeswara Rao, another Communist leader, was largely influenced by Frierich Engels Anti-Dihring. [4] The books of John Strachy, Edgar snow, Maxim Gorky and the writings of Lin Yutang and Pearl Buck were extremely popular among the youth.[5]

The first Andhra Provincial Congress Socialist Party's conference was held at Rajahmundry in 1936 and there arose a split within themselves. One group which had rightist leanings was represented by Rangasai and K. Linga Raju. The other, the leftists, who later became Communists was led by P.Sundarayya. During 1936-38 the Andhra Communists tried to organise strikes on the agricultural front in Nellore, Guntur, Krishna and Godavari districts under the leadership of P. Sundarayya and J. Ramalingayya. They purused the Leninist tactics of splitting up peasantry and agricultural proletariat after the Russian fashion.

As stated above, from the time of the establishment of the Congress Socialist Party in 1934, number of Telugu writers also were influnced by Marxist philosophy and began to propagate it through their writings. Therefore large number of Telugu books on Communism were published. They began to create hatred and contempt among the people of the country against the rich and the British Government. So the British Government, to continue their exploitation and rule in India, introduced a number of repressive measures. As part of it they proscribed number of Telugu books on Communism.

"NETI RUSSIA"

The first book on Leftist literature proscribed in entitled "Neti Russia" [6] (Modern Russia) written by Narla Venkateswara Rao, printed at Andhra Vani Press, Bezwada and published by Narlavaru, Kowtharam, Krishna district. The book is devoted to a description of the political, slocial, economic and cultural life prevailing in Russia under the "present" Soviet regime. The book is calculated to publish what the Communist Party has been able to achieve in Russia and what Communism is capable of achieving. The author gives various references and profusely quotes authorities like H.G.Wells, Bertrand Russel, Bernard Shaw, John Strachey A.D.,Monzie and C.E.M.Joad, etc. and gives excerpts from some of their books. The book is presented in an analytical, appealing and readable manner; the style is simple. It also contains photographs of Lenin, Stalin, Trotsky and Litvinoff.

The book begins with the advent of Lenin and the revolution and the seizing of political power by Lenin and the revolutionary party overthrowing Kerensky regime. The author gives a picturesque and striking description of Lenin's character and personality saying that he stood for stern justice and the triumph of Communism unaffected by personal relationships, prejudices, etc. He then sums up the implications of the membership of the Communist Party.

The author says that the duty of Indians is to know everything about Russians' endeavour because "there are at present only two movements in the world, Communism and Fascism". There are but two leaders Lengin and Mussolini. Indians must follow one of these two movements and one of these two leaders. Otherwise Indian nation and civilization already half-dead sink into oblivion.

At the beginning of this work the author has given a detailed account of political, social, economic and cultural life of the ten Russia with a view to bring to the knowledge of the Indians and through it he tries to inculcate an awareness of the disparities which exist in India when compared to the then existing Russia.

The author quotes famous authorities to support the system of Communism. The book also contains the photos of famous Communist leaders. The displaying of photos in the books is also a technique to attract the people and to create inspiration among the people. So the author used it in his book.

He also appreciated the introduction of five year plans in Russian administration and its results, the measures which were taken to remove illiteracy, jail administration of Russia, the formation of Soviet Union by the indpendent states and their rights to remain in the Union or two leave when they desired, and criticised the miserable life of the prisoners in Indian jails. Such a Soviet society the author wanted to establish in Indian soil.

The Government ordered to forfeit this book Neti Russia and all the documents containing copies, reprints or translations of or extracts from the said book on the ground that it contains matter of the nature described in Section 4 (1) of the Indian Press (Emergency Powers) Act, 1931 (Act XXIII of 1931) as amended by Section, 16 of the Criminal Law Amendment Act 1932. hence it was forfeited by the Madras Government.[7]

Life of Lenin and the Evolution of Russia (Article)

The second work on the aforesaid literature is a Telugu weekly newspaper entitled the Krishna Patrika[8] edited, printed and published by Kota Subba Rao at the Kistna Swadeshi :Press, Masulipatam, Krishna District. In its issue dated the 14th July, 1934, it published an article entitled "Life of Lenin and the Evolution of Russia."

The article contained passages such as the following: After his victory Lenin made a proclamation. In it he said that people should never leave these mean rich people. They were as it were young snakes. Indescribable were the atrocities perpetrated by them against labourers, peasants and people. When the downtrodden people had the power of legislation in their hands, they could kill the rich people who were the freebooters and robbed the poor. The rich people alone were responsible for the many hardships faced by the leaders of the peasants. It was on account of the dirty activity of the rich people that thousands of youth were hanged in Russia, that thousands of them were deported to Siberia, that thousands of Russian mothers lost their sons and that many women were obliged to become widows.

Lenin had suggested that people should not forget those who sacrificed their lives for the sake of Russia and those brethren who had undergone their sentences of transportation in Siberia, expecting death at every moment. Lenin questioned how Russian people could afford to forget the heroic women who had become widows as a result of their having offered their husbands as a sacrifice to the country. Further he suggested people should not forget those scenes of flogging administered on the hands of labourers who were made to stand naked in the very hot sun of summer and should not forget the scenes of aeroplanes raining bombs and gunshots upon Russian people.

Therefore Lenin said that the atrocities perpetrated against unarmed and starving labourers and peasants should be duly retaliated., Money, land and wealth all these were the property of labourers and peasants, and nobody should exercise any control over them. People should prepare themselves to secure powers which were their birthright., Even the mightiest forces in the world had to bow down their heads before labourers' and peasants' unbounded capabilities.

Mahatma Lenin was born to protect labourers and pesants in Russia from the atrocities perpetrated by the Government of the Czars. He left the world after achieving his object.

In this work the writer described the proclamation of Lenin after the establishment of the Communist form of Government. In it Lenin criticised the atrocities of the rich on peasants and labourers. He eulogised the sacrifices of the downtrodden classes in the crushing the Czar Government. He suggested to the people not to forget the sacrifices of the people, those who lost their lives for the establishment of Communist form of Government in Russia. He appealed to the peasants and labourers to recognise their strength and safeguard their rule for ever. The intention of the write in the publication of this article was to create awareness among the peasants and labourers in India and to eliminate their hardships through the establishment of their rule.

The Madras Government thought that this article attempted to create class war between labourers, peasants and rich people. Therefore the Governor in Council in exercise of the powers conferred by Section 19 of the Indian Press (Emergency Powers) Act, 1931. (act XXIII of 1931) declared it to be forfeited, [9] all copies wherever found of the issue, dated the 14th July, 1934 and all other documents containing copies, reprints or translations of or extracts from the said article in as much as it contains matter of the nature described in Section 4 (1) of the said Act as amended by Section 16 of the Criminal Law Amendment Act, 1932 (Act XXIII of 1932).

Samrajyavadamu

The third work on aforesaid literature Samrajyavadamu[10] (Imperialism), is stated to be a Telugu translation of Lenin's treatise on imperialism. It was written by 'A Communist', printed at the Panduranga Press, Eluru, West Godavari district. It was published by the 'Adarsa Grandhamandali of Elamarru, Gudivada Taluk, Krishna District as the 9th of their series of publications knows as the Adarsa Granda Mala. Lenin's treatment of imperialism is recommended as being impartial scientific and glowing tribute is paid to him. The capitalists are making profits as they like, having improved industries. If they are confronted with competition from any foreign country, they would deceive the people by means of big speeches urging that the country should be protected from foreign assassins, national efficiency maintained and peace established in the country. They would impose duties on foreign imports and raise tariff walls for the country's protection in the representative legislatures. Thus, they would not hesitate to carry on plunder both at home and abroad having established their dictatorship all over the country in this manner, these plunderers would goad the people to work for their own selfish ends. Nominally they say that the country belongs to the people, that the people's prosperity lies in the country's well being and that the country's progress alone constitutes the peoples improved standard of living.

It is obvious that the whole country is ruled not by institutions known as representative councils but by banks. The economic effect of imperialism has been to intensify the exploitation of workers and peasants which was brought about by capitalism. Labour regiments are increasing. While money is accumulating in heaps on the one hand, the wails of hunger are rending the air on the other.

Some countries in the world have advanced industrially while some others have remained very poor without any industries at all. The latter are known as uncivilized countries. Industrial countries have invested capital in such uncivilised countries and have freely been plundering the latter's mineral resources anriches. They would construct railways in such countries (not for the convenience of travel of the people) for the promotion of their own business. They would build forts. Having occupied the country by means of the army, they would use it in many ways. There is an important motive in exporting money to foreign countries. Militarism is becoming dominant in every state. This is the reason why the establishment of empires is going on unchecked.

The biggest capitalist countries namely Britain, France, Germany, Italy, America and japan are alleged to have already divided the whole world, among themselves and the sole concern of each of them now is to protect itself against every contingency of aggression by others by increasing its own armaments at a huge cost. It is asserted that international trade associations formed by capitalists can never quench the thirst for profits among their founders and can never lead to the establishment of permanent peace in the world "as hoped by some writers" and that world wars are inevitable.

In this work the aurthor appeals to the working class to recognise the cost of their labour and loss of their energy. He bitterly criticised the imperialist exploitation and suggested to the working class to establish a Communist form of Government to solve their problems.

On the basis of the report furnished by the Telugu translator the Government, felt that the book seeks to establish that imperialism is the last phase in the development of capitalism. Indirectly Communism is held out as the only panacea for the evils of imperialism.

So the book Samrajyavadamu and all other documents containing copies, reprints, or translations of or extracts from the said book in as much as it contained matter of the nature described in Section 4 (1) (d) of the India Press (Emergency Powers) Act 1931 (XXIII of 1931) as amended by Section 16 of the Criminal Law Amendment Act 1932 (XXIII of 1932) were forfeited by the Madras Government. [11]

Amma

The fourth work on aforesaid literature entitled Amma[12] (Mother) is said to be a translation of the book Mother written by Maxim Gorky (Maxim Gorky was the pen name of Aleksei Maksimouich Peshkov) of Russia. Charles Edward Russels wrote the forward to Mother. [13] In 1934 it came out in Telugu, translated by Krovvidi Lingaraju Krovvidi made his translation in prison after being convicted for his activities in the freedom movement. It was printed at the Sri Lakshmi press, Masulipatam and published under editorship of Gadde Lingaiah Choudhari as the tenth production of a series known as the Adarsa Grandha Mandali, Elamarru,

Gudivada Taluk, Krishna district. It has gone through seven reprints since 1934. It is this translation that earned Lingaraju and title "Andhra Gorky'.[14]

The summary of the novel is as follows:- In the beginning of the novel the author vividly described the daily life of the workers particularly on Sundays. Mikhail Vlassov was a hairy, sullen mechanic. He was the best mechanic at the factory and the strongest man in the settlement. Palagea Nilovna was his wife. People were afraid of him, because of his cruelty. He always called his wife a bitch. She was being beaten by her drunken husband. He spoke little and son-of a bitch was his favourite epithet. He used it every where. He died due to ill-health. In his life time he never took care about his son Pavel Vlassov and did not talk to him. On a Sunday, two weeks after the death of his father, Pavel came home dead drunk. Mother suggested to her son not to drink liquors. Time brought change in him. He would read them only the sly and always hide them when he had finished.

After two years of strange, silent life, full of obscure thoughts and ever increasing apprehension, one evening Pavel's mother asked him what he was reading all the time. He replied that he was reading forbidden books. They were forbidden because they tell the truth about workingmen. They were printed on the sly, in secret, and if the Government found him with them, they would put him in jail, he added. Mother asked him why he should do that he replied that he wanted to know the truth. Mother was frightened when she heard these hard, ringing words.

Natasha, Andrei, Nakhodka, Nikolai Ivanovich, Nikolai Vesovshchikov, Soshenka, Ivan Bukin, Yakov Somov Feodor Mazln, some of them local people and other from nearest town, met in Pavel's house and discussed the then prevailing social and economic conditions. Pavel said that the workers should prove that they were not inferior to others. Khokhol said that "we must build a bridge across the swamps of this rotten life to the future kingdom of human brotherhood. That's the task facing us comrades".

In the course of their discussion they announced that "We are socialists" and declared that "we know no tribes or nations, only comrades, only enemies. All workingmen are our comrades; all rich men, all Governments are our enemies".

The little house on the outskirts of the settlement attracted peoples attention, its walls had already been carefully examined by dozens of suspicious eyes. The sported wings of rumour fluttered anxiously above it. The people advised Mother to keep an eye on her son's activities.

People in the settlement began to speak about the socialists who were distributing leaflets written in blue ink. These leaflets harshly criticised the management of the factory, told about strikes in Petersburg and in the south of Russia, and called the workers to unite in the defence of their own interests. These leaflets were distributed by Pavel. The police inspector searched Pavel's house and arrested Nikolai, Nahodka, Vesovshchikov, Busin, Sam Sam Dilov, Somov and five others. Mother visited the jail to see Andrei and others.

The settlement paid more and more attention to Pavel's little grew house. This attention was tinged with suspicious and unconscious hostility, but a trusting curiosity was also aroused. Gradually people came to respect Pavel who spoke so simply and daringly.

The new director of the factory decided to drain swamp in order to extract the peat and make profit from the land. On the pretext of doing this for the sake of improving living conditions of the workers, the director gave an order to deduct one kopek from each ruble paid in wages for the draining of the swamp.

The senior workers Sizov and Makhotin and others requested Pavel to represent this issue to the director. Pavel write a note on kopek and entrusted the work to his Mother to deliver the note to their newspaper and said that it was absolutely essential that the story about the kopek got into the next issue. This was the first task, her son had ever entrusted to her.

At factory before gathering of workers Pavel said "Comrades, workers were the first to work but last to get consideration". No body cares for us. "We never win a lot for ourselves until we realise that we're all comrades, a family of friends lightly bound by the single desire to fight for our rights." The workers did not declare strike as instructed by Pavel. He failed to achieve success in kopek issue. But he won particular prestige after the incident with the "Swamp Kopek".

The police officer searched the house and took Pavel to jail. Mother suffered because of Pavel's arrest. After his arrest, Mother began to take interest in the movement. She understood much of what comrades said and stood for. She felt that they had discovered the true source of human sorrow and she agreed with most of their claims. Formerly she had never felt that anyone needed her, but now she clearly saw that many people needed her and this was a new and pleasant thing which made her lift her head. She carried the leaflets regularly to the factory, looking upon this as her duty. After some time Pavel was released from jail and Mother felt very happy.

Preparations were begun for celebrating May day. Leaflets explaining the significance of this holiday were scattered through the factory and settlement.

Almost everynight appeals to the workers to take part in the May day celebrations were posted on fences, and everyday they were found at the factory. May day procession was led by Pavel, Andhrei Feodor Mazin and Mother also participated in it. At the procession Andhrei criticised the exploitation of the rich and said, "In the world there are two people one is the rich and other is the poor. The police force would also join with us if they realise the exploitation of the rich". Pavel cried, "long live workers class", and in response to it hundreds of voices roared back"long live the Social Democratic Workers Party". They sang songs Pavel, Andrei and some others were arrested by the police.

Nikolai Invanovich was one of the comrades living in town. Nikolai entrusted to Mother and Sophia, his eldest sister, the work of handing over some books and newspapers to Rybin (one of the comrades working in a village). Passing through the streets of the town and the fields they arrived at their destination on the third day. They met Rybin, Yegim Yakov, Ignat Savely and conversed many things and handed over the books and newspapers.

Natasha took a teaching position in a school connected with a weaving mill and Mother began supplying her with illegal Pamphlets, proclamations and newspapers.

She continued her active participation in the activities of socialists. Several times a month she disguised herself as a nun or a peddler of laces and homespun linen, a well-to-do woman or a pious pilgrim and wandered through the gubernia with a bag over her shoulder or a suitcase in her hand. In trains, on boats, in hotels and inns she was the same calm, simple person who spoke the first word to strangers, fearlessly drawing attention to herself with her sociability and the self-assurance of a person who had seen a lot in her time.

One day Mother arrived at Niholscoy, big village, to handover leaflets and newspapers to Rybin. But he was arrested and beaten by the police. Before the crowd Rybin cried, "Peasants, everything comes from peasants. Peasants are the greatest force on this earth and you have no rights. Peasants have only the right to die of starvation" and he questioned"why should you go on starving to death. Once you get your freedom, you'll have bread and justice. That's what, Farewell, good people". Mother saw and heard of what happened there.

Mother said that "All those who have a life, all those who are worn out by violence and need, all those who have been ground down by the rich and the servants of the rich-all those should go forth to join the ones who perish in jail and give themselves to deadly torture for the sake of the people. With no thought themselves, they point the way to happiness for all people." She was happy to be doing something she had long wanted to do. She herself was telling the people the truth.

Mother thought of the innumerable villages cringing so humbly against the earth, and of the people who were secretly awaiting the advent of jusrtice and of the thousand of people who spent all of their lives at senseless work, unprotestingly, without hoping for anything better.

Mother said that "we need to assign special people to work in the villages. People we don't have enough of them.. We need hundreds". Mother felt the workers merged into one great fearless individual who was moving slowly but surely over the earth clearing away the century old mildew of lies in order to show people the clear and simple truth of life. And this great truth renascent would summon all without discrimination, would promise everyone emanicipation from greed and spite and falsehood-three monsters terrorizing and enslaving the whole world with their cynical force.

The police arrested the five ryot comrades including Mihail. Ignat escaped from them before arrest.

In response to Nikolai's letter Mother secretly received a letter from Pavel in jail. He wrote, "we shall not attempt an escape comrades. We cannot, None of us can. We would lose our self-respect if we did". He suggested to them to extent co-operation to Rybin to escape from jail. So with the assistance of the comrades Rybin escaped from jail.

To hear the judgement, Mother attended the court Pavel Andrei (Khokhol) Feodor Mazin, Gusev brothers, Somoslov, Bukin, somov and five others were presented before the judge. Pavel said before judges "there are no criminals and judges here" "There are only captives and victors".

Pavel on behalf of his comrades said "I shall attempt to explain to you those things which you have not understood. The prosecutor has called our demonstration under the banner of Social-Democracy a revolt against the ruling poswer, and he has at all times looked upon us as people trying to overthrow the Czar. We do not consider the monarchy the only chain bonding our country, it is only the first and not the most accessible chain from which it is our duty to free the people". Further he criticised the exploitation of rich and said "our slogans are simple enough 'Down with private property' 'All means of production in the hands of the people', 'All power in the hands of the people', 'Work is the obligation of all'. From this you can see that we are not mere rebels. "We are revolutionaries and will continue to be so as long as some only boss and others only work. We are against the society whose interests you have been ordered to defend. We are its irreconcilable enemies, as well as yours, and no reconciliation between us is possible until we have won our fight". They were sentenced to exile to Siberia "Long live the Russian workers" came a loud cry. Mother smiled and pressed people's hands while her throat contracted with tears of joy.

The activists of the movement decided to print and distribute the speech of Pavel in the court. Meanwhile the police arrested Nikolai. So some of the comradses cyclostyled his speech. The distribution of the leaflets in the village was taken up by the Mother.

Mother said, "our children are marching over the earth. That is what I understand. Our children are marching over the earth, over the whole earth from all corners, to one goal. It is like a new God being born to people. Everything for all; all for everything; that is how I understand it. In very truth we are all comrades, all kindred spirits, all children of one mother, who is truth".

Mother reached railway station and got into the train. But she was caught by a spy. He said, "You are a thief". She replied, "I am no thief. Yesterday there was a trial of political offenders, and among them was my son Pavel Vlassov. He made a speech. I am taking it to the people; they can read it and know the truth".

She waved the leaflets in the air and tossed them into the crowd. The Mother saw them snatch up the leaflets and stuff them inside their coats and into their pockets.

Further she said, "poverty, hunger disease, that's what people get for their work. Everything is against us. All of our lives, day after day, we give our last ounce of strength to our work, always dirty, always fooled, while others reap all the joy and benefits, holding us in ignorance like dogs on a chain – one don't know anything. And in fear we're afraid of everything. Our lives are just one long dark night".

Someone struck her in the breast and she fell on the bench. She cried, "Don't let anything frighten you. Nothing could be more bitter than the lives you live".

They pushed her in the back, in the neck., beat her over the shoulders and the head. Again she cried "Not even an ocean of blood can down the truth". A gendarme seized her by the throat and began to choke her.

In this work the author gave a detailed account of the day to day life of hardships of the working class with a view to emphasize the disparities between them and the capitalists. He encouraged the working class to read the Communist books to know the truth written for their awakening. The author gave a call to all workingmen to unite to solve their problems and to establish their Raj. He encouraged writing and distribution of leaflets and pamphlets among the working class to let them know the nature of exploitation by the capitalists and to unite the labourers to fulfil their interests. The author depicted Pavel as an exemplary person to be followed by others. The Mother began to enter into the propagation of workers' cause with the initiation of her son. The author also described the hardships of the peasants.

He appealed to the police force to join with working class and informed them how the police force was utilised by the rich to safeguard their exploitation. Mother played an important role in the propagation of revolutionary activities for the interests of the working class. The intention of the writer is to awaken the peasants on the Communist principles and unite them with industrial working class. Mother sacrificed her life for the cause of working class. The hope of the writer is to make women to actively participate in the struggle for working class independence and to establish Socialist form of Governmment.

The novel Mother which portrays the awakening of political consciousness in a common worker, revealed to the Indian people the finest tracts of the Russian national character. It is an expression of Gorky's faith in man's eventual triumph over evil and his better future.

The Government of Madras felt that the said book advocates violent revolution as a means for the establishment of the Communist rule. As the said book contained matter of the nature described in section 4 (1) of the Indian Press (Emergency Powers) Act, 1931, as amended by Section 16 of the Criminal Law amendment Act, 1932 (XXIII of 1932), in exercise of the powers conferred by section 19 of the Indian Press (Emergency Powers) Act, 1931 (XXII of 1931) the Governor in Council declared the book to be forfeited.[15]

In August 1937, Krovvidi Linga Raju requested the Government to life the proscription. The Congress Government which was in power after considering all the relevant aspects cancelled forfeiture order on the said book.[16]

Karmika Bhajanavali

The fifth book on the aforesaid literature, entitled Karmika Bhajanavali was edited by Swami Narayanananda, and published in memory of late Uppu Peddhanagasangappa who worked as secretary for Youth Association, Nandyal and died at the age of 32, on 31st June, 1934. It was printed at the Pandu Ranga Press, Nandyal on 28th March 1936 and published on 1st April 1936.[17] It is a compilation of songs by various writers. The style is simple and attractive.

The book contained fourteen songs written respectively by different authors. The songs Aarti, Deenulu, Bhagyavantula Pettanemu were written by Uriti Suryanarayana Rao, C.H.P. Choudhari and P.C.Choudari. the songs Maajanda, Karmika Sodara, Coolipata, Coolie, Kadupumanta, Geyam, Kalado-ledo (is there God or not) written by Narla Venkateswara Rao. Anyaya Kalamu (injustice time) written by Garimella Satyanarayana. Mringivestunnaru from Raitu Bhajanavali and Devudunte written by Vasireddy Nageswara Rao, taken from Raitu Bhajanvali or from the now defunct Communist journal Prabha of Masulipatam. This book also contains another song Samatadharmam (Communism). It was taken from the novel Malapalli of Unnava Lakshmi Narayana.

In these songs the writers depicted the miserable conditions under which the labour class was living; they also criticised the rich class for exploiting the labour class for their well-being. The rich were leading a luxurious and careless life, whereas the labour class had to work for their masters without getting their due. The labourers were treated as slaves and starvation for them was a regular feature. For this purpose some of the writers suggested to the labour class to unite and fight for their rights, even by resorting to strikes.

In the song Samatadharmamu (Communism) the writer, through the character Takkella Jaggadu, traced the emergence of distinctions based on money and status and stressed the necessity of establishing Samatadharmamu. The following is gist of the song: At the beginning of time all were brothers. All forests and beasts, the four oceans, mountains, rivers, ponds, brooks, crops, vegetables, fruit and houses were the property of all people irrespective of differences in status. There was enough to eat and spare for others. The world was getting on without any such difference as 'Mine' and 'yours'. All were equal servants without any difference of high and low. There were no differences at all of master and servant. No gradations of rich and poor raised their heads. No ailments due to indigestion and hunger made their appearance then. Evil days of Mammon worship did not set in. Poor people did not cringe before the rich for alms.

The blind and the lame were not hard put for want of food and clothing. Malas (Adi Andhras) did not undergo abject starvation day and night. Doras (Rulers) were not rolling intoxicated in low pleasures, and they did not allow themselves to be under the delusion that it would be beneath their dignity to do any manual labour at all.

All the principles of Kritayuga (the Golden Age) have been upset and the Kaliguga (the present Age) has become ripe with sin. Sinful tenets have spread all over the world. Owing to the prevalence of commotion, evils, competition and unrest everywhere, it has become difficult to lead a righteous life. All the money in the world has passed into the hands of misers. "A miser having become an Emperor, he would be ruling the world". Each person says that everything belongs to him. The days when all people said that everything was their common property having gone by the children of millionaries are heirs to huge properties, reversionary rights extending to generations together. Rich people would only be sitting comfortably without work and without thinking of the welfare of others. All the poor have become the slaves of the rich. They toil day and night for a morsel of food and the employers are not satisfied with the amount of work turned out by them.

Therefore the coolies should realise there is value to their labour. The coolies should be united and fight to seek real value for their labour, but the fight should be in the form of non-cooperation. It is a great weapon in the world. "Give up doubts and take a vow to establish Communism in the world; you would then be able to safely install the justice of Kritayuga (the Golden Age) all over the world".

It was proscribed on 22nd October 1936 inter-alia on the following grounds:

1. that it promoted feelings of enmity or hatred between the rich capitalists and the poor workers.
2. dissemination of contents of proscribed documents, that it contained passages from the Telugu book entitled Malapalli. It was proscribed by the Madras Government part I and II in G.O. No.396 Public Department dated the 14th May 1923 and part III in G.O. No.620 Public Department, dated the 8th August, 1923 but later the author was allowed to publish a revised edition as amended and approved in G.O. No.307, Public Department, dated the 30th March 1928. This revised edition was also proscribed in G.O. No.1203, Home Department the 3rd July, 1936. The book, under review only contained passages from the revised edition and was published before the revised edition was proscribed. Dissemination of contents of proscribed documents is punishable with imprisonment which may extend to six months or with fine or with both as per Government order.

3. that it reproduced some of the songs already published in the defunct Communist Telugu Journal Prabha of Masulipatam.

The Government also warned the keeper of the press for printing this book.[18]

The Krishna District Youth conference held at Moova on 27th august, 1937 has passed a resolution requesting the Government to remove the ban on certain Telugu books. One of the book was Karmika Bhajanavali.

According to Public (General) Department, Miscellaneous Series, Confidential, G.O.No.2171, dated 13th November, 1937, forfeiture orders were cancelled on the ground "There being no incitement to violence, the question is reduced to this, shall we put a ban on this book of songs merely on the ground that it verisifies the talk, which cannot be stopped of labour being exploited by the rich". The said Government decided that these books in particular would not materially add to the mischief nor a ban on them reduce the propaganda of hatred against the rich.

Karl Marx Upadesamulu

The next work on above said literature, entitled Karl Marx Upadesamulu[19] (The teachings of Karl Marx) was a Telugu translation of Lenin's The Teachings of Karl Marx. The Telugu translator of the book was Mahidara Jaganmohan Rao. It was the publication No.6 of Viswa Sahityamala and was printed at the Sree Lakshmi Printing Works, Jagannaickpur, Cocanada. Lenin's "The Teachings of Karl Marx", was publuished by Martin Lowrance Ltd. As Volume I of the Little Lenin Library. The book in English is a prohibited publication.

The chapters entitled – the Editor's Preface, Life of Karla Marx, Marx Teachings, Philosophic Materialism, Dialectics, Materialist Concep-tion of History. Class Struggle, Marx Economic Doctrine, Socialism and Tactics of the class struggle of the proletariat are translations of the corresponding chapters of the English book. The chapter on bibliography of Marxism in the English book is omitted in the Telugu adaptation.

In the chapter entitled "Editor's Preface" the author of the Telugu translation added his own opinion in the Telugu book. The added paragraph is as follows: "We can state that books of this type are not available in Telugu. Need it be mentioned that efforts should be made to freely publish books of this type in our languages. Unless such valuable scientific treatises are published and are accessible to the masses, there can be no salvation for us from our present deplorable condition. We deasire that youth should not mererly read these books for pleasure, but study them with zeal and decide on what they should do".

A number of chapters were thought to be containing objectionable matter. The chapter on Class struggle contains translations of extracts from the Communist Manifesto. These extracts stressed the singnificance of the proletariat and stated that "the proletariat alone is really revolutionary". It criticised the Capitalists for exploiting the labourers. It also forecast "a progressive dimunition in the number of Capitalist magnates" and "a steady intensification of the wrath of the working class."

In another chapter Capitalism was criticised as a system which while improving the system of production contributed to the ruin of the producers. The various stages of "class war" were also described in the book.

In the book there were also critical observations regarding "the state" and its ultimate removal" by Socialism. The state is described as a specific system organised for the purpose of repression. The existing Government of those days was characterised "as a Government of Capitalist looters", who exploit labourers. By destroying classes Socialsm wlould remove the above described "State".

The need to enlist peasants into the Communist movement in agricultural countries was also urged in the book.

It is evident from the foregoing passages that the object of the translator is not merely to present this book as one of academical interest but to urge the readers to put these Communist principles into practice.

The said book contained martter of the nature described in Section 4 (1) of the India Press (Emergency Powers) Act, 1931 as amended by Section 16 of Criminal Law amendment Act, 1932 (Act XXIII of 1932). Therefore the Madras Government forfeited[20] the said book and all other documents containing copies, reprints or translations of or extracts from the said book.

Russia Viplavamu:

The seventh work of the Leftist proscribed literature entitled Russia Viplavamu, 1905[21] was the 11th publication of the series in Telugu of Viswa Sahitayamala of Munganda, Amalapur Taluk, East Godavari District. It was printed at Srinivasa Press, Rajahmundry. It is stated to be a translation of Mahidhara Jaganmohan Rao of the English book Russia Revolution, 1905 olf "the Little Lenin Library Series", Edited and Published by Mahidara Krishna Mohan Rao of Munganda.

The book comprised one lecture delivered on the 22nd January, 1917 at a conference of young workers held in Zurich and six essays contributed to Russian newspapers between the 31st January 1905 and 11th September, 1906 by Lenin on the Russian Revoltuion of 1905. The articles contained in this book were written during and after the period of the revolution. They would afford invaluable help in devising projects and in the matter of practical working. Though 'in times of peace' no marked difference may appear to exist between the programmes of the various parties from the ordinary view point, this difference would become evident during revolution. These articles were helpful in enabling one to understand how all other parties except the revolutionary party become reactionary parties, as the fight progresses from one stage to another.

The book started with a graphic description of the huge Russian workers' strike and the procession to the Czar's palace in St.Petersburg and the subsequent opening of fire on the procession by the Russian Government military forces under the Czar's personal direction on the 22nd January, 1905 known as the Bloody Sunday. The book explained the value of economic and political strikes in preparing the Proletariat for revolution and the need for well-organized armed fighting, for the ultimate overthrow of the existing autocratic Government and the reasons for the failure of the Revolution of 1905. It advocated the unification of the Revolutionary Social Democratic Party with traditional revolutionary Bourgeois Democracy and openly urged 'summary murder' by the revolutionist party of all the civil, police and military officers in Government employ whenever the latter should fall into its hands. Lenin characterised the revolution of 1905 as a bourgeois democratic revolution and attributed the subsequent revolutions in Turkey, Persia and China only to its influence on the people of those countries.

Lenin wrote that the provision of a well-organized militia of the People's Revolutionary Party in any country was generally a prerequisite for the attainment of independence. The main support for independence lied in the armed masses. The working class should wear arms. "it is only when the workers are prepared to carry on strikes and revolution and show their readiness to fight, the (Government) military would be in a dilemma and the (Government)soldiers would realize the self-deception they had been practising". The soldiers would at once turn against the very same devilish Government, the very same cruel demons, on whose behalf they had tormented unarmed workers. Women and children would join the side of the people. The Petersburg rebellion would lead to a better disciplined and dynamic revolution. It was a stepping stone to that revolution. The Government may succeed in putting off temporarily the day of the revolution to some future date.

Further he wrote that the revolutionists would have an opportunity organize all revolutionaries into regiments and to broadcast throughout the country the story of Petersburg revolution which was started by the workers of Petersburg. Then only would all the workers give up their respective jobs, leave mills and factories, collect arms and join the fight. The whole country and the entire population of ryots, workers and poorer classes in every town and village would resound with slogans of the war of independence. Revolutionary organizations would spring up in every factory and in every ward of a town and the revolutionary populace would destroy all the departments of the Czar's Government and summon a Constitutent Assembly. The immediate duty of all revolutionaries belonging to the various parties in the country was to arm the workers and the masses, rally together all the forces of revolution for the purpose of destroying Government officials and institutions. The Russian workers have started with great courage the task of destroying the Emperor Czar. It was a milestone of change in the world's history. The Revolution of 1905 would render the task of other nations in other countries easy.

The workers could never forget the power to which the Czar yielded. It was by application of force of their power of organization, by their power of union, by their own boldness and courage that they were able to obtain a small bit of paper from the Czar, a shadow of independence called the Manifesto. Workers should utilize all the additional privileges conferred by the Czar's Manifesto, organize workers meetings and decide there how strikes should be conducted and how workers should carry on agitation for the release of all prisoners.

The people must carry on an armed rebellion with firm determination and intense force. A peaceful strike by itself was not enough to secure success in the fight and an armed fight must be carried on by the people fearlessly and mercilessly. A tremendous propaganda should be carried on among the masses about the need for an armed fight. The methods for the manufacture of bombs on a large scale should be taught to workers' regiments.

Lenin commented that in 1881 Empoeror Alexander II was murdered by the terrorists. They showed self-sacrifice of a very high order and captivated the world by their acts of daring and methods of violent fighting. Whether directly or indirectly they lent support to the education of the Russian people in revolution, though they failed to incite a revolution of the people.

Lenin wrote that the Ryots used to gather in groups to discuss their conditions and all of them were gradually drawn into the revolutionary fight. Formed themselves into hugged gangs they started an agitation to rebel against Zamindars. They looted their zamins and buildings, carried away paddy and other food-stuffs, burnt the buildings, killed the police and placed all the big Zamindars under the control of the people.

The summary of the Telugu Translator was that the book aimed at stirring up the peasants and ryots against the landed aristocracy and pointed out that the salvation of the peasantry lied in strong agitation and open rebellion against Zamindars. The book aimed at a violent overthrow of the Government and the then order of society and advocated for this purpose militant action such as armed revolution and mass action culminating in armed insurrection.

The C.I.D. reported that the ban under the Sea Customs Act on the importation into India of certain types of Communist literature did not in itself authorise action against translations of such literature made in India. Action against such publications could be taken only under the Press Act or under Section 99-A of Criminal Procedure Code.

In exercise of the powers conferred by Section 19 of the Indian Press (Emergency Powers) Act 1931 (XXIII of 1931) the book would fall with in the Section 4 (1) of the Indian Press (Emergency Powers) Act, 1931 as amended by Section 16 of Criminal Law Amendment Act 1932 (Act XXIII of 1932). The Government of Madras considered that the book contained passages tending to incite armed rebellion and the commission of offences involving violence and that it was expressly published to serve as a help in devising programmes and in working them out in practice. Therefore the Government directed that all copies of the said book, wherever found, and all other documents containing copies, reprints or translations of or extracts from it to be forfeited.[22]

The District Magistrate, East Godavari, as per Government order warned the keeper of the press and cautioned the keeper that action will be taken under Section 3 (3) of the India Press (Emergency Powers) Act 1931 if he again printed or published matter of the nature described in Section 4 (1) of the said Act.

ANNA

The eighth work of the aforesaid literature entitled Anna[23] is a Telugu translation of Barricades in Berlin, which is presumably an English rendering of the original German work. Telugu book Anna was printed at Sree Rama Press of Messers P. Prakasa Rao and Bros, Rajahmundry in 1938. It was written and published by Darbha Sri Ramamurthi of Bhimavaram, West Godavari district as publication No.1 of "Proletarian Series".

The author of the English edition was Claw Nue Cranz. To inspire the readers the Telugu translator Darbha Sree Ramamurthi has given a brief life history of the English author Claw Nue Cranz in the Preface. Therefore I am presenting a few lines of the life history of Cranz. He was born in a rich family. He took an active part in the youth movement even in his boyhood. He was a volunteer in 1914 and served for four and half years in the war. He came to know of Socialism for the first time in his life, in the summer of 1919 from Mr.Hugo Hassi. There after he read many books. Having tried a number of professions, he became a Communist between 1923-1925 when Communism was prohibited in Germany. Subsequently he was on the editorial staff of Weltuamia Bend (an evening newspaper of Berlin labourers). Working as its editor, he rendered useful services to the revolutionary workers' Party. Subsequently he stayed in Russia for a long time, and returned to Berlin where he was working as a labourer. He had considerable experience of the revolutionary movement. His writings depict the stages of workers' classwar and serve as models.

The translator's foreward states that though the book is written in the form of a novel, it depicts real characters and is based on actual occurances. It illustrates certain stages, which are necessary for "the workers' class war" and the incidents should serve as models. By means of quotations, the book also upholds the view that armed revolt is natural and proper. These admissions and circumstances leave no doubt as to the objective of the publication.

The book describes the celebration by the Communists in Berlin of the May Day in 1929 in contravention of the orders of the Police President, Comrade George Bell, a social Democract. The clashes of the Communists with the police on the May Day as well as on the following five or six days, accompanied by violence on both sides are vividly described.

Anna is the wife of Curt Gimmerman, a prominent leader of the German Communists living in Wedding Stracey. In this street the workers erected improvised barricades with iron pipes and wooden pieces to prevent the on rush of the police. Anna with her child in arms came out along with Curt at dusk on the 2nd May, just to see for herself the situation in workers' quarters. They got into the back-yard of a house at 10 P.M. and attended a huge meeting addressed by Herman, the Communist Chief. When the crowd was emerging out of the back-yard, it was faced by a police force and a general stampede followed. Curt tried in vain to take out Anna to a place of safety. The police made a lathi charge. Anna received a blow on the back of her head, dropped the child on the ground and fell down. She was arrested with a number of other male workers and was taken to the police station in a lorry. In the police station, all the arrested persons with the exception of Anna, were subjected to further lathi charges. Eventually Curt received a communication from the police stating that Anna was lying as a patient in the jail hospital in Werter. Stracey Curt saw Anna in the hospital, found in her a stronger Communist than before and departed with the hope of getting her back soon as an ideal comrade.

In part I of the Novel the Social Democratic Party of Germany was attacked. More than three fourths of the members and leaders of the party were holding Government jobs and eating their money and associated themselves with the Capitalist system. So Socialist Democratic Party could never become the party of the workers class.

The author paid a tribute, in the following terms, to the influence of revolutionaries on workers in the matter of celebrating the May Day. As a result of the May day celebrations of the previous year, it was noticed that all the workers acted upto the instruction of revolutionaries. As a result, it was transformed into the people's revolutionary political activity.

Part II of the novel begins with a quotation from Lenin's work. In this quotation Lenin stresses that "Incidents like these clearly show that armed revolt against autocratic Governments does not develop merely as an item in the programme of work of revolutionaries or as a phantom of their brains, but materialises as the next natural, practical and inevitable step in the movement. Armed revolt is nothing but the result of the growing indignation, suffering and courage of the masses'.

The author further stated the views of Anna on Communists and the attitude of Government towards them in the course of her husband's interview with her in jail hospital. In this interview she stated that the Government would have to be resisted in every fight which would be launched for the rights of workers. She stated that those who support the Government were the inveterate enemies of workers. They were using the authority of the Government for the protection of the interests of Capitalists and for the suppression of the rights of workers. She felt that the leaders of Social Democratic Party would have to be destroyed as they were lending their support to the administration of the Government.

The summary of report of the Telugu translator to Madras Government was that though the book did not contain vehement attacks against Capitalists, it commened political strikes on a nation-wide scale and firm, violent resistance on the part of workers against a Government that exercised its authority for the furtherance of Capitalists' interests and suppression of the rights of labourers. Officers of the Social Democratic Party of Germany and its president comrade George Bell, came in for a lot of hostile criticism as "traitors of the workers' cause".

The gist of the report of the Superintendent of Police, Special Branch, Criminal Investigation Department was that the author of this novel stated that it was based on actual happenings in Berlin, but from the very outset it was seen that the book was not merely a historical account but a piece of party literature calculated to promote the interests of the Communist party and to encourage armed resistance against the representatives of law and order. So, he suggested that it should be forefeited.

The opinion of the Madras Government was that it would foster and encourage physical resistance to the representatives of law and order and the commission of offences involving violence and this comes within the purview of Section 4 (1) (a) and (b) of the Indian Press (Emergency Powers) Act, 1931. Therefore the said Government directed that all copies of the said book, wherever found and all other documents containing copies, reprints or translations of or extracts from it to be forfeited.[24]

World War – Our Duty (Editorial)

The ninth work of the aforesaid literature was the editorial in the Telugu Socialist weekly newspaper entitled Navasakti [25], dated 6th September, 1939, under the caption "World War – Our Duty". It was printed and published at Navasakti Press, Bezwada, Krishna District. The Publisher and Editor of the paper was Maddukuri Chandrasekhera Rao. It contained matter of the nature described in Section 4 (1) (d) (f) and (i) of the Indian Press (Emergency Powers) Act 1931 (XXIII of 1931), as amended by Section 16 of Criminal Law Amendment Act, 1932 (XXIII of 1932). So all the copies of the said newspaper, wherever found, and all other documents containing copies, reprints or translations of or extracts from the said editorial were forfeited by the Madras Government. [26]

The summary of the editorial is as follows:- For a second time a work Imperialistic war begun. Britain and France were fighting against Germany. But the British Government was blowing its own trumpet declaring that they were fighting Germany, the aggressor, for justice, peace and democracy and to preserve and safeguard the democracies of minor countries. This war was nothing but a war intended to preserve the greatness of ther British Government. It was not a war fought for preservation of justice, peace and democracy.

Indians had sympathy towards Poland but Indians hatred towards the British Government was much more than Indian sympathy for Poland. If the British Government was really, fighting for preserving the democracy of Poland, they should not prevent the attainment of Indian independence.

The author further described the condition of India. In India everything was under the control of Britishers. Here once again the author gave an idea of what was meant by independence. Every adult, man or woman, about 18 years of age must possess the right of franchise. They must elect representatives from among them. This body was to be known as the Constitutent Assembly. This body must decide Indian Political Programme.

There will be no place in India for the British Army, British officers, or for the Governors or Viceroys. In their place there would be provincial presidents and an All-India President elected by the people. These would abide by the decisions, arrived at by Indian Parliament which would exercise its fullest rights. In the place of the British Army, arrangements should be made to give military training to all the people and to create a National Army.

Indians hope that their leaders would refuse any help to the British Government, before complete independence is granted to India and they should not be satisfied with petty reforms. It was ridiculous to say that independence should be obtained by stages. "it is not independence at all if it is not complete. That is slavery and may be political slavery".

The Congress resolution clearly stated the duties of Indians. Indians want complete independence immediately. No help should be rendered to the British Government in any war. Indians must start their national struggle and vigorously carry it out when the British Government is entangled in a war. It is clear that the British Government would not grant independence to Indians by means of negotiations for a compromise. It is also clear that the British Government would try its best to suppress any agitation that Indians might start against the British Government from this moment.

The British Government will not allow any open propaganda or any sort of agitation which may be directed against it. To fight the British Government, therefore, it is imperative that work should be carried on secretly. To work secretly does not mean that we should give up the work which Indians have been doing in various organisations and hide themselves. The author reported that about the end of 1933, Gandhiji said that secret propaganda was sinful, but Jawaharlal Nehru opposed it and said that it was no sin but privacy. Such people will have to move freely among the people and work. They must work through their association so long as they are not banned. As soon as they are banned they must mix with people like ordinary men and carry on their work.

Indians must bring to the notice of the public, not as propaganda, but as general news, how a man meets with violent death and is maimed by poison gas in the war and how many have already lost their lives since joining the army. Wide publicity, by way of rumours, must be made and hatred must be created against war and against British Imperialism. It is not to Indian advantage that so many people have died nor is it in the cause of Indian independence. It is to the advantage of British Imperialism. Such ideas must be inculcated in the minds of people. They must also create the impression that joining the army is only for the advantage of the British Capitalists.

During the war time all opportunities must be fully utilised which would cause loss to the British Government and embarrass it. All people must withdraw their deposits from the post office savings banks and from Government banks. No fresh deposits should be made. Nobody should purchase should help ther Government for any loan raised by it. British Banks and British Insurance Companies should be completely boycotted.

The Swaraj Government will not repay any debts contracted by the British Government. Propaganda work must also be done that there is no hope of recovery of any loan given to the British Government. If the above suggestions are not followed the Government will be in a position to raise loans. The Government will raise loans from the Postal savings Banks and British Banks. Therefore it is obligatory that these should be boycotted.

Taxes must be held up and paid as late as possible. By this means the Government will be put to inconvenience because it will have no ready money. Articles and chiefly food stuffs intended by the Government for foreign export should not be sold. Goods useful for war purposes should not be sold to the Government, or only sold at very exorbitant prices. Prices will rise as soon as war breaks out. Attempts must be made, therefore to obtain higher wages for the factory coolies. Attempts must be made to prevent overtime work.

Agitation must be started to reduce the taxes paid by the ryots and for getting for them better water facilities. The Government must be worried to show and find employment for the unemployed and if that is not possible to give an unemployment dole. Agitation must be started for rendering necessary help to the people in times of famine.

Strong anti-war feelings must be created in all bus drivers and motor car drivers, in all workers of the railways and the harbour and generally in all workers. In the same manner propaganda work must be done in armament factories.

Patriotism must be taught to the students and hatred against the British Government must be created. None should accept the post of an Honorary

Magistrate or any other honorary post. No one should enlist as a special constable even if he is paid. Every opportunity must be availed of in every department to create inconvenience to the Government and such work must be carried on.

In addition to the above mentioned things, simultaneously strikes in all railways and factories must be brought out. The Indian troops also must join hands with the general popular fight which will come out of it. Then it would be possible to drive away the British army from India and to achieve independence.

Besides the said paper's forfeiture the Government decided to demand from T. Venkataramayya, the keeper of the said press to deposit with the District Magistrate of Krishna on or before the 10th October, 1939 security to the amount of Rs.1000/-. Later the Government came to know that the above paper had ceased publication, and with held its order.

The articles on the lives of Azad and Khudiram Bose in the Telugu newspaper entitled Navasakti[27] dated 16th August, 1939 and 23rd August, 1939,were written by comrade Gadde Lingayya. They were printed and published at Navasakti press, Bezwada, Krishna district.

The author described the life history of Azad in an inspiring way. Azad was the "Commander-in-chief of the Hindustan Socialist Republican Army". Though the methods of the terrorists were not fit to follow, the patriotism, the self sacrificing spirit, the courage and daring of the terrorists deserved to hold as ideals and imitated zealously by every young man and it was with that idea the author placed it before the people. Azad participated in the non-cooperation movement. For that the Magistrate became enraged and ordered that fifteen lashes should be given to him. Though these lashes were dealt on his body in the court, they only wounded his heart. From that day he turned a "traitor". The desire to avenge that inhuman punishment took deep root in his mind. The non-cooperation movement subsided and the enthusiasm of the people cooled down. The suspension of the struggle by the Congress leaders was not relished by the youth. Sorrow and despair overtook Azad. He lost all faith in non-violent Satyagraha. He got disgusted with non-violence and began to seek a new method. Though he was engaged in the task of enlisting new members to the (Revolutionary) party and organizing volunteer corps, he participated in the affairs of the struggle with greater zeal.

An all India organization called the Hindustan Republican Association was started and Azad, Bhagat singh and others joined it. From that time Azad had worked in that body. At Lahore under the leadership of Lala Lajapat Rai, the people, with a black flag procession, greeted the Simon commission. Lajapat Rai lost his life as a result of the lathi charge made on the procession. Both the leader and the people from all parts of India severely condemned the action of the Government. But youth were differently constituted. They were not satisfied with mere criticism and protests. Retaliation was their answer. After killing Saunders, Bhagat singh and Rajguru entered D.A.N. College, with Azad in the rear, when Cheman Singh, a policeman followed them. Azad warned the policeman to go back but policeman persisted in following them. Azad was then forced to shoot Cheman Singh. From that day onwards, not only the United Provinces Government but the Punjab Government also bore grudge against Azad. Their attempt to arrest Azad was not successful. Azad escaped from Lahore in the guise of a Sadhu (Saint) deceiving the police.

A Superintendent of Police took Azad unexpectedly in the Alfred Park and ordered him to hold up his hands, pointing a revolver at him. He was not afraid as he was prepared at all times for such an occurrence. He at once drew out his fully loaded pistol and fired at the Superintendent who lost grip of his revolver, being wounded in the arm. With the loss of his weapon, the Superintendent took refuge behind a tree but Azad continued to discharge shot after shot until the Superintendent lost his life. Azad was then surrounded by policemen who rained bullets at him from all directions. Even in that helpless condition, Azad attacked them to the last with his pistol. Bullets hit him from all sides. His body was filled with bullet holes. Such was the manner heroic Azad gave up his life. Imperialistic power was not only not able to take him alive but could not even go near him. The author also praised enthusiastically the extraordinary practical ability and unparalleled spirit of sacrifice of Azad.

The second article in the newspaper was published on 23rd august, 1939 on the life of Khudiram Bose. The essence of the article is as follows:- The Government resolved to clap the terrorists youth in jail. A number of officials spared no pains to stem the desire for independence of those youths by inflicting cruel punishments on them and subjected them to torture. The terrorists made it their duty to do away with those high-handed officials and many sacrificed their lives as a result of it. Khudiram Bose, the hero of this article was one such. Khudiram Bose happened to come into contact with the terrorists even in his student days. Ideas of independence sprang up in his mind. His mind longed to break the fetters of slavery. He became the member of the (terrorist) party and usesd to scrupulously obey the orders of the leaders.

Kingsfort, the then District Collector at Calcutta, cruelly inflicted long-term imprisonment on several editors of newspapers. The terrorist party could not tolerate his high-handedness. The terrorists thought that it was shameful for soldiers of independence to merely express their resentment and keep quiet. They decided to meet violence with violence. The terrorist party deputed two youth to answer Kingsfort. They were Khudiram Bose and Profulla Kamara Chaki. Kingsfort was transferred to Muzafarapore. The party ordered two two youth to proceed there and fulfil their task. They both thought of throwing bombs on Kingsfort on his way back from the club in the evening. They entered the arena fully prepared therefore. They waited in ambush like hungry lions by the side of the road near the Muzafarapore club with bombs in their hands. After throwing the bombs on Kingsfort car they ran away in different directions. Two ladies who were seated in the car were both killed. Some mean-minded persons chased Khudiram with the object of obtaining reward by capturing him and handing him over to Government. The people for whom Khudiram was prepared to sacrifice his life, those very people brought him into trouble. Throwing of bombs, in the eyes of Imperialism, was a great offence in those days. The only punishment for that offence was gallows. Khudiram admitted that he himself and thrown the bombs which meant inviting death. A sentence of hanging was imposed on him, a boy of 17 years, without any mercy.

The people who gathered in devotion rushed for the ashes of Khudiram. Everyone picked up a little in his hands and all of them smeared it on their foreheads and bodies and preserved the rest safely. Though Khudiram disappeared from this earth, his ideas remained in the minds of the people.

Bal Gangadhara Tilak, in a leading article in his paper Kesari, commented that it was but proper to kill highhanded officials who subjected the people to suffering. But the Imperial Government which ruled the country with brute force, sentenced Bal Gangadhar Tilak also to six years imprisonment for his views.

The Madras Government decided that the said two articles contained matter of the nature described in clauses (a) and (b) of sub-section (1) of Section 4 of the Indian Press (Emergency Powers) Act, 1931 as amended by Section 16 of Criminal Law amendment Act 1932 (Act XXIII of 1932). Therefore all copies of the said issued of the above newspaper, and all other documents containing copies, reprints or translations of or extracts from, the said articles were forfeited.[28]

Samrajyavada Yuddhanni Bahiskarinchali (Pamphlet)

The eleventh work of the Leftist proscribed literature was a pamphlet entitled Samrajyavada Yuddhanni Bahiskarinchali[29] (Imperialist war should be boycotted). It was printed at Venktateswara press, Cocanda, East Godavari district.

In the beginning of the Second world War period the East Godavari District Socialist Party published the said pamphlet. The publishers stated that it was the right opportunity for the attainment of independence, because the World War had started. Europe had changed into a big battlefield. India could not affored to forget its duty under such critical conditions. Though the whole country resolved repeatedly that it should not render help in connection with the war, British Imperialism had decided to make use of India and Indian wealth for the war. The Government propagated that whole India would participate in war by the operation of a device from Simla.

The British Imperialism prepared to put down whatever opposition that would arise against the war. It had promulgated ordinances to repress those who were opposed to the war. It had put down the freedom of the press. Traitors to independence shamelessly supported the British war preparations. The traitorous Zamindars and rulers of Indian states chanted the hymn of loyalty in all its sacredness. Communalists like Sikhandar Hyat Khan strengthened the British Imperialist war. Moderates wanted to help the Imperialist war in the name of "independence, democracy and peace".

The Congress Working Committee met on the 11th August and passed a resolution that India would stand opposed to the war. It also resolved that Congress Ministers should be faraway from war preparations that Congress members of Central Legislative Assembly should boycott the Assembly for the Government had dispatched troops to other countries from India without Congress consent. But, it had not given any programme of work to the people and to India. It had not come forward to implement the anti-war resolution under such critical conditions when there was an opportunity to overthrow British Imperialism. The Congress party had not, at least, encouraged any kind of popular demonstrations. The publishers felt that it appeared that the Indian national leaders were satisfied with some political rights and to enter into a compromise with Imperialism.

Newspapers like Times of India and the Statesmen supported the British Imperialism because in their opinion Britain may safeguard peace and independence. Even The Hindu, which passes for a nationalist paper was not different from them. These traitorous newspapers condemned in unequivocal terms the Communists, the Socialists and the extremists who strongly opposed war.

Further, the publishers stated that the Viceroy might on account of the urgent need of the war, tactfully appeal to the national leaders asking them to forget the previous differences of opinion with a view to purchase the help of India. At this critical juncture when Imperialism was weak and when it could not stand the opposition of a united India, it would try to disrupt forces of independence, make empty promises, persuade by flattery and repress extremist forces. All these would injure the future India.

The Congress passed resolutions many times opposing war in umabiguous terms. If the war was foisted on India forcibly, India would deal a strong blow. India would not enter into any sort of compromise with Imperialism. India would on the other hand sever all her connection with Imperialism. It was the true meaning of the Congress resolution on war. The entire future of India was in the hands of Indian masses. The publishers suggested that a hartal should be obsereved throughout the country as the first step in opposing the war.

Under the leadership of chamberlain the British Governmenrt deceived Abyssinia, cheated Spain and sold Czechoslovakia to Hitler. Britain practised fraud on China. Britain alone was the root cause for the atrocities perpetrated by the Nazis and Fascists. While reminding the Indians of these atrocities, the publishers advised the Congress Ministers to work as Ministers opposing war, and war preparations from their places of advantageous position, challenge the Governors of Provinces, carry on anti-war and anti-recruitment propaganda, carry on intense boycott propaganda against the export of war material and against subscribing to war loans.

Under these critical conditions national solidarity should be maintained with all care. India helped Britain twenty five years ago in the war of plunder, which the latter proudly called a sacred war. Gandhiji and other leaders fell into snares of Britain and helped her. In return Indians had heavily reaped the fruit of that folly. The Rowlatt Act, the Jallianwallah Bagh massacre, the demonical acts of Dyer were the results of the blunder that India committed in 1914. These could not be forgotten. India would not repeat the same mistakes. Congress leaders might be clapped in jail. India would not change her opinion that she should oppose war. Imperialism could not destroy the fight for independence. The author gave the following slogan at the end of the pamphlet:

"Do not Help the Imperialistic War
Carry on the fight for Independence
Victory to Independent India".

The Madras Government opined that it contained matter of the nature described in clauses (bb), and (i) of sub-section (1) of section 4 of the India Press (Emergency Powers) Act 1931. Hence the Governor of Madras was directed that all copies of the said pamphlet, wherever found, and all other documents containing copies, reprints or translations of or extracts from it be forfeited.[30]

Just and Unjust Wars (Article):

Another work on the aforesaid literature is an article entitled Just and Unjust Wars in the Telugu weekly newspaper Vahini[31] dated 1st October 1939. It was printed and published at the Kisan press, Georgetown, Madras. The superintendent of Police, special Branch, Criminal Investigation Department, on 5th October, along with the said article's translation, wrote a letter to the chief secretary to the Madras Government, Fort St. George, Madras. The summary of the letter is that the said article was written by Dr.K.B.Krishna who recently returned to India from England. On his arrival at Madras a considerable quantity of prohibited Communist literature was seized from his baggage. He was the author of the book Problem of Minorities in India. Copies of this letter were forwarded for information to the Director, intelligence Bureau, simla, the Central Intelligence officer, Madras, and the Special press Adviser, Madras.

The essence of the said article is that the Histroy of the Communist Party of the Soviet Union was a valuable and authoritative book relating to Marxism and Leninism. This was the proper book for everyone who wanted to understand the problem of the lowest class of community. It did not contain merely the history of the Communist Party. It was a good exposition of Marxism, besides, it contained hints for and advice to the revolutionaries.

It would give concrete form to the ideas of Lenin about just and unjust wars. Lenin said that the war craze was a part of Capitalism. To rob other countries, to strive for superiority in colonies and to provide facilities for the sale of goods produced in their countries were the causes for the wars wages by the Capitalist Governments. Capitalists thought that wars were just and necessary. Lenin and his followers described and explained with the evidence, that 1914-1918 World War was due to the above causes. Two Imperialist organisations carried on that war. Britain was on one side.

When all the countries had blindly entered the war, it was only Bolshevik party that discovered the real nature of the war and utilized it to achieve a successful revolution.

Lenin was not totally opposed to war. According to Marxist principles, wars are of two kinds. Bolsheviks also believed in this theory. First kind of war is just war. In this category when a Capitalist Government wage war against a Free state, any way entered into, for the purpose of protecting the independence of the latter against the aggressor, is a just and righteous war. Similarly wars waged to liberate slave countries are just wars. Second kind of war is unjust wars. In this category wars were undertaken in selfish commercial speculation and to extend Empires. The main object of these wars was to enslave other countries. Bolsheviks weaged first kind of war (i.e. just wars). An outbreak of the second kind of war (i.e. unjust wars) should be availed of to bring about a revolution and to overthrow the Capitalist Government.

Therefore, the attitude of the international workers and peasants would depend on the causes and objects of the war. Lenin declared the 1914-1918 war as an Imperialist war. He concluded that the objects of both the parties were not reasonable and he stated that the readers could understand whether the second World War was a just war or an unjust war.

In this work the intention of the writer is to propagate and create confidence in Communism. He propagated Lenin's opinion on war to popularise Communism. He stated that Lenin proved that the First World War was the result of Capitalistic ambition. The Capitalists supported wars for their control on colonies and their trade. But Lenin did not completely oppose the wars, because he supported the just wars to preserve the independence of a nation and to liberate a slave country.

The Madras Government decided that it contained the matter of the nature described in clause (bb) of sub-section (1) of Section 4 of the Indian Press (Emergency Powers) act, 1931. So the Government of Madras directed that all copies of the said newspapers, wherever found, and all other documents containing copies, reprints or translations of or extracts from the said article to be forfeited.[32]

Viplava Yugamu:

A book in Telugu entitled Viplava Yugamu[33] (Illustrated Terrorist History of India) written by Kranti Kumar and printed at Kranti Press, swechapuram was the next book that was proscribed by the government.

While reviewing the atrocities perpetrated by Imperialist and Facist countries and British propaganda about Germany and Japan the author questioned the British statement, that the British were at war with Germany to safeguard democracy. On the other hand the author stated that the inhumanities done by Germany and Japan would pale into insignificance before the atrocities perpetrated by the British Government in putting down First Indian War of Independence.

The author had traced the history of errorism from a Marxist point of view, and commented on the futility of individual terrorism, and the recent drift of terrorists towards Marxism; but he did not condemn ther cult of the bomb anywhere. On the other hand he criticised those orthodox Congressmen who described terrorists as decoits and desparadoes. Further he stated that in every country terrorism raised its head and disappeared after the mass movement had strengthened. In Soviet Union too it was so. Though the cult of the bomb prevailed at first after the advent of Lenin, it was the movement which overthrew the autocratic Czarist Government. Whenever police officers, informants or opprovers were described graphically, they were referred to as imperialist hirelings who deserved the fate they suffered at the hands of terrorists.

British in India did not hesitate to exploit the poor. The women folk of poor ryots who failed to pay their taxes were forcibly removed to bungalows and raped. The fingers of expert weavers who disobeyed their orders were cut off. To attain freedom Indians must march with sword and lance in hand and cut down India's enemies by hundred and sacrifice themselves on the nation's battlefield. Not only that, the blood of those who defiled Indian holy dharma should flow. Indians would kill and then die. The author supported the view i.e. murder of an enemy for a great cause was not a sin.

The terrorists believed that murder of certain autocrats would fuse consciousness among masses though it may not bring Swaraj. And they believed the army too would join them. Inspector Nandalal had arrested a terrorist. For that he was promoted and commended for his bravery by the British Government. The terrorists too had given him a hot reception by shooting him down in broad day light in Calcutta. With his blood they performed the funeral rites of Chaki (Terrorist).

The terrorists did not commit murders or dacoities for selfish gain. The stolen money was utilised for revolutionary purposes for securing arms and bombs. The people whom they murdered were obstacles in the way of getting Swaraj for India. They only robbed the rich but not the common people. The terrorists wanted to engineer an all India armed rising in open resistance to establish authority. They tried hard to create consciousness in the army. They committed murder only in self defence. The author also praised Azad for his exemplary courage, sacrifice and creative powers.

The Inspector General of Police (Lowmen) was high handed and cruel. In 1916, he tortured several terrorists and torture was a child's play to him. He who came here for his livelihood, misused his power and the youth could not bear it. Vinaya Krishna Bose fired three shots at Lowmen and after two days he died. His murder struck terror into the hearts of Imperialist slaves in Bengal. When there was no safety for the principal police officers what about the fate of others? People were struck dumb by the bravery displayed by Vinaya Krishna Bose who escaped after successfully accomplishing his mission.

In the Secretariat incident in Calcutta some youth opened fire on European officers but they did not touch the ordinary staff. Their object was to destroy the white insects exercising autocratic powers.

In the conclusion the author stated that history tells that the terrorist movement was not merely the death cry of an isolated few, but an all India issue and anti-Imperialist agitation. It started with middle class discontent, spread to several provinces and lasted for several years. Inspite of several hard hits, the author expressed his hope, that would it continue to become more and more severe.

The opinion of the Madras Government was that it was a most objectionable book as it contained a history of the terrorist movement in India. Lives of prominent terrorists and their photographs were reproduced. The publication of the lives of terrorists with their photos, whose only claim to notoriety was the fact that they killed treacherously, was a direct incitement to violence. Their description as martyrs was calculated to incide unbalanced youth to follow their example.

The book contained material that fell under Section 4 (1) a, b, c, d and h of the India Press (Emergency Powers) Act, 1931. Therefore the Madras Government ordered that the said book and all other documents containing copies, reprints, extracts, and translations be forfeited.[34]

Paris Commune

The fourteenth work of leftist proscribed literature was Paris Commune.[35] It was a translation of a book written by Lenin. The translator was Mahidara Jaganmohan Rao. It was printed at the Srinivasa press, Rajahmundry, East Godavari District and published by the Viswasahityamala as its publication No.13. The said book was seized in the local library at Atukur village of Gudivada Taluk. It dealt with the incident leading to the Communist revolution of Paris, and its significance in relation with the ideals and principles of Communism. The Telugu book appears to have been published early in June, 1938. then its proscription was considered not necessary.[36]

The Communist revolution of Paris was a first rehearsal for the ultimate world revolution: to exterminate the plundering administrative state control and to bring to the forefront the working classres in every part of the world. This revolution acts as an eye opener and forms an invaluable asset. The Modern era has begun with Communism. It consists of rule by the Proletariat and the workers classes. That was Communism in its real sense. It came into lime light as a result of the struggle between the officialdom and the workers. That was the beginning of the prosperity of the workers. Change of administration did not mean change of control of the militia from one hand to another in previous times. It means a total and thorough destruction of military. Communism has as its main objective, the complete extermination of the administrative plunderers and to install in their places the rule of the hard-working labourer.

Describing the incidents that led up to the revolution, Lenin wrote in his characteristic passionate style. The revolution had to face an allround attack by the Paris Bourgeois, landlords, stock-brokers, factory owners and officials – big and small alike. Those were all backed by Bismark. But all their efforts could not stem the tide of the Communist success. The proletariat had ultimately hoisted a flag over Paris. He had to depend solely on selfhelp for his very existence. Inspite of all these hardships and the short lived nature of the revolution, Communism could still achieve some notable results. It is only through those incidents during the subsequent to the revolution that one could understand the objects and significance of Communism. It had destroyed completely the military which was but a toy in the hands of bureaurcratic officials and had in its stead, a better organised militia. It had proclaimed to the world that religion had nothing to do with politics and administration had stopped all conrtributions by the state to religious organisations and institutions.

Further the author stated that it deprived the ranks of their life. It had opened the public eye to the fact that the state was primarily responsible for the public education. It had also taught that education in its real sense was complete education, unconnected with religion. It had banned the system of fining the workers. To the world that was then based upon slavery and official plunder, the acts of the Paris Commune were heart-rending. The efforts of the aristocratic classes to stem its advance were a cry in the wilderness. The elevation of the world all round depended upon the emancipation of the workers. This, in short, is the significance of "The Paris Commune".

Detailing the several lessons that the public had to draw from a study of these facts, Lenin had laid emphasis in particular of a thorough extermination of the state administrative machinery and its power and to get in its place the rule of the officials elected by the masses.

The Krishna District Magistrate opined and reported that the book bristles with dangerous statements drawn from sciences or experiences such as setting up of internal war with deadly weapons if necessary, the overthrow of organised administrations and militia wherever found, ruthless destruction of enemies, condemnation of religion as a subject of study, denial of relationsnhip between politics and religion and lastly stoppage of all state contributions to all religious organisations and institutions. The book affords an invaluable guide to a flaming youth for an organisation of the workers' and the peasants' revolutions on a large scale for the overthrow of organised administrations to wrest power. He considered that books of this kind were just the type that did not deserve to be in public circulation. He therefore recommended that the book might be proscribed and necessary action taken in the matter.

The Madras Government decided that it contained prejudicial reports. Therefore in exercise of the powers conferred by clause (b) of sub-rule (1) of rule 40 of the Defence of India rules, the said booklet and every copy or translation thereof or extract therefrom, wherever found, to be forfeited.[37]

The following books, along with other books were investigated by the Government with a view to find out whether they were against the interests of the British Raj. The subordinate officers to the Government of Madras suggested proscription of some of the books. But the Government did not do as they suggested, on the ground that the works were not against the British interests.

Samyavada Sidhantalu[38] which forms the eighth of the series of publications known as Adarsa Gandha Mandali of Elamarru, is stated to be a Telugu translation of the "Principles of Socialism" by Friederich Engels. It was printed at Sree Panduranga Press, Ellore, West Godavari District.

The treatise seeks to give an exposition of Communistic principles in the form of a catechism. The author described the differences between a slave and a labourer. A slave is one who has been fully sold away, while a labourer sells himself for an hour or a day. A slaves life would not be so very contemptuous as that of a labourer. His master is bound, in his own interest, to his life. As all the goods in the world are in the possession of the Capitalists, the labour and energy of labourers are being sold in accordances with the requirements of this bureaurcracy. In this aspect the intention of the author is to awaken the working class and encourage labourers to destroy the Capitalist private property, and establish Communist form of Government. He criticised the exploitation system of the rich and highlighted the benefits of Communism.

The Registrar of books, Madras, suggested the proscription of the book because the intention of book seems to promote feelings of enmity or hatred between Capitalists and the labourers and to incite the latter to revolution. But the Government did not proscribe it. It remained as an investigated work.[39]

Karl Marx (A Modern Saint) [40] was a Telugu rendering by Kundurthi Narasimha Rao, Guntur, of Lala Haradayal's English sketch of Karl Marx. It was printed at Lalita Mudrakshasarasala, Tenali and published by Kommuri Kasiviswanadham, Tenali.

It is a thrilling narrative of the struggles undergone and the sacrifices made by Karl Marx and his wife for the furtherance of the workers' cause. The style employed by him is so passionate as to readily catch the hearts of the readers.

Marx's spirit of self sacrifice, perseverance, earnestness of purpose, self-confidence and intense sympathy for the poor had been well depicted in the book. The author vividly described how the peasants and labourers were subjected to starvation. The author praised the greatest achievements of Karl Marx. Marx had brought the latent power of the workers to the notice of eminent persons.

The author wrote this book with the idea of bringing home to young India – the life story, the pleasant and painful experiences and the activities of the great man, the famous saint and seer whose name is being meditated upon with profound reverence day and night by millions of people all over the western countries. It was a well investigated work. [41]

"Comrade Damitroff" [42] was printed in the Minerva Press, Masulipatam and published by Adarsa Grandha Mandali, Masulipatam. "Comrade Damitroff" is a short sketch in telugu of the life the Bulgarian Communist, Damitroff, with special reference to the Reichstag burning of 1933 in which he was tried as one of the accused and finally acquitted on the orders of Hitler, Damitroff left Germany. Then he settled in Russia with his old mother. The Soviet Government welcomed him and conferred on him all the rights of Russian citizenship.

The government's opinion was that the intention underlying the publication of this book seems to spread communism and to support class war carried on by the peasants. There is however no incitement to violence or advocacy of militant action or armed revolution or mass action. On the whole the book may be said to be a mild type.

Dhanaprabhavamu[43] is the seventh in order of a series of pamphlets published by Cooly Samrakshka, Sangham (Workers protection Society)" of Guntur. It was printed at the Ramakrishna Press, Tenali, Guntur District. The publishers stated that the pamphlet dealt with a tiny story that demonstrates the intolerable condition of workers under capitalist regime.

This pamphlet is more a workers' manifesto than a story. Interest centers round the gradual evolution of credulous, unquestioning, religious God-fearing and servile workers' into self-conscious, self-respecting, inquisitive, irreligious, Godless, defiant and dynamic Socialists, yearning for freedom and transformation of the present Capitalist society into a Socialist order. This theme is expressed in the form of a story.

Sandesamu[44] is said to be a Telugu translation of "Appeal to the Youth" by "The French Anarcho Communist", Prince Kroporkin. It was printed at Sree Lakshmi printing works, Jagannaick Pur, Cocanada, and issued as No.5 of the series of publications known as Viswa Sahitya Mala of Munganda, East Godavari district, by Mahindhra Ramamohan Rao, the editor of the series. The author's name has not been given.

The book reads like an address delivered at some university convocation, to an audience composed of youth who are about to start on their respective walks of life as doctors of medicine, scientists, advocates of law, engineers and the like. It passionately exhorts them all to utilise their talents and resources for the destruction of the then social system and imperialism and for the spread and triump of Communistic principles.

Socialism (Samyavadamu) Ante[45] was written by Ravu Vankata Jagga Rao and printed at Sree Venkateswara Press, Pittapur, East Godavari district. In this work the author mainly concentrated on propagation of communistic principles, Congress Socialist Party objects, the inequalities prevailing among the people in India, the exploitation of rich, the causes for the starvation of peasants and labourers, and the relative merits of the Indian National Congress. The author stated that Marxism alone is the universally acknowledge form of Socialism at the present day. Its object is to remove by a thorough nationalisation all the means of production, the existing inequalities between man and man in respect of wealth, education and general comforts of life.

"Hindudeasamu Rajakiyamulu[46] (Indian Politics) was written by comrade Kameswara Sastri. It was printed at the Box printing press in 1939, Rajuhmundry, and was published by the New Political Publishing House, Rajahmundry.

The author was a known socialist and was one of the accused in the Cocanada conspiracy case. He has traced the history of India from the Marxist point of view, and shown how the British Capitalists, holding the strings of the British Government of India, were systematically exploiting the resources of India.

Hailing the Congress Socialist Party as a move in the right direction he deplored the malicious propaganda carried on by interested right wing leaders against the party and narrated how the Congress Ministers were freely resorting to the use of Imperialist forces to put down agitation by the labourers.

"Akalimantalu" (The Flames of Hunger) and Communistulu-Congress (Communists and the Congress) were jointly submitted for perusal of the Government of Madras. [47] They were written by Settipalle Venkataratnam and Tantia respectively. The first book was issue No.6 of the Ryotanga Grandhamala, Gudivada, and was printed at Krishnanda Press, Powerpet, Ellore. The Ryotanga Grandhamala was started by N.G.Ranga with an editorial board consisting of active Kisan sabhaites of Andhra. In this book the author had depicted the poverty and misery prevailing among the working classes of India. He suggested that the formation of workers rule is the remedy to their hardships.

The second bolok was published as issue No.20 of the Adarsha Grandha Mandali, Elamarru. It was a left book publishing company run by an Andhra communist Gadde Lingayya. The said book was printed at the Usha Printing Press, Telaprolu in January, 1939.

It was a thesis on the role of the Indian Communists in the struggle for complete independence of India. It urged that the Communists should become a decisive force inside the Congress itself, unifying the entire left and its Socialist core.

Communistulu Koredemiti[48] (what do the Communists want?) was printed at Navasakti Press, Bezwada and published as No.4 of Navasakti Publication. In the course of his foreward the editor of the publication said that the book was a translation of the last chapter of the autobiography of "Comrade Morris Thoreau, the French communist Party Leader". He considered that the book was a reply to the many wrong notions that prevailed even in countries other than France and hoped that "it would be of use to the vast number of people in India also who get frightened at the mention of Communists". The name of the translator was not given.

In this work the author pointed out the plunder, robbery, violence of the Capitalists on working class. He depicted Russia as an exemplary country in the world in every aspect. The Government of Madras felt that it was a work advocating Communistic ideas. [49]

Balidana Sphulingamulu[50] (Sparks of self sacrifice) is said to be a translation translator Seerla Brahmayya and an adoptation from the 'Prajamitra' with certain modifications. It was printed at Dhanalakshmi

Press, Tadepalligudem, west Godavari districts, and punblished as publication No.2 ("2nd drop of hot blood of Sowkya Sadhana Prachara Grandhamala.)

The book depicted how a hero (Prince Charming) and a heroine (Nane) bound to each other by strong love, helped Lenin and his followers in the overthrow of the Czar and the murder of the Royal family at the cost of their lives.

Socialism-Charitrakam-Siddhantam[51] publication No.23 of Viswasahitya Mala was printed at Avanti Press, Munganda, in July 1940. It was a translation by Darsi Subhadramma of the three chapters entitled "General, Historical and Theoretical of the "Anti-Duhring" by Friedrich Engels which was translated into Englisdh by Emil Burns. The book was edited by Mahendra Jaganmohan Rao. Besides the introduction by the editor, wherein he praised the services rendered by Darsi Subhadramma to the cause of Telugu literature, the book contained a life sketch of Friedrich Engels by Darsi Subhadramma.

This book dealt with the general, historical and theoretical features of Socialism. The author described in the first chapter the origin and development of Socialism in Europe upto the time of Herr Duhring and how the Capitalists and land lords were exploiting the working classes.

The second chapter, while tracing the history of Socialism, characterised the old school of Socialism as static and the new school as dynamic.

In the third chapter the author said that a community was organised on the basis of production of articles and their disrtribution. The production of articles, the method of production and distribution of articles divided the community into several classes. There was always a clash between the forces and the method of production. It subjected the working class into miserable poverty, servitude and misery. He stressed that Socialism was the only remedy to eliminate the hardships of the working class.

Comrade Lenin[52] by Joseph Stalin was printed at the Srinivisa Press, Rajahmundry and published by the Athika, Rajakiya Vignana Parishat, Cocanada. It contained Telugu translations of two lectures delivered by Stalin on Lenin and an article contributed by him to "Pravda". All the three dealt with the exceptional qualities of Lenin as a leader.

Stalin promised to safeguard the ideology of Lenin and Communist principles, the union of ryots and workers and strengthen and widen the United Soviet Republic. He laid stress on Lenin's deep desire on the duty of the Soviets to strengthen the revolutionary movement in every country in the world. He indicated how the Communist Party was established by Lenin in the face of antagonistic elements and how it was strengthened by him.

Superintendent of Police, Special Branch, Criminal Investigation Department, suggested the book for proscription as per Rule 40 of the Defence of India Rules. The Government felt it was not inflammatory or as tending to incite the reader to violent or terrorist activities.[53]

Soviyat Rasyalo[54] (In Soviet Russia) was printed at the Lakshmi Power Press, Tenali and published by Navya Sahitya Mala, Anatapuram. The author was not known. The book dealt with the social, economic and political life of the people in Soviet Russia. The author traced the growth and development of the Union of Soviet Socialist Republic and described at length the economic life of modern Russia, her industries, railways, education, mineral resources and system of agriculture. The author criticised the attitude of 'capitalist' countries, Britain, France and America towards Soviet Russia.

Jatiyaikyataku Soviet Choope Margamu[55] (the way which the Soviet Russia shows towards National solidarity) was the 55th book in the series of publications known as "Prajasakthi Prachurana", Bezwada, and printed at the Prajasakthi Press, Bezwada. The book purports to be a translation of a speech delivered by comrade Dr.Adhikari at a meeting held under the auspices of Soviet Friends Union in Bombay. The translation into Telugu was done by Ananda Mohan.

The ideas underlying the book is that the Soviet leaders successfully solved their racial and minority problems by means of the principle of the self-determination. The author said that India at this time (1944) was facing problems similar to those which Russia faced during 1926-36. According to the author, India also could adopt the methods which were followed by Russia, with some modifications to solve her own communal and racial problems and achieve national independence and solidarity. The author tried to establish communal harmony by exemplifying Soviet Russia. The author mentioned the differences between the Monsheviks and the Bolesheviks in Russia. The author stated how the Russians established harmonious and financially sound conditions in the Russian society with a view to create inspiration among the Indians in favour of the Communist form of Government.

Since 1934 the publication of Communist literature began in India. By this time the Salt Satyagraha and Civil Disobedience movements subsided. Since 1920 Gandhiji began to participate actively in the freedom struggle. He brought the struggle to the masses. So masses were awakened. This was a most dangerous thing to the British. In addition to that, the publication and propagation of Communism by Leftists among the masses would become a serious problem to the British to protect their rule in India. With the influence of Communist literature the working class became united and held strikes, hartals and protests. Particularly they were prepared to overthrow the British rule through various conspiracies. At the time of ban on them, they joined with Indian National Congress and Congress Socialist Party with their own object to create unity and awakening among the working classes to overthrow the British Raj. The proscription of Leftist literature itself shows how the people were inspired by the literature. Apart from the ban on literature, they prohibited the entrance of Leftist literature from Leftist countries into India. To prevent the Leftist ideology and implementation of the Leftist policy in India, even they seized Leftist literature from patriots in jails.

NOTES

1. Order No.NF 718/38 Dt. 23rd July, 1934. Vide Home Department F.N. 7/13/34 – Political.
2. C.Rajeswara Rao, Party Organisation, p.16
3. D.Chenchayya, 'Nenu-Nadesamu' (Autobiography) (Telugu) pp. 337-338.
4. Ibid, p.340.
5. N.G.Ranga, Fight for Freedom, p.238.
6. Government of Madras Public (General) Departmenrt G.O.No.1059, Dt. 16th October, 1934.
7. Government of Madras Public (General) Department G.O.No.1059, Dt. 16th October, 1934.
8. Government of Madras, Public (General;) Department, G.O.No.1183, Dt. 26th November, 1934.
9. Government of Madras, Public (General) Department G.O. No.1183, Dt. 26th November, 1934.
10. Government of Madras, Public (General) Department G.O.No.823, Dt. 23rd May, 1935.
11. Government of Madras, Public (General) Department, G.O.No.823, Dt. 23rd May, 1935.
12. Government of Madras, Public (general) Department, Confidential, G.O.No.1180, Dt. 18th July, 1935.
13. Mother was translated into Bengali in 1925 by Nripendra Krishno Chattopadhyaya. Bimol shen also translated it into Bengali. The first translator of Mother into Hindi was Chandrabhal Jauhari, who published his translation in the 1930s. Another translator of the book into Hindi was Chhabinath Pandey. It was translated into Assami by Phani Bora; Punjabi by Nirender singh Socha in the early 1940s and later by Gurbaksh Singh; Marathi by Prabhakar Undhvaresh in the early 1940s. An abridged Tamil translation was published in Madras in the mid 1930s and complete translation into Tamil was brought about by Chidambara Raghunathan. It was translated into Urdu in 1946 by Makhmur Jalandhari.

The British colonial authorities tried to keep Mother from becoming popular in India. The newspaper Advance, on 17th April, 1937, carried a report of Communist literature seized during the arrest of some Indian patriots including Mother by Gorky and some of his other works.

14. He was justly honoured with the Soviet Land Nehru Award in the year 1965.
15. Government of Madras, Public (General) Department, Confidential G.O.No.1180, Dt. 18th July, 1935.
16. Government of Madras, Public (General) Department, MS. Series, Confidential G.O.No.2044, Dt. 27th October, 1937.
17. Government of Madras, Home Department, G.O.No.2833, Dt. 22nd October, 1936.
18. Government of Madras Public (General) Department, MS. Series, Confidential, G.O. No.2072, Dt. 14th December, 1936.
19. Government of Madras Public (General) Department, G.O. No.925, Dt. 19th May, 1937.
20. Governmdent of Madras, Public (General) Department G.O. No.925, Dt. 19th May, 1937.
21. Government of Madras Public (General) Department, G.O. No.668, dt. 11th April, 1938.
22. Government of Madras, Public (General) Department G.O. No.668, Dt. 11th April, 1938.
23. Government of Madras, Public (General) Department G.O. No.1834, Dt. 5th November, 1938.
24. 24. Government of Madras, Public (General) Department, G.O. No.1834, Dt. 5th November, 1938.
25. Government of Madras, Public (General) Department, MS. Series, G.O. No.1606, Dt. 26th September, 1939.
26. **Ibid.**
27. Government of Madras, Public (General) Department, MS. Series, G.O. No.1625, Dt. 28th September, 1939.
28. Government of Madras, Punblic (General) Department, MS. Series G.O. No.1625, Dt. 28th September, 1939.
29. Government of Madras, Public (General) Department, MS. Series G.O. No.1702, Dt. 11th October, 1939.
30. Government of Madras, Public (General) Department, MS. Series, G.O. No.1702, Dt. 11th October, 1939.
31. Government of Madras, Public (General) Department, G.O. No.1790, dt. 23rd October, 1939.
32. Government of Madras, Public (General) Department, G.O. No.1790, dt. 23rd October, 1939.
33. Government of Madras, Public (General) Department, Confidential, G.O. No.832, dt. 25th April, 1941.
34. Government of Madras, Public (General) Department, Confidential, G.O.No.832, dt. 25th April, 1941.
35. Government of Madras, Public (General) Department, G.O.No.416, Dt. 10th February, 1945.
36. Government of Madras, Public (General) Department, Confidential, G.O.No.1430, dt. 18th August, 1938.
37. Government of Madras, Public (General) Department, G.O.No.416, Dt. 10th February, 1945.

38. Government of Madras, Public (General) Department, MS. Series Confidential, G.O.No.932; dt. 5th June, 1935.
39. Government of Madras, Public (General) Department, MS. Series Confidential, G.O.No.932, dt. 15th June, 1935.
40. Government of Madras, Public (General) Department, MS. Series, Confidential, G.O.No.1015, dt. 15th June, 1935.
41. Government of Madras, Public (General) Department., MS Series Confidential, G.O. No.1015, dt. 15th June, 1935.
42. Government of Madras, Public (General) Department., MS Series Confidential, G.O. No.1753, dt. 25th October, 1935.
43. Government of Madras, Public (General) Department., MS Series Confidential, G.O. No.2077, dt. 4th December, 1935.
44. Government of Madras, Public (General) Department, MS. Series, Confidential G.O. No.462, Dt. 5th March, 1937.
45. Government of Madras, Public (General) Department, MS. Series, Confidential G.O. No.1833, Dt. 27th September, 1937.
46. Government of Madras, Public (General) Department, MS. Series, Confidential G.O. No.1277, Dt. 1st August, 1935.
47. Government of Madras, Public (General) Department, MS Series Confidential, G.O. No.1276, dt. 1st August, 1939.
48. Government of Madras, Public (General) Department, MS Series Confidential, G.O. No.1557, dt. 20th September, 1939.
49. Government of Madras, Public (General) Department, MS Series Confidential, G.O. No.1557, dt. 20th September, 1939.
50. Government of Madras, Public (General) Department, MS Series Confidential, G.O. No.1978, dt. 14th November, 1939.
51. Government of Madras, Public (General) Department, MS Series, G.O. No.2061, dt. 17th October, 1940.
52. Government of Madras, Public (General) Department, MS. Series, Confidential; G.O.No.293, Dt. 12th February,1941.
53. Government of Madras, Public (General) Department, MS. Series, Confidential, G.O.No.293, Dt. 12th February,1941.
54. Government of Madras, Public (General) Department, MS. Series, Confidential, G.O.No.167, Dt. 15th Januuary,1942.
55. Government of Madras, Public (General) Department, MS. Series, Confidential, G.O.No.2022, Dt. 3rd July,1944.

8

PILLARS OF THE PROSCRIBED LITERATURE

The course of the freedom struggle in Andhra from 1920 to 1947 depended mainly on the decision of the Indian National Congress. The local leaderas closely followed these decisions. In popularising the various movements political leaders, philosophers, writers, poets, orators, dramatic associations, literary institutions played an effective part. In addition various propaganda techniques were also used. Some of them spent their lives as freedom fighters-cum-writers and poets. They performed dual role to free the nation from the British. The large number of writers in Andhra, wrote number of books, novels, dramas, Harikathas, Burrakathas on the then political, social, economic and cultural conditions of India as well as Andhra with main stress on the propagation of struggle of independence. Among them I have taken four important personalities to estimate their contribution to free the nation. They are Unnava Lakshmi Narayana, Garimella Satyanarayana, Damaraju Pundarikakshudu and Vaddadi Sitaramanjaneyulu. They were freedom fighters-cum-writers and poets.

Unnava Lakshmi Narayana and Damaraju Pundarikakshudu have a special place in national literature, vis-à-vis Guntur district. They belonged to the district. Besides being first ranking political figures of the district they were also writers of eminence. They ably used their pen to rouse national consciousness, and point out the glaring social and economic injustices.

The freedom movement began to intensify from 1920 onwards for many reasons. So the writers were influenced by the movement and the movement was intensified by the writers through their writings. At the same time the repressive policy was also intensified by the Government. So the Government began to proscribe a number of books. The aforesaid writers books were banned between 1920 and 1923. This is the beginning of intensification of proscription. Except a few all the major works of the aforesaid persons were proscribed. In addition to that they were freedom fighters. So I called them the pillars of the proscribed literarture of my period of study.

The aforesaid freedom fighters-cum-writers' books are in spoken language. How they stirred political consciousness, social awakening, pointed out economic injustices and brought the people into the struggle for independence are described in the following pages.

UNNAVA LAKSHMI NARAYANA (1877-1958)

Early Life and Education:-

Unnava Lakshmi Narayana was born on 4th December, 1877,[1] at Unnava village, Pattipadu Taluk, Guntur District.[2] So he was popularly known as Unnava Lakshmi Narayana. His father was Sriramulu, mother Seshamma. They belonged to a middle class family His father was a teacher. He studied primary education at Vemulurupadu and Amenabad; high school study was at A.E.L.M. School (present Andhra Christian College, Guntur); passed matriculation examination in 1897, and completed F.A. in Guntur. While working as a teacher he completed the law course and with the encouragement of Kandukuri Veeresalingam Pantulu he jolined Teacher Training College at Rajahmundry and completed it in 1905-1906. He went to Ireland to study Barrister course in 1913 and completed it in 1916.

Professional Activity

To earn a livelihood for himself and his family he joined as a Teacher after completion of F.A. course, 1900. Apart from his job, he completed law course and took to lawyer's profession in 1903. But he went to Rajahmundry to complete Teacher training with the encouragement of Veeresalingam. After completion of it, Veeresalingam offered him a job to work as a superintendent to his widow-shelter. This job he performed for one year only and left this job due to differences of opinion towards the British Raj. Kandukuri was a supporter of the British while Unnava was against it. So differences arose between them.[3]

Therefore he returned to Guntur and joined as a teacher in a school where he studied. In this job, he worked as an ideal teacher. In 1907 Unnava and Jonnavittula Gurunadham jointly wrote a Telugu book entitled India Rajyatantram. In this work they described the disastrous conditions of India and the exploitation by the British Government. So the Guntur

District Collector cautioned the principal of the school. The principal cautioned Unnava, and Unnava left this job.

UNNAVA LAKSHMI NARAYANA (1877-1958)

Then he joined as a cashier in the Rally Company, but the Company owners disliked the political speeches of Unnava and at the same time Unnava hated the exploiting business system of the Company. So he resigned the job. For some time he worked in the post office. Thereafter he again took to lawyer's profession. Simultaneously he acrtively participated in political, social and cultural activities in Andhra. For a short while he went to Ireland to study Barrister course and after its completion he returned to India and began practicing in Madras High Court in 1917. He was successful in this profession both professionally and financially. But due to the ill-hgealth of his wife Lakshmi Bayamma and attraction of the local Guntur political issues he returned to Guntur. From this time onwards he began to participate completely in the poilitics. During these days non-cooperation movement started in India in 1920. With the call of Gandhiji he left his lawyer's profession. From that time onwards he completely dedicated his life for the liberation of the country and to social reform.

Apart from his educational qualifications, he was a poet, playwright and novelist but he never tried to live by them nor did he seek patronage from any patrons.

Participation in the Freedom Struggle

Unnava while studying Matriculation in Guntur in 1897, learnt leadership qualities and idealistic principles from his Head Master, Pasupuleti Venkata Subbayya Naidu. Naidu also worked as a Municipal chairman, Guntur. Unnava was influenced by him.

In 1900 Unnava and some other educated youth founded Youngmen's Literary Association in Guntur. In the beginning it was used as a reading room. Afterwards it was changed into a library.[4] In this place occasionally they conducted discussions on political, social and cultural aspects. The Government suspected it and kept an eye on the institution.

While he was working as a teacher in Guntur, Vandemataram movement was going on in India. In this context he conducted meetings and gave speeches in Guntur. He also translated some of the speeches of Bipin Chandra Pal, when he toured Andhra. He was influenced by Pal's speeches.

He had some connection with organising revolutionary activities upto 1911. Their activities were mainly academic and had very few sympathisers. All such revolutionary activities however subsided after 1911.

The Governor – General Hardinge issued a declaration on 11th December 1911, stating that India would be divided into states on the basis of language. On the basis of it Youngmen's Literary Association started a movement for separate Andhra State. It was the beginning of Unnava's political life.

Andhra Movement – Unnava

Unnava in consultation with Jonnavittula Gurunadham, prepared Visalandhra map which contained the Telugu Districts of Madras Presidency, Mysore, Hyderabad. Maharashtra and Orissa. Unnava attended Krishna, Guntur political and social conferences. In May, 1912 Krishna Guntur Mandal joint conference was held. In arranging this conference Unnava played an important role. He circulated the idea of and the need for the establishment of Andhra State and Andhra University among the people of the conference.

In 1913 the 1st Andhra conference was held at Bapatla under the presidentship of B.N.Sarma. Konda Venkatappaiah worked as a Reception Committees president. Unnava worked as the Committee's secretary. For a short period Unnava went to Ireland to study Barrister Course. Meanwhile in the Andhra conferences of 1914 (Bezwada), 1915 (Vizagapatam) and 1916 (Cocanada) a resolution was passed for a separate Andhra State.

He returned to India after completion of Barrister course in 1916. He acted as the President of the Guntur District Social Reforms Conference held at Repalle, and Krishna Mandal Reform Conference held at Kovvuru. In these conferences Unnava inspired the people. Guntur Mandal political conference was held at Sattenapalli under the presidentship of Unnava in 1918. In 1918 under the Presidentship of Kasinadhuni Nageswara Rao a state conference was held for stressing the need for a separate Andhra State.

In this conference Unnava condemned Montague Reforms. He was arrested on the occasion of no tax campaign in Palnadu. After his release he became the president of Andhra conference held in Chittoor in 1922. he paid keen interest on formation of Andhra State, Andhra University, development of Telugu language and protection of Andhra culture.

After the formation of Andhra state in 1953 Unnava appealed to the Government to make Guntur as the capital of Andhra State. He also appealed to the Government of India. [5] But he failed to make Guntur the capital. He tried hard for the formation of Andhra state from the beginning but he did not get his due place as he was away in Ireland. He occupied second place in the formation of Andhra State. But he fulfilled his deep desire with the establishment of Visalandhra in 1956.

Sinn Feini Movement – Unnava

In 1913 Unnava went to Ireland. While he was there the Sinn Feini movement was going on in Ireland. Sinn Feini meant the representatives of the people. The Irish people led a movement against the British dictatorship and their exploitation. All this was seen by Unnava and was influenced by it. With his co-Indians who were studying in Ireland Unnava boycotted the foreign cloth and customs. He attended every political conference held in Dublin and read many books on Socialism and also made an acquaintance with the Sinn Feini movement leader Devilaru.

In the vacation he came to Guntur and presided over the Andhra conference in Guntur. In this context he said that without political independence any reform movement would not yield fruitful results and appealed to people to fight against the British like the Irish people.[6]

Unnava returned to India in 1916. He started a hurricane campaign demanding self Government. Most of the supporters of the movement were Congressmen. However at Bezwada[7], Gudur[8] and some other places the members of the local Theosophical Societies also joined the league (Home Rule League Andhra Branch) and helped to intensify the agitation. Public meetings were addressed by prominent leaders like Konda Venkatappaiah and Unnava.

At the Andhra patrika office, Madras, the Andhra leaders held a conference and passed a resolution to establish a society reconstruction institution. For this institution Unnava was elected as a secretary.

He came to Guntur due to the aforesaid reasons on the eve of the non-cooperation movement. He gave up his highly profitable profession (lawyership) in response to the call of Congress.

At the Guntur Disrtrict Conference held in June 1921 discussion went on for two days on a resolution on civil disobedience moved by Unnava and seconded by Gollapudi Sitarama Sastry, two of the top ranking leaders of the time.

Palnad Satyagraha

While the non-cooperation movement was at its height the Andhra Provincial Committee appointed a committee in July 1921 consisting of Unnava and Madabhushi Vedantam Lakshminarasimachari to enquire into the grievances of the people of Palnad. The presence of these leaders served as a new incentive to the agitators and further worsened the relations between the authorities and the people. The leaders visited many villages in the Taluk, preached to the people on the necessity of non-cooperation and exhorted them to observe strict non-violence. At Macherla they were arrested on the ground that their speeches were provocative and were imprisoned in July 1921 in Rayavellore jail where he wrote a famous novel entitled Malapalli.

Violation of the Government order

Gandhiji appointed a committee to observe how the non-cooperation movement was going on in various parts of the country. On behalf of the committee Motilal Nehru, one of the members of the committee came to Andhra while Unnava was the president of Guntur District Congress. To prevent such enquiry the Government authorities declared Section 144 in Guntur. But Unnava violated it and sent volunteers to the Railway station. The police arrested volunteers instead of the leaders Unnava and T.Pakasam. On this occasion Unnava himself mingled with the arrested volunteers. The police also noticed the enthusiasm of Unnava in the freedom struggle.

Swarajya Party-Unnava

Unnava was brave enough to advise Congress to suspend the non-cooperation movement, since it failed and favoured Council entry. His courageous lead was taken later by Motilal Nehru and C.R.Das and Swaraj party took shape out of their efforts. Andhra Congressmen were by and large too orthodox in politics also and so would not countenance any such departure from Gandhian policy.

There was however, a certain section of Congressmen who fell in with the views of C.R.Das and his party. They formed themselves into an Andhra Swarajya party which met in Bezwada on 18th April 1923 and elected a provincial committee with V. Ramadas as President, K.V.R.Swami as Vice-President and Unnava, B.Ramalingam and V.L.Sastry as secretaries. District Swarajya Parties were formed and Kolli Satyanarayana Chowdari, Unnava and several other prominent workers became members[9] of the party.

By this time T.Prakasam the dominant leader came round to Unnava's point of view and joined the Swarajya party. Unnava found himself without funds to think of standing for any legislature. He realised the extreme need for money in such political election campaign and the realist and genuine patriot that he was, he decided not to venture into election politics by himself and to be content to help others. He disliked the caste orientation of electioneering. He was too independent minded to gain the support of the Congress bosses. He hated bossism and so, did not try to become a partner in the political combinations. So he abstained from election politics without any regrets. Such was the noble conception of politics, so dutiful and altrustic. In 1923 elections to Assembly he actively campaigned for his comrade Rama Swami.

Guntur Patrika

After his release from Rayavellore jail Unnava began to run a newspaper entitled Guntur Patrika and also he worked as its editor. In this paper he discussed the political, social and religious matters. But he gave importance to local issues. For some time Jamili Nammalwaru worked as the editor for this paper. But it did not run for long.

Salt Satyagraha – Unnava

Unnava played an important role in Salt Satyagraha in Andhra. He used a new technique in the propagation of Salt Satyagraha in Andhra and particularly in Guntur. He and his volunteers built a thirty feet high Prabha. In this Prabha, they stitched the photos of Bharata Mata and Congress leaders, named it as Swarajya Prabha and held street processions. Unnava and others prepared salt at the house of Konda Venkatappaiah. In this context his wife Lakshmi Bayamm with two hundred volunteers participated in the Salt Satyagraha. The Government resented it and arrested Unnava and Lakshmi Bayamma. He was imprisoned in Rajahmundry, Tiruchurapalli, vellore jails. Lakshmi Bayamma was also imprisoned. Due to Gandhi-Irwin pact, Unnava was released two months earlier than due on 12th March, 1931.

Palmyra trees Satyagraha – Unnava

As a part of anti-drink programme of Gandhiji, Unnava led a movement of cutting of Palmyra trees and broke up the pots on palmyra tres. This kind of activity was not suggested by Gandhiji.

Local Politics – Unnava

In the local politics Unnava acted in favour of Jagarlamudi Kuppa swami and against Nadimpalli Venkata Narasimham in the Guntur District Board Presidentship. So the latter remained a foe to Unnava.

Individual Satyagraha – Unnava

Unnava a participated in the individual Satyagraha. So Government imprisoned him for two months on 4th April 1941 and released him on 3rd June, 1941.

Quit India Movement – Unnava

In the context of Quit India movement a conference was held at Guntur. Police fired on the gathering. So Unnava and others established Azad Hind Government in Guntur in 1943. They brought Government officials of Guntur into their custody one by one for half an hour and released them. The Government came to know of this activity and arrested Unnava on 8th February 1943 and imprisoned him for six months. In august he was released. Lakshmi Bayamma was also arrested by the Government.

Unnava continued to be true to his revolutionary role he wished to assume. So when Rama Swami, his friend, stood against the Swarajya candidates in Assembly elections, he supported him. When N.G.Ranga stood as a Congress candidate, the candidate of landlords and other Justicities, he supported Ranga. When Gandhiji started the anti-untouchability campaign, he joined it.

Gandhiji said that the reformation movement relating to untouchables should come from higher castes with their broadening of their hearts whereas Unnava said that the said reformation movement should come from untouchables and with their self confidence.

Unnava was influenced by Pal, Talik, Gandhiji,C.R.Das, whereas many leaders were influenced by Unnava.[10] He believed in God and thought that he realised communion with God. In fact many of his disciples believed that Unnava was himself a Siddhi Purusha and he, in his turn, looked upon Gandhiji as an Avatar. It was but natural for him to deal with the role of God in discussing such vital social questions as poverty, exploitation of man by man and age long social injustices. His wife Lakshmi Bayamma died on 29th February, 1952. Unnava died on 27th September, 1958.

Political and Literary Works

Unnava wrote a number of ballads in various contexts. In his ballads he used spoken language of the people and gave importance to meaning. His famous ballads are Elapata, Burrakatha, Aavulakaparulu, Tandhana Pata,

Rotipata, Deyyalapata or Pralaya Geetam, Yasodavaibhavam, Puvvupata, Mekapata, Budabukkala Jyoshyam.

In these ballads he described patriotism, Palnati charitra, social conditions and customs of the people, the necessity and importance of religion in human life, upliftment of Harijans. All his ballads in the form of a book entitled Bhavatarangalu was printed in Chennapuri Mudraksharasala and published in 1933.

Unnava translated some of Bipin Chadra Pal's speeches into Telugu and printed them in Bezwada Vani press and published them in the form of book in 1907. Unnava and J. Gurunadham jointly wrote a Telugu book entitled India Rajyatantram, a political treatise. It was published by Swadesi press, Masulipatam in 1907. Unnava wrote a Telugu book entitled Life of Akbar in 1906. In this work Unnava highlighted the reign of Akbar and criticised the rule of the British. The main intension of Unnava in writing this work was to keep alive the national feelings among the Andhras. It was printed in Krishnadesi press, Masulipatam, and published by Andhra Bhashabivardini Sangam in 1908.

His famous novel Malapalli[11] is separately discussed. His another novel Tikkana is a historical novel but it is uncompleted. His historical drama Nayakuralu (Palnati war) is a Six Acts drama and it was written in 1925. It was printed in Triveni press, Masulipatam and was published in 1926. Later it was published four times. His playlets Annamamba was published in Andhra Patrika Ugadi[12] Annual Number in 1946, Sangeeta Napasani, Sailaja Publication, Guntur in 1933 and in 1958. Sodoyamma Sodi is a political playlet. It was published in Krishna Patrika on 11th November, 1933. In this playlet Unnava described the Salt Satyagraha. He also wrote essays on politics, social reformation and vedantam (philosophy).

SOICIAL REFORM:

Unnava Widow Re-marriage

The performance of Sati (dying on the funeral pyre of her husband) was one of the most cruel customs of the Indian society. To prevent it the Governor-General William Bantinck passed legislation on 4th December, 1829. Prohibiting sati in Indian society. For the first time Raja Ram Mohan Rai, began social reform movement in India. This movement was continued by Eswarchandra Vidyasagar. In Andhra Kandukuri Veeresalingam Pantulu began social reform movement. Veeresaligam, led the way for South India in espousing the cause of women and pleaded for the right of child-widows to remarry and demanded equal educational and cultural rights for women along with men and made a bold attack on religious bigotry, untouchability, caste taboos.[13] Unnava accepted Veeresalingam's teachings against casteism and worked for the widow remarriage movement. He founded a home for widows at Guntur 1902. On 11th October 1902 Unnava performed the first widow remarriage under the presidentship of Veeresalingam. He displayed as long back as 1905-1910, his special characteristic of acting according to his convictions, unmindful of social or religious or even political consequences and painful penalties that resulted therefrom by aiding Veeresalingam in organising marriages of Hindu widows, whenever the concerned parties wished to get married, despite the opposition of their respective families and leaders of their castes. Lakshmi Bayamma cooperated with him boldly. They faced the ban issued against them by local Brahmins and their high priests. They provided shelter to the Brahmin widows who wished to re-marry and they braved the legal actions instituted by the parents of these widows and thus strengthened the social revolution initiated by their leader Veeresalingam. To have to face such social persecution and painful rigours of Brahminical bans, even during Gandhiji's national campaign against social orthodoxy, for the sake of Swaraj was dreadful enough. But to have openly invited that persecution from the then almost all powerful orthodoxy and challenged it to do its worst, two decades before Gandhian era was indeed a terrific task and Unnava and his wife proved their mettle by shouldering that extremely dangerous mission on the inspiration of Veeresalingam. Veeresalingam and Unnava faced social ostracism in heroic manner and emerged as "triumphant templars" of social revolution and thus paved the way for the later Gandhian age.

SARADA NIKETAN: (Residential Social Reform Girls High School):

Unnava and Lakshmi Bayamma founded the residential institution of Sarada Niketan on 24th November, 1922 in Guntur, soon after their return from jail, because they realised the importance of recruiting, training and sponsoring young leaders among Indian women folk, especially of rural areas. It was not easy to persuade peasant families to send their grown-up girls to such institutions in distant towns in those days. In the establishment of this institution he was financially assisted by many persons.[14] He introduced in this institution, Telugu, Sanskrit, Hindi and English. English was introduced to send students to Benaras Matriculation Examination. To study in this institution, women from other countries also came.[15] He admitted Harijan girls into the beloved institution. He also introduced the training in handicrafts and fine arts in this institution. The students of this institution extended their assistance in organising political conferences in Guntur. They transformed the Congress movement into a people's movement. Gandhiji visited this institution. In 1944 it became affiliated institution to Andhra University. The Silver Jubilee celebrations were held in 1948. In 1956 Kalluri Chandra Mouli the then state Endowment Minister brought this institution under the control of Andhra Pradesh Government.[16]

Unnava made this institution the training ground for many a spirited competent women leader for the later decades of Kisan, Congress and Women movement of South India. Thus he carried on Veeresalingam's tradition and broadened his revolution's ambit through the constructive work for Indian women.

Many a full-pledged public worker, among Indian leaders of women who have be come freedom fighters, like Smt.Annapuranamma, former member of Parliament from Karnataka, Sangam Lakshmi Bayamma former Parliamentarian and Deputy Minister from Telangana, Pushkaramba, artist from Andhra have gained their spiritual back ground and cultural attainments and self-confidence from Unnava and Lakshmi Bayamma.

This institution also produced B. Sakuntala Devi, Masumdar Savitri, who studied in this institution. Later on she worked as a principal to this institution. Unnava Kalyani, the adopted daughter of Unnava also studied in this institution and participated in Salt Satyagraha and was imprisoned for three months in Rayavellore jail. Bharati Devi wife of N.G.Ranga was also a student of this institution.

Harijan-Upliftment:

For the upliftment of Harijans Unnava and a few others[17] founded Krishnasramam in Podapalem village, Guntur district in 1916. Through his novels Nayakuralu and Malapalli, he tried to propagate reformation in the Hindu society and tried to bring the Harijans into the streamline of the society. When most of the Congress Brahmins were not yet ready to join in organising inter dining with Harijans in large scale public dinners in rural areas and especially in Harijan areas, Malapallis, Unnava gladly joined N.G.Ranga, Bharati Devi and Desoddharaka.[18]

In 1933 Gandhiji toured entire India in connection with his Harijan upliftment movement. During Gandhiji's visit Unnava and Kasinadhuni Nageswara Rao and other Congress leaders arranged inter dining with Harijans in the Harijan street at Aaremanda village, Bapatla Taluk.

Proscribed works and contribution to Freedom Movement:

Unnava was a great scholar in Telugu. He believed, like Veeresalingam, in the need for democratising Telugu prose and poetry so as to make it the vehicle of revolutionary thoughts and the emerging educative medium of expression for the feelings and thoughts of the suffering and struggling masses. So he wanted to write a novel in the language of the masses.

Unnava was aware of the cataclysmic social challenge that Lenin's Russia posed to the whole of the world. Unlike most other nationalists and even poets and thinkers of the Congress, he realised that sooner or later, India too would have to face up to the socio-economic conflicts that were latent in the Indian economic life and find a solution to the age old disease of exploitation that was eating into her vitals.

Unnava read Tolstoy's novels Resurrection and Anna Karenina and the English novel Silas the Mariner and H.G. Wells novel, New World for the Old. He knew also about the British socialist approach. He wanted to prepare the Andhra Congressmen and other nationalists as well as the youth to face up to not only world's struggle against imperialism and to India's immediate need for Swaraj but also inescapable problem of Indian masses to liquidate social and economic exploitation and achieving equal human relations among all classes and castes. Around this principal ideological approach Unnava wove the plan for his novel Malapalli.

October Revolution of Russia had its profound impact on Unnava. It is difficult to accept this assertion, as Unnava wrote much that was opposed to Marxism in Malapalli. Still as Kasinadhuni Nageswara Rao in his foreward to Malapalli says "it is a peerless work" and Unnava's attempt to reconstruct life on a new rational basis" was most commendable.[19] Malapalli (The Adi-Andhra Hamlet) or Sanga Vijayamu (The Triunph of Sangadas) [20] was written by Unnava Lakshmi Narayana while confined in the central jail, rayavellore and published in 1922 in contravention of the terms on which permission was granted by the Andhra Parishad, Bezwada. It was proscribed and forfeited by the Madras Government on 14th May, 1923 by the powers conferred by section 99-A of the Code of Criminal Procedure 1898 as it contained seditious matter the publication of which was punishable under Section 124-A of the Indian Penal Code. [21] It was proscribed for twice.

Setting, background and time of action were early 1920s, a village in the Andhra region. The principal characters are Choudarayya, head of a high caste (Kamma) a family of landowners, his wife Lakshmamma, their adopted son Venkatayya, their own son Rama Naidu, his wife Kamala. A cousin of Rama Naidu was Mohan Rao; Ramadas, head of a Harijan family, his wife Mahalakshmamma, their sons Venkatadas (Takkela Jaggadu), Sangadas and Rangadu, their daughter Jyoti. Appadas, a Harijan boy working in their house, in love with their daughter was another character.

The summary of the novel is as follows :

There lived in Mangalapuram in the Guntur district a wealthy land-Lord named Choudarayya who was, acutely conscious of his social status (as a member of the high-caste) as well as of his wealth. He was greedy and callous. His younger son Rama Naidu received education. Rama Naidu married Kamalamma, a handsome young lady, had a son, Sahu by name, and devoted himself to the uplift of the Adi-Andhra community. Choudarayya felt very sad because his son Rama Naidu fraternising closely with Sangadas, son of Ramadas. He wanted that each one should know his place and keep it at all cost.

In a hamlet adjoining the village lived Ramadas, an Adi-Andhra. He was a man of culture and refinement. He lived a happy and contended life on his small plot of land with his wife and children. Philosophical by temperament and religious by family tradition, he spent his spare time in discoursing on the teachings of holymen. His family was an example of obedience in life. In the task of reforming his community he was greatly assisted by Rama Naidu in his social work.

These two young men, Rama Naidu and Sangadas, fomented strikes among the coolies, with a view to secure increased wages for them. On the return of the latter from Bezwada, whither he had gone to attend an Adi-Andhra conference, Choudarayya, his master, felt displeased with him for inciting the coolies, and dealt a heavy blow on his head which proved fatal, though death had never been intended by the murderer. The police appeared on the scene, received bribes and hushed up the case.

Shocked by this murder Ramadas derived some consolation from his son's memory perpetuated in the founding of a school (Sangamandiram) for the untouchables with the active co-operation of Rama Naidu. But this was not the end of the troubles of Ramadas. Choudarayya would not let him live in peace. With the connivance of Revenue officials, he managed to evict Ramadas from his land. Armadas and his family found themselves thrown on the streets. He was forced to work as a common labourer.

Rama Naidu had thus lost a comrade in social service, and now worked single-handed. His wife Kamalamma had eloped with his cousin Mohan Rao, and left her son, Sahu, behind.

Appadas, a nephew of Ramadas opened an Adi Andhra School in Sangamandiram. Ramadasu's daughter, Jyoti, a grown up girl of noble qualities was his student in this school. They passionately loved each other and wished to be united in wed-lock.

Venkatadas, the eldest son of Ramadas, unable to withstand the injustice done to his father, turns a rebel. Under the an assumed name (Takkella Jagannadham or Jaggadu) he organised a gang of robbers, plundered the rich and supported the poor all over the land. Among the followers of Jaggadu were Santhans (a hill trible) who were a terror to the authorities.

With a view to break up the gang of Jaggadu, Government kept many members of the depressed classes, who had been suspected to be his followers in the Criminal Settlement. Ramadas, his wife, daughter, and the third son were removed to the Settlement at Seetanagaram, near Bezwada Paul, the evangelist of the Settlement was inspired with love for Jyoti and proposed to her father, that she might be given to him in marriage, which neither the father nor the daughter liked. Indignant at this, Paul and Anderson (The Superintendent of the Criminal Settlement) got Ramadas and his wife imprisoned on the allegation that he (Ramadas) and some others had fled away from the settlement. One morning Paul had tried to seize Jyoti, who in spite of her being purused by her adversary, escaped from his, threw herself into the river Krishna and got drowned in it. Hearing the news of the tragic death of Jyoti, Appadas who had lover her and wished to marry her, flung himself into the river and followed her to the other world.

Foresaken by Mohan Rao, Kamalamma returned home in the guise of a servant. Sahu, Kamalamma, Choudarayya and his wife had died one after another, and left a large prosperity, all of which Rama Naidu and his elder brother devoted to the organisation of labour unions. The authorities imprisoned Rama Naidu for doing work on behalf of these unions.

The sin of seducing Kamalamma pursued Mohan rao, who proceeded to the Sabarmati Asramam, where he met with an untimely death. He made over his property to the labour unions.

The Government agitated by the escapades of the gang of robbers laid a trap for Jaggadu. Coming to know of this he decided to fight it out. In the encounter that ensued he was seriously wounded and captured. He was tried and sentenced to simple imprisonment for six years. He had spent some time with his parents, who were in the same prison, and died soon after his confinement there.

Swaraj was at last granted to India by the British Parliament. All the Europeans withdrew from the country, and the prisoners were let off. Ramadas once again joined Rama Naidu and his brother and proceeded with the task of the organisation of the labour unions and the uplift of the depressed classes.

Unnava chose rural India as the panorama for his story, village life as its canvas and the class as well as caste struggle between the land holding village bosses on one side and the landless workers on the other. He found the class struggle inextricably inter-twined with the intercaste antagonisms and rivalries. He found village-life so full of social disparities, caste rivalries and spirit of vengeance poisoning social relations and untouchability butteressing economic exploitation.

Unnava displayed his uncompromising passion for social revolution in the title Malapalli, he chose for his novel; that is the ghetto of the untouchable tribe, called Malas. He hated the segregation of Harijans from the rest of the village folk, a segregation that the defeated and submerged Harijans must have bargained for at the time of their political fall so as to be free from daily and intimate interference of the aggressive victors in their social relations or the victors had forced on the vanquished as a token of their subordination. He wanted to highlight the utterly unconscionable and socially degrading nature of such isolation and thus shamed society for its callous apartheid policy and practice.

The father of his hero, Ramadas was fashioned after Gandhiji and the character of Sanga Das probably took shape after himself. He made Sanga Das and Venkata Das, the other principal characters to typify a Gandhian and a Leninist, one practicing non-violence, the other choosing violence as their means for achieving te desired social revolution. He developed the dialectical themes, conversations and disputations between these protagonists with great skill, and literary excellence. Unnava's heart was consecrated to Gandhian means.

Around these social approaches, along these themes, Unnava developed his great novel of about 1000 pages, so rich in its discussions about the nature and place of religion, literature, songs family loyalties etc. all woven into a beautiful multi-faceted Kalankari of literature.

An active nationalist and committed social reformer, he brought to bear on the novel his felt experience of rural life in all its diversity and even before Gandhiji's Harijan movement had its pervasive impact, Unnava saw in the upliftment of the lower classes the vital clue to national regeneration. It was out of this firm conviction regarding the vital role of the lower classes in any programme of social advancement that he created one of the most memorable characters in Telugu fiction.

He also criticised the corruptive British administrative system of criminal settlements, police departments and jails.

It has come to be one of the noblest literary achievements of contemporary India. Its translations have appeared in Hindi, English, Russian and Kannada. It ranks among the best world classics of 20th century.

The essence of the objectionable matter (as per Government opinion) of the novel is as follows:- While describing the policies of the Government the author said that like the buffaloes which had fallen into a lotus tank, the British rulers had completely destroyed the institutions of the village administration wonderfully organised by the ancient kings in every village.

Bolshevism means the opinion of the majority of the people. The Czar of Russia had become a puppet in the hands of the capitalists and the zamindars, and tormented the people at large, according to ther wishes of the former. This wicked Government had continued for more than a hundred years. The people were immersed in unbearable poverty. At last, in the European war (First World War) the capitalist and the labour communities sank like the kolair lake. A Panchayat Government was set up and panchayats were established all over the country.

The Bolsheviks main doctrines are that all have the right to enjoy the store of things in creation; that all should work and enjoy it, and it is not just that while some were burnt fiercely without food and raiment, some other should sink in and flour on luxuries and wicked passions. It is not possible for anyone to say that their doctrines are wrong.

While describing the corruption of the Government the author said through the character Pantulu, to the wife of Choudarayya, in connection with the hushing up of a case of homicide, from the village munsiff right upto the Deputy superintendent of police all their mouths has to be shut with bribes. Four or five bags of rupees were lost to us. Inspector Sastri collected four bags of money and distributed them, one bag for Ayyangar, who was the Deputy Superintendent of Police, one bag for the Inspectors of Police, one bag for the police establishment, and one bag for the people of the village.

Small pox raged at Mambalam, near Madras and the authorities disposed of the dead. As the corpses had increased in number, they threw them into the same motor lorry, mingling them with living patients. When valuable articles were found they would load the articles into another motor lorry. With the stolen cloths and articles the polkice set up a big trade in the city. Police stole the money from the houses and disrtributed it among themselves.

The author described the activities of the Government courts such as the District Munsiff of Bapatla who would forcibly compromise the parties in some cases; dismiss certain cases by taking advantage of the absence of pleasders; adjourn the cases in which witnesses were present; put up for enquiry the cases where witnesses were absent; and would thus lighten his work and in some cases the Munsiffs took bribes from the respective parties.

Further the author described the activities of Jaggadu as known to the inhabitants of the village of Kondavidu: that the gang of Takkella Jaggadu (the decoit-leader), had besieged the District Superintendent of police and his staff, caught them, tied them up to trees and went away.

The author kept in mind the policies of the Government and he said through the character Rama Naidu, that the Government was thinking of uprooting the labour unions. No movement could go on without the advent of Swaraj. If the Government continued in this fashion, Bolshevism would spread in India.

The British troops had encountered the gang of dacoits of Jaggadu. He was imprisoned by the Government. His statement in the court made all thoughtful men realise that on account of the wilful destruction of the indigenous industries in the interest of England, the poorer classes lost their livelihood and it was a mighty cause for the increase of the dacoits in India. Legal thefts to more harm to the world than illegal thefts. "What is useful to the rich is lawful, while that which is not is a crime". The wealthy themselves were the demons of this age. This demonical nature was derived from the tormentation of the poor. If the wealthy did not change their conduct, the poor themselves would alter the laws and establish a heaven on earth in the universe.

Ramadas said "if the police department is abolished, there will be much reduction in the number of cases. The gain derives from the abolition of police department will be greater than the loss sustained by it".

As already stated Malapalli was written by U. Lakshmi Narayana of Guntur while under going simple imprisonment in the central jail, Rayavellore. The manuscript was forwarded to Government by the Inspector General of Prisons. The Telugu translator to Madras

Government supplied areport on the book together with a translation of certain passages in it which were considered objectionable. In the report he stated that The author snatches every opportunity or creates an opportunity where none exists, to denounce most unsparingly the system of criminal settlements, police, jails, courts etc. He does not stop here, but zealously preaches at some length the principles of Bolshevism, and the creed of non-cooperation in such a manner and in such language as would assuredly bring Government into hatred and contempt in the country". "personally, I feel convinced that its publication, if allowed by Government, will do incalculable harm to the country and its people." [22] The translator was clearly of opinion that the book would bring the Government into utter hatred and contempt among the people of the country.

The translation was referred to the Advocate General for his opinion. He pointed out that many of the passages offended against Sections 124-A and 153-A of the Indian Penal Code. The Government therefore proscribed the book under the Public Department G.O. No.396 dated 14th May, 1923. Swarajya newspaper severely criticised the proscription of Malapalli novel and wrote that "......it is deplorable that a book of surpassing literary charm should have been proscribed by the Government of Madras on the ground that it was seditious.......we rejoice that the Government have afforded the most eloquent illustration of the truth that "all looks yellow to the jaundical eyes".[23]

In answer to a supplementary question in the Madras Legislative Council on the subject of lifting the ban on the novel in 1927 the then law member agreed to allow the publication of a revised edition of the book provided six or seven objectionable passages were expunged from it. The Advocate General after personal discussion with the author indicated six passages which should be modified or expunged in order to make the publication unobjectionable. The author agreed to carry out all the omissions and alterations except one poem in Volume III. The advocate General suggested waiver of objection to the retention of the above poem. The Government accepted the suggestion and accordingly the author was permitted to publish a revised edition as amended and approved in G.O. No.307 Public dated 30th March 1928, subject to a further condition that the copies should bear the words 'revised edition'.

On 19th July 1928 at a prize distribution at the Krishna Ashram, Guntur, for Adi Andhra a copy of the proscribed book was given as a prize. On inspection by the District Superintendent of Police it was found that all pages objected to except page 114 of part III had been torn out. The District Superintendent of Police had the house of Lakshmi Narayana searched and recovered one copy. The author then gave a statement to the effect that all copies (about 80) ahad been given to a press at Bezwada for rebinding after removing objectionable portions and that he, by oversight failed to tear out page 114 in the book which was presented. The explanation was accepted by Government and no further action was taken in the matter – vide G.O. No.701 Public dated 21st September, 1928. The revised edition was published in September 1935 by Andhra Grandhamala of Kasinadhuni Nageswararao.

Malapalli was prescribed as a non-detailed text book for the B.A. in the Andhra University – Vide Fort St.George Gazette dated 8th January, 1935, part I-B, Education page 27. At that time the Vice-Chancellor of Andhra University was S. Radhakrishna. On 7th February 1936 the chief Secretary to Madras Government wrote a letter to the Vice-chancellor of Andhra University. In it he wrote that there were many objectionable passages in the revised edition and gave reasons and stated that the Government was thinking to proscribe it – Vide Home Department G.O. No.1203 dated 3rd July 1936. Later the Andhra University authorities removed it from syllabus.

On 30th October, 1935 Madras special Branch C.I.D. sent a report to the Governmnet. The report stated that the revised edition contained objectionable passages which fell within the scope of section 4 (1) clauses (b) and (d) of the Indian Press (Emergency Powers) Act, 1931. Capitalists and bureaucrats were made out to be tyrants, and libellous statements about the police, the Magistracy, and jail department were made. The book was revised as amended and approved by Government in G.O. No.307 Public dated 30th March, 1928. If the revised edition contained objectionable matter the police might seize and forfeit to His Majesty under the forfeiture orders passed in respect of unrevised edition. No fresh order or notification was necessary. The C.I.D. however did not say that the author had failed to comply with the conditions laid down, permitting him to publish revised edition but only pointed out that the revised edition contained objectionable passages which fell under Section 4 (1) (b) and (d) of the Indian Press (Emergency Powers) 1931. The above act was not in force at the time when the book was amended and approved by the Government in 1928 and this probably accounted for the existence of some of the objectionable passages in the revised edition.

The C.I.D. suggested that the revised edition should be sent to the Telugu Translator to scrutinise with a view to see whether the conditions laid down by the Government were complied with. The review of the book and the translations of the objectionable passages furnished by the C.I.D. were also sent to the Translator for remarks as to whether they might be taken as substantially correct.

The Telugu Translator wrote that though the author had expunged strong words and passages which openly characterised the representatives of British Government in India as 'buffaloes' and their system of Government as a sort of legalised plunder, by carrying out the amendments, he had managed to retain the insidious poision of the latter practically in toto as it was, under the cover of 'literacy value' and under the pretext, that "it is not wrong to preach Communism or to encourage the union of labour against capital". A perusal of the passages actually omitted by the author in pages 221 to 222 of old edition side by side with the corresponding pages in the revised edition (pages 485 to 487) would show how meager the omission was and how ineffective and it meant that practically no revision was effected by the author. He asked the Government how permission had been accorded to the author to retain the poem in the old edition (pages 339 to 341 of the new edition). The translations of extensive parts of the poem would show how powerfully it advocated communism.

The report (16th January 1936) of K.V.Reddi Naidu (member of the Executive council) was "the whole book is nothing but communistic propaganda". To support this view he showed the song at pages 339, 340 and 341. He reported that "courts are described as despicable. The police are corrupt. They concoct false cases and torture the accused. The rich are robbers and do not hesitate to tell an oath the most naked lies. Dacoities are praised and even if property worth ten lakhs of rupees is robbed it is no sin because no murders have been committed in such dacoities. The miser having become an emperor is ruling in this world. If all the workers only unite, the world is theirs. If they swarm and strike, the world is theirs. In my opinion the whole book ought to have been proscribed".

In contrast to K.V.Reddy Naidu's report the Advocate General on 16th May 1936 sent a report to the Government. He stated that though some portions of the book are expressed in strong language it is susceptible of the interpretation that the writer is dissatisfied with the present social system and economic ordering society, points to certain abuses in the police and jail administration and thinks that the panacea for all these evils is the attainment of self Government and the reform of the existing system of administration" and he also reported that "the writer also emphasises that according to him the existing economic evils in the society tend to perpetration of crime and lawless acts on the part of the poor and oppressed in society". "The reference to the British flag being pulled down etc., is incidental to the fury which overtakes the gang. On the whole, taking all parts of the book into consideration, I cannot safely advise the Government to take proceedings to proscribe the book". He also cited an example i.e. a decision of a full Bench of the Allahabad High

Court, which appeared in the Hindu of the 14th instant, pointed to the conclusion that even the deliberate preaching of Bolshevism under particular circumstances might not bring the case under Section 124-A or under the Press Emergency Power Act. He also mentioned that "if proceedings are taken against the revised edition of the book, the action of the Government on the former occasion, though it may not preclude them from taking any proceedings may carry considerable weight with any court of law dealing with the case under Section 99-B of the Criminal Procedure Code".

Taking into the consideration the opinion of K.V. Reddy Naidu and C.I.d. reports the Government proscribed the said novel on 3rd July, 1936. The proscription orders were published in Gazette. But the occupation of the office of Prime Minister by Raja Gopala Chari the ban on the novel was lifted on 28th July, 1937[24] on the ground that the Governor stated that "It is a harmless and tedious bit of literature".

Conclusion

Unnava was a great writer, a prominent freedom fighter and dedicated social worker. His literary works especially his novel Malapalli and active participation in the political activities proved the zeal and devotion to free the nation from the yoke of British rule. Through these services and contribution he tried to generate new ideas and trends, necessary for reformation. He was one of the founder of the tradition of the novel in Telugu. He was the trend-setter to the revolutionary writers of the 1960-1980 generation.

He decided not to venture into election because he disliked the caste orientation of electioneering, bossim and so did not try to become a partner in the political combinations. It indicates his individuality and independent mindedness. He was not a leader of the masses but a number of mass leaders were encouraged by him. He sacrificed his life for the sake of the country.

Unnava had adopted Gandhiji as his political guru and accepted his cult of non-violence as the most effective weapon to achieve political and social revolution, and believed that it would assist the revolution and enrich the society. At the same time, he learnt to admire such revolutionaries as Tiwari and Alluri Sitaramaraju and appreciated the inestimable strength and spirit of their sacrifices. Unnava had two types of personalities to exemplify the two contending forces and means for achieving the revolution of the non-violent Gandhiji and violent Tiwari and Sitarama Raju.

GARIMELLA SATYANARAYANA (1893-1952)

Early Life and Education :

Garimella was born in 1893 (the date and month is not available) at Gonepalli Village Priyagraharam, Narasannapeta Taluk, Srikakulam District.[25] His father was Venkata Narasimham, mother Suramma. Venkata Narasimham had five sons and three daughters. Garimella was the eldest among them. He studied primary education in his own village. Higher education was at Vizianagaram and Masulipatam. For his education he received financial help from others[26] and got B.A. degree. He joined teacher training college in Rajahmundry in 1920. Majority of scholars opined that Garimella did not complete L.T. (teacher training). [27]

Participation in the Freedom Movement

Gandhiji's call made Garimella a freedom fighter and freedom movement made Garimella a poet. While he was studying B.A. in Vizianagaram he wrote the famous patriotic ballad Maakoddi Tella Dora Tanam (We don't want this White Government[28] in folklore style. While he was studying L.T. degree in the historic place Rajahmundry, he established relations with freedom fighters and patriots like Brahmajoshyula Subramanyam. It was the beginning of a new chapter in the life of Garimella. During this period he made some changes in the aforesaid ballad and enhanced it.

Influenced by Bipin chandra Pal's speeches, the A.I.C.C. conference at Bezwada and the approval of All India Congress Conference's non-cooperation resolution and its movement, Garimella decided to enter into the freedom struggle. He went to seek approval from his father, but his father refused. However, observing the zeal of his son he approved his participation in the struggle. At the same time he took promise from his son, not to say sorry to the Britishers under any circumstances. Thereafter Garimella entered into freedom struggle. He choose to take part in the freedom struggle through his writings on the nature of the British rule, Gandhian constructive programme like Anti-drink, Harijan upliftment, the propagation of the establishment of Raatnam and the then political, social and economic conditions and the need for the establishment of independent India. Another instrument he continuously used was the singing of ballads and gitas in various gatherings. He boycotted English education, and discontinued his studies, and he never took Government service even though many elders pressurised him; and he never wore British cloth and wore only khaddar till his death.

GARIMELLA SATYANARAYANA
(1893-1952)

For the propagation of freedom struggle, he used his first ballad "We don't want this white Government". He was not only a famous writer but also a famous singer, so he began to sing it in many gatherings and inspired the people. This news reached the British officials. Therefore East Godavari District Collector G.T.H.Braken brought Garimella before him and asked him to sing the said ballad. Garimella sang the ballad with his melodious and inspiring voice. Though Braken did not know Telugu language, he grasped the inspiration, potentiality and anti British attitude of the ballad. Immediately he ordered police to arrest him. He was arrested under section 108 Criminal Procedure Code and sentenced to one year imprisonment by the District Magistrate of Cocanada on 9th February 1922.[29] On this occasion Garimella gave a message to Andhras. This message was published in Hindu on 11th February 1922.[30] Later on it was proscribed and forfeited by the Government of Madras. This ballad was written by Garimella twenty one years prior to Gandhiji's Quit India movement of 1942. Gandhiji appreciated Garimella for writing this ballad and suggested to the gathered writers and poets before him on the occasion of writers and poets conference before Gandhiji, to write on the model of this ballad.

Another two Telugu volumes of Garimela, entitled Swarajya Gitamulu were published in 1921-1922. These two volumes were printed in Madras, because the local press owners refused to print them due to fear of Government. The Government scrutinised thesae two volumes and felt that they raised intense hatred and contempt among the people of the country against the British Government. The concerned officials took measures not to publish the third volume of "Swarajya Gitamulu". So the Government of Madras proscribed and forfeited the said two volumes. Five hundred copies of them were burnt by the Government.

A case was filed by the Government on Garimella against the aforesaid book and he was sentenced for two years of imprisonment. During this imprisonment his beloved father in 1923 and grandfather in 1924 died, but he did not attend the funeral. To keep the promise which was given to his farther, he did not ask permission from jail officials. On his return from jail, he received hearty welcome from Andhras as well as his native village people in 1924 and paid homage to his father and grandfather.

To create social consciousness, political awakening and to bring the modern ideas before the people, Garimella founded a printing institution called Sree Sarada Grandhamala[31] in his native place and printed seven books, but it did not yield fruitful results, because there was no publicity of the books in those days, in addition to that he was frequently at Rajahmundry, Bezwada and Madras. So the books were destroyed due to natural causes.

Professional Activity

Garimella's family profession was agriculture, but they lost their lands after the death of his father. After the completion of B.A. degree Garimella worked as a clerk in Collector Office Ganjam and a teacher in the Vizianagaram High School for some time.[32] For some time he worked as a Secretary for Gnanodaya Samaj Grandhamandala of his village. In this library there were 600 books. For livelihood Garimella and his family went to Madras in 1933. His fourth borther Suryanarayana maintained a hotel at Mylapore in Madras, the name of the hotel was Kalpaka Vilas.[33] But they did not make any profit from the hotel, so they closed it.

He worked as an Editor to K.N. Kesari's monthly magazine Gruhalakshmi, but he left it after some time. For some time he worked as a co-editor to N.G.Ranga's Vahini and Andhra Prabha, a daily newspaper. For some time he worked as a freelance journalist and an editor for Anandavani. He earned money from writing of essays to various newspapers and All India Radio, Madras. In addition he received financial help from some notable personalities.[34] Even then he was subjected to poverty and ill-health. Pasumarti Raghava Rao the editor of Penki Pilla, monthly journal, described the impoverished condition of Garimella and requested the people to extend financial help to Garimella.[35] His brother Ramalinga Murthy died in 1944 and also Garimela's wife Satyavathi died in the same year. His mother died in 1951. In addition to all these troubles he lost his vision in the later days.

He did not settle in any employment due to independent mindedness and straight forwardness. Apart from patriotism these qualities were responsible for his poverty. But he did not leave patriotism.

Political and Literary works

Gurajada Appa Rao, writer of the famous poem Desamante Matti Kadoyoi Desamante Manushuloi, died in 1915. In this context Garimella wrote an eighty-sentence memorial Gitam on Appa Rao. It was published in Krishna Patrika on 4th December, 1915.

In those days the songs of Garimella were very popular. Freedom fighter and famous writer Manikonda Satyanarayana appreciated Garimella for writing the song entitled Emayya Yuvaraja Endukochavayya,[36] in his book entitled Krishna Zilla Charitra (history of Krishna District). It was written at the time of Connaught (the British Royal family member) arrival to inaugurate the Dyarchy in India. This song was most popular in those days. He wrote a drama in Telugu entitled Manikyam in 1926.

His ballads Madyapana Nishedamu (prohibition of liquor), Nemali Pata (song peacock) "Andhra University" Rajabhakti Gitam were published on 2nd October 1926 in Krishna Patrika. Swarajyamunakokabata (A way to Swaraj) was published in Krishna Patrika on 2nd April 1927. In these ballads he propagated that the drinking of toddy and arrack was one of the responsible factors for the impoverishment of the people. If the people discarded this habit, it would give death blows to the British treasury and it would be useful as a weapon for the achievement of Swaraj. He discouraged the growing desire for foreign civilization among the Indian women. He appreciated the establishment of Andhra University in Andhra, but suggested the continuation of national education to the extent possible. He criticised the policies of Justice Party and praised the principles of Gandhiji; discouraged the differences among the Congressmen and the craze on foreign cloth. He highlighted the importance of Raatnam and Khaddar; propagated it as a symbol of independence and suggested to the people to fight against British Raj.

The ballads Congressulo Galabha was published in Krishna Patrika on 26th September, 1926, and Valapu-Vagalu was published in Bharathi in December 1926. In these ballads he described the differences among the Congressmen on the issue of entry into the Legislature. Gandhiji and some others were against the Council entry while Chittaranjan Das and some others were in favour of Council entry. So they separated themselves as Swarajyaists, but they obeyed the principles of Gandhiji. He admired Lajapat Rai, Malavya, Sreenivasaiyyangar, Showkat Ali, Kitchlu and Gandhiji. The misbehaviour in the legislatures was also criticised. In these ballads he mirrored the then political conditions.

His another work Nutana Jatiya Gitamulu was printed at Gautami press, Sitanagaram by Madduri Annapurnayya in 1926. He stated that he took all kinds of care in writing this work so that it might not be proscribed and to continue in the hearts of the people and to give inspiration to the people. This book contained songs entitled Vandemataram, Nirakaranam (non-cooperation), Congressulo Ikamatyam, Yotulapata, Chittaranjan Das, Kartavyam (duty), Desaaradhakulu Bhadalu (The troubles of Patriots) and Purvapu Sthithi.

In this work he worshipped Mother India and suggested to the people not to give vote to the Justice Party and condemned the role of money in the elections. He appealed to the thirty three crores of Indians to continue the system of Panchayats instead of the courts which were established by the British; encouraged non-cooperation, stressed the need for unity among the various sects of people; described the hardships of patriots in the freedom struggle in their day to day life including bearing the comments of jealous persons and supported the Congress, Gandhiji and compared him with God. He highlighted the troubles of labourers and peasants; the exploitation system of Britishers; suggested to the people to fight against the British in the method of non-cooperation; propagated Raatnam which would provide employment to poor and a blow to British trade. These ballads, songs and 'gitas' gained propularity among the people next to the ballad "We don't want this white Government".

Gandhiji's concentration on the removal of untouchability from Hindu Society has stirred the whole country in a manner that nothing else could have done. He had awakened the soul of the Harijans no less than that of the other Hindus. Gandhiji's slogan untouchability must die if Hinduism was to live and if untouchability was to live Hinduism had to die became popular in India. The upliftment of Harijans was one of the items in Gandhiji's constructive programme. At this juncture Garimella wrote Harijana Patalu in February 1933 and the book was published by Desoddharaka Nageswara Rao Pantulu, the then Andhra Rastra Harijana Seva Sangha President (1933). It contained ballads like Prardhana (prayer) Hindu Sanghiyulam, Sarvasammatam, Harijanulam, Bharatadesa Prathibha, Asuprusyata Siddanta Nirasanam, Nutana Tejam etc.

In these songs he gave an assurance on behalf of Harijans that every aspect of their day to day life would be cleaned and they would discard all evil habits like drinking toddy. He criticised the traditional high castes attitude towards Harijans. He said Gandhiji was against the seperation of Harijans from Hindu society and all were one, every body had to obey the orders of Eswara (God) and if so, there was beauty, strength and unity. He preached that all castes should work unitedly for collective prosperity; people must enjoy the wealth of land equally all are Hindus, "Vedas are ours". He hated untouchability and invited them to temples; eulogised the past glory of India.

After 1932 Salt Satyagraha, number of changes took place in the national politics such as rise of Extremism in the Congress, the establishment of Congress Socialist Party, propagation of Socialism by Communist party, the rise of labour and ryot movements, the formation of Congress Ministry in six States and Congress hung-Ministry in three states. The Congress Government released political prisoners, gave freedom to press and publication. Labour and ryot organisations raised their voice. All these changes influenced Garimella besides the influence of Mallikarjuna Rao, the Congress Socialist Party Secretary, Darsi Chanchayya, Gadar Party leader and later a Communist. Under these influences he wrote a revolutionary Gitam entitled Anyayakalam Dapurinchindipudi (injustice time prevailed now (1938). In this Gitam he described the impoverished condition of peasants and labourers, the exploitation of wealthy people. He hated disparities and tried to wake up the suppressed classes. He hoped that this injustice should die and preached the necessity of unity among the labour classes to eliminate this injustice.. It was published in Chitragupta.. this gitam is still relevant to the present society. The communists used this Gitam in their conferences and propagation of their party ideals. Some people thought it was written by a Communist. He also wrote religious songs.

He was also a famous essay writer. He wrote many essays on politics, social life, and literary aspects. His main object in writing these essays was the propagation of Congress principles. Bharati, Anandavani, Krishna Patrika, Trilinga, Dhanka published his essays. On 2nd October 1926, Krishna Patrika published his big essay on Nutana Sahitya Vijrumbhanam (Rise of Modern Lierature). In this essay he discussed Gita Kavitvam, Misra Kavyamulu, Prabhanda Vachanamulu, novels, Andhra dramas, Newspapers, Telugu spoken language etc.

In 1947, 1948 Danka Patrika published two essays of Garimella entitled Bharatadesamunku Kavalasina Socialist Vidhanam Bharatadesanug unamagu Communism Kavalenu. In these essays he stated that the concentration of wealth in a few hands was the resoponsible factor for the creation of conflicts among the people. If it was shared by everybody the differences in religious sects, and regions automatically would subside.

Garimela translated Pattabhi Sitaramayya's English work The Economic Conquest of India into Telugu entitled Bharata Khandam Paini Aardhikavijayam or British Samrajyam (limited). It was published by Hindustan Publishing Company in 1938. He wrote in English Heart of the Nation and Mother India poems, the latter was published in the name of S.N.Garimella. In this poem he supported the proposal for the establishment of Andhra University in Andhra, by the then Education Minister, A.V. Patro (Justice Party) in the Government of Madras.

During his imprisonment in Tiruchirapalli Jail, he learnt Tamil language from N.S. Krishnaswami Iyyangar and Holasyam Iyer. Tiruvalluvar's Tirukkural was a famous Tamil work. Tamils treated it as a Veda. It was translated into many languages. Many translations took place in Telugu for aforesaid book. Garimella was one of the first translators. It was entitled in Telugu as Ardhatraya Sarvasvam. Its first volume was printed at Sudharma Press, Masulipatam and published in 1926. for this contribution Garimella was appreciated by many stalwarts.[37] He also translated a Kannada work Tallikota into Telugu.

He stated that with the influence of Western civilization, literature and education many changes took place in the Telugu literature. A modern age began in Telugu literature Prabhanda Kavyas gave place to Khanda Kavyas and manay writers began to write Khanda Kavyas. Large number of writers began to use prose. All these are the features of modern age.

In his opinion the newspapers should be patriotic and fearless. Their object should be collective welfare. He realised the importance of editorials and criticised some of the newspapers for their narrow object.

His thinking, writings preached socialism and the essence of Upanishads. He appeared as a revolutionary poet but he was a national poet. He never supported the leftist parties.

Last Days

With his patriotism, literary contribution and freedom fighting, he occupied a prominent place in the history of freedom struggle in India. He spent his entire life in the service of his mother country. He expressed deep grief on the partition of India into two nations. Even after independence neither the Government nor any individual extended financial help to this freedom fighter, who sacrificed everything for the sake of the nation. He used to smile away his abject poverty and financial stress and strain saying "Some men at least should die of poverty; without this there cannot be independence for our country". He breathed his last on 18th December 1952 at the age of fifty nine, unhonoured, unsung and unwept. At the time of his death there was only a ten year old daughter took after him. His neighbours performed the obsequies.[38]

The Andhras have forgotten the great soul for forty five years. They did not give due recognition for his sacrifice and service. But now some of the freedom fighters and writers through their writings,[39] are recollecting the sacrifices made by Garimella.

Vavilla Venkateswara Sastrulu compared Garimella with Subramanya Bharathi of Tamil Nadu and called him Subramanya Bharati of Telugus.[40]

N.G.Ranga praised him as a Prajapatla Tyagayya.[41] The famous Telugu poet Viswanadha Satyanarayana called Garimella as Jatiyakavi Sarvabhoumudu.[42] Gurajada Raghava Sarma called him as Jatiya geeya Kavi sarvabhoumudu.

Within a span of forty-five years the people have forgotten the famous freedom fighter and writer. It is not the fault of the people, but it is the administrators, who are responsible for this. The Tamil people recognised and propagated the greatness of Subramanya Bharathi even after his death. But in the case of Garimella people have forgotten him. Whatever it is, people have now begun to recognise again the greatness of Andhra Jatiya Mahakavi Garimella.[43]

Proscribed works and contribution to Freedom Struggle

Among Garimella's inspiring political works the Government of Madras proscribed two important works of these two, the first and most important one is the Telugu ballad "We don't want this White Government". It was a balled of 162 sentences. It was the 'Magna carta' to describe the dependent, declining condition of India and for the propagation of Gandhiji's principles.

This song caught the imagination of young and old alike and soon became a symbol of the non-cooperation movement in the Telugu land. Here are a few excerpts from this lengthy ballad:

We don't want this White Government,
We dlon't want this White Government, my Lord,
It is after our lives,
And has stripped us of our honour,

For trade he came
Took over towns
Built an empire
Which he gifted to the Queen
He does violate
The Queen's assurances
And threatens with punishment
If you should but ask
Why it is so!

Even though the crops failed
The taxes are not curtailed
He sets the village officers on us
The taluk officers
Threatened with dismissal
He makes our homes
Nests of hardships
The taxes go up year by year
Finally he says the land is mine.
He makes us cultivate
The land for wages
And gives us the option
Of dying of hunger
Oh my God, he likes to become
An overlord of slaves.

Realise soon that it is a blackmark
To live by the service to the whites;
It is treason against the nation
And an offence against the Gods in heaven

Hark! You the cries of the motherland
The hearts of the whites have turned into stones
With whose permission did he
Commence his rule here?
And to whom is he responsible?
He does not follow a righteous path;
No parallel to his rule of terror.

The following description shows the importance of this ballad. This ballad began with "We don't want this white Government". Among all the problems, the food problem is most important one; so he described it first. He wrote thart a number of states were producing enormous food grains but the ordinary people were suffering from lack of sufficient food. They even whent to the extent of imposing tax on salt. The British came to India merely for trade, but in course of time they captured towns and after that they occupied entire India by illegal means, began to rule and finally handed it over to the British Crown.

The age-old functioning of Panchayats was destroyed and new courts were established by the British rulers. Through these they killed friendliness among the Indians and created many parties, differences and conflicts in the family and among the Indians. The rulers imposed heavy taxes on peasants and increased taxes year by year. They collected taxes by force, irrespecrtive of production of crops. The peasants were subjected to slavery and starvation. If the Government officials failed to collect taxes they used to dismiss them from jobs.

They imposed Section 144 and through it they closed the lips and tied the tongue of the people. The people had no right to question the injustice of the rulers. Even people had no right to talk. They curtailed singing and playing of National Anthem and forbade questioning the British administration, through cruel Acts. They insulted Indian women. Dyer ruthlessly killed several Indians by throwing bombs and opening fire, to continue their rule. Through their repressive laws they exploited the Indians.

They introduced toddy and arrack in India to fill their treasury. These were responsible to create calamities in the families, disturbed social harmony and even made some people to sell the Pustelu, [44] so the people lost their wealth and health.

The Britisheres removed the Indian flags at any and every place. To create fear among the nationalists the army petrolled the streets. They forced the Indians to salute the British flag (jack); they objected to the students going to schools wearing Gandhi cap. They severely opposed the establishment of Raatnam in the schools. Garimella criticised these activities of the British.

He highlighted the national feeling of chirala-Perala people and admired their courage to revolt. He criticised the British for their shamelessness after the seeing courageous and patriotic fervour of the people of Chirala-Perala.

He stated that the progress of a country or a movement would depend on the people's involvement and dedication. The dedication to the cause, based on dharma, would get victory. He stressed the necessity and importance of the unity among the Indians to get freedom and suggested that people should not leave Gandhiji's principle of non-violence even if the Britishers used violence.

He emphasised the importance of Raatnam to provide livelihood to the people. It would serve as a death blow to the British trade and a most powerful weapon to get Swaraj to Indians. He criticized the caste system which was existing in Indian society and suggested to destroy this evil system and invited Harijans into temples.

He compared jails with paradise, and invited the people into jails for liberation of mother country from the British yoke. He also stated that people need not live under cruel rule.

The author prayed God to remove the British authority on Indians, requested to protect the honour of the Indians and praised the ideas and policies of Gandhiji. He exactly estimated the significance of the movements advocated by Gandhiji and described Gandhiji's principles as powerful weapons. He praised Gandhiji for awakening the people and for involving them in freedom struggle by providing a unique type of leadership.

The ballad was written during the non-cooperation movement. It spread like wild-fire throughout the Telugu country and was recited by hundred of people during 1921-1923. this ballad gave utmost inspiration to the leaders as well as to the people. It was also recited by non-Andhra political prisoners who were the poet's comrades in jail. He was imprisoned for sedition for one year and those that sang the songs of Garimela were likewise imprisoned.

The ballad was tuned by Band troops and sang on the occasion of marriages. It indicated how much popularity this ballad had inspired and worked as a powerful weapon.

The Government of Madras decided that it raised intense hatred and contempt among the people of the country against the British Government. Hence it was proscribed and forfeited as per the powers conferred by sub-section (1) of the Section 99-A of the Code of Criminal Procedure 1898.[45]

In this ballad the author used most powerful and beautiful language. No poet, or singer or a famous political leader had not written such a powerful ballad in the country. Garimella preached the upliftment of panchamas (untouchables) in 1921, even before the Gandhiji's Harijan movement in 1930-32. Every question in this ballad was a powerful arrow to the heart of British Raj. It was learnt by heart by children, propagatoras, beggars and was sang by girls in houses, cattle keepers in agricultural fields. It ended with an exhortion that Indians should get their independence, protect their honour even at the cost of their lives. It was a mirror to the then prevailing political, social and economic conditions. By the influence of this ballad thousands of people began to participate in the freedom struggle.

Garimella's ballad "We don't want this white Government" was one of the most inspiring ballads during the period of freedom struggle. Its beginning is marvelous. Its greatness is contained in the beginning of the ballad. The beginning sentences of the ballad showed the people's desire towards independence and their anger and hatred towards the British Raj. Each sentence, each word, worked as a powerful weapon to break the heart of the British Raj.

It is an extraordinary ballad in its language, meaning and style. This ballad became the war cry in various stages of the freedom movement. It attained such a force due to British imperialistic administration, dictatorship and exploitation.

Garimella, in this immortal song, strongly condemned the imperialist rule of the whites. He appealed to his countrymen to forget their differences on consideration of castes and creeds. He decried untouchability. He exhorted the people to unite and revolt against the injustice under the unique leadership of Gandhiji, the new force and the new hope.

The tremendous popularity of the song with "its simplicity and catching rhythm disturbed the then Government in an unprecedented way". Any one who sang a bit of it was vigorously attacked by the police force and was ultimately imprisoned.

The song of Garimella went direct to his audiences mostly composed of the uneducated rural folk. The language and style of the song were suited to their comprehension capacity.

Garimella's another work entitled Swarajya Gitamulu[46] in two volumes was printed by C. Muniswami Mudaliyar & sons at the Sivakami Vilas Press, 41 Ling chetti Street, Madras. They were published by the Indian Agency Bureau, Triplicane, Madras. They were printed and published in 1921.

The first volume consisted of the following Gitamulu. Matrusthavam, Melukolupu, Raatnam, Panchalam, Swarajyam, Gandhi, Gramam (village), Angleyavidya (English Education), Courts, Kallu (toddy), Panchamulu (untouchables), Khilafat Presna (Khilafat question), Rajyameludam, Manchisamayamiderara, Radham Pata, Koyyudu Gitamulu, saitan Prabhuta (Devil Government).

The second volume consisted of Prardhana (prayer), Sasanasabhikudu (legislative member), Mantalu (flames), Gandhiji-Irwin Sambhashanam (conversation), seemaguddalu (foreign cloth),Kallu (toddy), Tragudu (wine drinking), Dasara Padyamulu (Dasara Poems), Bharatamata, Kastamulu (troubles), Swarajyam (indepenence), Karuvu (famine), Raatnam, Ikamatyam (unity), Selav, Dharmamu (justice), Dipavali (Divali), Saitan Prabhuta (Devil Government), Mangalam.

In these ballads the author described how the Britishers came to India for trade. But they began to commit theft. He, through his Gitamulu, appealed to Bharata Mata (Mother India) not to take revenge against the Jallianwalla Bagh atrocities and prayed her to provide food, clothing and shelter to the poor and to liberate the people from foreign yoke. He condemned the British for their biassed attitude towards General Dyer and exhorted the people to follow the Congress principles.

The author vividly described the disadvantages from the addiction of toddy and arrack. The people began to sell the pustis of their wives. For asking the people not to drink toddy, the Government killed number of people at Dharwar.

The British created differences even among the brothers in a family by the establishment of courts and caused the destruction of panchayats. The courts were one of the reasons for poverty of ryots. Further the author described the impoverished conditions of the peasants. He blamed the British for the unnecessary expenditure on army and condemned the patrolling army in Guntur.

He highlighted India's past glory from the beginning of Puranas and stated that India had enjoyed in the past harmonious and prosperous conditions in the political, social, economic and cultural fields. He encouraged Swadesi education and condemned the foreign education.

The Britishers cut off the thumbs of Indians who spun yarn. They had imported foreign (England) cloth and destroyed Swadeshi spinning yarn through the foreign trade. They took to Britain many crores of rupees. So Garimella suggested not to purchase foreign cloth. Wearing Khaddar became an offence and the Government on that account killed number of people in Malabar.

The author discouraged the service of Indians in the Government offices. The British followed a policy of divide and rule to create conflicts among the Hindu castes in the recruitment of Government jobs. He expressed confidence in achieving Swaraj within short period and encouraged the Indians by telling them that they were not inferior to the Hungarians, the Koreans, the Irish and the Egyptians and criticised the British for the introduction of Martial law. He crirticised the inefficient administration of the British.

Garimella recognised the importance of villages in India. He thought that the villages are the backbone to development. So he gave utmost priority to the village people and pleaded for the re-installation of Raatnam and some other small scale industries to provide employment to the villagers. He criticised the cruel policy of the British transferring the Indian raw materials to England and sale of finished goods in India. So he said "We don't tolerate this Satanic Government" and suggested to the people to destroy the dictatorship. He supported the rule of the representatives of the people.

The author criticised the taxation system of the British, Rowlatt Act. The entrance of some of the Indians into the Legislatures and the policy of Britishers prior to first World War and after towards Khilafat. He suggested that the Hindus should now assist the Muslims in this regard and jointly fight for the protection of Mohammadan religion.

He said that the British treated patriotism as a crime and subjected it to punishment and claimed large number of lives. He appealed to higher castes to treat the untouchables with requal social status. He praised the characters of gandhiji, Malavya, Chittaranjan Das, Ali Brothers and preached importance of Gandhiji's non-cooperation movement and asked the people to follow Gandhiji and appealed to the people to sacrifice individual benefit and work for the collective welfare.

The Government felt that it created hatred and contempt among the people in the country against British India. Therefore it was proscribed and forfeited by the Government as per the powers conferred by the Government by sub-section (1) of Section 99-A of the Criminal Procedure Code 1898.[47]

For the writing of the above said books Garimella was imprisoned in Tiruchurapalli and Kalalur Jails. Even the copy of the said book which was sent by the District Magistrate, was burnt by the Government of Madras fearing that on the basis of it, we might understand the inspiration it had. The publishers and printers were also subjected to punishment.

In this context while contesting the case in Madras court Garimella began to read out his statement but the Judge refused him permission to read it out. His statement was published in Andhra Patrika on 28th July 1922.

In his statement he appealed to the people not to compromise with bad deeds; lack of unity is an obstacle for the development. He preached non-cooperation movement, wearing Khaddar and encouraged people to eliminate foreign rule truth was treated as a crime by the British; eulogised the national leaders such as Tilak, Maulana, Lajapat Rai and Gandhiji, love and non-violence would win the world; the imprisonment of freedom fighgers, poets and writers would not solve the problem of the British; their goal would be establishment of National Government. The burning of 5000 copies of this bòok would increase inspiration of the people towards freedom movement.

Garimella was a staunch follower of Gandhiji in every aspect of life. He and members of his family wore Khaddar not only as a symbol of Swadeshi but also as followers of Ganddhiji. He discouraged the study of English education by his children. He hated violence; a revolutionary should not support violence. It is the essence of Gandhism. Garimella was a socialist; many ballads indicates this view. He was the first man to write a ballad which created tremendous fear in the hearts of the British Raj. He was a scholar, good in music and literature. He sacrificed his life for the sake of the country.

As already stated, Garimella wrote a ballad "We don't want this white Government" twenty one years prior to gandhiji's Quit India Movement. The necessity of the upliftment of Harijans was recognised by him and he preached it in 1921 even before Gandhiji's harijan movement in 1930. This helps us to estimate the patriotism and social awareness of Garimella. He established Sarada Grandhamala to create social consciousness and political awakening. This contribution is also significant to understand the then contemporary period. He realised the importance of the development of villages as the backbone of the country i.e. he showed keen interest on villages in his ballads. Even the prostitutes were influenced by his ballads.

Some of his writings have a relevance to the present society, because the age-old evils like poverty, unemployment, illiteracy are prominent in the society. To eliminate these evils his writings are useful.

Such a patriot was reduced to write a ballad on Amrutanjanam advertisement for a little remuneration. The advertisement ballad was published in Bharati, Divali Sanchika November, 1947 and he was even reduced to begging in the Madras streets. But till his death he remained a patriot.

He occupies a prominent place in the history as well as in the hearts of the people of Andhra. Poets and writers are the forerunners of the people's life. So his writings are still relevant to solve our social, economic, religious differences in India.

DAMARAJU PUNDARIKAKSHUDU (1896-1976)

Damaraju Pundarikakshudu was born on 5th June, 1896 at Patibandla, Sattenapalli Taluk, Guntur district. He was the son of Gopalakrishnaiya and Rangamamba. His Father was an advocate and poet. He worked as an editor for a newspaper Ram Raj for some time. He was a District Court Vakil, Guntur.

Participation in the Freedom Struggle

From 1920 Gandhiji became the leader of the Indian freedom struggle. His principles and programmes attracted both the masses and classes. Freedom fighters and writers came under his influence. Damaraju Pundarikakshudu also came under his influence and wrote a number of dramas based on the Gandhian programmes and in support of the Congress activities. In 1920 Damaraju founded Sanghasevana tyamandali and through it he made all arrangements to perform his dramas.

He established an organisation called Swarajya Sowpana Pankti Publications. Through it he not only published his own dramas and books but also works of others. It was established solely and purely with the object of bringing out the non-violent spirit of Mahatma Gandhi and educate the masses on the principles of non-violence and Satyagraha as enunciated by Gandhiji. He translated into verse and dialogues the various preachings of the then leaders of the Congress, bringing about at every stage the purity and supremacy of Gandhiji's ideals and principles.

DAMARAJU PUNDARIKAKSHUDU
(1896-1976)

Damaraju toured the entire Andhra country and propagated the Congress Movements. He wrote several dramas with patriotic themes. Some of his dramas were proscribed. Actors were imprisoned and books worth Rs.50,000/- were burnt down by the Government of Madras. His writings greatly inspired the people during the freedom struggle apart from their intrinsic literary value.

He took part in the non-cooperation movement in 1921. at that time he was a student. He was lathi-charged at Guntur and Mangalagiri and arrested and detained for twenty days in the Guntur sub-jail. He was again arreasted and detained at Cocanada for three months.

Political and Literary Works

Besides his proscribed Telugu dramas he also wrote Sanghasamasya Anu Samskarini in 1922. In this drama he described the hardships of people from the beginning of casteism to the modern period. His another social Rupakam entitled Missvihar Anu Kaliyugabharatam in 1936. In this work he described the advantage of widow remarriages, and intercaste marriages. His another work was Guntur Goppa (Pannula Nirakaranam) (non-payment of taxes in Guntur).

Pundarikakshudu's other dramas were Bhagavan Narada in 1935, Bhakta Potana in 1940, Tara Sasankam, Kumbharana in 1938, Votlaprahasanam Anedi Prahasanam. All these dramas were not published but performed on the stages and got popularity from the people.

Proscribed works and contribution to Freedom Struggle

The dramas of Pundarikakshudu were used as instruments to intensify the political propagation in Andhra during the freedom movement. When the actors enacted the dramas[48] of Pundarikakshudu, the people used to go home fully convinced that the ejection of the British from India alone lay their salvation. The authorities therefore created much trouble to Pundarikakshudu and the actors of the Nataka Samajam. Before one play was proscribed by the authorities, another was forthcoming from the pen of Pundarikakshudu. He used the pen as his sword and that was why he came to be widely known as Andhra National Poet. [49] The plays and poems of Pundarikakshudu produced many patriots in the district.

We may divide the Telugu National patriotic dramas into three kinds. The first one was Mythological dramas. In this kind the writers through the mythological characters explained the slavery of India and the advantages of independent life. The writers indirectly, through mythological characters, propagated the ideas of independence. For the indirect propagation, the mythological dramas were used as powerful instruments.

The second catgegory is Historical dramas, for example the dramas like Sivaji, Ranapratap, Rasaputra Vijayadi etc. The Historical dramas also inspired and brought the people into the way of freedom struggle. The chronicles like the battle of Bobbili also played an important role in inspiring the people.

The third kind of dramas which may be termed as political dramas began from 1920. this year onwards the writers began to write directly on the activites of the then political conditions, particularly the activities of the Congress. This kind of dramas became more popular because these dramas mirrored the political conditions of the times. In writing this type of dramas Pundarikakshudhu was one of the important writers.

The Government of Madras proscribed five books of Damaraju. One book was taken for investigation. The first book that was proscribed was Navayugarambham or Gandhi Mahodayam (New Era or the Rise of Gandhi). It was a drama, dealing with imaginary Gods, democratic Parliament, Tilak's death, Mahatma Gandhiji's advent into politics, inauguration of his Satyagraha movement and non-violence and invocation to Bharatamata.

Navayugam – Gandhi Vijayam, the second book, dealt with the emergence of Mahatma as the leader of Congress at Nagpur and his hold on other leaders. It also contained the exact speeches of the Congress leaders.

The third book Panchala Parabhavam dealt with the Punjab atrocities. The violence was at every stage discouraged and Gandhiji's divine hand was depicted and preached as the best and upper-most.

The forth book Swarajya Mahasabha or Ahmadabad Congress dealt with the Punjab atrocities, criticised the repressive policy of the Government and threatened the Government with the inauguration of civil disobedience movement.

Subsequently he wrote a fifth book Gandhi Mahatma Anu Kaliyuga Prahlada (Mahatma Gandhi, the Prahlada of the present Age) in a Harikatha form. This book contained Gandhiji's activities and was a compilation of some portions from the previous one, two and three books.

His another Telugu drama entitled Sangasamsya Anu Samskarini was investigated by Government. It was not proscribed. The object of the work is already stated.

His first book Navayugarabham or Gandhi Mahodayam (New Era or the Rise of Gandhi) was a Telugu drama. It was a three Act drama. This book was first brought to the notice of the Government by the C.I.D. in 1921 vide C.I.D. note in page 1 of Government order No.198, Public dated 7th April 1921. The Telugu translators reported on the book and the translation with select paragraphs are in pages 4-10 of the Government Order. It was then considered unnecessary to proscribe the book under the Press Act 1910 vide decision in page 14 of the Government order. Later the District Magistrate of Ballary moved the Government to prohibit the performance of the drama under the Dramatic Performance Act vide letter in Page I of the Government order No.520. Public Department, dated 17th August 1921. The Government accordingly prohibited the performance of the drama within Madras Presidency.

In this drama the author gave a detailed account of Gandhiji's principles and tried to spread them throughout Andhra.

The characters of this drama were Desa Bhakta, Desa Sevaka, Aurobindo Ghosh, Bal Gangadhar Tilak, gandhiji, Sri Rama, Sri Kirshna and Parasurama and others. It was the first drama in Telugu with political theme.[50] The language of this drama was very simple because the author intended to make it understood even by illiterates.[51] To educate poilitically the illiterates this drama was performed in many places prior to prohibition.

In the first Act the author described the ten incarnations. Then he treated Bal Gangadhar Tilak as the eleventh incarnation. After discussing the purposes of eleven incarnations the author stated that the God must incarnate as Gandhiji for his twelfth incarnation.

In the second Act the death of Tilak and the great qualities of Tilak imbibed by Gandhiji were described.

In the third Act God's conference wsas convened to welcome Tilak and to bless Gandhiji's incarnation. It was announced that Gandhiji was born as the twelfth incarnation. "From yesterday world's nature has completedly changed i.e. an era under the leadership of Gandhi Mahatma the nation would be liberated". The Gandhiji mentioned that India must get independence within one year. He stated that the means for this was Satyagraha. In this drama the author on the basis of the Puranic beliefs of the people proposed God's new incarnation.

His second book entitled Navayugam – Gandhi Vijayamu was a political drama. It was printed at Andhra Grandhalaya Press, Bezwada. It contained a series of dramatic dialogues and advocated Gandhiji's non-cooperation scheme. It was suspected to contain objectionable matter. The Telugu translator to Government of Madras translated some passages from the book.[52] The Advocate General felt there was no necessity to take any action against the book. The book was however brought to the notice of the Government again by the Criminal Investigation department in 1932 and it was proscribed as falling under the Press Act vide Government Order No.1006, Public Department dated 21st July, 1932.

In this drama Damaraju described the actual deeds which happened in India from the beginning of Gandhiji's entrance to Indian freedom struggle to the completion of Nagpur session. He vividly described the proceedings of Calcutta and Nagpur sessions. The intention of Damaraju was to display the then history to the then society. It was a five act drama.

The men characters of this drama are Desabhaktudu, Desasevaka, Aurobindo ghosh, Gandhiji, Shaukat Ali, Lajpat Rai, Bipin Chandra Pal, Chittaranjan Das, Muhammad Ali, Nehru, Madan Mohan Malaviya, Selam Vijaraghavachari, Kasturi Rangaiya, Konda Venkatappaiah Pantulu, Bapireddy, Gopisetti, Ramayya, Swabhilashi, Sagarvi, Adhikarabhilashi, Nyayavadi (Lawyer), Ryot, Students, Vedgewood, Bezmafar, Jinnah, Bala Bhaktudu (Boy Soldier), etc. The women characters are Sarada Devi and Annie Besant.

In the beginning of this drama, Damaraju, through the characters, praised Gandhiji's success in South Africa and Chaparan through the Satyagraha weapon. He compared Gandhiji with God and said he was one of the incarnations. So he need not have the assistance of Army and Armoury to free the nation from the yoke of British.

He stated that the entrance of Gandhiji in the freedom struggle would pave the way for the unification of Modrates and Extremists, elimination of Brahmin and non-Brahmin feelings and eradicate caste and religious distinctions.

The Ryots were subjected to many hardships due to lack of good harvest and the heavy taxation system of Government. In addition to that there was income tax.

He stressed the need for unity between Hindus and Muslims in their struggle for the liberation of the country and highlighted the co-existence of Hindus and Muslims for centuries.

The author expressed his hope that the end to all the atrocities of the wicked administration had neared. India was day by day reduced to humiliating condition. The administration of the Government was becoming worse day by day and knew no bounds. Both life and self-respect were at a stake.

The author pointed out that the whites (British) were enjoying high positions taking big salaries while the Indians were becoming poor day by day. He also asked the people to judge the utility of following non-violence to subdue the British autocratic Government which had taken deep roots in India. However he did not advocate violent methods.

The third book of Damaraju was Panchalaparabahavam[53] (The Punjab outrages or the insult offered to Panchala) was a drama printed at the Chandrika Press, Guntur. The Government of Madras thought that it was calculated to excite feelings of disaffection towards Government established by law in British India. So, it was proscribed and forfeited by the Madras Government as per the powers conferred by sub-section (1) of Section 12 of the Indian Press Act 1910. [54] The above said book contained matter of the nature described in Section 4 (1) of the Indian Press Act 1910. [55] The local government were of the opinion that the said drama about to be performed in a public place in the Guntur district as already said was likely to excite feelings of disaffection to the government established by law in British India. So under the Dramatic Performance Act 1876, it was ordered to prohibit the performance in any public place within the (Madras) Presidency.

Panchalaparabhavam was a drama in five acts in which the author described the political history, commencing from the awakening of the Satyagraha vow and concluded with Amritsar session of the Congress.

This book was dedicated to the memory of the heroes of the Punjab who laid down their lives, moved by an enthusiasm for the service of the country.

Everything written in Panchalaparabhavam was based on the chief incidents of the horrible massacres perpetrated in the Punjab while Sir M.O.Dwyer was the Governor and Lord Chelmsford was the Viceroy. These incidents were massacre in the Jallianwallah Bagh, the enormities in the crawling lane, the punishments inflicted on the school-boys by Johnson, the stopping of the marriage procession, etc.

His fourth book Swarajya Mahasabha or the Ahmedabad Congres[56] was printed at Aryavaisya Press, Guntur. In this book the author appealed to the people to be conscious about the political situation in India, and praised the imprisoned leaders like Chittaranjan Das, Lala Lajpat Rai, Jawaharlal Nehru and the Ali Brothers.

The Punjab was compared with the Panchali (Drowpati, the wife of Pandavas in Mahabharatam). For their evil actions Dyer and O' Dwyer were compared with Dusyasana and Duryodana (Mahabharata). The author warned the British Government that the Indians wlould not tolerate any type of slavery and disintegration. The author advised the British Government to avert the Indian agitation and possible civil war. He further warned the British government not to commit atrocities against Indian women.

The Government itself was responsible for creating Mappilla riots and nobody could tolerate the repressive policy adopted by it there. The author stressed that the mighty India was struggling for the birth of independence. We could not cooperate with this unholy Government. The author threatened the British Government with guerilla warfare if necessary. The non-violent and non-cooperation movement had greatly damaged the reputation of the British Government.

The author cautioned the British Government of dangerous consequences for obstructing freedom of speech and freedom of meeting. "In regions where the martial law is put into force, we should, if need be, be prepared even for war". The Indians should not agree to any compromise except Independence. The British Government could not survive by creating differences between the Hindus and the Muslims. The author requested the students to co-operate in obtaining freedom.

The Government of Madras felt that it induced great hatred and contempt among the people of the country against the British Government. Therefore it was proscribed and forfeited by the Government as per the powers conferred by the Section 99-A of the Code of Criminal Procedure 1898.[57]

His fifth book entitled Gandhi Mahatma Anu Kaliyuga Prahlada[58] was printed at the Chandrika Press, Guntur and was published in the same place which is the fifth in the series of publication entitled the Swarajya Sowpana Pankthi (the flight of steps to Swaraj). It was in Harikatha form and it contained Gandhiji's activities and was a compilation of some portion from the Navayugarambham or Gandhi Mahodayam, Gandhi Vijayam and Panchala Parabhavam. The author acknowledged his indebtedness to Vadlamudi china Basavayya who helped him with funds to print the book.

Prahlada[59] had most bitterly been tormented by his father for his intense devotion to God Vishnu till he was rescued from such a miserable state by the latter who killed his father. Kaliyuga Prahlada means the Prahlada of the "Present age". The author called Gandhiji by this name and the book was a history in easy verse of the Satyagraha movement from the time of the Punjab murders and the appearance of the Khilafat question.

The author in this book praised the activities of Gandhiji in south Africa to save his countrymen through his non-violent methods. He criticised the people who were engaged in the toddy and arrack business. This drinking habit contributed to the deterioration of the Indians socially and economically. Through these items the British were amassing money in their treasury. The Government repressed those who had preached against the drinking of toddy and arrack.

The author said that the great happiness, might prosperity, celebrity, heroism, purity, the wealth of learning, the fruit of peanance, the merit of religion and the fortune of reputation of the Indians were destroyed by the British. The Mother India had been humbled under the British rule. Mahatma Gandhi had great mental anguish at the afflictions suffered by the Mother Country.

The author expressed his hope in the following way: The divine vow of Satyagraha alone would grant emancipation to Indians. The way of Prahlada, who saw the grace of God Vishnu in a steeel pillar would do good. No other would serve the purpose. Alal the people of the earth should not quit the path of Gandhiji's Satyagraha. It was only the satyagraha vow of Prahlada, that was the novel road suited to the natural disposition of the Indians.

Satyagraha would not touch weapons. Whoever practices this vow; would have the purification of the soul, a life of perfect purity, liberation from servitude and the attainment of Swaraj within a period of unparalelled shortness. Thus did the holy Mahatma Gandhi preach the vow of Satyagraha to all the people of the earth and saved India.

While the people were thus beside themselves in a mighty uproad, the eys of Dyer and O'Dwyer, who saw this and became jealousy were very much inflamed with wrath. They put the Martial law into force, repressed the people and perpetrated such deeds as were not to be found anywhere in countries inhabited by human beings. They had laid the offence on sons of valour Kitchlew and Satyapal and arrested them.

The cruel demon of Dyer had come to the meeting in the Jallianwallah Bagh, and besieged the place with an army saying, who are these fellows that brush aside the order and hold the meeting without any regard whatsoever. In a minute he fired at the audience. Hundreds and thousands had perished and gone to heaven as heroes.

However, much of the dreadful deeds had become publicly known. On the contrary instead of giving punishment to the demons such as Dyer and O'Dwyer, the Government in England improved their honourable positions.

On the pretext, that Turkey had joined Germany, the Europeans undertook to wreak their former grudge. While the whole continent of Europe was the play-ground of the Christians, there was in the midst of them, as if in mokery, Turkey a region belonging to an alien religion. Saying that the opportunity had come, they made the terms of the treaty very rigid. Through the operation of the fate of the followers of Islam, the destruction of the sense of respect for their own creed had happened.

Up to this movement the Muslims of India appeared to have love for the British rulers; but after this incident, they are inspired with a sense of indignation. The murders of the Punjab in India, the dishonour done to all the Muhammadans, the long standing slavery of the Indians became fuel to the fire which uplifted country.

With the great dawn of the sun of Gandhiji his luster had spread to the corners of the earth. All the people woke up as one man while the thick darkness had left them.

The Ali brothers had come out from prison and sprang like the Cobra whose tail had been trodden upon, because of the destruction of the sense of respect for their own religion.

The author further tried to propagate through this book that all pleaders should give up their profession and establish panchayats. People should not resort to court. Students should at once boycott educational institutions of the Government. No one should take part in the Legislative Council elections to be held under the new redforms act of Montague and Chelmsford. Candidates would withdraw their candidature. All the people should not vote. The reforms act itself was boycotted. Thus it happened that the elections became the butt of ridicule; that the reform Act suffered ruin and that some nameless men sat in the Legislative councils with some ten or fifteen votes. Then the faith of the people in the country in the non-cooperation movement greatly increased. Another important thing was that people should not purchase the cloth manufactured in alien countries, wear only the cloth woven with the yarn prepared in our country. "God" Gandhiji says, "this is not great task and that if you accomplish this, swaraj will draw near. Fulfil this and in three months India will obtain liberation and attain Swaraj".

The tone and contents of the book were of such a highly objectionable and seditious nature as would bring the Government into utter-hatred and contempt among the people of the country. Hence the book was forfeited[60] and also all other documents containing copies of translations of or extracts from the said book in as much as it contained matter the publication of which was punishable under Section 124-A of the Indian Penal Code.

The Drama Sanga Samsya Anu Samskarini[61] (the social problem or the Reformer) was written by Damaraju. It was scrutinised by the Madras Government, but it was not proscribed. The papers were recorded for the purpose of future reference.

In this drama the author introduced characters like Dharma Siddhanti, Achara Siddhanti, God Brahma, Jagannatga. The South African Indians – coolies a man and a woman, Rajamma, Yamini Sundari, Mastan Kasim and Britishers first Dorai and second Dorai.

The author in this drama stated that the white men looked upon all the Hindus as base slaves and used them as menial servants. The author gave a detailed account of the conditions of Indians in South Africa. The Indians migrated to south Africa for livelihood, but they were helplessly suffering through ignorance, want of food for the stomach, house to dwell in and cloth for (to protect) modesty and from the absence of protection. The White men called Indians in south Africa as 'black men', 'nego folks' low fellows and 'the slaves of dorais (Europeans) that was the condition of Indians in South Africa.

The author gave a description of the evils of prostitution and miserable life led by the dancing girls and discouraged the drinking of toddy and appealed to listen to the teachings of Mahatma Gandhi.

Conclusion

Damaraju was a great writer and staunch supporter of Gandhian principles and programmes. Through his works he popularised the Gandhian principles and brought the people into the steamline of struggle for independence. He realised the importance of dramatic performances which were the most influencial instrument to attract, mould and awaken the public to fight for struggle for independence. So he made all arrangements for the dramatic performances. He led his life as a lawyer, publisher, writer and freedom fighter. He spent his life for the liberation of country. So he occupies a prominent place in the history of freedom struggle in Andhra. He breathed his last on 10th November, 1976.

VADDADI SITARAMANJANEYULU (1900-1993)

Early Life and Education

Vaddadi Sitaramanajaneyulu was born on 5th July, 1900 in Doddammapeta near Draksharamam, East Godavari District. His father was Bhimasankaram and mother Venkataratnam. Bhimasankaram was a poet and he worked in the Doddammapeta Zamindar. The Zamindar made matrionial relations with Kasimkota Zamindar, Vizagapatam District (Visakhapatnam). In this context Bhimasankaram and his family came to Kasimkota.[62]

VADDADI SITARAMANJANEYULU (1900-1993)

Vaddadi studies in Kasimkota up to first form, up to third form in P.R. College High school, Cocanada, fourth form in Municipal High School, Anakapalli, fifth form in M.R.College High School, Vizianagaram and S.S.L.C. in A.V.N.College High School, Vizagapatam in 1919.

Parrticipation in the Freedom Struggle

Vaddadi was independent minded and an adventurist. From his childhood he evinced keen interest in freedom struggle. He used to read a number of books and newspapers containing information about the freedom struggle. His life and career were influenced by the political situation and by some personalities. The first personality to influence him both politically and literallay was Puranam Suryanarayana Thirdhulu. In 1914 in a political conference at Anakapalli Puranam Suryanarayana Thirdhulu read some songs relating to Indiana Freedom Struggle. Vaddadi was so much impressed by the songs and the scholarship of Thirdhulu that he became his disciple.[63] The second person to influence him was Gandhiji. While he was studying S.S.L.C., he read the speech of Gandhiji in the newspaper. The Hindu, in 1919 (Just before Gandhiji's entrance into Freedom Movement). He was impressed with the ideas and principles of Gandhiji and began to hate foreign education and discontinued his studies and entered into the propagation of Congress programme in the public.

At Vzagapatam he came under the influence of Vasanta Rao Bucchi Sundara Rao. Buchhi Sundara Rao was a famous young lawyer and a patriot belonging to Vizagapatam. In 1920 Vaddadi introduced himself to Sundara Rao. Sundara Rao also was impressed by the lecrturers and the actuive interest that Vaddadi was showing towards freedom struggle. He studies a number of books such, as prosperous British India, Indian War of Independence, India, in the library of Sundara Rao. Vaddadi used to go to Vizagapatam beach every day along with a chair and place the photo of Gandhiji on the chair and sing a song on the freedom struggle. After people gathered he used go begin his lecture on freedom struggle and on the principles of Gandhiji. Sometimes Sundara Rao presided over the beach gathering lectures of Vaddadi. With the help of this technique he tried to inclucate in the minds of the people the feeling of patriotism. This technique was followed by Vaddadi in the propagation of Congress programme. He was not only the first popular freedom fighter but also the first non-cooperator in the non-cooperation movement in Vizagapatam.[64]

Vaddadi went to nearby villages of Vizagapatam to propagate Congress programme on freedom movement and constituted Congress Committees in the villages.[65] With the influence of non-cooperation movement

Vaddadi wrote a lengthy song entitled Dandalu Dandalu Bharata Mata. It was sung by Vaddadi at A.I.C.C. meeting in 1921 at Bezwada. Afterwards it was sung by Vaddadi in a number of meetings. It was published in 1921[66] in the book Swarajyageetamrutamu. It was one of the most popular songs in those days in Andhra.

For fifteen days Vaddadi and Duggirala Gopala Krishnayya jointly propagated the Congress programme in 1924-1925. In 1926 Vizagapatna Mandal Congress Conference was held at Madugula under the Presidentship of Duggirala Gopala Krishnayya. This context brought Vaddadi closer to Tenneti Viswanadham, one of the famous freedom fighters of Andhra.

In November, 1922 Vaddadi was imprisoned for one year for his "seditious" writings i.e. Swarajyageetamrutam. It was discussed In the next para. After his release from jail Vaddadi continued his political and literary activities. He also wrote a Telugu booklet entitled Atmasiksha. It was proscribed and forfeited by the Government of Madras. With the inspiration of Buchhi sundara rao, Vaddadi opened Swasekti Press in Vizapatam.[67] In the press premises Vaddadi held political and literary discussions with his friends frequently. In the same place Kavita Samiti was established in 1926. Its firsrt conference was held in the same year.[68] The first committee was constituted with Vaddadi, Puripanda Appaswami and Srerangam Sreenivasa Rao. The Kavita Samiti elected Marepalli Rama Chandra Sastry as the President for his life time. Vaddadi maintained relations with the Samiti for a decade from its inception.[69]

Besides Congress programme propagation, Vaddadi in the company of V.B.R.Sundara Rao, collected Paisa fund for the Congress from the people.

Professional Activity

Vaddadi passed Ubhaya Bhasha Praveena (Telugu Pandit Diploma) in 1936. He joined as a Telugu Pandit in a High School in Vizagapatam District for his livelihood. He worked as a Telugu Pandit in the schools at Kasimkota, Nakkapalli, Munagapaka, Sompeta, Salur and retired in 1960. Even during his employment period, he secretly propagated the Congress principles without any designation till the advent of independence. During the Second world War an unknown person filed a case against Vaddadi stating that he had relations with the Japanese. But the court acquitted him for lack of sufficient evidence.[70] At the time of independence he was working as a Telugu Pandit at Sompeta. At the request of people of Sompeta, Vaddadi hoisted the Indian flag on 15th

August 1947. After 1965 he settled in Visakhapatnam and maintained relations with such political leaders and Tanguturi Prakasam and Tenneti Viswanadham.

Political and Literary Works

After indpendence Vaddadi completely left politics. He object was to get independence for India. He never expected any offices or favours. He disliked to participate in Indian politics and concentrated on philosophical and religious writings. His total works are one hundred and thirty. Out of them thirty works were published.

Puligoru Satakam, Phalanjali, sree Ranga Nayaka Sthotra Mangari, Chaleesa Manjushu, Radhakrishnodaharam, Tikkana Bhagavatgeeta, Pushpa Bana Vilapamu (translation), Bhakta Sanzeevini, Thrylinga Swami, Sree Veeranjaneya Sthotra Taravli Sahita, Sree Veera Hanumanuti Vimsati, Chanukya Neeti Sangraham, Kanka Dhara Sthavam were his major works based on philosophical and religious themes.

He also wrote two dramas Bhuvanavijayam and Gurudakshina and dedicated them to V.V.Giri a former President of India and Puranam Thirdhulu, his beloved teacher respectively. Bapujee, Bharatiya Probhodam and Saraswata Chendrika were his other noteworthy writings.

In recognition of his services rendred to the freedom struggle he was awarded Tamrapatra. The Andhra Pradesh Government and a number of other Associations felicitated him.[71] This freedom fighter-cum-poet of north coastal Andhra died on 14th april 1993 at the age of ninety two years in Visakhapatnam.

Proscribed Works and Contribution to Freedom Struggle

Bala Kavi Vaddadi Sitaramanjaneyulu and Pudipeddi Kasi Viswanadha Sastry, residents of Vizagapatam jointly wrote a Telugu book entitled Swarajyageetamrutamu[72] (The nectar of Swarajya Geeta – song of Swaraj). It was printed at the V.N. Press, Rajahmundry, Godavari District. This book contained the popular song Dandalu Dandalu Bharata Mata, Rakthabhisheka (Blood bath) Panchala[73] Mana Bhangam (The outrage of Punjab) The Pisacha (devil) of Misfortune, The Pasupatha (Divine Missile) of Non-Cooperation.

In this work the authors worshipped and requested Bharata Mata (Mother India) to protect the people's honour from the exploitation of British.

They criticised the repressive, exploiting, ruthless rule of the whiteman. The taxation system which was imposed by the Britishers was very heavy. They imposed a tax on salt as if they had excavated all the ocean. The economic exploitation in all forms was burden some and unbearable to the Indians. The Britishers were collecting one hundred and ninety crores of rupees in the shape of land tax and they spent only twenty three crores of rupees for the welfare of the people. People could not speek the truth. It was obscene to utter 'Rama'. The authors compared Britishers with cobras. Indians honour was all stained. Hindu religion was lost, their customs were stamped out.

The rulers robbed the liberty and honour of the ruled. They showed all their might in the Punjab. They made tender infants stand in scorching Sun. They ruthlessly whipped to death innocent children with big horse-whips and killed many people in the Punjab. They bathed with blood and rejoiced.

The authors criticised the English education system on the ground that it destroyed the people's ideas of freedom and "brought us up as slaves". They compared English language with Keesara Bhasha (the uncivilised people's language).

The authors discouraged the foreign cloth; described the poverty of the Indians and the importance of Raatnam; criticised the establishment of courts which were responsible for the creation of parties, and conflicts and reduced people to poverty; criticised the corrupt Government administration and its divide-and-rule policy, and the dictatorship and monopoly of trade. The authors described the legislatures as useless institutions. Labourers were not enjoying the fruits of their labour; the fruits of the labour were exploited by the British. They also criticised the Indians who were crazy to receive the honourary titles which were issued by the then British Government. They highlighted the personality and principles of Gandhiji.

The authors reminded the people of the devotion and patriotism of Sivaji, great bravery of Tippu sultan, great intellectual power of Nana Saheb and the splendour of the character of Jhansi Lakshmi Bai. So they exhorted the Andhras to wake up and preserve dharma. Further they said that Ravana who tried to violate the character of Sita Mahalakshmi met with destruction the Kauravas were burnt down when they tried to violate the modesty of Drowpati.

The Pasupata of non-cooperation sent by the Vijaya (Arjuna) of the Congress of the Parthasaradhi (Krishna) of Gandhiji, guarded Indians. British Ingratitude and their cannon perished in it.

The fire of the Pasupatha of non-cooperation blazed forth quickly filling all the universe spite and deceit fell to the ground. Despotism of the English Government their bad ways could no longer succeed and they had no place to set their foot in India. The time of their destruction drew near.

The Government of Madras felt that it contained matter of the nature described in section 4 (1) of the 1910 Act. Therefore the Government as per the powers conferred by sub-section (1) of Section 12 of the Indian Press Act 1910 proscribed and forfeited the[74] book.

The Government of Madras was not satisfied with the proscription of the book. Before filing a case against the authors, the said Government tried to seek an apology from the authors before the East Godavari District Collector. But the authors did not agree and opposed the Collector. But the father-in-law of Pudipeddi Kasiviswanatha Sastry brought him before the Collector of Cocanada and made him apologised and gave an assurance not to do such work in future, whereas Vaddadi escaped from police for months. The Government filed a case against him and subjected him to rigorous imprisonment for nine months and fine rupees five hundred, but he did not pay the fine. So he was imprisoned for another three months. [75] At that time he was 21 years old. The co-prisoners of Vaddadi were Annaparagada Kameswara Rao and Bhimasankaram of Cocanada at Central Jail, Rajahmundry.

Another book that was proscribed by the Government was Atmasiksha[76] (self-discipline). It was composed and published by Vaddadi Sitaramanjaneyulu and Pudipeddi Kasiviswanatha Sastri, and printed at Sri Krishna Mudraksharasala at Chodavaram.

The authors stated that the "yarn of the disc" in the hand of God Vishnu would hunt the enemies (the British) and then would come the "kingdom of liberation". If you conquer the foes within you, and flourish, will not all the external foes (the British) be speedily destroyed in a twinkle? It was the religious duty of the Indians to refuse cooperation with men of wicked conduct (the British). Britishers were vile 'wretches' 'Burst as under' skillfully, the fraud decvised by the Britishers. Indians should not obey the "demonical" laws of the British. Besides the laws were made without representation from the Indians and to rob Indians prosperity. Shove out the British with all your might. It was a false notion that justice clould be had from British. The Britishers did not care to show toleration towards India. So the Indians too followed the same policy. If Indians had wanted liberation, the fiend of the authority of the Britishers who broke to pieces Indians progress and committed treachery, should be rooted out by force. The sparkling of great humility would consign the empires of the vile 'wretches' (the British) to fire. There was the authority to Indians to wage war. It was the ordained duty of the Indians to break the British rule without hesitation.

Further the authors stated it was the ordained duty of Indians to kill sinners and the traitors in the world (the British); prepare yourself to wage war; arise forthwith, with redoubled vigour and bravery for war, to speedily cut the British to pieces; wage the war of righteousness bravely, 'If Indians do not wage this war of righteousness, fame will be uprooted, and sin will arise; take the sword of wisdom, with intellectual skill cut the crowd of Britishers who are the cause of ignora nce'. In order to shove out the Government of British, Self-Government should be set up as a substitute for it.

The Government of Madras felt that it was of highly seditious nature, and as would assuredly bring Government into utter hatred and contempt among the Telugu speaking people. Hence it was punishable under Section 124-A of Indian Penal Code.[77] Therefore as per the powers conferred by Section 99-A of the code of Criminal Procedure 1898, it was proscribed and forfeited.[78]

Vaddadi invented a new technique of propagation of freedom movement through beach speeches. As already stated he was the first non-cooperator during the non-cooperation movement and first popular freedom fighter from Vizagapatam District. It was a significant event in the life of Vaddadi as well as in the history of the freedom movement in Vizagapatam district. This credit goes to Vaddadi.

He propagated the Congress programme from village to village and constituted Congress committees there. His song Dandalu Dandalu Bharatamata was very popular in those days in Andhra. He established Swasekti Press to awaken political consciousness among the people and founded Kavita Samithi for literary development and to exchange the ideas on freedom movement and literary fields among the poets and writers. Through these he proved his patriotism towards his mother country.

As a government employee he propagated the Congress programme secretly. He never expected any office during the freedom movement. In his book Swarajyagitamrutam and Atmasiksha he described the then political, social and economic conditions which prevailed in those days and encouraged the people to fight against the British. Like other writers he also paid keen attention to the political economy of the country.

For these writings he suffered one year of imprisonment. He occupied an important place in the history of freedom movement in Vizagapatam as well as in Andhra.

NOTES

1. The date, month and year is a controversial fact but majority of the scholars agreed on the above date.
2. Ch.Lakshmi Rajyam, Sree Unnava Lakshmi Narayana Gari Jeevitamu, Sahityam, p.3 (unpublished Thesis, Andhra University). This information was furnished by Are Bhushayya, the husband of Unnava Kalyani who is the adopted daughter of Unnava. Unnava himself gave this information to Bhushayya. Bhushayya's native place is Kopparru, three miles from Unnava village. This fact is known only to those closest to him.
3. Kandukuri Veeresalingam – Autobiography.
4. The members in this Association were Unnava Lakshmi Narayana, J. Gurunadham, Challa Seshagiri Rao, Nyapati Narayana Rao, Chatti Durgayya, Gollapuri Sitarama Sastry and some others.
5. Unnava, Vavilala Gopalakrishnayya, Siram Subbarao prepared themselves to go to Delhi to meet Nehru the then Prime Minister of India. But Unnava and Subba Rao gave up the idea in Bezwada Railway Station due Unnava's old age and heavy crowds in the train.
6. Andhra Patrika, Telugu Newspaper, 23rd September, 1922.
7. A Short History of the West Krishna District Congress, p.8.
8. G.V.Subramanyam, History of Satyagraha Struggle, p.78.
9. M.Venkatarangaiya, Freedom Struggle in Andhra Pradesh (Andhra) Vol.IV, Document No.77, pp.609-610.
10. Mancherla Gopala Rao, Nadimpalli Venkata Lakshminarasimhama Rao, Darshi Chechhaiah, Annapragada Kameswara Rao, Nadendla Krishnaiah and others.
11. It is highly appreciated by Krishna Patrika, Modali Nagabhushan Sarma, Pervaram Jagannadham, Akkiraju Ramapti Rao, K.V.Rama Reddi and others.
12. Telugu New Year.
13. For a detailed account of the life and work of Veeresalingam see John Greenfield Leonard, Kandukuri Veeresalingam, Hyderabad, 1991.
14. Kasinadhuni Nageswara Rao, Munagala Zamindar, Rajanayani Venkata Ranga Rao Bahudar, Konda Venkatapapaiah.
15. Lakshmi Devamma came from Rangoon in 1923 and studied upto 1929. Ch. Lakshmi Rajyam, **Sri Unnava Lakshmi Narayana Gari Jeevitam – Sahityam,** p. 22.
16. G. V. Subbaiah, Sangha Samskarta – Unnava, p. 27.

17. Nallapati Hanumanta Rao, P. Lakshminarayya, V. Sitaramayya and others.
18. N.G.Ranga, Distringuished Acquaintances, Vol.II, p.370.
19. Unnava Lakshmi Narayana, Malapalli (Sangavijayam), p.8.
20. Government of Madras, Public (General) Department, Ordinary Series, Confidential, G.O. No.396 Dt. 14th May, 1923.
21. **Ibid**.
22. Bangorez Malapalli Navalpai Prabhutva Nishedalu (Telugu) Appendix-2.
23. Swarajya, Editorial, 18th May, 1923.
24. Government of Madras, Public (General) Department Confidential G.O. No. 1441, Dt. 31st July, 1957.
25. Gurajada Raghava Sarma, Garimela Satyanaraya Jeevita Charitra (Telugu); M.V. Sastry, "Garimella Satyanarayana", an English essay, Teluguvani, July-September, 1979; Tekumala Kameswara Rao, Naa Vangmaya Mitrulu, (Telugu) 1966, p. 327.
26. Land-lords, Garimella's relative Barrister Kammepalli Lakshminarasimham and Palakodeti Sreepada Kameswara Rao.
27. Challa Radhakrishna Sarma, Garimella Sahityam (Telugu) p.6.
28. Challa Radhakrishna Sarma Swatantra Samaramulo an article in Eenadu dt. 15th July, 1993.
29. The Hindu, Dt. 5th April, 1922.
30. Dear Brothers and sisters,

    I have done my little work and am going to a comparatively long rest. The British bureaucracy have determined to lull my pen and my voice for a period of one year. It pleased them to think that I am dangerous to the 'Public tranquility' which means its own existence. Certainly it is a revelation to me. If I am really such as it suspected me to be, it certainly caught me too late an hour. I have given out to the country what is best to me. My physical body is to be locked up, but my soul I have let off into the country through literature. Let it be gathered, consolidated and worked out. It will work more than my frail body. The times are past when the Government" proscription or prohibition could gag our liberties. I often times wished to move among my people through my songs than through my person. The Government have created that peculiar opportunity if the people can avail themselves of it. I feel that I am most hollow now and may God grant that I should return into your midst for the sake of singing the establishmnt of Swarajya and the glory of your achievements'.
31. Garimella received financial help for the maintenance of Grandhamala from Sri Sailapati, Kasinadhuni Nageswara Rao, Bikkini venkata Ratnam and Vavilla Venkateswara Sastry.
32. Challa Radhakrishna Sarma, Garimella Sahityam, p.6.

33. Narasinga Rao in his letter mentioned it as Srivas hotel. The famous patriot and well known doctor Guduri Namassivaya wrote in his letter that Garimella had run the said hotel.
34. Desoddharaka Nageswara Rao Pantulu, Bhashoddharaka Vavilala Venkateswara Sastrulu and some others extended financial help to Garimella.
35. Penkipilla Journal, May, 1946.
36. It is a manuscript in Telugu and is available in Andhra Pradesh Government Oriental Manuscript Library, Hyderabad, Vol.I, p.97.
37. Vikramadev Varma, Lakshminarasimham Pantulu, Marepalli Ramachandra Sastry Kavi, Tadepalli Venkata Krishnayya.
38. Bulusu Venkata Ramanayya's letter Dt. 17th January 1984.
39. Tekumalla Kameswara Rao, K.V.Ramana Reddy, Chadrasekara reddy, Gurajada Raghava Sarma, Challa Radhakrishna Sarma, Mallela Srirama Murthy, Arudra, Pandrangi Rajeswara Rao and M.V.Sastry.
40. Tekumalla Kameswara Rao, Naa Vangmaya Mitrulu, p.326.
41. Challa Radhakrishna Sarma article on Garimella Eenadu, daily Telugu Newspaper Dt. 15th July 1993.
42. Challa radhakrishna Sarma, Garimella Sahityam, p.25.
43. Akhilandhra Veerasamsmarana Mandali, Kovvuru, published Garimella's comprehensive life history. Andhra Pradesh abhyudaya Rachaitala Conference was held at Trirupati in July 1987. In this conference one of the writers presented a research paper on Garimella's ballad "We don't want this white government and its historicity". Challa Radhakrishna Sarma published a research book entitled Garimella Sahitayam in February 1989. B. Krishna Kumari did M.Phil degree on Garimella. The title of her topic is "Garimella Sahityam – Vimarsanbatmakaparisilana, under the guidance of Telugu Department, Madras University (1990).

    All India Telugu Conference was held at Banglore in March 1990. In this conference Vavilala Gopalakrishnaiya Mahidara Rama Mohana Rao and Parakala Pattabhirama Rao, presented six page folder on behalf of freedom fighters, entitled "Andhra Jatiya Mahakavi Garimella Telugujati Vismarinchadaguna". It was distributed in the conference and sent to many persons in Andhra. It would popularise Garimella's contribution in Andhra Pradesh.

    With the initiation of the aforesaid freedom fighers C. Narayana Reddy the then Vice-Chancellor of Telugu University, Hyderabad, the 98th Birth day celebration of Garimella was celebrated on 15th July 1990. Famous freedom fighers and writers were invited by the said institution. In this celebration Jonnalagadda Prabhavathi (Garimella's daughter) was felicitated with great pomp.
44. A small disc around the neck sacred to the married women.

45. Government of Madras, Public Department, G.O. No.331, Dt. 15th April, 1922.
46. Government of Madras, Public Department, G.O.466, Dt. 26th May, 1922.
47. Government of Madras, Public Department G.O. No.466, dt. 26th May 1922.
48. Patri Seenappa and his company (Guntur) performed the proscribed dramas of Pundarikakshudu. Seenappa acted as Gandhiji, Jagarlapudi Lakshminarasimha Rao as Bhagat Singh, Eeka Anjaneyulu as Desbhaktudu, Vinjamuri Sreenivasachari as annie Besant and Singh as dyer.
49. Madala Veerabhadra Rao, Desabhakta Jeevita chritra (Telugu), pp.68-69.
50. D. Pundarikakshudu, Navayugarambham, Introduction, p.6.
51. Ibid.
52. The contents of the drama are in pages 1-12 of G.O. No.93, Public Department Dt. 1st February, 1922.
53. Government of Madras, Public (General) Department, G.O. No.792, Dt. 12th November, 1921.
54. Government of Madras, Public (General) Department, G.O. No.792, Dt. 12th November, 1921.
55. Ibid.
56. Government of Madras, Public Department, G.O. No.153, Dt. 27th February, 1923. thirty Sixth Indian National Congress held at ahmedabad on the 27th and 28th December, 1921. The Preasident of the session was Deshbandhu Chittaranjan Das.
57. Government of Madras, Public Department, G.O.No.153, dt. 27th February, 1923.
58. Government of Madras, Public (General) Department, Ordinary Series, G.O. No.413, Dt. 18th May, 1923.
59. Bhagavata, a mythololgical story. Prahlada was the son of Hiranyakasepa.
60. Government of Madras, Public (General) Department, Ordinary Series, Confidential, G.O. No. 413, Dt.18th May, 1923.
61. Government of Madras, Public (General) Department, G.O. No. 942, Dt. 15th December, 1922.
62. Personal Interview with Vaddadi Sitaramanjaneyulu, Dated 31ast August, 1988.
63. Puranam Suryanarayana Thirdhulu was a famous scholar – poet of Vizagapatam. He ran the monthly journal Kameswari for some time. He wrote five hundred poems relating to Home Rule Movement of Annie Besant.
64. Attaluri Narasimha rao, an article on Vaddadi Sitaramanjaneyulu in Rachana, July 1993, a monthly Journal from Visakhapatnam.
65. Ibid.

66. The song was separately published in 1977.
67. Madi Suryanarayana (Masuna) an article on Vaddadi entitled "Swearajya Kavi Vaddadi" published on 15th August 1987, in Andhra Bhoomi, a daily Telugu Newspaper.
68. Ibid.
69. Ibid.
70. Attaluri Narasimha Rao, op.cit.
71. Personal Interview with Vaddadi Sitaramanjaneyulu, Dt. 31st August 1988.
72. Government of Madras, Public Department G.O. No.816, dt. 19th November 1921.
73. Thiș contains a pun in connection with the Panchali Manabhanga the outraging of modesty of Drowpati, the wife of Pandavas by Dussasena., the brother of Suyodhana in Mahabharatha. Suyodhana in the story of Challeanges. Drowpati to sit on his thigh which he beats with his hand.
74. Government of Madras, Public Department, G.O. No.816, Dt. 19th November, 1921.
75. Ibid.
76. Government of Madras Public Department G.O. No. 137, Dt. 22nd February, 1923.
77. Government of Madras, Public Department, G.O. No.137, Dt. 22nd February, 1923.
78. Government of Madras, Public Department, G.O. No.137, Dt. 22nd February, 1923.

9

SUMMARY AND CONCLUSION

An attempt has been made in the fore-going chapters to analyse and assess the contribution of Proscribed Telugu Literature to the national movement in Andhra during the period between 1920-1947. This chapter attempts to draw some conclusions on the influence of the proscribed literature on the people of Andhra.

The nationalist intelligentsia of Andhra during this period participated in the struggle for freedom indirectly, through their wrotomg and contributed profusely to free the nation and made the people to participate actively in the struggled. Some of them toured the towns and villages to intensify the movement through the singing of songs, ballads and Harikathas. Some of them propagated their writings with the help of thousands of volunteers. On the basis of it we can estimate their zeal, patriotic fervour, and enthusiasm to liberate the country from slavery.

They were the persons responsible for propagating the Gandhian ideology and Congress programmes to every nook and corner in Andhra region. They extended their staunch support and actively participated to make the freedom struggle as a mass movement based on Gandhian ideology and principles. During this entire period Gandhiji preached to the people the efficacy of Satyagraha as an effective weapon in all spheres of life. To him, satyagraha was nothing else but a moral revolution and civil resistance was only a necessary part of it. Therefore majority of writers tried to popularise the Satyagraha weapon of Gandhiji. In Andhra a large number of works were written on Gandhiji as the writers as well as the people believed him to be an avatar.

In rendering service to the nation the nationlist writers who were associated with the proscribed nationalist literature had to make many sacrifices and their sacrifices were in no way less important than the sacrifices made by the elite-political leaders and their followers. In spite of the innumerable limitations imposed on them by repressive laws, hostile officialdom, family sufferings, and poor finances the performance of the writers was praiseworthy.

These nationalist writers were Andhra in character and Indian in spirit. They wrote for the national interest in a selfless spirit and with a missionary zeal. Whether they wrote on Gandhiji or Swadesi or on socialist ideas their object was to achieve freedom for India. They tried to bring out a collective movement for collective purpose. They faced the repressive actions of the Government without fear and preached patriotism and nationalism to the masses and strongly attacked the imperialist policies of the Colonial Government.

The writers did not concentrate on the writing of fiction. They, being writers of national movement, did not construct an imaginary past. They attempted to grasp and interpret a vast present for a bright future. They created political and economic awakening among the people by highlighting the national and international political and economic situation. The emergence of Mahatma and his mob mobilising programmes created self-confidence among the writers. They derived satisfaction that they were doing good to the people by supporting a wrothy cause at any cost. They attached to his charismatic image many Messianic elements and described him as the only leader who could lead the masses and achieve independence to the country. The personality of Gandhiji and his unique techniques, when propagated by the writers, made Gandhiji dear and near to the people and created self-confidence among the people also. Thus the literature served as a weapon to keep alive the sense of patriotism and the spirit of sacrifice.

The nationalist literature in Andhra between 1920 and 1947 was able to influence the people at large in many ways. The immense contribution made by the nationalist literature to the national movement and the impressive influence it excercised over popular mind is evident from the very fact that the colonial Government had to enact during this period a series of Press Acts of varying stringency. Throughout this period the nationalist writers in Andhra published many Telugu books, dramas, pamphlets and newspaper articles to propagate the Gandhian charisma, to spread leftist ideas and to bring ideas of nationalism and freedom to wider and wider sections of the Andhra people. They created rich Telugu nationalist literature trying to impregnate the classes and masses with the spirit of nartionalism and self-sacrifice.

To explain the proscribed Telugu literature's relationship with national movement in Andhra this literature is classified into Gandhian literature, patriotic literature, Leftist literature and literature in the form of drams for a better analysis and a close examination.

In writing this literature the writers were influenced by the then political environment. It was the period of strains and stresses, excitement and exasperation, hopes and fears, sacrifice and surrender, repression and rejection and unique programmes and novel strategies. The generally acknowledged leader, was Gandhiji. He was the elite of the elite political leaders. Before the emergence of Gandhiji there were Vandemataram movement and Home Rule movement at the national level and their repercussions in Andhra were the Rajahmundry college incident, the Cocanada riot and the starting of a branch of the Home Rule League of Annie Besant in Andhra with Gadicharla Harisarvothama Rao as the secretary, Rowlatt Act, the Jallianwala Bagh massacre and Khilafat movement made Gandhiji take part in the freedom struggle and slowly but steadily he was accepted and the prominent leader to lead the struggle of liberation. From that time onwards the programmes and movements – the non-cooperation movement, civil disobedience, salt satyagraha and Quit India movement of Gandhiji decided the course of the national movement. In Andhra the elite political leaders and the nationalist intelligentsia and, under their leadership, a wider section of the people participated actively in support of the movements and programmes enunciated by the national leaders.

During this period the national movement in Andhra was studded with episodes like Chirala-Perala Satyagraha, Palnati forest satyagraha, no-tax campaign in Pedanandipadu firka and Sitaramaraju's (Rampa) Rebellion which at times wrung admiration from the people and leaders of the whole country. It also saw the emergence of new parties with leftist orientation. The people of of Andhra responded very well to the movements and constructive programmes of Gandhiji. The nationalist writers contributed richly to influence the popular mind. The political environment shaped the writings of the nationalist intelligentsia and they in turn influenced the political environment to a great extent.

The nationalist literature gained momentum with the advent of Gandhiji on the national scene and touched all branches of Telugu literature – poetry, novel, drama etc. for spreading the Congress ideology and methods of political struggle among the masses and to mobilize the villagers in support of the Gandhian movements, the nationalist writers of this period wrote dramas. They were the most popular means which exercised tremendous influence on the people. So popular and so much was the impact of the dramas on the people and so "seditious" were thse dramas that the Government by invoking the Dramatic Performance Act of 1876 proscribed the published texts and prohibited their performance. Whenever the Government intervened and banned the staging of these dramas the nationalist writers used to write new ones. This was the case especially with Damaraju Pundarikakshudu of Guntur. His dramas proved to be the most inspiring and powerful. His political dramas **Navayugarambham, Gandhivijayam** and **Panchalaparabhavam** were written and staged to evoke sympathy for nationalism and Gandhiji in the minds of the people. In all these plays Gandhiji was the hero and contemporary politics provided the main theme. They were "aimed at" in the words of the author "reaching the illiterate common people and developing political consciousness among them."[1] In these dramas the old mythology was reinterpreted to show the then colonial reality, so that it would easily reach the hearts of the illiterate masses. In all the above political dramas almost all important Hindu Gods and Kings, popular Muslim leaders and Congress personalities come to the stage in one scene or the other to strengthen the myth that Gandhiji was the incarnation of the Lord of the Universe. These dramas projected Gandhiji into popular psychology as the saviour from above who came down to redress the grievances resulting from colonialism and establish Swarajya and cought the imagination of the masses in the villages. Many theatre groups staged his dramas at different places and acted as "political agents" for the Congress party both in urban and rural areas. The report of a Police Inspector about the influence of a play on the audience which "impressed very well on the audience and in my humble opinion even several non-cooperative meetings could not impress so well" [2] was the best compliment to the contribution of the nationalist dramatic literature to the national movement. This particular observation is true of all the "seditious plays" of this period. Thus the contribution of a political drama if staged properly proved to be more powerful than the speeches of a number of leaders for a number of times at a number of places. Political dramas politicized the masses and created a very wide social base for the national movement.

Next to dramas songs were used effectively to spread national consciousness among the people. The perceptions, which they disseminated through songs and poems, were the same perceptions that were embodied in the plays, writings and speeches. However unlike in the other forms, songs and poems covered a wider spectrum of Gandhian programme and national movement. They were written on Gandhiji's, "holy image", Khaddar, Charaka, temperance, triple boycott, Harijan uplift, national flag, national movement and political personalities.

Of the proscribed songs the most popular and the most influential song of the period was **"Maakoddi Tella Dora Tanam** by Garimella Satyanarayana of Srikakulam, which, in fact was on the lips of every contemporary nationalist. In this nationalist song the author "projected the basic contradiction with colonialism" and "brought to surface popular grievances vis-a-vis colonialism" and emphasized the spirit of patriotism and nationalism. He gave a call to the people to participate in the national movement and be prepared to any kind of sacrifice, his dedicated life being exemplary. This song influenced all sections of society during thre days of national movement. In those days everyone in Andhra hummed this tune.[3]

Another proscribed song that was very popular in the north coastal Andhra was **"Dandalu Dandalu Bharata Mata"** by Vaddadi Sitaramanjaneyulu of Visakhapatnam district. In this song the author criticised the imperialistic rule of the colonial Government and supported the non-cooperation movement of Gandhiji.

These and other songs, simple and direct, mixed with folk traditions and age old myth's were sung in the streets, at the functions in the houses, pilgrim gatherings, festival congregations, marriage functions and political meetings to rouse the sentiments of nationalism among the Telugu people. These songs inspired them to become a part of the national liberation struggle. The Congress volunteers used to sing these songs, tuned to ragas early morning everyday to keep alive the spirit of nationalism in the hearts of the village people.

From 1930s onwards the nationalist intelligentsia influenced by the Russian Revolution, Marxist ideology and socialist ideas, contributed immensely to the leftist (proscribed) literature. Some of the works were by Andhra writers and some were translations of the works by foreign authors.

Some of the eminent persons ready socialist literature and they began to translate Marxist literature into Telugu and began to propagate it with an object of overthrowing the British Imperialism in India and to establish workers Raj in India.

With the imposition of ban on Communists in 1934 the Communists in Andhra began to establish **Coolie Rakshana Samithis** (workers protection organizations) and through them they tried to achieve their objects. These organisations were established in towns, such as Guntur, Bezwada, Nellore, Bandar, Tenali, Bhimavaram, Visakhapatnam, Rajahmundry and so on. Through the railway labourers, agricultural labourers the Communists propagated their Socialistic principles.

Newspapers undertook the responsibility of propagation of communism. For example **Navasakti**, a weekly contributed much for spreading communism. To bring the Marxist philosophy before the people separate publishing organizations were established. Such were **Adarasa Grandha Mandali, Visva Sahitya Mala, Ativada Grandha Mala, Pragathi Prachuranalayamu, Cooly Samrakshaka Sangham, Ryotanga Grandhamala, Navasakti Publication, Sowkhya Sadhana Prachara Grandhamala, Athika Rajakiya Vignana Parishat** and **Prajasakti Prachurana**.

Prior to the establishment of Communist Party of India there were Andhra Ryot Association and Ryot Associations in three districts but they were not full fledged in their activity. So after the establishment of Communist Party of India, they established Ryot Associations in every district and towns. The Communists played an important role in the Ryot Movements in Andhra.

This party tried for the unification of agricultural labourers and conducted strikes for the achievement of their rights against landlords and money-lenders. They fought for the achievement of freedom for the country and separate state for Andhras.

Between 1936 and 1939 it established labourer, peasantry, agricultural coolie, students, youth, women associations and they provided the leadership in their movements and created political, and class consciousness among the working class.

With the outbreak of Second World War the British Government imposed repressive laws on the Communist Party of India and other extremist parties and imprisoned prominent leaders and party workers under Defence of India rules. Number of works on Marxist literature were prohibited and the Government imposed a ban on party newspapers. So the publication of **Navasakti** stopped. Some of the Communist leaders and party workers went underground.

Neti-Russia, Samrajyavadam, Amma, Karmika Bhajanavali, Karl Marx Upadesamulu, Russia Viplavamu, Anna and **Tirugubatu** were some of the important works on leftist ideology. In these works the writers gave an account of the political, social, and economic conditions, prevailing in those days in the Soviet Union, traced the life history of Lenin, criticised the imperialistic policies of the colonial powers, praised Russian Revolution and labour movements, detailed the teachings of Karl Marx, highlighted the miserable life of the working class, tried to awaken the ryots and proletarian class, condemned the Zamindari system and landlordism, attempted to popularise socialist ideas and advocated boycotting of imperialistic war.

The leftist writers encouraged inter-caste marriages, widow remarriages, denounced untouchability, propagated equal social status for women and encouraged women's participation in political, social, cultural movements. They fought for social justice to all through their writings. The writers used spoken language of the people in their writings. Because of this the people easily understood the socialist theory and it enriched the Telugu language.

They also wrote a number of dramas on political, economic and social exploitation. So it acted as a mass media. Street dramas also were written during this period. These works also propagated patriotism.

Thus the leftist writers attempted to awaken the peasants and working class against the capitalist exploitation and Zamindari suppression. They encouraged these classes to fight for their rights. During the period of ban the underground party leaders and party workers got support and cooperation of the people who had socialist leanings. Large number of people joined this party and began to spread to many villages. The leftist literature, published by the publication organizations mentioned above, played an important role in spreading the leftist ideology among the people. These writings first influenced the party workers and they, by undertaking the programme of propagation, influenced the working classes and peasants.

Of all the nationalist writers who wrote on the national movement in Andhra the writings of "four great singers of freedom" stand out as prominent. These four 'greats' of the proscribed Telugu literature of this period were Damaraju Pundarikakshudu, Garimella Satynarayana, Unnava Lakshmi Narayana and Vaddadi Sitaramanjaneyulu. Of these Damaraju and Unnava belonged to Guntur district, a politically advanced District and Garimella belonged to Srikakulam District and Vaddadi belonged to Visakhapatnam District, the backward districts of North Coastal Andhra. These four were writers and freedom fighters. Of these four Garimella stands out as supreme for his sacrifice and dedication. Damaraju's dramas, Garimella and Vaddadi's songs and poems and Unnava's novel, **Malapalli**, enriched the proscribed Telugu literature and left their imprint on the national movement in Andhra.

Another point that emerges from this study is the lack of contribution of women to the nationlist literature during this period. There was only one women writer who translated a work relating to the leftist ideology. That lady was Dari Subhadramma. She translated a work of Engels from English to Telugu. The details of the work are mentioned in the chapter "Proscribed Leftist Literature". It is not an original work, only a translation. The year in which it was translated was 1940. The work was only investigated but the proscribed. This shows the then existing gender inequality prevailing in the then Indian society and domination of men in the world of politics and nationalist literature.

It is true that there was no suffragette movement as such in India as in England and much less in Andhra. Neverthless Andhra women too, unhesitatingly marched abreast with men to face troubles and tribulations. There were women freedom fighters. As the analysis points out there were no nationalist women writers who contributed substantially to the national movement.

"Ideas become the material force when they reach out to the people". To prevent ideas reaching the people the British Government subjected the Press to restrictions and the writers to suffering and punishment. As it was reluctant to satisfy the aspirations and grant the demands of Indian nationalism, the Government passed a series of Press Acts of varying stringencies to curtail the liberty of press and circulation of printed material. It imprisoned the writers, and proscribed and forfeited their works on the ground that these writings created an atmosphere conducive to the spread of illfeelings and violence and seditious in nature and spirit. It did not proscribe some works which it considered were not of defamatory nature and gave warning to the writers and sometimes to the publishers. It also did not proscribe those works which were not against the interests of the colonial Government. It only proscribed those works which were critical of the political and economic policies of the Government.

It is clear from this that the nationalist literature of Andhra between 1920 and 1947 played a glorious part in promoting economic nationalism and national consciousness among the people and encouraged their participation in the national movement. Unless this 'Satanic' Government "is really destroyed, we cannot establish another Government" was the gist of their works. They tried to spread national consciousness among the masses, both as a mode of communication and method of mass political mobilization. All this literature and propaganda exerted a powerful influence, to use the words of Georges Lefebvre, upon the evolution of "the collective mentality".

NOTES

1. Modiali Nagabhushana Sarma, Telugu Sahityam: Gandhi Prabhavam, pp.124-126.
2. Quoted in S. Theodore Bhaskaran, The Message Bearers: The National Politics and the Entertainment Media in south India,. 1880-1945, (Madras, 1981), pp. 126-129.
3. N. Venkatarao's article "Adhunikayugam – Gandhi Sahityam" in **Andhra Patrika**, Annual Number, 1973-74, p.17.

APPENDIX

In this Appendix I have given only the relavent section of the Acts pertaining to the Proscribed Telugu Literature, of my period of study from 1920 to 1947.

THE INDIAN PENAL CODE (ACT XLV 1860)* (6th October, 1860)

Preamble: Whereas it is expedient to provide a general Penal Code for British India, it is enacted as follows:-

Section 117 Abetting Commission of Offence by the Public or by more than ten persons. Whoever abets the commission of an offence by the public generally or by any number or class of persons exceeding ten, shall be punished with imprisonment of either Description for a term which may extend to three years, or with fine, or with both.

Section 124 A Sedition Whoever by words, either spoken or written or by signs, or by visible representation, or otherwise, brings or attempts to bring into hatred or contempt or excites or attempts to excite disaffection towards Her Majesty, or the Government established by law in British India shall be punished with transportation for life or any shorter term, to which fine may be added, or with imprisonment which may extend to three years to which fine may be added or with fine.

Explanation – 1 :- The expression "disaffection" includes disloyalty and all feelings of enmity.

Explanation – 2 :- Comments expression disapprobation of the measures of the Government with a view to obtain their alteration by lawful means, without exciting or attempting to excite hatred, contempt or disaffection do not constitute an offence under this Section.

Explanation – 3 :- Comments expressing disapprobation of the administrative or other action of the Government without exciting or attempting to excite hatred, contempt or disaffection, do not constitute an offence under this Section.

Section 143 : Punishment Whoever is a member of an unlawful assembly shall be punished with imprisonment of either description for a term which may extend to six months or with fine, or with both.

Section[1] 153A Promoting enmity between Classes. Whoever by words, either spoken or written or by signs, or by visible representation, or otherwise promotes or attempts to promote feelings of enmity or hatred between different classes of Her Majesty's subjects, shall be punished with imprisonment which may extend to two years or with fine or with both.

Explanation:- It does not amount to an offence within the meaning of this section to point out, without malicious intention and with an honest view to their removal, matters which are producing or have a tendency to produce feelings of enmity or hatred between different classes of Her Majesty's subjects.

THE PRESS AND REGISTRATION OF BOOKS ACT, 1867* [Act XXV of 1867]

(Passed on the 22nd March, 1867)

An act for the regulation of printing presses and Newspapers for the preservation of copies of books printed in British India and for the registration of such books.

Preamble: Whereas it is expedient to provide for the regulation of printing presses and of periodicals containing news for the preservation of copies of every book printed or lithographed in British India, and for the registration of such books; it is hereby enacted as follows:-

Section 3 (a) Particulars to be printed on books and papers. Every book or paper printed within British India shall have printed legibly on it the name of the printer and the place of printing, and (if the book or paper be published) [1] (the name) of the Publisher and the place of publication.

Section 5 Rules as to publication of printed periodicals containing Public news. No printed periodical work, containing public news or comments on public news, shall be published in British India, except in conformity with the rules containing public news hereinafter laid down:

1. The printer and the publisher of every such periodical work shall appear before the Magistrate within whose local jurisdiction such work shall be published, and shall make and subscribe, in duplicate, the following declaration:

   "I A. B., declare that I am the printer (or publisher or printer and publisher) of the periodical work entitled.......and printer (or published, or printed and published as the case may be at........."

   And the last blank in this form of declaration shall be filled up with a true and precise account of the premises where the printing of publication is conducted.

2. As often as the place of printing or publication is changed, a new declaration shall be necessary.

3. As often as the printer or the publisher who shall have made such declaration as is aforesaid shall leave British India, a new declaration from a printer or publisher resident within the said territories shall be necessary.

Section 12 Penality for printing contrary to rule in Section 3 (a) Whoever shall print or publish any book or paper or otherwise than in conformity with the rule contained in Section 3 of this Act shall on conviction before a Magistrate, be punished by fine not exceeding[1] (two thousand) rupees, or by simple imprisonment for a term not exceeding [2] (six months) or by both.

THE DRAMATIC PERFORMANCE ACT, 1876 (ACT XIX OF 1876)* (16th December, 1876)

An Act for the better control of Public Dramatic Performances.

Preamble : Whereas it is expedient to empower the Government to prohibit public dramatic performances which are scandalous, defamatory, seditious or obscene, it is hereby enacted as follows:-

Section 3 : Power to prohibit certain dramatic performances – whenever the provincial Government is of opinion that any play, pantomine or other drama performed or about to be performed in a public places is (a) of a scandalous or defamatory nature or (b) likely to excite feelings of disaffection to the Government established by law in British India, or (c) likely to deprove the corrupt persons present at the performance, the Provincial Government, or outside the presidency towns and Rangoon the Local Government or such Magistrate as it may empower in this behalf may be order prohibit the performance.

Explanation:- Any building or enclosure to which the public are admitted to witness a performance on payment of money shall be deemed a "public place" within the meaning of this Section.

Section 10 : Power to prohibit dramatic performance in any local area, except under licence – whenever it appears to the Provincial Government that the provisions of this section are required in any local area, it may words "with the sanction of the Governor-General in Council" (were repealed by the Decentralization Act 1914 (4 of 1914) declare by notifiation in the official Gazette, that such provisions are applied to such area from a day to be fixed in the notification.

On and after that day, the Provincial Government may order that no dramatic performance shall take place in any place of public entertainment within such area, except under a licence to be granted by such Provincial Government, or such officer as it may specially empower in this behalf.

The Provincial Government may also order that no dramatic performance shall take place of public entertainment within such area, unless a copy of the piece, if and so far as it is written, or some sufficient account of its purport, if and so far as it is in pantomime, has been furnished not less than three days before the performance, to the Provincial Government or to such officer as it may appoint in this behalf.

A copy of any order under this Section may be served of any keeper of a place of public entertainment; and if thereafter he does or willingly permits, any act in disobedience to such order, he shall be punishable on conviction before a Magistrate with imprisonment for a term which may extend to three months, or with fine or with both.

THE CRIMINAL PROCEDURE CODE 1898 (ACT V OF 1898)*

An Act to consolidate and amend the law relating to Criminal Procedure whereas it is expedient to consolidate and amend the law relating to Criminal Procedure. It is hereby enacted as follows:-

Power to declare certain publications - Forfeited and to issue search-warrants for the same.

Section[1] 99-A (1) where

(a) any newspaper, or book as defined in the Press and Registration of Books Act, 1867 or

(b) any document,

Wherever printed, appears to the Local Government contain any seditious matter[2] (or any matter which promotes or is intended to promote feelings of enmity or hatred between different classes of His Majesty's subjects or which is deliberartely abd maliciously intended to outrage the religious feelings of any such class by insulting the religion or the religious beliefs of that class that is to say, any matter the publication of which is punishable under Section 124 A [3] (or Section 153 A ir Section 295 A) of the Indian Penal Code, the local Government may, by notification in the local official Gazette, stating the grounds of its opinion, declare every copy of the issue of the newspaper containing such matter and every copy of such book or other document to be forfeited to His Magesty, and there upon any police officer may seize the same, wherever found in British India, and any Magistrate may by warrant authorize any police officer not below the rank of Sub-Inspector to enter upon and search for the same in any premises where any copy of such issue or any such book other document may be or may be reasonably suspected to be.

2. In sub-section (1) "document" includes also any printing drawing or photograph or other visible representation.

Section 108 Security for good behaviour from Persons disseminating seditious matter. Whenever a chief presidency or District Magistrate, or a Presidency Magistrate or Magistrate of the first class specially empowered by the Local Government in this behalf, has information that there is within the limits of his jurisdiction any person who, within or without such limits either orally or in writing, or in any other manner intentionally, disseminates or attempts to disseminate or in anywise abets the dissemination of a. any seditious matter, that is to say, any matter the publication of which is punishable under Section 124 A of the Indian Penal

Code, or b. any matter the publication of which is punishable under Section 153 A of the Indian Penal Code, or c. any matter concerning a Judge which amounts to criminal intimidation or defamation under the Indian Penal Code.

Such Magistrate, if in his opinion there is sufficient ground for proceeding may (in manner hereinafter provided) require such person to show cause why he should not be ordered to execute a bond with or without sureties, for his good behaviour for such period, not exceeding one year as the Magistrate thinks fit to fix.

No proceedings shall be taken under this section against the editor, proprietor, printer or publisher of any publication registered under, and edited, printed and published in conformity with, the rules laid down in the Press and registration of Books Act 1867, with reference to any matter contained in such publication except by the order or under the authority of the Governor-General in council or the Local Government or some officer empowered by the Governor-General in council in this behalf.

THE INDIA POST OFFICE ACT, 1898 * (ACT VI OF 1898)
(Passed on the 22nd March 1898)

An act to consolidate and amend the Law relating in the Post Office in India.

Whereas it is expedient to consolidate and amend the Law relating to the post office in India; it is hereby enacted as follows:-

1(Section 27(B) (1) of the Indian Post Office Act 1898 dealt with any officer of the post office authorised by the Post Master General in this behalf may detain any postal article in course of transmission by post which he suspects to contain –

(a) (i) any newspaper or book as defined in the Press and Registration of Books Act (XXV of 1867) 1867, 2 or

(ii) any document; containing any seditious matter, that is to say, any matter the publication of which is punishable under Section 124A of the Indian Penal Code, or

(b) any newspaper as defined in the press and Registration of Books act, 1867, edited (XXV of 1867) printed or published otherwise than in conformity with the rules laid down in that Act, and shall deliver any postal article so detained to such officer as the Local Government may appoint in this behalf.

(2) any officer detaining any postal article under the provisions of sub-section (1) shall forthwith send by post to the address of such article notice of the fact of such detention.

(3) The Local Government shall cause the contents of any postal article detained under sub-section (1) to be examined and, if it appears to the Local Government that the article contained any newspaper, book or other document, of the nature described in clause (a) or clause (b) of sub-section (1), may pass such orders as to the disposal of the article and its contents as it may deem proper, and if it does not so appear, shall release the article and its contents, unless the same be otherwise liable to seizure under any law for the time being in force.

Provided that any person interested in any article detained under the provisions of clause (a) of sub-section (1) may, within two months from the date of such detention, apply to the Local Government for release of the same, and the Local Government shall consider such application and pass such orders thereon as it may deem to be proper.

Provided also that, if such application is respected the applicant may, within two months from the date of the order rejecting the application, apply to the High Court for release of the article and its contents on the ground that the article did not contain any newspaper, book or other document containing any seditious matter.

(4) In this Section "document" includes also any printing drawing or photograph or other visible representation.

THE INDIAN PRESS ACT, 1910 (ACT I OF 1910)*
(Passed on the 9th February, 1910)

An Act to provide for the better control of the Press where it is necessary to provide for the better control of the press. It is hereby enacted as follows:-

Section 4 (a) (1) Power to declare security forfeited in certain cases Whenever it appears to the Local Government that any printing press in respect of which any security has been deposited as required by Section 3 is used for the purpose of printing or publishing any nrewspaper, book or other document containing any words, signs or visible representations which are likely or may have a tendency directly or indirectly whether by inference, suggestion, allusion, metaphor, implication or otherwise – a. to incite to murder or to any offence under the Explosive substances Act, 1908 or to any act of violence, or b. to seduce any officer, soldier or sailor in the Army or Navy of His Majesy from his allegiance of his duty, or c. to bring into hatred or contempt His Majesty or the Government established by law in British India or the administration of Justice in British India or any native prince or chief under the suzerainty of His Majesty, or any class or section of His Majesty's subjects in British India, or to excite disaffection towards His Majesty or the said Government or any such prince or chief, or d. to put any person in fear or to cause annoyance to him and thereby induce him to deliver to any person any property or valuable security or to do any act which he is not legally bound to do, or to omit to do any act which he is legally entitled to do, or e. to encourage or incite any person to interfere with the administration of the law or with the maintenance of law and order, or f. to convey any threat of injury to a public servant or to any person in whom that public servant is believed to be interested, with a view to inducing that public servant to do any act or to forbear or delay to do any act connected with the exercise of his public functions.

The Local Government may, by notice in writing to the keeper of such printing press,. Stating or describing the words, signs or visible representations which in its opinion are of the nature described above declare the security deposited in respect of such press and all copies of such newspaper, book or other document wherever found to be forfeited to His Majesty.

(b) Explanation – 1: In clause (c) the expression "disaffection" includes disloyalty and all feelings of enimity.

(d) Explanation – II :- Comments expressing disapproval of the measures of the Government or of any such native prince or chief as aforesaid with a view to obtain their alteration by lawful means, or of the administrative or other action of the Government or any such native prince or chief or of the administration of injustice in British India without exciting or attempting to excite hatred, contempt or disaffection do not come within the scope of clause (c).

Section 12 (1) Power to declare certain Publications forfeited and to Issue search warrants for same. Where any newspaper, book or other document wherever printed appears to the local Government to contain any words, signs or visible representations of the nature described in Section 4, sub-section (1), the Local Government may, by notification in the local official Gazette, stating the grounds of its opinion, declare such newspaper, book or other document to be forfeited to His Majesty, and thereupon any police officer may seize the same wherever found, and any Magistrate may by warrant authorise any police officer not below the rank of Sub-Inspector to enter upon and search for the same in any premises where the newspaper, book or other document may be or may be reasonably suspected to be.

THE CINEMATOGRAPH ACT, 1918 (ACT II OF 1918) *
(Passed on 6th March, 1918)

An Act to make provision for regulating exhibitions by means of cinematographs.

Whereas it is expedient to make provision for regulating exhibitions by means of cinematographs, it is enacted as follows:-

Section 7 Sub-section 5 Certification of films : The District Magistrate, or in a presidency town or in the town of Rangoon, the Commissioner of Police, may, after recording his reasons in writing, by order suspend the certificate of any film pending the orders of the Local Government, and during such suspension the film shall be deemed to be an uncertified film in that district or town. He shall forthwith forward a copy of his order to the Local Government to which he is subordinate and such Local Government may, in its discretion, either discharge his order or, by notification in the local official Gazette, direct that the film shall be deemed to be an uncertified film in the whole or any part of the province.

THE INDIAN PRESS (EMERGENCY POWER) ACT, 1931 *
(ACT No.XXIII of 1931
(9th October, 1931)

An Act to provide against the publication of matter inciting to or encouraging murder of violence.

Whereas it is expedient to provide against the publication of matter inciting to or encouraging murder or violence, it is hereby encated as follows:-

Control of Printing Press and Newspapers

3(1) Any person keeping a printing-press who is required to make a declaration under Section 4 of the Press and Registration of Books Act, 1867, may be required by the Magistrate before whom the declaration is made, for reasons to be recorded in writing, to deposit with the Magistrate within ten days from the day on which the declaration is made, security to such an amount, not being more than one thousand rupees, as the Magistrate may in each case think fit to require, in mo ney or the equivalent thereof in securities of the Government of India as the person making the deposit may choose:

Provided that if a deposit has been required under sub-section (3) from any previous keeper of the printing-press, the security which may be required under this sub-section may amount to three thousand rupees.

(2) Where security required under sub-section (1) has been deposited in respect of any printing-press, and for a period of three months from the date of the declaration mentioned in sub-section (1) no order is made by the Local Government under Section 4 in respect of such press, the security shall, on application by the keeper of the press, be refunded.

(3) Whenever it appears to the Local Government that any Printing-Press kept in any place in the territories under its administration, in respect of which security under the provisions of this Act has not been required, or having been required has been refunded under sub-section (2), is used for the purpose of printing or publishing any newspaper, book or other document containing any words, signs or visible representations of the nature described in Section 4, sub-section (1), the Local Government may, by notice in writing to the keeper of the press stating or describing such words, signs or visible representations, order the keeper to deposit with the Magistrate within whose jurisdiction the press is situated security to such an amount, not being less than five hundred or more than three thousand rupees as the Local Government may think fit to require, in money or the

equivalent threreof in securities of the Government of India as the person making the deposit may choose.

Power to declare security or press Forfeited in certain cases. 4 (1) Whenever it appears to the Local Government that any printing-press in respect of which any security has been ordered to be deposited under Section 3 is used for the purpose of printing or publishing any newspaper, book or other document containing any words, signs or visible representations which –

(a) incite to or encourage, or tend to incite to or to encourage, the commission of any offence of murder or any cognizable offence involving violence, or

(b) directly or indirectly express approval or administration of any such offence, or of any person, real or fictitious, who has committed or is alleged or represented to have committed any such offence.

The Local government may, by notice in writing to the keeper of such printing-press, stating or describing the words, signs or visible representations which in its opinion are of the nature described above -

(i) Where security has been deposited, declare such security, or any portion thereof, to be forfeited to His Majesty, or

(ii) Where security has not been deposited, declare the press to be fordfeited to His Majesty, and may also declare all copies of such newspaper, book or other document wherever found in British India to be forfeited to His Majesty.

Explanation:- No expression of approval or admiration made in a historical or literary work shall be deemed to be of the nature described in this sub-section unless it has the tendency described in clause (a)

(2) After the expiry of ten days from the date of the issue of a notice under sub-section (1) declaring a security, or any portion thereof, to be forfeited, the declaration made in respect of such press under Section 4 of the Press and Registration of Books act, 1867, shall be deemed to be annulled.

Section 16 (1) Power to seize and destroy news sheet and newspaper. Any Police Officer, or any other person empowered in this behalf by the Local Government, may seize any unauthorised news sheet or unauthorised newspaper, wherever found.

Special Provisions Relating to the seizure of certain documents

Section 19 Power to declare certain Publications forfeited and to issue search warrants for same. Where any newspaper, book or other document wherever made appears to the Local Government to contain any words, Signs or visible representations of the nature described in Section 4, sub-section (1), the Local Government may, by notification in the local official Gazette, stating the grounds of its opinion, declare every copy of the issue of the newspaper, and every copy of such book or other document to be forfeited to His Majesty, and thereupon any Police Officer may seize the same wherever found in British India, and any Magistrate may by warrant authorise any Police Officer not below the rank of Sub-Inspector to enter upon and search for the same in any premises where any copy of such issue or any such book or other document may be or may be reasonable suspected to be.

Section 22 : Power to detain and being transmitted by post. Any officer in charge of a Post Office or authorised by the Post Master General in this behalf may detain any article other than letter or parcel in course of transmission by post, which he suspects to contain-

(a) any newspaper, book or other document containing words, signs or visible representations of the nature described in section 4, sub-section (1), or

(b) any unauthorised news-sheet or unauthorised newspaper, and shall deliver all such articles to such officer as the Local Government may appoint in this behalf to be disposed of in such manner as the Local Government may direct.

ORDINANCE NO.II OF 1932 *
(4th January, 1932)

An Ordinance to confer Special Powers on government and its officers for the purpose of maintaining law and order.

Whereas an emergency has arisen which make it necessary to confer special powers upon Government and its officers for the purpose of maintaining law and order;

Now therefore, in exercise of the power conferred by section 72 of the Government of India Act, the Governor-General is pleased to make and promulgate the following Ordinance:

(1) This Ordinance may be called the Emergency Powers Ordinance, 1932.

This Section and Section 63 shall come into force at once, and the Local Government may by notification in the local official Gazette, direct that any or all of the remaining provisions shall come into force in any area to which they have been extended, on such date as may be appointed in the notification.

Section 63. So long as this Ordinance remains in force, in sub-section (1) of Section 4 of the India Press (Emergency Powers) Act, 1931, the following clauses shall be deemed to be added to clauses (a) and (b) namely:-

"(c) to seduce any officer, soldier, sailor or airman in the military or naval or air forces of His Majesty or any Police Officer from his allegiance of his duty, or

(d) to bring into hatred or contempt to His Majesty or the Government established by law in British India or the administration of Justice in British India of any Indian Prince or Chief under the suzerainty of His Majesty, or any class or section of His Majesty's subjects in British India or to excite disaffection towards His Majesty or the said Government or any such Prince or Chief, or

(e) to put any person in fear or to cause annoyance to him and thereby induce him to deliver to any person any property or valuable security or to do any act which he is not legally bound to do, or to omit to do any act which he is legally entitled to do, or

(f) to encourage or incite any person to interfere with the administration of the law or with the maintenance of law and order, or to commit any offence, or to refuse or defer payment of any land-revenue tax, rate, cess or other due or amount payable to Government or to any local authority, or any rent of agricultural land or anything recoverable as arrears of or along with such rent, or

(g) to induce a public servant or a servant of a local authority to do any act or to forbear or delay to do any act connected with the exercise of his public functions or to resign his office, or

(h) to promote feelings of enmity or harted between different classes of His Majesty's subjects, or

(i) to prejudice the recruiting or persons to sercve in any of His Majesty's forces or in any police force, or to prejudice the training discipline or administration of any such force",

and the provisions of that Act shall apply accordingly.

ORDINANCE NO.X OF 1932 *
(30th June, 1932)

An Ordinance to confer Special Powers on Government and its officers for the purpose of maintaining law and order.

Whereas an emergency has arisen which makes it necessary to confer special powers upon Government and its officers for the purpose of maintaining law and order:

Now therefore, in exercise of the power conferred by section 72 of the Government of India Act, the Governor General is pleased to make and promulgate the following ordinance:

1. (1) This Ordinance may be called the special Ordinance, 1932.

   (2) This Chapter and Sections 64, 74, 75, 76, 77, 78, 79 and 80 extend to the whole of British India, including British Baluchistan and the Sonthal Parganas, and the Governor-General in Council may, by notification in the Gazette of India, extend any or all of the remaining sections to the said area or to any province or part of a province specified in the notification.

   (3) This Chapter and Sections 64, 74, 75, 76, 77, 78, 79 and 80 shall come into force at once, and the Local Government may, by notification in the local official Gazette, direct that any or all of the remaining provisions shall come into force in any area to which they have been attended, on such date as may be appointed in the notification.

   Section 77: so long as this Ordinance remains in force in sub-section (1) of Section 4 of the Indian Press (Emergency Powers) Act, 1931, after clause (b) the following words and clauses shall be deemed to be inserted namely:-

   "or which tend, directly or indirectly -

   (c) to seduce any offi cer, soldier, sailor or airman in the military, naval or air forces of His Majesty or any Police Officer from his allegiance or his duty, or

   (d) to bring into hatred or contempt His Majesty or the Government established by law in British India or the administration of justice in British India or any Indian Prince or Chief under the suzerainty or His

Majesty or any class or section of His Majesty's subjects in British India or to excite disaffection towards His Majesty or the said Government or any such Prince or Chief, or

(e) to put any person in fear or to cause annoyance to him and thereby induce him to deliver to any person any property or valuable security, or to do any act which he is not legally bound to do, or to omit to do any act which he is legally entitled to do, or

(f) to encourage or incite any person to interfere with the administration of the law or with the maintenance, or law and order, or to commit any offence, or to refuse or defer payment of any land-revenue, tax, rate, cess or other due or amount payable to Government or to any local authority, or any rent of agricultural land or anything recoverable as arrears of or along with such rent, or

(g) to induce a public servant or a servant of a local authority to do any act or to forbear or delay to do any act connected with the exercise of his public functions or two resign his office, or

(h) to promote feelings of enmity or hatred between different classes of His Majesty's subjects, or

(i) to prejudice the recruiting of persons to serve in any of His Majesty's forces, or in any police force, or to prejudice the training, discipline or administration of any such force, and the provisions of that Act shall apply accordingly.

THE CRIMINAL LAW AMENDMENT ACT, 1932 *
(Act No.XXIII of 1932)
(19th December, 1932)

An Act to supplement the criminal law.

Whereas it is expedient to supplement the criminal law and to that end to amend the Indian press (E.P.) Act, 1931 and further to amend temporarily the Indian Criminal Law amendment Act, 1908 for the purposes hereinafter appearing; it is hereby enacted as follows:-

Section 16. Amendment of Section 4 Act XXIII of 1931. In sub-section (1) of Section 4 of the Indian Press (Emergency Powers) Act, 1931:

(a) after clause
(b) the following words and clauses shall be inserted, namely:-

"or which tend, directly or indirectly

(c) to seduce any officer, soldier, sailor or airman in the military, naval or air forces of His Majesty or any Police Officer from his allegiance or his duty to or

(d) to bring into hatred or contempt His Majesty or the Government established by law in British India or the administration of Justice in British India or any class or section of His Majesty's subjects in British India, or to excite disaffection towards His Majesty or the said Government, or

(e) to put any person in fear or to cause annoyance to him and thereby induce him to deliver to any person any property or valuable security or to do any act which he is not legally bound to do, or to omit to do any act which he is legally entitled to do, or

(f) to encourage or incite any person to interfere with the administration of the law or with the maintenance of law and order, or to commit any offence, or to refuse or defer payment of any land-revenue, tax, rate, cess or other due or amount payable to Government or to any local authority, or any rent of agricultural land or anything recoverable as arrears of or along with such rent, or

(g) to induce a public serva nt or a servant of a local authority to do any act or to forbear or delay to do any act connected with the exercise of his public functions or to resign his office, or

(h) to promote feelings of enmity or hatred between different classes of His Majesty's subjects or

(i) to prejudice the recruiting of persons to serve in any of His Majesty's forces, or in any police force, or to prejudice the training, discipline or administration of any such force",

(j) the Explanation shall be numbered as Explanation.1, and after the Explanation as so numbered the following Explanations shall be inserted, namely:-

"Explanation 2 – comments expressing disapprobation of the measures of the Government with a view to obtain their alteration by lawful means without exciting or attempting excite hatred, contempt or disaffection shall not be deemed to be of the nature described in clause (d) of this sub-section.

Explanation 3 – comments expressing disapprobation of the administrative or other action of the Government without exciting or attempting to excite hatred, contempt or disaffection, shall not be deemed to be of the nature described in clause (d) of this sub-section.

Explanation 4 – words pointing out, without malacious intention and with an honest view to their removal, matters which are producing or have a tendency to produce feelings of enmity or hatred between different classes of His Majesty's subjects shall not be deemed to be words of the nature described in clause (h) of this sub-section".

DEFENCE OF INDIA ACT 1939 AND RULES MADE UNDER THE DEFENCE OF INDIA RULES *

10 (1) (a) Unlawfully enter or board any Vehicle, Vessel or aircraft used or appropriated for any of the purposes of this Majesty's service, or trespass on premises in the vicinity of any such vehicle, vessel or aircraft or

(b) Trespass on, or on premises in the vicinity of, any premises used or appropriated for any of the purposes of His Majesty's service or for defence against, or protection from an enemy.

If any person contravenes any of the provisions of this rule he shall be punishable with imprisonment for, a term of three years and shall also be liable to fine or with fine or with both.

Prevention of prejudicial Acts and control of Information. In this part unless there is any thing repugnant in the subject or context.

34 (6) "prejudicial Act" means any act which is intended or is likely -

(e) To bring into hatred or contempt, or to excite disaffection towards, His Majesty or the Crown Representative or the Government established by law in British India or in any other part of His Majesty's dominions.

(f) to promote feelings of enmity and hatred between different classes of His Majesty's subjects.

(g) to cause fear or alarm to the public or to any section of the public.

(k) to influence the conduct or attitude of the public or of any section of the public in a manner likely to be prejudicial to the defence of British India or to the efficient prosecution of war.

34 (7) read with rule 34 (6) (g) of Defence of India Rules.

34 (7) "prejudicial report" means any report, statement or visible representation, whether true or false, which, or the publishing of which is, or is an incitement to the commission of a prejudicial act as defined in this rule.

[1](40) (1) Where in the opinion of the Central Government or the provincial Government any document made, printed or published, whether before or after the ordinance came into force, contains any confidential information, any information likely to assist the enemy or any prejudicial report, that Government may by order: -

(a) addressed to the editor, printer, publisher or person in possession of such document -

(i) require to be informed or the name address of any person concerned in the supply or communication of such information or in the making of such report:

(ii) require the delivery of such document and every copy thereof to an authority specified in the order;

(b) prohibit the further publication, sale or distribution of such document including, in the case of a newspaper or other periodical, the publication, sale or distribution of any subsequent issue thereof;

(c) declare such document and every copy thereof to be forfeited to His Majesty.

(2) Where in pursuance of sub-rule (1) any document is required to be delivered to a specified authority, that authority may enter upon and search any premises whereon or wherein such document or any copy thereof is or is reasonably suspected to be.

(3) Where in pursuance of sub-rule (1) any document has been declared to be forfeited to His Majesty, any police officer may seize any copy thereof, wherever found in British India and any Magistrate may by warrant authorise any Police Officer not below the rank of Sub-Inspector to enter upon and search any premises whereon or wherein such document or any copy thereof is or is reasonably suspected to be.

(4) If any person contravenes any order made under this rule he shall be punishable with imprisonment for a term which may extend to three years and shall also be liable to fine.

NOTES

* **The Criminal Court Manual (Imperial Acts)**, Second Edition, Vol.II, Major Acts, Published by The Madras Law Journal Office, Mylapore, Madras, 1936.

Section 153A was added by section 5 of the Indian Penal Code Amendment Act 1898 (4 of 1898).

* P. Hari Rao and S. Kasturi Rangacharian (Editors) **The All India Cfriminal Court Manual, Imperial Acts**, vol.I, published by T.A.Venkata Swamy Row and T.S.Krishna Swamy Row, Proprietors, The Law Printing House, Madras and the Layers Companion Office, Trichinopoly, Madras, 1919.

1. These words wre inserted by Amending Act, 1891 (12 of 1891).

These words substituted for the words "five thousand" by Section 3 and first Schedule of the Press Law Repeal and Amendment Act, 1922 (14 of 1922).

These words were substituted for the words "two years" by Section 3 and first Schedule of The Press Law Repeal and amendment Act, 1922 (14 of 1922).

* V.R.Manohar and W.w.Chitaley (Editors) **The A.I.R. Manual, Unrepealed Central Acts, Civil and Criminal,** Vol.XV, Fourth Edition, 1979, All India Reported Ltd., Congress Nagar, Nagpur.

* **The Criminal Court Manual (Imperial Acts)** Second Edition, vol.II, Major Acts, Punblished by The Madras Law Journal Office, Mylapore, Madras, 1936.

Sections 99 a to 99 G were inserted by the second schedule of Act XIV of 1922.

Inserted by Act XXV of 1927, Section 3.

Ibid.

* Government of India, Legislative Departmenrt. The Indian Post Office Act, 1898, as modified upto the 1st July 1922, Calcutta, Government Printing, India, 1922.

1. this Section was inserted by Section 6 and Fourth Schedule of the Press Law Repeal and amendment Act, 1922 (14 of 1922).
2. General Acts Vol.I.

* P.Hari rao and s. Kasturi Rangachariar (Editors), "The all India Criminal Court Manual", **Imperial Acts**, Vol.I, published byT.A.Venkata Swamy row, and T.S. Krishna Swamy Row, Proprietors, The Law Printing House, Madras; and the lawyer's Companion office, Trichinopoly, Madras, 1919.

* V.R.Manohar and W.W.Chitaley (Editors), **The A.I.R.Manual**, unrepealed Central Acts, Civil and Criminal, Fourth Edition, Vol.III, 1979, All India Reporter Ltd., Congress Nagar, Nagpur.

* **The Madras Law Journal**, Vol.LXI, July – December 1931, R. Narayana Swamy Iyer, Advocate, High Court, Mylapore, Printed at the Madras Law Journal Press, Mylapore.

1. The Act of 1931 originally a temporary Act, it was made permanent in 1935.

* Nripendra Nath Mitra (Ed.) **The Indian Annual Register : An Annual Digest of Public Affairs of India**, Vol. II, January – June, 1932, published by the Annual Register Office, Calcutta.

• Nripendra Nath Mitra (Ed.) **The Indian Annual Register : An Annual Digest of Public Affairs of India**, Vol. II, January – June, 1932, published by the Annual Register Office, Calcutta.

* **The Madras Law Journal**, Vol.LXI, July – December 1931, R. Narayana Swamy Iyer, Advocate, High Court, Mylapore, Printed at the Madras Law Journal Press, Mylapore.

* Defence of India Act 1939 and Rules made thereunder The Defence of India Rules (Being Rules reprinted as amended upto and including 30th September 1940). Published by the Manager of Publications, New Delhi, 1940.

Substituted by Defence Coordination Department Notification No.347 OR/40 dated the 14th June, 1940 for original rule 40.

BIBLIOGRAPHY

Primary Sources

Records of the Government of Madras

Proceedings of the Government of Madras, 1920-1947, Home Department, Public Department, Judicial Department.

Fortnightly Reports (Confidential) of the Government of Madras.

Madras Police Abstracts of intelligence (Secret) Reports 1920-1947.

Native Newspaper Reports of the Madras Presidency 1920-1947.

C.I.D. Reports of Madras Presidency (Confidential) 1920-1947.

History of Freedom Struggle in Andhra (H.F.S. typed material) 1920-1947.

Proscribed Books, Pamphlets, Leaflets, Newspapers and Periodicals.

Madras Legislative Council Proceedings 1920-1947.

Records of Government of India

Sedition committee Report 1918.

The Press Law Committee Report 1922.

The Civil Disobedience Movement, 1930-1934.

Coatman, J., India in 1925-26

---------------, India in 1926-27

---------------, India in 1928-29

---------------, India in 1929-30

Secondary Sources

Abbas, M.H., All about the Khilafat, Calcutta, 1923.

Andrews, C.F. and Mookerjee, Girija, The Rise and Growth of the Congress in India, London, 1938.

Anil Seal., The Emergence of Indian Nationalism, Cambridge University Press, 1968.

Anjaneyulu, Kodali., Andhra Pradeshlo Ganbhiji (Telugu), Hyderabad, 1978.

Appa Rao, G., Kanyasulkam (Telugu), Machilipatnam, 1969.

Appa Rao P.S.R., Telugu Nataka Vikasamu (Telugu), Secunderabad, 1967.

Argov, Daniel., Moderates and Extremists in the Indian National Movement, 1833-1920, Bombay, 1967.

Arudra, Samagra Andhra Sahityam (Telugu), Vol.XIII, Vijayawada, 1991.

Baker, C.J. and Washbrook, D.A. [Eds] South India – Political Institutions and Political Change 1880-1940, Delhi, 1975.

Baker, C.J., The Politics of South India 1920-1937, Delhi, 1976.

Bangorey (Ed.), Letters from Brown History of Telugu Journalism, Nellore, 1973.

Bipin Chandra, The Rise and Growth of Economic Nationalism in India, Delhi, 1969.

------------------, Malapalli Navalapai Prabhutva Nishedhalu (Telugu), Madras, 1979.

Barnett., Catalogue of the Telugu Books, London, 1912.

Bhatnagor, G.S., Education and Social change, Calcutta, 1972.

Bhattacharjee, Arun., The Indian Press Profession or Industry, Delhi.

Bhuyan, A.C., The Quit India Movement, The Second World War and Indian Nationalism, New Delhi, 1975.

-----------------, Essays on Indian nationalism, New Delhi, 1993.

-----------------, Freedom Struggle, New Delhi, 1972.

Bipan Chandra and others, India's Struggle for Independence, Delhi, 1989.

Bamford, P.C., History of the Non-Cooperation and Khilafat Movements (Reprint), Delhi, 1974.

British Paramountacy and Indian Renaissance, Vol.IX, Part I, Vol. X, Part II, Bharatiya Vidyabhavan Series, Bombay, 1963.

Chalapati Rao, I. V. Duggirala Gopala Krishnaiah, Hyderabad, 1988.

Chalapati Rao, M., The Press, New Delhi, 1974.

Chintamani, C. Y., Indian Politics Since the Mutiny, Waltair, 1937.

Chowdary, Sukhbir, Growth of Nationalism in India, Vols. I and II, Delhi, 1973.

-----------, Indian People Fight for National Liberation 1920-1922, Delhi, 1972.

Dantwala, M. L., Gandhism Reconsidered, Bombay, 1944.

Das, M.N., India Under Morley and Minto, London, 1964.

Desai, A.R., Social Background of Indian Nationalism, Bombay, Fourth Edn., 1966.

---------(Ed.), Peasant Struggle in India, Bombay, 1979.

Devanesen, Chandran, D.S., The Making of the Mahatma, Madras, 1969.

Dhawan, Gopinath, The Political Philosophy of Mahatma Gandhi, Ahmedabad, 1957.

Diwakar, R. R., Glimpses of Gandhiji, Hind Kitabs, Bombay, 1949.

-----------------, Gandhi's Triple Message (Sri Venkateswara University Endowment Lectures), Bombay, 1966.

Durga Das Basu, Law of the Press in India, New Delhi, 1980.

Dutt, K. Iswara, Andhra Souvenir, Delhi, 1963.

-----------------, The Congress Encyclopedia, Vol. I, Delhi, 1967.

Dwyer, Michael, O., India as I knew it, London, 1938.

Easton, Jeamette, Gandhi: Fighter Without Sword, New York, 1950.

Furneawx, Rupert., Massacre at Amritsar, London, 1963.

Gandhi, M. K., Satyagraha (Non-violent Resistance), Ahmedabd, 1951.

-----------------, Women and Social Injustice, Ahmedabd, 1942.

Ganguli, B. N., Indian Economic Thought, Delhi, 1977.

Gerald Barrier, N., Banned Controversial Literature and Political Control in British India, New Delhi, 1977.

Ghose, Aurobindo., The Doctrine of Passive Resistance, Pondicherry, 1952.

Ghose Sanker, The Renaissance to Militant Nationalism in India, Bombay, 1969.

Ghosh Hemendra Prasad, The Newspaper in India, Calcutta, 1952.

---------------, Press and Press Laws in India, Calcutta, 1930.

Girija, S., Freedom Movement in India – Nellore District, New Delhi, 1990.

Gopalakrishnan, S., Political Movements in South India 1914-1929, Madras, 1981.

Griffiths Sir Percival, the British Impact on India, Lodon, 1952.

Guha, A.C., First Spark of Revolution: he Early Phase of Indian Struggle for Independecne 1900-1920, Bombay, 1971.

Gupta, D.C., Indian National Movement, Delhi, 1970.

Hanumantha Rao, K., Sweeya Jeevita Sameeksha (Telugu), Rajahmundry, 1973.

Hari Rao, P. and Kasturi Rangachariar, The All India Criminal court Manual, Imperial Acts Vol. I, Madras, 1919.

Irschick, E.F., Politics and Social Conflict in South India, London, 1963.

Jawaharlal Nehru, The Discovery of India, Bombay, 1961.

Judith, M. Brown, Gandhi's Rise to Power in Indian Politics 1915-1922, Cambridge, 1972.

-----------, Gandhi and Civil Disobedience.

-----------, The Mahatma in Indian Politics 1928-1934, Cambridge, 1977.

-----------, Modern India : The Origin of An Asian Democracy, New Delhi, 1984.

Kaleswara Rao, A., Najeevitakatha Navyadhram (Telugu), Vijayawada, 1959.

Kamesewara Rao, Tekumalla, Naavangmaya Mitrulu (Telugu), Chittore, 1966.

Kapil Kumar (Ed.), Congress and Classes, New Delhi, 1988.

Kaushik, P. D., The Congress Ideology and Programme, Bombay, 1964.

Keswa vanarayana, B., Political and Social Factors in Andhra, 1900-1956, Vijayawada, 1976.

Krishnamacharya, Samudrala, Malapalli-Vimrsanatmaka Pariseelana (Telugu), Warangal, 1990.

Krishna Rao, Y. V. and Balaramamurthy, Y. (Ed.), Andhra Pradesh Darsini, Vijayawada, 1976.

Krishna Rao, Y.V. and Nageswara Rao, Andhra Pradeshlo Communist Party 50 Ella Porata Charitra (Telugu), Hyderabad, 1985.

Kumar, R. (Ed.), Essays on Gandhian Politics : The Rowlatt Satyagraha of 1919, Oxford, 1971.

Lakshmi Narasimha Kavi, Chilakamarti., Sampoorna Grandhavali 8 Vols. (Telugu), Sastipoorthi Mudranamu, 1927.

Lakshmi Ranjanam Khandavalli and Balendra Sekharam Kandavalli., Andhrula charitra-Samskruti (Telugu), Madras, 1974.

Leonard, J.G., Kandrukuri Veeresalingam, Hyderabad, 1991.

Lovett, Verney, A History of the Indian Nationalist Movement, Delhi, 1972.

Madhurashri, Alluri Sitaramaraju, Hyderabad, 1967.

Majumdar, A.K., Advent of Independence, Bombay, 1963.

Majumdar, B.B., History of Indian Social and Political Ideas, Calcutta, 1967.

Majumdar, R.C., History of the Freedom Movement in India, Vol.I & II, Calcutta, 1962, Vol. III, Calcutta, 1963.

Mangamma, J., Book Printing in India, Nellore, Bangory Books, 1975.

--------------, Alluri Sitaramaraju (Telugu), Hyderabad, 1983.

Margarita, Barns, the Indian Press (History of the Growth of Public Opinion in India), London, 1940.

Masselos, Jim., Nationalism on the Indian sub-Continent – An Introductory History, Melbourne, 1972.

Indian Nationalism – An History, Adelhi, 1985.

Maxim Gorky., Mother, Moscow, 1949.

Menon, K.B. The press Laws of India, Bombay, 1937.

Mitra, D.K., Press and Press Laws in India, Calcutta, 1930.

Mosley, Leonard., the Last Days of the British Raj, London, 1961.

Nagabhushana Sarma, Modali, Telugu Sahityam – Gandhiji Prabhavam (Telugu), Hyderabad, 1970.

Nagendrudu, Karyampudi, Andhra Ratna Duggirala Gopala Krishnayya (Telugu), Chirala, 1976.

Naraian, V.A., Social History of Modern India, Meerut, 1972.

Narasimha Rao, S. Natasthanam (Telugu), Komeripalem (A.P.), 1974.

Narasimha Rao, Y., History of Alluri Sitaramaraju, Hyderabad.

Narasimha Rao, K.V., the Emergence of Andhra Pradesh, Bombay, 1973

Naidu, Ch. M., Salt Satyagraha in the Coastal Andhra, Delhi, 1986.

Narayana Reddy, C., Aadhunikandhra Kavitvamu Sampradayamulu Prayogamulu (Telugu), Secunderabad, 1967.

Narayana Swamy Iyer, R. (Publisher), The Madras Law Journal Vol. LXI July-December, 1931, Vol. LXIII July-December, 1932, Madras.

Narja, V. R. , Veeresalingam, New Delhi, 1968.

Natarajan, S., A Century of Social Reform in India, Bombay, 1959.

---------------, A History of the Press in India, Bombay, 1962.

Nirmal, C. J., Nineteenth Century Press and the Development of Indian Nationalism, the Lajapat Rai centenary Lectures, Madras University, Madras, 1970.

Panigrahi, D. N., Quit India and the Struggle for Freedom, New Delhi, 1984.

Penderel Moon, Gandhi and Modern India, London, 1968.

Poornachandra Rao, Adsumilli., vennela Velugulu Padmabhooshan Sri Vennelakanti Raghavayyagari Jivita charitra (Telugu), Vijayawada,. 1982.

Pattabhirama Rao, Parakala , (Ed.), Gerimella Geyalu (Telugu), Hyderbad, 1992.

Pyarelal, Mahatma Gandhi, The Last Phase, Vol.II, Navijiwan, Ahmedabad, 1959.

Radhakrishna, P. Manyamlo Viplavam (Telugu), Ellore, 1964.

Raghavana Sarma, Gurujada (Ed.), Jatiya Gitalu (Telugu), Hyderbad, 1973.
Rajaram, The Jallianwallah Bagh Massacre: A Premeditated Plan, Chandigarh, 1969.

Raju, P.A., Social and Political ideas of Kandukuri Veeresalingam (A study in Political thought), Allahabad, 1986.

Ramana Reddy, K.V. (Ed.) Unnava Rachanalu Konni (Telugu), Kavali, 1970.

Ramu, P.S., Home Rule to Satyagraha-Prelude to Quit India, New Delhi, 1993.

Ramanuja Rao, Devulapalli, Teluguseemalo Sanskricika Punarujjeevanamu, Hyderbad, 1962.

Ranga, N.G., History of Kisan Movement, Madras, 1939.

---------------, Distinguished Acquaintances, Vol.II, Hyderabad, 1976.

Ranga Devi, Vallabhaneni, Navyandhra Divya Jeevamulu (Telugu), Eluru, 1964.

Rothermund, Dietmar, the Phases of Indian Nationalism and Other Essays, Bombay, 1970.

---------------, Mahatma Gandhi : an Essay in Political Biography, New Delhi, 1991.

---------------, India in the Great Depression, New Delhi, 1992.

Rudrayya Choudaruy, G., T. Prakasam – A Political Study, New Delhi, 1971.

Rushbrook Williams, L.R., India in 1923-24, Calcutta, 1924.

Sankar, R.C.S., The Press in India, New Delhi, 1984.

Sarma, P.S., Compiler Bharata Swatantra Samaranganam Lo Godavari Theeram Vol.I and II (Telugu), Kakinada, 1987.

Sarojini Regani, Highlights of the Freedom Movement in Andhra Pradesh, Hyderabad, 1972.

---------------, Who is Who of Freedom Struggle in Andhra Pradesh, Vol.I and II, Hyderabad, 1978.

Satyanarayana, Bh., Sri Alluri Sitaramaraju Prasamsa (Telugu), Rajahmundry, 1925.

Satyanarayana, Kambampati,Andhra Pradesh Lo Communist Udyama Charitra (Telugu), Vijayawada, 1983.

Satyanaraayana, S.V., Telugulo Udyama Gitalu (Telugu), Hyderabad, 1991.

Sen, S.P., (Ed.), The Indian Press, Institute of Historical Studies, Calcutta, 1967.

Seshagiri Rao, B., History of Freedom Movement in Guntur District, Ongole.

Seshagri Rao, K.R., studies in the Histroy of Telugu Journalism, Delhi, 1968.

Shankar, Girija, Socialist Trends in Indian National Movement (A Study of the Congress Socialist Party), Meerut, 1987.

Shiva Rao, B., India's Freedom Movement : Some Notable Figures, Delhi, 1972.

Shridevi, S., Mahatma Gandhi and Emancipation of Women in India, Hyderabad, 1969.

Sitapati, G.V., History of Telugu Literature, New Delhi, 1968.

Sitaramayya, Pattabhi, B., History of the Indian National Congres Vols. I & II, First Reprint, New Delhi, 1969.

Subba Reddy, Madduri, Telugulo Jatiyaodyama Kavitvam (Telugu), Tirupati, 1982.

Subramanyam, K., the Press and the National Movement in South India, Andhra 1905-1932, Madras, 1984.

Suda, J.P., Indian National Movement, Meerut, 1973.

Sundaralingam, R., Politics and Nationalist Awakening in South India, Arizona, 1974.

Sunil Sen, Agrarian Relations in India, 1793-1947, New Delhi, 1979.

Surya Prakasa Rao, Kalapala, (Ed.), Krishna Zilla Swatantra Porata Charitra (Telugu), Masulipatnam, 1975.

Surya Rao, A., (Ed.), Mahakavi Diareelu (Telugu), Gurajada Rachanalu, Vijayawada, 1954.

Sumit Sarkar, Modern India, 1885-1947, Delhi, 1983.

Sushila Agrawal, Press, Public Opinion and Government in India, Jaipur, 1970.

Tarachand, History of Freedom Movement in India, Vols.I to IV, Delhi 1972.

Tendulkar, D.G., (Ed.), Mahatma : Life of Mohandas Karamchand Gandhi, 8 Vols. 2nd Edn., New Delhi, 1960-63.

Tamlinson, B.R., The Indian National Congress and the Raj, London, 1976.

Tripathi, N.M., The Law of Sedition in India, Prepared under the auspices of the Indian Law Institute, New Delhi, 1964.

Vaidehi Alladi, 1857 and After – Epic Struggle for Freedom in India, Hyderabad, 1984.

Vaikuntham, Y., Education and Social Change in South India, Andhra 1880-1920, Madras, 1982.

Veerabhadra Rao, Madala, Sri Sarvottama Jeevitamu (Telugu), Vijayawada, 1965.

--------------------, Desabhakta Jeevita Charita (Telugu), Machilipatnam, 1966.

--------------------, Andhrodyama charitra (Telugu), Hyderabad, 1982.

Venkatarangaiya, M., Angleyasamrajya Charitramu (Telugu), Vizianagaram, 1921.

--------------------, Bharata Swatanrtrodyama Charitra, vols. I to III (Telugu), Secunderabad, 1974, 1976, 1977.

--------------------(Ed.), The Freedom Struggle in Andhra Pradesh (Andhra), Vols. I to IV, Hyderabad, 1965, 1969 and 1974.

Venkatarangaiya, M. and Innaiah, N., Andhraloo Swatantra-Samaramu (Telugu), Hyderabad, 1972.

Venkata Subbayya, Gorrepati, Desoddharaka Charitra, (Telugu), Vijayawada, 1961.

Venkata Subbayya, G., Sangasamskarta Unnava (Telugu), Hyderabad, 1977.

Venkata Subba Rao, Gummidithala, Sree Gopalakrishnayya, Amalapuram, 1967.

Washbrook, David, Political change and the Madras Presidency 1880-1921, Cambridge, 1971.

Washbrook, D.A., the Emergence of Provincial Politics: The Madras Presidency 1870-1920, Delhi, 1976.

Unpublished Dissertations

Atlury Murali, 'Social Change and Nature of Social Participation in National Movement in Andhra 1905-1934', Ph.D.Thesis, Jawaharlal Nehru University, New Delhi, 1985.

Lakshmi Rajyam, ch., 'Sri Unnava Lakshmi Narayana Panthulu Gari Jivitam – Sahityam', Ph.D., Thesis, Andhra University, Waltair, 1987.

Some Speeches and Writings

Arundale, G.S., (Ed.), Annie Besant : speeches and Writings, Madras, 1942.

-----------, The Sprit of Freedom, Madras, 1917.

Gandhi, Mohandas Karamchand, Young India 1919-1922, Madras, 1922.

-----------, Hind Swaraj or Indian Home Rule, Madras, 1927.

-----------, Swaraj in One Year, Madras, 1921.

Nehru, Jawaharlal, A Bunch of old letters, Bombay, 1958.

Vijayaraghavachariar, C., Swaraj Constitution : An Address to the Delegates of the Indian National Congress, Madras, 1927.

Periodicals and Journals

Andhra Patrika (Telugu), 1920-1930

Andhra Saraswatha Patrika (Telugu), 1920-1946.

Bharatti (Telugu), 1926-1935.

Griha Lakshmi (Telugu), 1928-1935.

Indian Economic and Social History Review, 1968-1978.

Indian Historical Review, 1974-1977.

Indian History Congress Proceeding Volumes, 1950-1979.

India Quarterly, 1951-1961.

Indian Social Reformer, 1920-1930.

Indo-British Review, 1973-1978.

Itihas.

Journal of Andhra Historical Research Society, 1954-1966.

Journal of Indian History, 1950-1978.

Krishna Patrika (Telugu), 1920-1930.

Modern Asian Studies, 1971-1977.

Modern Review, 1955-1968.

Quarterly Review of Historical Studies, 1965-1977.

Reddi Rani (Telugu), 1923, 1924.

The Indian Quarterly Registers.

Rachana, (Telugu), July, 1993.

Autobiographies, Biographies and Reminiscences

Aiyar, C.P.Ramaswamy, Annie Besant (Builders of Modern India Series), Delhi, 1963.

Aiyar, A. Rangaswamy., Dr.Annie Besant : Her Work for Indian Swaraj, Madurai, 1955.

Gandhi, Mohandas Karamchand., An Autobiography or The Story of My Experiments with Truth, Ahmedabad, 1966 Edn.

---------Gokhale My Political Guru, Ahmedabad, 1955.

Jog., N.G., Lokamanya Bal Gangadhara Tilak, (Builders of Modern India Series), New Delhi, 1970 Edn.

Kaleswara Rao, a., Naajeevita Katha (Telugu), Vijaywada, 1959.

Krishna Rao, M., Sri Alluri Sitharamaraju Charitra (Telugu), Rajahmundry, 1959.

Nair, K. Madhavan, Malabar Kalapam (The Malabar Rebellion in Malayalam – Postumously Published), Calicut, 1971.

Nanda, B. R., Mahatma Gandhi, a Biography, London 1959.

Nehru, Jawaharlal, an Autobiography, Bombay, 1962.

Prakasam, T., Naajeevitayatra (Telugu), Machilipatnam, 1972.

Ramakrishna Rao, V. and Rama Rao, T., autobiography of Kandukuri Veeresalingam Pantulu (Translated into English), Rajahmundry, 1970.

Rama Rao, Padala., Alluri Sitaramaraju Natakamu (Telugu), Hyderabad, 1961.

Subba Rao, G.V., Andhra Ratna Sree Gopakrishnayya, Amalapuram, 1967.

Veeresalinvam, Kandukuri., Sweeya Charitramu (Autobiography) in (Telugu), Vol.I & II, Rajahmundry, 1954 Edn.

Venkatappaiah, Konda., Sweeya Charitra (Autobiography) in (Telugu), Vol. I & II, Rajahmundry, 1954 Edn.

Venkatappaiah, Konda., Sweeya Charitra (telugu), Vijaywada, 1952.

Venkateswarlu, V., Andhra Kesari Sri Tanguturi Prakasam Pantulu Gari Jeevitamu (T. Prakasam's Biography in Telugu, Madras, 1951.

Souvenirs

Andhra Pradesh, annuals, 1920-1947.

Gurazada Satavarshika Jayanthi Sanchika, Gurazada Shatavarshika Jayanti Sangm, Hyderabad, 1962.

Half-way, the Golden book presented to Sri V.R.Narla on his fifty first birth day, 1958.

Krishna Patrika a Diamond Jubilee Souvenir, 1964.

Kaviraju Smaraka Sanchika, Kaviraja Vardhanti Vutsava Committee, T. Nagar, Madras, 1972.

Madras Tori Centenary Commemoration volume, Madras, 1939.

Samadarsini Annual, 1928-1931.

Souvenir, Telugu Federation of Theosophical Society (First Conference, 1959). The Souvenir Sub-Committee of the Reception Committee, Hyderabad, 1959.

Telugu Samachar, annual supplement, Bombay, 1927.

Articles

Ahluwalia, M.M., "Press and India's Struggle for Freedom", Journal of Indian History, December, 1960.

Arudra, "Modati Telugu Patrikalu" (Telugu) Andhra Jyoti 24th May, 1968.

Bipan Chandra "The Long Term Dynamics of the Indian National Congress" Proceedings of the Indian History Congress, Amritsar, 1985.

Chandrasekhara Reddi, Rachakpalem, "Tirugubatu Bata Garimella Pata" (Telugu) Andhra prabha, 30th October, 1983.

Gerald Barrier, N., "South Asia in Vernacular Publications – Modern Indian Language Collections in the British Museum and the India Office Library, London", The Journal of Asian Studies published by the Association for Asian Studies, INC, Vol.XXVIII, No.4, August, 1969.

Kalpana, B., "The Nationalistic Indian Press, Vis-à-vis The Constructive Anglo-Indian Press on Nascent Indian Nationalism", The Quarterly Review of Historical Studies, Vol.VIII, 1967-68, No.1.

Krishna Gopal, "The Development of the Indian National Congress as a mass Organisation, 1918-1923", the Journal of Asia Studies, XXV, 3, (1968)

Linga Raju, K., "Telugu Patrikalu" (Telugu) Samadarsini, (Annual) 1930-1931.

Leonard, J.G., "Politics and Social Change in South India – A Study of Andhra Movement", Journal of Commonwealth, Political Studies No.1 (1967).

Low, D.A., 'The Government of India and the First Non-Cooperation Movement 1920-1992', The Journal of Asian Studies, XXV 2, 1966.

Masuna, "Swarajyakavi Vaddadi", (Telugu), Andhra Bhoomi, Dt. 15th August, 1987.

Murthy, E.S., "The Rampa rebellion of Alluri Sitaramaraju, South Indian History Congress, Volume pp. 125-127, 1981.

Misra, G, Socio-Economic Background of Gandhi's Champaran Movement", the Indian Economic and social History review, 3., (1968)

Naidu, C., Ch. M., "The Role of Press in the Madras Presidency During the Pre-Gandhian Era (1885-1918)", The Quarterly Review of Historical Studies, vol.XXI, 1981-82, Nos.2 and 3.

Radhakrishna Sarma, Challa., "Maakoddi Tella dora Tanam" (Telugu), Andhra Prabha Newspaper Dt. 21st August, 1985.

-----------------------, "Garimella Vivarinchina Gandhiji Sandesam" (Telugu) Andhra Prabha, Dt. 10th December, 1985.

-----------------------, "Rajakeeeyalanunchi Kavitva Vishayalu" (Telugu) Andhra Prabha, Dt. 21st August, 1987.

------------------------, "Garimella Ghanatha" (Telugu), Andhra Prabha dt. 5th July, 1987.

------------------------, "Bharati, Garimella: Telugu Tamil Kavula Saamyalu" (Telugu), Andhra Jyoti, Newspaper, Dt. 13th November, 1982.

Ramakrishna Sastri, V., "Desabhasha Patrikalu Jateeyodyamamu" (Telugu) Trilinga, Dt. 16th June, 1930.

Rao, P., Rajeswara, "Alluri Sitarama Raju : Doughty Freedom Fighter", Sunday Standard, dt. 4th April, 1968.

Sastry, M.V., "Garimella Satyanarayana", Telugu Vani, Vol.4, July-September, 1979.

Sastri, Dwana, "Jatiya Geyakavi Sarvabhouma Garimella" (Telugu), Andhra Prabha, Dt. 14th August, 1988.

Sree Rama Murthy, M., "Maakoddi Telladoratanam" (Telugu), Andhra Patrika Newspaper Dt. 30th June, 1985.

Subramanyam, K., "Telugu Journalism", Andhra Bhoomi, Newspaper, Dt. 12th April, 1975.

The "Congress" Telugu weekly of Madduri annapoornaiah, Dr. K. Subrahmanyam, Itihas, A.P. state Archives, Publication, July-December, 1984.

Venkata Rao, N., "Prachinaandhra Vaarta Patrikalu" (Telugu), Bharati, May, 1929.

Watson, A.H., "The Growth of the Press in English in India", The Asiatic Review, Vol.44, 1948.

Yasoda devi, V., "History in Modern Telugu Literature" (Paper presented at the Eighth annual conference of the Institute of Historical Studies, at Jodhpur, 1970).

GLOSSARY

Ahimsa	:	Non-violence
Aryavarta	:	Land of the Aryans.
Ashram	:	A spiritual retreat; place where a Hindu devotee or Religious community lives.
Avatar	:	Incarnation
Bigha	:	A measurement of land; in Chaparam 1.16 to 1.40 acres.
Crore	:	10,000,000.
Darshan	:	Sight or view, generally of a holy man.
Dharma	:	In Hindu though a person's allotted role in life.
Dhoti	:	Loin Cloth.
Gitam:	:	Song
Guru	:	Spiritual Teacher.
Hartal	:	Strike, traditionally used to indicate mourning or protest.
Karma	:	In Hindu thought fate or destiny resulting from actions committed in successive states of existence.
Khadi	:	Hand-spin cloth.
Khalifah	:	Successor to the prophet as ruler of Muslims; The Sultan of Turkey, from this Khilafat, used of The post – First World War movement to protect The Kalifah.

Kisan : Peasant

Lakh : 1,00,000.

Mahatma : Title of respect; literally 'Great Soul'.

Maulana : Title of respect given to a learned Muslim.

Panchayat : Court of arbitration, from Panch meaning five.

Puja : Worship.

Raatnam : Spinning wheel.

Ryot (Raiyat) : Peasant.

Raj : Rule.

Sabha : Assembly, Association.

Sadhu : Hindu Ascetic.

Satyagraha : 'Truth force' 'Soul force'; Gandhian passive Resistance. From this, Satyagraha one who Practices Satyagraha.

Sepoys : Soldiers.

Seva Samiti : Social Service Organization.

Taluka : Division of a district for land revenue purposes.

Tahsil : The revenue sub-division of a district.

Vaishnava : Relating to Vishnu; worshipper of Vishnu.

Vakil : Pleader, Indian Lawyer.

Zamindar : Landholder; paying revenue direct to Government.